Stars of David

Stars *of* DAVID

PROMINENT JEWS

TALK ABOUT

BEING JEWISH

Abigail Pogrebin

BROADWAY BOOKS
New York

BROADWAY

PRINTED IN THE UNITED STATES OF AMERICA

BROADWAY BOOKS and its logo, a letter B bisected on the diagonal, are trademarks of Random House, Inc.

Pages 389–90 constitute an extension of this copyright page.

Visit our website at www.broadwaybooks.com

First edition published October 2005.

Book design by Patrice Sheridan

Library of Congress Cataloging-in-Publication Data
Pogrebin, Abigail.
Stars of David : prominent Jews talk about being Jewish / Abigail Pogrebin.
p.   cm.
ISBN 0-7679-1612-3 (alk. paper)
1. Jews in public life—United States—Biography. 2. Jews in public life—United States—Interviews.
3. Jews in public life—United States—Attitudes. 4. Jews—United States—Identity.
5. United States—Ethnic relations. I. Title.
E184.37.A163 2005
920'.0092924073—dc22
[B]   2005042141

1 3 5 7 9 10 8 6 4 2

For Dave, Benjamin, and Molly—
the luminous stars in my life—
who make me feel grounded and blessed.

Contents

Stars of David

Prologue

WHEN I WAS TWENTY-FIVE YEARS OLD and dating an Irish Catholic, my very liberal Jewish mother became an instant reactionary. All her
teachings about tolerance and open-mindedness seemed to evaporate
overnight. When she suddenly grasped that I might actually end up married
to this man, and produce grandchildren who would celebrate Christmas, she
panicked. The tension between us was startling. It lasted almost two years.

I didn't end up with Michael, but two lessons stayed with me: first, that
my mother had one benchmark issue that was nonnegotiable. And two,
that no matter how angry I was at the way she handled it, when I really
played out what my life would be like with a non-Jewish husband, I
couldn't do it. No matter how close I was with Michael, there was some
unmistakable barrier. I knew that navigating our different backgrounds
would be too hard.

Jewish identity has crept up on me. And now that I'm forty and ten
years married (to a Jew from Skokie), with two young children who are
ours to shape, I'm aware of both how connected I feel to other Jews and
how confused I feel about Judaism.

Which is what led me, in part, to this book. I found myself looking at public figures that happen to be Jewish and wondering how Jewish these people felt. It occurred to me that we might share a kind of figurative secret handshake—not just pride in the heritage and endurance of the Jewish people, but uncertainty about what it means to be a Jew today. Was their ethnic and religious identity crucial to them, incidental to their lives, or meaningless? If they were raised with rituals, had they maintained them? Did they care if their Jewish daughter decided to marry a Michael?

I realize that choosing to talk to prominent Jews instead of regular folks is slicing off a narrow population, but that was the point. I consider myself a journalist, not a sociologist, and I wanted to focus on one snapshot of American Jewry—albeit a random sample within that group—who have in common a level of achievement that represents the American Dream. If an obvious goal of Jewish immigrants was to reach the highest rungs of American success, then what happened to the religious underpinnings of their children and grandchildren? Did being in the American spotlight require them to neutralize their ethnicity? Had they felt pressured to downplay their Jewishness at any point in their careers? Or had they benefited from it? Been ashamed of it?

Adam Sandler's "Chanukah Song" (in which he lists—and in some cases, outs—famous Jews) is hilarious precisely because it gets at something true. Jews feel a particular ownership of public figures who are members of the so-called tribe. We see Steven Spielberg and Joe Lieberman, for instance, as representing us. I know my parents still look at the newspaper headlines and cringe when a Jew is the one indicted, feel proud when it's a Jew who's won the Pulitzer. I wondered, is that a generational phenomenon? Do we still feel that any Jew fortunate enough to have become famous has a duty to be a credit to the Jewish people because their behavior reflects on us all? And if that's true, are Jewish celebrities aware of it and do they embrace or reject this burden?

The majority of prominent Jews are not prominent for being Jewish. Most Jews with boldface names don't hide their Judaism, but they don't flaunt it either. And it's certainly not a staple of the typical celebrity interview. So I set out to ask how being Jewish fits into a public life.

For my parents' generation—children of immigrants or first-generation Americans—the framework for being Jewish was heavily influenced by their parents' experience of poverty, bigotry, and the Holocaust. They absorbed a sense of peril, the need to prove themselves, to stay connected to the Jewish community and hold fast to rituals that were ingrained since childhood. My generation, on the other hand, has been given Cafeteria-Style Judaism: We can pick and choose. Nothing is required. There's no sense of urgency or menace, of having to boost up or protect our people. Some of my friends fast on Yom Kippur, others come to our annual breakfast party having already eaten. Some go to synagogue only on the High Holy Days, others only when they're invited to a wedding. I have no close friends who attend Shabbat services regularly or build a sukkah every fall. Many are sending their kids to Hebrew school, but few could say exactly why. Because they think they should, or because they went, or because they want their children to have more Jewish education than they did. My sense is the decision is often more reflexive than considered.

I was interested in what people who happen to be Jewish and happen to be famous think about being Jewish today, when à la carte Judaism is the norm and when strict observance and fervent Zionism have largely fallen away.

For a book that features conversations with sixty-two well-known high-achievers, it seems like the ultimate in hubris to start by talking about myself. But it also feels compulsory, because clearly I came at these interviews from my own vantage point. Though I consider myself a fair reporter, it would be disingenuous to call myself completely disinterested when it comes to this particular maze.

The fact is, I'm curious about all of this because I'm Jewish, but also because I'm not sure how Jewish I am. Judaism wasn't a huge part of my growing up, though I was surrounded by Jews on New York's Upper West Side. I was raised with occasional shabbos, synagogue twice a year, two seders, and eight nights of Hanukkah. My mother, who was raised in a Conservative home in Queens, given an extensive Hebrew school education, and a bat mitzvah, which was unusual for her era, turned her back on formal Judaism at the age of fifteen. This was because when her mother died, she was excluded from the mourners' minyan (at that time, a quorum of ten men) solely because she was female. After she married my father, she maintained a home-based Judaism that involved intermittent Shabbat dinners and the celebrations of every major Jewish holiday—including the warmest overpopulated Hanukkah party every year, with latkes dipped in sour cream and a gift for every guest. She also helped found a makeshift congregation in Saltaire, Fire Island—a church was borrowed for the High Holy Days—where she was the cantor and people worshipped in bare feet.

My father was a Jew without portfolio: no Hebrew school, no synagogue (until he met my mother), and no belief in God. But he was utterly Jewish in his sensibility, sense of humor, tastes in culture and penchant for Talmudic argument.

My siblings and I were not sent to Hebrew school, nor given bat or bar mitzvahs, which my mother regrets to this day, especially now that she's a fairly observant, involved Jew again. Eventually, she found her way to a more egalitarian practice that includes women without over-modernizing or abandoning the basics. She writes about Jewish issues and tries to regularly attend Friday night services. But by the time she had her "rebirth," when she was in her late forties, my Jewishness was already formed in its fragmentation and ignorance.

I took Introduction to Hebrew in college because I wanted to try to catch up. My professor taught us vocabulary by having us memorize the Israeli Top 40, which she recorded off a shortwave radio. After graduation, I visited Israel and was very popular there because I knew all the latest hits. Now, eighteen years later, I can't put a Hebrew sentence together.

That trip was actually kind of a bust. It was my parents' graduation gift to me and my twin sister, Robin: They booked us on what they thought would be a spirited bus tour. When we arrived at the departure lounge at Kennedy Airport, everyone in our group was geriatric. Somehow the American Jewish Congress had assigned us to the wrong itinerary. Despite our disappointment, we still got on the plane and managed to enjoy the trip. Robin and I became the communal grandchildren, and there was something more poignant about touring the "homeland" with people who remembered its founding and who had lost family in the Holocaust.

I met my husband, David, on a blind date in 1993 and married him the same year on a mountaintop in St. Lucia; we imported our college friend and newly minted rabbi, Mychal Springer, to officiate, and brought our own kosher wine for the vows. It was the first Jewish wedding the Caribbean hotel had ever hosted, and their staff referred to the *chuppah*— the traditional wedding canopy—as the "hooper."

David grew up in Skokie and Evanston, Illinois, and was bar mitzvahed in his neighborhood shul. I keep his bar mitzvah invitation in a frame on my bureau because the pencil drawing of his thirteen-year-old self in 'seventies big hair and yarmulke make me smile. He wants to give our children a religious education, but his emotional connection to Judaism is vague and tenuous. Our ease together as a couple is not based in faith at all, though I'm aware that so much of our common vocabulary—our humor, eccentric relatives, close siblings, focus on food—feels somehow quintessentially Jewish.

Since the arrival of our two children, I've tried to figure out how to incorporate rituals that acknowledge the sacredness in our daily lives. But my efforts still feel stilted, forced. I light candles on Friday nights when we're home, and savor watching our son, Benjamin, rip into the challah and pass pieces around the table. I love watching our daughter, Molly, imitate me sweeping my hands three times over the candles. Before the meal, I say out loud what I was grateful for that week and Ben and Molly pipe up with some thanks of their own. We all trade kisses and say "Good shabbos." But I feel David's discomfort—he lacks my sentimentality, and ritual doesn't come naturally to him—and that makes me self-conscious.

I pray briefly before bedtime most nights, thanking God for the health and safety of my children. But I worry that my appeals are too self-centered.

I'm still in synagogue twice a year on the High Holy Days. I've always loved the chaotic family suppers before we rush out to evening services: Mom sets a beautiful table with lace and silver, there are the round, shiny challahs, apples dipped in honey, familiar blessings. But I get annoyed by my mother's explanations; they feel like a reproach, a cue that I should know more about the symbolism of things.

In synagogue on Kol Nidre—the eve of Yom Kippur—I always feel hypocritical confessing my sins. But that doesn't stop me from asking God for clemency: My list of lapses is always easy to summon up. During one service recently, I found myself weeping during the Shehechianu (the blessing that thanks God for giving us life, sustaining us, and allowing us to reach this moment). I was overcome by the singing, everyone standing and swaying, arms around neighbors they didn't even know. Of course, minutes after that transcendent moment, I found myself flipping ahead in the prayer book to see how much of the service was left.

Every year, my husband says he doesn't know why he's fasting or going to temple since he doesn't feel anything there. When I suggest that maybe we ought to tell each other our sins for the year, he says he can't have that conversation when he's so hungry.

I go to two seders every year, but I grew up attending three. The first two were the typical Passover gatherings, one at cousin Danny's on Long Island, the other at Aunt Betty's in Larchmont—same Haggadah, same undersalted matzo ball soup, same chocolate macaroons, same thirty people around the table. The third seder was the feminist adaptation, co-conceived by my mother, who seemed to be the only one of the five so-called Seder-Mothers not dressed in a bohemian caftan. I remember feeling moved by a room full of articulate, animated women sitting on cushions on the floor, making the themes of the Haggadah relevant, seeming interested in my nascent opinions. But that same comforting circle would turn on each other in later years—fighting over who should be invited—and the event would sour in my mind.

I know I've inherited my mother's superstitions. I close the shades when there's a full moon, toss salt over my shoulder after it spills, and say "tuh, tuh, tuh" when a bad thought creeps into my head. My fear of tempting the evil eye goes even further than my mother's: I feel convinced that cancer is just around the corner and I've written notes to my children in case I go down in a plane.

I've tried to resist my mother's prejudices: her cringing at Christmas carols playing in every store, the involuntary recoil at the sound of a German accent, the sense that Jews are the supreme sufferers. I'll never forget, when I was dating Michael, that I was stupid enough to venture to my mother that Jews are not the only people whose ancestors had endured massive, premeditated persecution. I mentioned the Irish potato famine as an example. Not wise. *You're comparing the Shoah to the Potato Famine?* She looked as if she wanted to disown me—rip her shirt as is the Jewish custom when a child is considered symbolically dead.

Michael was a great boyfriend, but there was undeniably a cultural chasm between us. He didn't "get" my family's *mishigas,* let alone find a way to deal with it. And when I was with his family on Easter, sitting quietly around the table, I missed my family's tumult. It was unsettling to go with him to Midnight Mass on Christmas Eve, no matter how merry. I couldn't imagine my children taking the sacrament and crossing themselves. Baptism was out of the question. It bothered me, when we watched the film *Music Box*, about a woman who discovers her beloved father's Nazi past, that Michael had no personal link to that story. We didn't share an indigenous sorrow. He would never feel entrusted with or obligated by the responsibility to carry Judaism on. I realized that no dash of Christianity, however modified, would ever be palatable for me.

I also realized I'd have to work harder to keep my own family Jewish than I would if I'd just married another Jew. I wanted the Jewishness to just be there: in my children's faces, in their food, in their celebrations. I wasn't sure enough of my own faith and history to be confident I could effectively pass it on.

My religious identity used to be informed entirely by my mother: She made the holidays sparkle, she made me feel there was a privilege and weight to being Jewish, she made me feel lazy for not doing more to understand it. But now I'm wading in in my own way, on my own time. And this book felt like one step in that direction.

The specificity of each person's Jewish chronicle was unexpected. The fact that Mike Nichols still feels, at his core, like a refugee; that Edgar Bronfman Jr. initially rejected Judaism because he rejected his father; that Beverly Sills felt uncomfortable enrolling her deaf Jewish child in a Catholic school, chosen because it specialized in educating deaf children; that Alan Dershowitz gave up his Orthodox observance because he couldn't defend it to his children. That Justice Ruth Bader Ginsburg spurned Jewish ritual because of its sexism; that Barry Levinson believes Jewish Hollywood executives abandoned his film *Liberty Heights* because it was "too Jewish"; that Mike Wallace—long labeled a "self-hating" Jew because of his coverage of the Middle East—recites the Shema, Judaism's most hallowed prayer, every night; that Natalie Portman feels ashamed of her Long Island hometown's materialistic Jewish values; that Kati Marton never quite forgave her parents for hiding the fact that she was Jewish; that Kenneth Cole has misgivings about agreeing to raise his children in his wife's Catholic faith. My conversation with Leon Wieseltier upended my approach to Judaism because he challenged my justifications for remaining uninformed about it.

These portraits are micro snapshots: They are private, often boldly candid, idiosyncratic, scattershot, impressionistic. They are not exhaustive, they do not purport to answer the macro questions about assimilation, anti-Semitism, or Jewish continuity. They are highly personal stories from people we feel we kind of know—stories that hopefully peel back a new layer. I was not investigating how many powerful Americans are Jewish, or how much power powerful American Jews have; what interests me is how Jewish those powerful Jews feel they are.

I intentionally chose not to underscore the commonalities among these voices because I believe they will reverberate differently for each reader. Recurring themes, including the tendency to abandon childhood rituals, the thorny questions of intermarriage, the staunch pride in history, and the ambivalence about Israel, will undoubtedly feel familiar depending on one's experience.

I understand the temptation to turn first to chapters about the people one already admires, but some of the best nuggets lie among the least known. Even if you've never read a Jerome Groopman piece in *The New Yorker*, it's intriguing to hear this doctor's views on the clash between science and faith. Even if you're not a *Star Trek* fan, it may surprise you to learn how Leonard Nimoy based Spock's Vulcan greeting on a rabbinic blessing. Even if you disagree with every word "Dr. Laura" has ever said on the air, you may feel a pang of sympathy for her once you read about the vitriol she endured from other Jews after her conversion to Judaism.

We are living in a period of heightened religious awareness. Our political leaders cite biblical verses and claim to act in the name of God. Popular magazines run cover stories on spirituality. From Chechnya to Iraq, from Rwanda to Bosnia, we've seen how ethnic loyalties can bring out the worst in people. What I've attempted to probe in this book is how those Jews who are major players on the stages of American politics, sports, business, and culture feel about their Jewish identity and how it plays out in their daily lives. Just as these public Jews have entered our collective consciousness through their outsized accomplishments and celebrity, we can find parts of ourselves in their honest, intimate personal stories.

Dustin Hoffman

DUSTIN HOFFMAN VIVIDLY RECALLS ONE AFTERNOON, sitting in his apartment on 11th Street in New York City, talking on the phone to Mike Nichols. The director was trying to convince Hoffman to audition for the part of Benjamin Braddock in *The Graduate*. "Mike was asking, 'What do you mean you don't think you're right for the part?'" Hoffman says. "'Because you're Jewish?' I said, 'Yeah.' Mike said, 'But don't you think the character is Jewish *inside*?'" Hoffman reminds me that Braddock was originally written as a thoroughbred WASP. "The guy's name is Benjamin *Braddock*—not Bratowski," Hoffman says with a smile. "He's a track star, debating team. Nichols tested everybody for the part—I think he tested Redford, who visually was the prototype of this character."

Hoffman finally agreed to fly to L.A. to audition. "That day was a torturous day for all of us," he says. "I think I was three hours in the makeup chair under the lights. And Mike was saying with his usual wry humor, 'What can we do about his nose?' Or, 'He looks like he has one eyebrow'; and they plucked in between my eyebrows. Dear Mike, who was, on the one hand, extremely courageous to cast me, in the end was at the same time aware that I looked nothing like what the part called for." Hoffman laughs.

We're having breakfast in a Columbus Avenue restaurant near his apartment in New York City. He arrives in buoyant spirits, dressed in jeans, white T-shirt, and blue blazer. Right away he befriends the waitress—"Where did you grow up?" She turns out to be from his childhood neighborhood in Los Angeles: Orlando Street. "Oh my God," he says, "I grew up on Flores!"

He orders very specific "loose" scrambled egg whites with one yoke thrown in, plus onions, salsa, and garlic. "Not too dry, no milk, no butter; a little olive oil." Hoffman shakes his head when I order my omelet. "Omelets aren't the best way to go," he advises me. "Scrambled is tastier. But you go ahead with your omelet."

Back to 1967: Nichols, who had seen Hoffman in an off-Broadway play, invited him to California to audition: "I flew out to L.A. with very little notice, and of course hadn't slept," says Hoffman. "I was very nervous. And in my memory, it was an eight-page or ten-page scene in the bedroom, and of course I kept fucking it up. I distinctly remember Mike taking me aside and saying, 'Just relax; you're so nervous. Have you ever done a screen test before?' I said, 'No.' He said, 'It's *nothing*; these are just crew people here; you're not on a stage. This is just film; no one's going to see it. This isn't going into theaters.' And I nodded and I was so thankful that he was trying to soften me; but then he put his hand out to shake mine, and his hand was so sweaty that my hand slipped out of it. *Now* I was terrified. Because I knew, '*That man is as scared as I am.*'

"I felt, from my subjective point of view, that the whole crew was wondering, 'Why is this ugly little Jew even trying out for this part called Benjamin Braddock?' I looked for a Jewish face in the film crew, but I don't think I sensed one Jew. It was the culmination of everything I had ever feared and dreaded about Aunt Pearl." He's referring to his Aunt Pearl, who, upon learning that "Dusty" wanted to become an actor, remarked: " 'You can't be an actor; you're too ugly.' " "It was like a banner," Hoffman continues: " '*Aunt Pearl was right!*' She'd warned me."

Hoffman reaches into the bread basket to break off small chips of a baguette. "It was probably one of the more courageous pieces of casting any director has done in the history of American movies," he continues. "And an act of courage is sometimes accompanied by a great deal of fear."

Obviously the film went on to become a classic and made Hoffman a star. But even after becoming a Hollywood icon, with memorable roles in such films as *Midnight Cowboy, Marathon Man, Kramer vs. Kramer, Tootsie,* and *Rainman*, at the age of sixty-eight, Hoffman says he's still being "miscast": "Someone told me about a review of this movie I did, *Runaway Jury*, which indicated that I was miscast because the part was a Southern gentleman lawyer. Which must mean to that critic, 'He shouldn't be Jewish.' The unconscious racism is extraordinary—as if there are no Southern gentlemen Jews. So he implied I was miscast. And I mentioned that to my wife and she said, 'Well, you've always been miscast.' And she's right. The truth is that you've got two hundred million people in this country and I don't know the number of Jews—are there six or seven million? [An estimated 5.7 million.] I think there's thirteen million in the world [13.9]. So in a sense, we're miscast by definition, aren't we? That's what a minority is: It's a piece of miscasting by God."

Hoffman grew up unreligious—"My father later told me he was an atheist," he says of Harvey Hoffman, a furniture designer. Though they celebrated Christmas, one year he decided to make a "Hanukkah bush" instead. "About the time I realized we were Jews, maybe when I was about ten, I went to the delicatessen and ordered bagels and draped them around the tree."

But when it came to Hoffman's neighborhood friends, something told him he should deny his Jewishness. "It was so traumatic to me, before puberty, realizing that Jews were something that *people didn't like.* I have a *vivid* recollection—literally *sensory* feeling—of the number of times people would say to me (whether they were adults or kids), 'What are you?'" Hoffman pauses. "It was like it went right through me." He twists his fists into his belly. "It was like a warning shock—painful. And I *lied* my way through each instance of that kind of questioning. So here would be the dialogue: You ask me, 'What are you?'"

POGREBIN: "What are you?"
HOFFMAN: "American."

He gives me direction: "Now you press."

POGREBIN: "What kind of American?"
HOFFMAN: "Just American."
POGREBIN: "What are your parents?"
HOFFMAN: "American—from Chicago."

More direction: "Keep pressing—because they would. They'd ask, 'What *religion* are you?' And I'd play dumb."

So he knew that being Jewish was something to hide? "Oh God, yes," he replies immediately. "I didn't want the pain of it. I didn't want the derision. I didn't come from some tough New York community where I'd say, 'I'm Jewish—you want to make something out of it?' There was an insidious anti-Semitism in Los Angeles."

It's one of the reasons he was impatient to move to New York, which he did, at age twenty-one. "I grew up always wanting to live in New York, even though I'd never been here. And what's interesting is that all people ever said to me and still say is, 'Oh, I always assumed you were from New York!' Even now, if you look Jewish, you're from New York. I didn't know that most of the Jews in America live in New York. But I did know it inside. I flew to New York to study acting in 1958; I took a bus from the airport terminal to New York City and they let me off on Second Avenue. It was summer, it was hot, and I walked out of the bus, and I saw a guy urinating on the tire of a car, and I said, 'I'm home.' " He smiles. "The guy pissing on the tire must have represented to me the antithesis of white-bread Los Angeles: New York City was the truth. It was a town that had not had a face-lift, in a sense—that had not had a nose job."

Despite the city's ethnic embrace, when it came to open casting calls, Hoffman learned quickly into which category he fell. "Character actor," he says with a grin. "The word 'character' had a hidden meaning: It meant 'ethnic.' 'Ethnic' means nose. It meant 'not as good looking as the ingenue or the leading man or leading woman.' We were the funny-looking ones."

I ask whether it frustrated him—being pigeonholed. "Sure. But everything frustrates you when you're not working." He pauses. "I think I just gave you the glib answer. I think the non-glib answer would be how quickly you accept the stereotype that's been foisted on you: 'They're right; I'm ugly.' You learn that early, before you even think about acting. You learn that in junior high school."

I assume that changed for him when he became a bona fide movie star whom many considered adorable. "I still don't feel that, by the way." He shakes his head. One's self-image, he maintains, is indelibly shaped in adolescence. "You're really stuck with those first few years," he says. "That's what stays with you. It takes a lot of therapy to break through that."

What about all the women who must have thrown themselves at him at the height of his fame? "It doesn't matter," he insists. "If you're smart, you know you're interchangeable. It's like people coming up and asking for your autograph; they'll ask any celebrity." He also says he realized after a while that the shiksa conquest has little staying power. "The cliché from the male point of view—which is another interview—is the number of times we men in our youth would talk about girls that we had bedded down. And there was often the comment, 'What a waste; I mean here she is—a model, gorgeous—and she's just a lox.' " He laughs. "I mean, you learn. That outward stereotype only goes so far."

But the short Jewish guy with the nose did choose the trophy wife for his first marriage. "The first wife was Irish Catholic, five-foot-ten, ballet dancer." He smiles. "I don't want to discredit this ex-wife, but the grandmother of my current and lasting wife, Lisa, her grandmother Blanche once referred to my first wife as," Hoffman dons a husky voice, " 'He married a bone structure!' " He laughs. "I mean, that was the prize."

I wonder if he himself ever thought about changing his appearance? "No, but my mother asked me to. When I was a teenager, when she got *her* nose job, I remember she wanted me to get one, too. She said I would be happier."

I tell him it's probably a good thing he didn't. "Oh but I did," he jests. "You should have seen it before!"

He says his first set of in-laws—from Chappaqua, New York—weren't thrilled about their daughter's choice in husbands. "I think there was a certain amount of ambivalence on her parents' part that she was marrying a Jewish guy. I don't think they were tickled about me before I became famous and I think they were a little more tolerant afterwards."

Didn't he feel some vindication once he became prominent—a kind of "I showed them" to his in-laws, to Aunt Pearl, and to all the casting directors who'd once dismissed him? "I can't say yes because I don't remember that feeling. On the contrary, I tried my hardest after *The Graduate* to defame myself. I was *sent* scripts for the first time, and I just kept saying, 'no, no, no.' I did not want to be a part of this party joke that I was now a leading man." Hoffman is almost never still; he keeps tearing at the baguette, adjusting the sugar packets, the flatware. "None of this is simple," he says.

His second and current wife, Lisa Gottsegen ("We just celebrated twenty-three years," he announces proudly), took him on a more Jewish path. "My wife changed everything," he says. "Two sons bar mitzvahed, two daughters bat mitzvahed." They have four children together (he also has two children from his first marriage, one of whom was a step-daughter). Their family rabbi, Mordechai Finley, who Hoffman describes as "a red-headed Irishman with a ponytail"—is someone to whom Hoffman speaks candidly about his misgivings about faith. "I said, 'Mordechai, can I tell you the truth? I used to live on East Sixty-second Street—years ago, when I was still married to my first wife—and there was the Rock Church (it's still there) across the street. And I'd hear the singing and the clapping and I loved it.' I said to Mordechai, 'I always wanted synagogue to be like that.' "

Hoffman acknowledges he hasn't given the time to his Judaism that he has to his acting. "I have no one to blame but myself, because I could have learned it," he says. "Every one of my kids that has had a bar or bat mitzvah, I've had to learn my part phonetically; it's uncomfortable for me." The family observes all Jewish holidays, though Hoffman noticed his son Max didn't go to synagogue on Yom Kippur in Providence, where, at the time we meet, he's just started Brown University. "We called up Max in Rhode Island, and the first thing he said was 'Good Yom Tov.' But he didn't go to services. He just said it to say, 'See, I know what today is.' "

Hoffman is, in fact, planning to drive up to Brown after our breakfast: It's parents' weekend. "My son met a girl who we'll probably meet and her name is Brittany from Mobile, Alabama; I don't think that she's Jewish." He smiles. "But I don't care." His cell phone rings: It's Lisa wondering when he's coming home. "Can you give me ten, fifteen minutes?" he asks her. "Okay, my dear. I'll hurry."

He and Lisa were spotted on camera a couple of nights earlier at the Yankee playoff game against the Boston Red Sox. "Because the New York fans are so devout, if the Yankee pitcher strikes somebody out, everybody stands," he says. "Then they sit down. And then they stand for the next guy. And the next. They sit down, they stand up, sit down." He demonstrates. "And at one point, Lisa said, 'This is worse than temple.' "

He says Lisa cares deeply about Jewish tradition, while his connection is more unconscious. "I have very strong feelings that *I am a Jew*." He punctuates the declaration with his fist. "And particularly, I am a *Russian, Romanian* Jew. I love herring and vodka; I feel it comes from something in my DNA. I do love these things. And I know I have a strong reaction to any anti-Semitism."

He recounts a story that was clearly disquieting. It happened when he took his family to the premiere of his film *Outbreak* in Hamburg, Germany—the hometown of the film's director, Wolfgang Peterson. "I said to my wife before we left, 'Are there any concentration camps around there? Because I think these kids are now finally at the age when they can handle it.' We found out that Bergen-Belsen was forty minutes south. That is where Anne Frank was taken."

They decided to go the morning after the premiere, and Hoffman took an early walk from the hotel to buy some provisions for the drive. "I heard there was a nearby fancy bakery, and I could get wonderful German pastries and sandwiches. And this place had all these little tables, like this," he gestures around our restaurant, "and against the wall were these beautiful pastries and the waitresses were very attractive German girls in their striped uniforms—it was as upscale as you would come across. And I'm aware of the fact that no one is coming up to me—because when you're a celebrity, you're aware of when you're being recognized—and they were quite respectful.

"I'm waiting in line to pay, and as I start to pay, a man is sitting at a table—a man in his twenties—short haircut, drinking coffee, well dressed. And he starts yelling, '*Juden!*' " Hoffman pauses. "And the place stops. In my memory, it was like a movie: Suddenly everyone stops like this." He freezes. "And he repeated it: '*Juden!*' " Hoffman is inhabiting this character now, shouting threateningly—with an accent: '*Dostin Hovvman! Juden!*' I remember my brain had to do some work, but I had already done *Merchant of Venice* in London and I remembered that Shakespeare had used the word in the play. So I made the connection: 'Oh, that must mean Jew.' It was an extraordinary moment. The irony of hearing this when I'm buying German pastries to go to a concentration camp.

"Finally I turned to this guy and he's just with his coffee—he's not drunk. And I'm aware of men in overcoats walking over to him," Hoffman acts this all out, "and they didn't grab him; he just stood up and they followed him out. And I go back to pay, and there was complete, total denial. All of us. Everyone in the room, including me." He pantomimes paying his bill. " 'Thank you very much.' And I walked out in a kind of haze. And of course, when I get a block away, I think of what I should have done. I should have gone over to him and said, 'Yeah—and? *And? What of it?*' "

Hoffman may have drawn a blank in that instance, but he didn't

hesitate years earlier, when there was an artistic dispute as to how his character in *Marathon Man* should handle an anti-Semite. "The big sticking
point in *Marathon Man* was the ending," he explains. "I was called on, as
the character, to fire point-blank at the Laurence Olivier character, Dr.
Szell [a Nazi dentist], and kill him in that last scene. And I said that I
couldn't do it. The screenwriter, William Goldman, was quite upset about
it, because first of all, how dare I? He wrote the book. 'Your job isn't to
rewrite; your job is to play it as written.' I think we had an outdoor meeting in L.A. at the home of the director, John Schlesinger—there was me,
Goldman, and Schlesinger around the table—and it got nasty. I said, 'Go
hire someone else'—Pacino wanted the part—'Go get Al.'

"I remember Goldman saying, 'Why can't you do this? Are you such
a Jew?' I said, 'No, but I won't play a Jew who cold-bloodedly kills another
human being. I won't become a Nazi to kill a Nazi. I won't demean myself. I don't give a fuck what he did. Even though he tortured me, I won't
do it.' And we worked it out—it's in the dialogue. Olivier says"—Hoffman
does the German accent—" 'You can't do it, can you? You don't have the
guts.' So I don't shoot; he comes at me, there's some wrestling or whatever,
and I throw the diamonds at him. *That* I wanted to do. That I dearly loved
doing because I believed it. I throw the diamonds at him and they're all
falling in the grate around him, he is losing them. And I say, 'I'm going to
keep throwing them at you until you eat them.' I say, '*Essen, essen*' ["Eat,
eat"]. Because I didn't mind torturing him; but I wasn't going to shoot him
point-blank. I wanted to do what felt like the Jew that's in me. I want him
to swallow those fucking diamonds for all those people that he tortured and
he killed—'Eat these fucking diamonds because that's what it was all about
to you.' "

He describes how Dr. Szell ultimately falls and impales himself, and
then Hoffman's character walks to the Central Park reservoir. "There's a
great moment for me—I mean it's just a movie, but nevertheless—there's
this music playing, and there's the fence, and I just go," he reenacts it, "I
wind up my arm and throw this gun over the fence into the reservoir. And
I just keep walking. And it's the end of the movie." He pauses. "And that's
important to me: that I didn't shoot him in the end. Being a Jew is not losing your humanity and not losing your soul. That's what they were unable
to do when they tried to erase the race; they tried to take the soul away.

That was the plan." He gets choked up and excuses himself to go to the bathroom.

When he returns, neither of us refers to the moment before. He asks if I want to walk with him the few blocks to his home and, as we chat, we end up talking again about the Yankee game he attended a few days ago. "I didn't have any identity on—neither a Yankee hat nor a Red Sox hat," he says, "and this one woman said, 'Are you neutral?' And before I could stop myself, I said, 'No, I'm Jewish.'" He chuckles. "That would never have happened a bunch of years ago. Some part of me wants to advertise it now. Finally."

Ruth Bader Ginsburg

JUSTICE RUTH BADER GINSBURG HAS A RUN in her stocking, which, I must admit, puts me at ease. It's my first time in a U.S. Supreme Court Justice's chambers—even that word, "chambers," conveys hushed, erudite activity—and it's strangely comforting to see that this tiny woman with the giant intellect gets runs in her hose like the rest of us. "Why don't we just sit here." She gestures to a couch in her sitting area.

Ginsburg, often described as small and soft-spoken, appears almost miniaturized in her sizable office space, formerly occupied by the late Thurgood Marshall. Dressed all in black—slacks, blouse, stockings, sandals, a shawl draped around her shoulders—she looks like a frail Spanish widow rather than one of the nine most powerful jurists in the land.

But it's clear that despite her petite frame, small voice, and a recent battle with colon cancer, Ginsburg—age seventy when we meet, the second woman on the bench in the court's history and its first Jewish member since Abe Fortas—is formidable. She tells one story that illustrates her intrepid style: "My first year here, the court clerk, who is just a very fine fellow, came to me and said, 'Every year we get letters from Orthodox Jews who would like to have a Supreme Court membership certificate that doesn't say *In the year of our Lord*. [She's referring to the certificate lawyers receive when they become members of the Supreme Court bar.] So I said, 'I agree; if they don't want that, they shouldn't have it.'

"So I checked to see what the federal courts and circuit courts were doing and discovered, to my horror, that in my thirteen years on the D.C. circuit, the membership certificate has always said *In the year of our Lord*. So I spoke to the chief judges of all the circuits, and some of them had already made the change, others were glad to make the change. Then I came to my Chief and said, 'All the other circuits give people a choice.' " Her "Chief," William Rehnquist, recommended she raise the issue "in conference" with her fellow justices, which she did. "I won't tell you the name of this particular colleague," she says, "but when I brought this up and thought it would be a no-brainer, one of my colleagues said, '*The year of our Lord* was good enough for Brandeis, it was good enough for Cardozo, it was good enough—' and I said, 'Stop. *It's not good enough for Ginsburg.*' "

Significant laws have been changed over the last few decades because the status quo wasn't "good enough for Ginsburg." She is known as a pioneer in the field of antidiscrimination law, a founder of the Women's Rights Project of the American Civil Liberties Union, the first female tenured professor at Columbia University Law School, and the lawyer who argued six women's rights cases before the Supreme Court and won five of them.

She abandoned Judaism because it wasn't "good enough for Ginsburg" either. Its exclusion of women from meaningful rituals was painfully brought home to her at age seventeen, when her mother, Celia Bader, succumbed to cancer a day before Ruth's high school graduation. "When my mother died, the house was *filled* with women; but only men could participate in the minyan [the quorum required for public prayers of mourning]." It didn't matter that the young Ruth had worked hard to be confirmed at Brooklyn's East Midwood Jewish Center—"I was one of the few people who took it seriously," she remarks, or that at thirteen, she'd been the "camp rabbi" at a Jewish summer program. Having a Jewish education counted for nothing at one of the most important moments in her life. "That time was not a good one for me in terms of organized religion," she says with typical understatement. I ask her to expand on how Judaism made her feel secondary. "It had something to do with being a *girl*. I wasn't trained to be a yeshiva *bucher*." (She uses the Yiddish word for "boy.")

Later, she was also turned off by the class system in her family synagogue. "This is something I'll tell you and you know it exists: In many temples, where you sit depends on how much money you give to the shul. And my parents went to the synagogue, Temple Beth El in Belle Harbor, Long Island—it's right next to Rockaway. When my mother died and my father's [furrier] business went down the drain, he was no longer able to contribute to the temple. And so their tickets for the High Holy Days were now in the *annex*, not in the main temple, although they had been members since the year they married. And I just—that whole episode was not pleasing to me at all."

Neither was the time when she tried to enroll her son, James, in Sunday school at Temple Emanu-El on Fifth Avenue in New York City. "The rabbi told me to fill out the application for membership 'as though I were my husband,' " she recalls with indignation. "I said, 'Well I haven't consulted him; I don't know if he wants to be a member of Temple Emanu-El.'

"The idea was, as a woman, if you were not single, widowed, or divorced, you could not be a member. If you were married, then your husband was the member. I was still teaching at Rutgers—it was 1972. And I remember how annoyed I was. Still, I wanted James to have something of a Jewish education. So I said, 'I will make a contribution to the temple that is equivalent to the membership, if you will allow my child to attend Sunday school.' "

I ask her if these bouts with sexism were what kept her from embracing Jewish observance. Again she's not expansive. "Yes," she answers softly. "Yes."

Despite giving up synagogue attendance, Sabbath candle-lighting, and fasting on Yom Kippur, Ginsburg did go to her husband's parents' home for Passovers. "That was always a great time for the children," she says. "I think even more for my children than it was for me." Her husband, Martin Ginsburg, a respected tax lawyer and an accomplished cook, occasionally dabbled in Jewish ethnic cuisine. "In his very early days he made his mother's chopped liver," she says with a smile.

Her children were bored with Sunday school, and she didn't urge them to stick it out. "James was not bar mitzvahed," she says of her younger son, "and that was his choice. He didn't want to do the studying. We were living in California at that time—we were at Stanford [where she was a Fellow at the Center for Advanced Study in the Behavioral Sciences]. James did not like the Sunday school there, and I didn't want to have one more issue in his life."

Her daughter, Jane, ducked Sunday school more cannily. "She made a deal with us." Ginsburg smiles. "We were then going to a much nicer Sunday school at Shaaray Tefilah on East Seventy-ninth Street in New York City, but Jane didn't like it very much. She is ten and a half years older than her brother. One Sunday morning, when he was an infant, I overslept; she took care of him and didn't go to Sunday school. And I was so glad that she did such a good job. So she said that she would make a deal with us: If she didn't have to go to Sunday school anymore, she would take care of James every Sunday morning. That was an offer I could hardly refuse. So that's when she stopped.

"But Jane became very Jewish again when she married a Catholic boy," Ginsburg continues. "First, she wanted to have a rabbi reassure her that even if her children were baptized—which they were because it was important to my son-in-law's Italian-Catholic mother—that it could still be a Jewish baby. And I thought that would be easy." Ginsburg shakes her neatly chignoned head. "But it was very, very hard to find a rabbi who would say that. Ab [Abner] Mikva was my chief judge on the D.C. Circuit Court. His daughter is a rabbi and she said, 'No, I won't tell her that.'"

I remark that this must have been very upsetting. "Yes," Ginsburg says with a nod, "but I said to Jane, 'This woman [the Italian-Catholic mother-in-law] is thinking that if her grandchild isn't baptized, *this child's soul will never go to heaven.* So it's just to put her at ease.'"

Did it matter to Justice Ginsburg that her children marry Jews? "No. Jane is married to a very fine man who is perfect for her. And she had anticipated all kinds of difficulties that didn't arise. There was a question of Sunday school and I said, 'Wait till George—my son-in-law—finds the church that he is going to enroll Paul and Clara in.' And he never did—to this day he hasn't. My granddaughter, who will be thirteen in October, is this summer—for the second time—going to a Hadassah-run camp on the French side of Lake Geneva. So now she knows more about Judaism than I have forgotten."

Ginsburg seems comforted by a sense that her grandchildren know what's at the heart of their birthright. "I think they have enough of an understanding that, when you are a Jew, the world will look at you that way; and this is a heritage that you can be very proud of. That this small band of people have survived such perils over the centuries. And that the Jews love learning, they're the people of the book. So it's a heritage to be proud of. And then, too, it's something that you can't escape because the world won't let you; so it's a good thing that you can be proud of it."

So what does it mean to be Jewish without rituals? "Think of how many prominent people in different fields identify themselves proudly as Jews but don't take part in the rituals," Ginsburg replies. She adds that even without observance, being Jewish still matters greatly to her. "I'll show you one symbol of that which is here"—she gets up—"if you come." We walk across her office, which is surprisingly ordinary—no dark paneled walls, in-laid desks, or library lamps. It looks more like a civil service office with gray carpeting, tan puffy leather chairs, and a round glass table (with a stuffed Jiminy Cricket doll sitting on top). The only clue to Ginsburg's personality is the profusion of family photos propped on her bookshelves—pictures of son, James, who produces classical music recordings from Chicago; daughter, Jane, who teaches literary and artistic property law at Columbia; the two grandchildren; and of course, the requisite Ginsburg-with-Presidents Series—Carter, Clinton, Bush Sr., George W.

She guides me to her main office door, where a gold mezuzah is nailed prominently to its frame. "At Christmas around here, every door has a wreath," she explains. "I received this mezuzah from the Shulamith School for Girls in Brooklyn, and it's a way of saying, 'This is my space, and please don't put a wreath on *this* door.'"

Her barometer for religious insensitivity rises not just around Christmastime, but at the beginning of each court term. "Before every session, there's a Red Mass [in a Catholic Church]," she says. "And the justices get invitations from the cardinal to attend that. And not all—but a good number—of the justices show up every year. I went one year and I will never go again, because this sermon was outrageously anti-abortion. Even the Scalias—although they're very much of that persuasion—were embarrassed for me." (She and Justice Antonin Scalia are close friends who have celebrated many New Year's Eves together, despite their profound ideological differences.)

Clearly, Ginsburg takes symbolism seriously. Though others might view it as nitpicking, she's always deemed it worth her effort and prestige to challenge small inequities, in addition to working toward large-scale reform. Thus, the changed language in the lawyer's certificate, the jettisoned wreaths, the boycotted Red Mass, and most recently the blacked-out First Monday in October: "We are not sitting on the first Monday in October this year and we will not sit on *any* first Monday that coincides with Yom Kippur," she says proudly. "Now, this is the *first year* that is happening. The first time Yom Kippur came up, it was an ad hoc decision—we were not going to sit that Monday. But now, this is the way it's going to be from now on." Having her comrade Jew on the court, Stephen Breyer, lobbying alongside her was crucial, she says. "In this great Yom Kippur controversy, it helped very much that there were two of us."

Her final show-and-tell items are framed, calligraphic renderings of the Hebrew command from Deuteronomy: "*Zedek, Zedek, tirdorf*"—"Justice, Justice shalt thou pursue." Ginsburg says it was her mother who put Jewish tradition in the context more of doing justice than of observance. "My mother had mixed memories of her Judaism because her father was ultra-Orthodox; she remembers her eldest brother worked very hard to ride a bicycle and then his father caught him riding on the Sabbath and broke it to pieces. So that type of fanatic observance my mother did not appreciate. On the other hand, she has very pleasant memories of the Sabbath and the smell of the bread; and it was the one day that her mother wasn't working—wasn't cooking all the time."

Ginsburg's mother, Celia Bader, pushed her daughter hard to succeed. "My mother told me to be independent. She thought that meant I'd be a high school history teacher." Does Ginsburg consider that emphasis on achievement to be Jewish? "Yes," she answers definitively. "I loved my mother dearly and she was constantly supporting my reading, sometimes pushing me to do things that I didn't really care about, like math. And she cared in a way that other mothers didn't. Our neighborhood was divided three ways—it was Italian, Irish, and Jewish in equal parts. And the Jewish parents were much more concerned about how their children were doing in school."

When Ginsburg stood at President Clinton's side during her nomination ceremony in 1993, she discussed the hurdles she faced at the start of her law career. "I had three strikes against me," she recalled. "I was Jewish, I was a woman, and I was a mother. So if a door would have been open a crack in either of the first two cases, the third one was too much." One of her first jobs—between college and law school—was in a Social Security office working for a man who'd never met a Jew before. "He wasn't entirely sure I wasn't hiding horns somewhere in my head," she says with a half smile.

In her first year at Cornell, she says, the anti-Semitism was visible but unspoken. "In the dormitory, all of the girls on both sides were Jewish," she recalls. "That didn't happen by chance. The houses were arranged so that we would not contaminate all the others. We were contained." She adds that this made for lasting bonds. "We are friends to this day—it was a wonderful group of people."

I ask if the "outsiderness" she felt over the years proved to be a motivating force. "Oh, it certainly is," she replies without her usual hesitation. "You've got to be sure you were better than anyone else."

So I ask the obvious question, "Does being Jewish affect the way you approach cases on the Court?"—expecting her to wave it off with some boilerplate version of *Justices can't let personal experience color their judgment.* Instead, her answer is more nuanced. "I don't think that I approach cases in a particular way because I am Jewish any more than I do because I'm a woman. I have certain sensitivities for both. You know the old expression, 'Is it good for the Jews?' For example, a lot of people want to have crosses in front of their town hall or whatever. They say, 'It doesn't hurt anybody.' We had one case where I was in dissent—it was about a cross in front of the Statehouse in Ohio. And to me, the photograph of that statehouse told the whole story of the case: Here is the Capitol in Columbus, and here is this *giant cross.* And what is the perception of a Jewish child who is passing by the Capitol? It's certainly that this is a Christian country. A person's re-action could be: 'There's something wrong with me.' *It's not a symbol that includes you.*"

The theme of exclusion runs through so many of her stories: the sting of being sidelined, legal cases about people who are made to feel unwel-come. A sad irony occurs to me, as she talks: As other institutions margin-alized her for being a Jew, her religion made her feel left out because she was a woman and thus lost her early on. When I ask if she misses Judaism, there's a long pause. "I wish that I could have the feeling for it that I once did. I don't think I ever will."

Steven Spielberg

"I THINK THE BREAKTHROUGH in my rediscovering the honor of being a Jew came *before Schindler's List,* when I married my wife, Kate." Filmmaker Steven Spielberg is sipping tea in the honey-toned conference room of Amblin Pictures, the production company built for him by Universal Studios after his 1982 blockbuster, *E. T.* He looks relaxed in jeans, sneakers, and a blue baseball cap. "Before I married Kate Capshaw, I only felt my Judaism when I was at the Milky Way Restaurant with my mom and stepfather." He's referring to the kosher café his mother owns in West Los Angeles. "Kate is Protestant and she insisted on converting to Judaism. She spent a year studying, did the *mikvah,* the whole thing. She chose to do a full conversion *before* we were married in 1991, and she married me as a Jew. I think *that,* more than anything else, brought me back to Judaism. I've actually said *Schindler's List* went a long way in getting me back into the fold, but it really was the fact that my wife took a profound interest in Judaism."

Did his wife convert solely for him? "I think she did that for *us,*" Spielberg replies. "But if you ask her that question, she'll probably say she found the history of the Jewish people to be the most compelling history she had ever read. Also, I think Kate saw the size of our family before we had our family, and she wanted us all to be on the same page with the same faith."

They have seven children between them: Capshaw has a daughter (not Jewish) from her first marriage, Spielberg has a son from his first marriage to actress Amy Irving, he and Capshaw have three biological and two adopted children. Four days before our meeting, Spielberg and Capshaw's son Sawyer became bar mitzvahed. Daughter Sasha and son Theo have also crossed that threshold. "Three down, two to go," Spielberg announces, obviously pleased. "The most amazing sight was Theo, who is almost seventeen now," Spielberg continues. "He's African American. I'd always said I wanted at least one of my sons to have the Orthodox bar mitzvah that I had. But Theo didn't want to have the Orthodox bar mitzvah—he fought me on it. He said, 'Dad, please let me be able to design my own coming of age.' And I said, 'You're my last chance and my *only* chance to see a strong, young black man standing in an Orthodox shul surrounded by the congregation of Saturday worshippers with the tallis over their heads.' I said, 'I know I'm not allowed to take photographs in an Orthodox temple, but I will take a photograph of that in my mind and I will know that you shared the same experience that I shared, going the whole formal route to confirmation.' Theo didn't want to do it, but in retrospect, he's many times thanked me for it."

As a black adopted Jew, Theo Spielberg must have felt the collision of his two histories. Spielberg shakes his head. "No. It's a beautiful thing to see Theo with his own history as an African American—his own cultural legacy of slavery and indentured servitude and an unholy host of sins perpetrated on *his* race. There is this symmetry in the sense that he was bar mitzvahed. It's something that he really sees and can talk about."

Spielberg's son Max, by Amy Irving (who isn't Jewish), chose not to become bar mitzvahed. "It was hard for me that Max wasn't," he admits. "Had Max been living with us on the West Coast, as opposed to with his mom, Amy, on the East Coast, I simply would have compelled Max to be bar mitzvahed. But I didn't want to impose that on Amy because she was his custodial mom and he was living under her roof."

He says Capshaw fuels his family's current level of observance. "My wife keeps the Jewish momentum flowing in our lives." He smiles at the irony. "This shiksa goddess has made me a better Jew than my own parents. We light the candles on most Friday nights. Kate hand-makes the challah. We observe Yom Kippur and Rosh Hashanah; nobody's compelled to fast, but I fast and Kate fasts; the kids had to fast on their bar mitzvah year—their rabbi insisted. We do Hanukkah *and* we do Christmas." Christmas in such a consciously Jewish home? "We do Christmas because it was a tradition in Kate's family and because it's the one holiday I wished I could have partaken in every year I was growing up."

His longing was especially acute as an eight-year-old in Haddon Heights, New Jersey. (His family would later move to Cincinnati, Phoenix, and then Northern California.) "I would go to my dad and say, 'Dad, why can't we put lights up? We're the only house on the block that doesn't have lights.' And my dad would say, 'We have a porch light.' I said, 'Dad, you know what I mean.' Our neighbors used to win these awards for decoration; every house was regaled with Nativity scenes and Santa's sleigh. There were lights on all the eaves, doorjambs, and windows, sometimes even outlining the shape of each house. Our neighborhood was like a light show, and we were the black hole of Calcutta. But my dad would never allow us to do anything. One time he said, 'If you want to, we can put the menorah in the window.' And I said, 'No, no, no! Then people will think we're Jews!' "

Come spring, Passover always brought the entire extended family together, and that continues to this day. "We all go to Arizona where we were raised," he says. "It's a wonderful reunion." Like so many others I spoke to, Spielberg recalls being young and impatient at the seder table. "It's a shame you can't eat first, and then have Passover," he says. "When you're a kid, all you want to do is get to the food; so the grown-ups could not pray any faster."

His family kept kosher for several years when they lived in Cincinnati with his kosher grandparents. But after leaving for Camden, New Jersey, and later for Phoenix, the Spielbergs were kosher only when grandparents came to town. "My parents would never say, 'Dada or Mama are coming to visit,' Spielberg explains. "I just heard the clanking of glass against glass and knew that *treyf* was being thrown away. I'd go into the kitchen and sure enough, my mom would be cleaning out the refrigerator, cleaning out the cupboards of all of her favorite delicacies—caviar, shellfish, cherrystone clams—which you could get in Arizona in those days because Flying Tiger

Airlines was shipping them into restaurants from Maine. All the *treyf* was on its way out. And then my grandparents would come and we would be kosher for a week. We went kosher for either side of the family."

When either grandmother visited, Spielberg's mother, Leah, reverted easily to their kosher dictates, but chafed at their cooking. "I remember great clashes in the kitchen about how much schmaltz to put in the chopped liver," Spielberg says. "My father's mother had a special way of making chopped liver which was contrary to the way my mother always prepared it, and they used to fight over how much minced onions and schmaltz go in the mix. I would just sit there and watch these two ladies fight. My mom only knew English, so she'd hurl invectives at my grand- mother in English. My grandmother would become so flustered, she'd start screaming at my mother in Russian and Yiddish. Most of the Yiddish I learned was during these conflicts in the kitchen."

His family's impious taste for seafood was nearly discovered one evening in their New Jersey home, when their family rabbi decided to pay a surprise visit. "Maybe this was God very carefully watching our sweet hypocrisy about being kosher and nonkosher, but my mom had just come back from the fish market and she had just brought in four live lobsters for dinner. Lobsters, as you know, are just behind pork as *sin food*. As she's tak- ing the live lobsters out of the bag and putting them on the counter, Rabbi Greenberg pulls into the driveway, unannounced. I remember my mom screamed, 'Quick! Hide these things!' She throws them in my arms. Luck- ily their claws are wrapped with rubber bands, and I run into my bedroom and put them on the bed.

"Well, the rabbi sometimes liked to come to our rooms and see how we were all doing; he would knock on our doors, and just say, 'How's school and how are you feeling? Any problems?' We had a wonderful rabbi. This particular night, I could hear his footsteps coming because my mom never uncovered the shag carpet from the clear plastic covering—only when special company came did we get to actually feel shag on our bare feet—we walked on plastic most of our lives. So I heard his squeaky Flor- sheims against the plastic coming down the hallway, and I took all the lob- sters and stuffed them under my bed, and the second I put them under the bed, the knock came on my door." Spielberg raps on the conference table. " 'Shmuel?' the rabbi says. (He called me Shmuel.) And I said, 'Yes, come in.' He comes in and sits next to me on the bed with his feet on the floor and he's asking, 'So how's school? How are things?' and suddenly I notice—but he doesn't—that two of the lobsters are crawling out from under the bed next to his left shoe. Two more lobsters are coming out next to my right foot. And the lobsters are starting to investigate my bedroom. My eyes are going all over the room because these lobsters are out, but he's just talking to me, making good eye contact. When he was finished, the rabbi just got up and left and never looked down at his feet. Those lobsters were in plain sight."

This rabbi was part of the Spielberg family—"My mom and dad went on camping trips with him," he says. When they moved to Phoenix, they were visited by their cantor, who came weekly to prepare Spielberg for his bar mitzvah. "I want to remember his name," he says, clearly laboring to recall it. "I really want to remember. Was it Cantor Rothstein? *Hey, Christy!?*" He's calling his assistant, who sits outside his office. "*Christy!?*" An aside: "This a Jewish house: we yell all the time." He tries another assistant: "*Ben!?*" Ben opens the door expectantly. "Call my dad and ask him, 'Did Cantor Rothstein prepare me for my bar mitzvah?' " Spielberg instructs. "Ask him who came to the house every Sunday for a year. I think it was Cantor Rothstein." Another sip of tea. "Of course the cantor couldn't accept any kind of gratuity; we had orange trees in our yard, so every Sunday I would have to prepare a box of oranges for him."

Spielberg felt puffed up on his bar mitzvah day. "I really felt that I was a man," he recalls. "Until I still had to go to bed at nine the next day. I couldn't reconcile my early bedtime with the lip service my parents and my friends were giving me that 'Today you are a man and forever shall you be.' "

As he grew out of adolescence, Spielberg grew away from observance. "I was privately proud to be a Jew but I was publicly humiliated to be one because I was living in a neighborhood of upward mobility where everybody was gentile. And we were always, if not the only Jews, some of the few Jews in the area. I think the Sussmans were Jewish—they lived across from us. He recalls kids ribbing him—"Mainly in Arizona; people sometimes walked past me and coughed 'Jew' into their hands like they were trying to clear their throats. It was always deeply humiliating for me to encounter anyone that didn't like me because of who I was."

He never let his parents know. "I didn't want them to call the parents of the kid harassing me," he explains. "I knew I would be doubly harassed if I told."

Though he felt shame in being different, there was no shame in the heritage itself. "We were involved in the synagogue, we had a lot of Jewish friends—my mom was a concert pianist and she played four-hand with other Jewish pianists that came to the house to perform. And my grandparents brought great old Russian stories about the Cossacks—most of them apocryphal, but nonetheless enjoyable, and stimulating to my whole being and imagination. So I wanted to be able to shout out I was a Jew, but I was a minority and was too afraid of the consequences. I also knew a lot about the Holocaust—my parents talked about it all the time—and so it was always on my mind: 'Look at what the Nazis did to the Jews—only a couple of decades ago, relatively speaking.' "

While he didn't dare tell his parents about being teased as a youngster, that secrecy became impossible in his teenage years. "My last year of high school—when we were living in Northern California—I really encountered anti-Semitism," Spielberg says. "That was the first time I was ever slugged in the mouth for being a Jew. That was the first time I was ever kicked in the groin for being Jewish. That was the first time I ever had pennies thrown at me in a very quiet study hall while a hundred kids around me were trying to study. That was the first time I saw people walking twenty yards out of their way to knock me into a wall on their way to class. It was the first time anti-Semitism became physical abuse. That had never happened before.

"My mom—which was even more humiliating—decided she would now drive me to school. We only lived within a fifteen-minute walk from the high school but my mom insisted on taking me in her army jeep and picking me up every day until this would end. But it never ended. It ended only when I graduated. Still, all that time I never went to a teacher. I never went to a dean. I never complained. I never turned anybody in." He was too fearful of reprisals from the kids responsible. "It was a group of about six seniors. We all graduated in the same class. I've never mentioned their names and I never will."

I assume he's been tempted, all these years later, to give them a call. "Actually, one of them called *me* after *Close Encounters* came out," he says, clearly aware that his fame had turned the tables. "I'd had these two big successful movies—*Jaws* [1975] and *Close Encounters [of the Third Kind,* 1977]*, and I got a call from one of these guys right here in my office at Universal Studios. He wasn't the worst of the group, and ironically he'd become a police officer, working in San Jose. We had a very nice conversation. I never brought it up; I should have. He never brought it up; he should have. And that was the last we spoke."

Why does he think he should have opened old wounds? "Because I had been fantasizing about getting all these guys in group therapy with me," he replies, with a deep laugh. "I just wanted to ask them, 'Why did you make my life miserable for a whole semester?' "

Spielberg says this hazing made him appreciate the sting of even small slights. "It gave me tremendous respect for any personal injustice meted out by people who are intolerant of the differences in others," he says. How does he react when he hears people say, in effect, 'Enough with this anti-Semitism stuff; it's not an anti-Semitic world anymore'? "I will join them in saying, 'Enough of this anti-Semitism stuff' once this 'anti-Semitism stuff' is over," Spielberg replies flatly. "I don't know when that's going to be. It may be over in Hollywood, where I've never experienced anti-Semitism anywhere inside the film industry in my entire career. But I know it exists all over the country in pockets. If it doesn't exist vocally, it exists in whispers."

He never felt bigotry after high school, but he observed it on the set of *Schindler's List* (1993)—his widely acclaimed, Oscar-winning film about Oskar Schindler, the German Nazi officer who saved more than 1,100 Polish Jews during the Holocaust by employing them in his factory. "Everybody experienced anti-Semitism in Poland when we were making the movie," he recalls. "They were putting all sorts of anti-Semitic slogans on the walls with spray paint, painting swastikas on our set. And there were incidents in our hotel, the Hotel Forum, between Ben Kingsley and a German businessman. Because I'd hired Jews to play Jews and Germans to play Germans, and suddenly this German businessman walks into the dining room of the hotel and he's surrounded by Israeli actors who I'd brought in from Israel to play the Jews in my movie, and he began loudly making disparaging remarks, until Ben Kingsley leapt across the table and brought him to the ground. And the hotel staff ran over and pulled Ben off of this guy, and told this guy never to come back."

Why did Spielberg feel so strongly that only Jews should play Jews?

"Because it's in my nature, I think—especially in a story about the Holocaust—to be able to commiserate and to tell the story with members of my own race. That was very important to me. In fact, I unfairly developed a very, very strong 'attitude'—in quotes—about the German actors playing the Nazis. These were just really good actors I had cast who wanted to talk to me about *E.T.* and *Close Encounters* and *Raiders of the Lost Ark*— they were fans—and I was giving them an attitude: 'I can't talk about that now; I'm too into this.' Whereas I would happily talk to the Israeli actors about anything they wanted to talk to me about.

"And then one day we had Passover at the Hotel Forum and we invited the whole cast and crew to come. The Israeli actors all came in and sat around me with the Haggadahs, and then all the German actors playing the Germans came in. And the Israeli actors took the German actors and shared their Haggadahs with them; they took them through the entire seder. I sat at the head of the table and I just cried like a baby. Nobody understood what was wrong with me—people kept coming over to me saying, 'Are you okay?' I was wrecked by that. And I apologized to a lot of the actors the next day when we began shooting again. I said, 'If you felt a distance or a coldness from me, it's the uniform. I'm having a real tough, tough time with the uniform you're wearing.' And I think everything changed for the better after that. The fact that the German actors took it upon themselves to come to a seder and sit with the Israeli actors and learn about the holiday was an epiphany for me."

Spielberg was given *Schindler's List,* the book by Thomas Keneally, in 1982 by then-president of Universal, Sidney Sheinberg, who'd found and bought the book for the studio. Spielberg waited a decade to make the film. "I put it off because I knew I wasn't ready to tackle that subject," he says. "I needed to know I was ready before assuming a maturity on film that I knew I didn't possess at that time, in the early eighties. I think making *The Color Purple* [1985] and making *Empire of the Sun* [1987] were the two stepping-stones that led to my feeling ready to direct *Schindler's List.* And without those two pictures, I probably would have had to find two more films of more mature, adult subject matter before I could have felt qualified—not just as a Jew but as a filmmaker—to tackle that subject and to acquit that film powerfully."

When it came time to start the project, he was still uneasy. "I was more frightened of bringing shame to a segment of the survivor population already devastated by what occurred. My big, big fear was that somehow the film would be too sweet and saccharine, too sentimental, and I could somehow trivialize the impact on film that the Holocaust had on the real people in real life. I didn't ever think a survivor would see the movie and say, 'That's exactly the way it was.' I was hoping they would see the movie and say, 'It was something like that, but worse beyond your imagination and beyond my communication.' So that would have been a great compliment. And indeed many, many survivors who saw the movie felt the film honored their experiences; but of course no book, no film, no television miniseries, no poetry or music can ever replicate the experience that the Holocaust survivors had firsthand. That's impossible. It will never be communicated in its savage intensity by any of the creative arts. I knew that going in, but I just didn't want to soft-pedal it. I didn't want to water it down. And I didn't care if it got an X rating. I would have been very happy to show the picture in the few movie houses that would dare to exhibit it."

He says he almost intentionally sabotaged its commercial viability. "Obviously I did a lot of self-destructive things: I shot it in black and white; the movie is three hours and fifteen minutes long; it's about the Holocaust; there's full-frontal nudity; there are unspeakable acts of horror and bloodletting—all based on the facts. But this was obviously a film—especially to Universal Studios—that was not going to make its money back. And I have to give credit to Sid Sheinberg, who had the courage first to buy the book, but more importantly to give it to *me*—a person who had just made a movie about a friendship between an alien and a human. For Sid to even have thought that someday in the future I could have been the right filmmaker for this—that's the most courageous thing Sid ever did—giving it to me and not Sydney Pollack or somebody else who had already proved themselves worthy of telling a story like that. But he gave it to me; I'll never forget him for that. Also for allowing me to make this picture in black and white, R-rated, over three hours long, with no punches pulled, and saying, 'I don't care if it does cost twenty million dollars'—which is how much the film cost to make—'if we lose every penny, it will have been worth it just to have released that picture.' That's what Sid said to me and that's why he's my hero."

I ask Spielberg how it felt to be the one to resurrect scenes of unspeakable horror—for instance, the scene where hordes of women are corralled into the "showers." "I felt shame," Spielberg recounts. "I felt shame for being a witness with my clothes on, in relative safety—standing in the shadow of the camera—while a hundred women disrobed, actually had their heads shaved, and were forced into these shower rooms. These actors portrayed women who didn't know whether there would be Zyklon-B gas or cold water coming from the taps. At Auschwitz, when the women were first taken off the transports, they didn't know whether it was going to be gas or water, because by then the rumors were all over that these were death camps.

"And it was also the feeling that I wanted to save everybody. I wanted to run in there and say, 'You don't have to take your clothes off, you don't have to go into the shower, this doesn't have to happen; the Holocaust *never should have happened.*' And then finally stopping those words from reaching my lips and realizing that we were here because the Holocaust *did* happen, and maybe we can do something about it never happening again, if I can be so pretentiously bold in making that statement. Because I really felt that if this film changed ten minds, it would have been worth the effort. If it could turn ten deniers into people who accept the statistics of the six million, it would have been worth the effort. If the film lost all its money—all twenty million dollars and all its marketing costs and everything else—but one teacher decided to show the film to his or her class, it would have been worth the effort. And that emboldened me to tell the story as powerfully as I knew how in 1993."

The film not only garnered Spielberg the kind of respect he'd had yet to earn from critics and from the Hollywood community (the film won the Academy Award for best director and best picture), but it was an unambiguous commercial success, grossing $100 million at the domestic box office and more than $320 million worldwide. "It was a complete affirmation of the fact that people *were* paying attention," he says. "They weren't going to forget about the Holocaust. And it also opened the door to the Shoah Foundation, which is now the reason I realize I made the picture. I didn't know why I made *Schindler's List*, but only in retrospect can I say I made it so the Shoah Foundation would exist."

The Shoah Foundation—Shoah means catastrophe in Hebrew and has become a synonym for genocide—was created by Spielberg to preserve the stories of Holocaust survivors from all over the world and to catalog them for use in schools and libraries. "I never would have imagined collecting the testimonies on videotape of survivors in sixty-four countries in thirty-seven languages—fifty-two thousand of them have already given their testimony—had it not been for some of the actual survivors depicted in *Schindler's List* coming up to me when they came to visit Poland for the first time since 1945 to try to get me to listen to their *entire* life stories. These survivors wanted to tell me not just about the segment of their life experience that we were depicting on film, but about all of it."

Obviously he's heard the sentiment that Jews shouldn't hold themselves up as the only people to have suffered a genocide, that they should let it go a little. "The Jews are just the people who *can't* let it go," he says fervently. "Because everybody *else* wants to let it go. If the Jews let it go, the entire roof falls in."

Kenneth Cole

THE FOG AND DRIVING RAIN don't detract from the majesty of Kenneth Cole's estate in Westchester. As I drive through the electric security gate (which he's left open for me), past wet green lawns and a tennis court, I can't help thinking, *This Jewish boy from Great Neck made good.*

He answers the front door himself—looking compact and younger than his forty-nine years—dressed in jeans and a gray cotton button-down shirt with a black T-shirt underneath. Very Kenneth Cole. I catch only a glimpse of the elegant foyer and sweeping staircase before he leads me into his office on the main floor—a cozy room with antiques, a mannequin torso, and a wall full of enlarged black and white photographs of his three photogenic daughters, products of his eighteen-year marriage to Maria Cuomo. (She is the daughter of former governor Mario Cuomo and chair of a national housing program for the indigent, HELP USA.)

Cole and I sit on opposite sides of his desk, his hands folded in front of him on a leather blotter. He has jotted down some notes on a legal pad, and the fact that he has prepared for this interview should not surprise me: It's clear early on in the conversation that Judaism is a subject to which he's given a great deal of thought, especially lately. He begins haltingly, explaining that it's a delicate time in terms of this issue. "Being Jewish was always something I was proud of, but it wasn't until my father passed away about twelve years ago that I became much more committed to learning about why my Jewishness mattered so much to me."

His father, Charles Cole—formerly Cohen—was a shoe manufacturer whose profession Kenneth initially rejected in favor of law school plans, but ultimately chose and pursued with astounding success. (His company, Kenneth Cole Productions, which he founded in 1982, has one hundred thirty stores in twenty-five countries, annual worldwide sales of over one billion dollars, and was ranked among the top one hundred New York companies in June 2003 and for the five years prior.)

Cole has often described his father as his greatest mentor, but Charles's death jolted Kenneth into an emotional reexamination of his dad and his heritage. "I think that maybe I just needed to connect a little bit more to *him* and to get a sense of him," Cole says now. "And through him, probably myself. I believe that we are all essentially the culmination of our life's experiences and relationships. And that relationship—for me and probably for most people—was as important as any."

He says he wasn't particularly curious about his religion growing up. "I didn't have a real understanding of what it meant to be Jewish—what those four thousand years of history had entailed. I knew that it was something that many people had committed their lives to. I knew that, over the years, it was as defining a characteristic of who someone was (or wasn't) as any. I also knew that so many Jews, whether they wore their Jewishness on their sleeves or not, had died just because they were. But I never really took the time to put any of it in perspective. I just hadn't felt a need to."

That changed when he was seventeen years old, in 1973. His parents, who he says always came up with "inspiring" summer adventures, suggested he work on a kibbutz in Israel—a farming collective where families live and labor together for the benefit of their shared community. "When I search back for one experience in my life where I learned and came away with the most, I think it might have been that summer," he says. It was harder work than he was prepared for. "The ritual essentially was: You woke up at four-thirty in the morning, had a quick something to eat—a piece of bread and a glass of juice—and you were in the fields by five picking peaches. And you worked three or four hours *very* hard and then you had your big meal—or the big breakfast—at about eight, nine in the morning. And then you got back to work, until about twelve o'clock, and then you'd rest." (His rhythmic, run-on cadence has the unmistakable feel of a rabbi telling an ancient parable; I can tell there's a lesson coming.) "And then you'd sleep because you'd worked hard and it was very hot and that was the most productive use of your resources and that was the way you were expected to contribute to this community—this idealistic settlement which was socialism in its purest form.

"So during the hot hours of the day, everyone took naps and rested. And then they woke up, exercised—usually soccer—and had a light dinner, and there was a little socializing and then eventually you'd go to bed.

"But for me it was different: When everyone started picking peaches, I would find the biggest peach I could and hide behind the biggest tree I could find and essentially napped, and picked one bucket of peaches for every eight or ten of everyone else's. And I thought that I had found the way to realize the same rewards as the next guy while doing far less. (Not uncharacteristic of much of what I did in those days.) And then, at the end of the day, while all the others rested, I would go off to look for excitement, young people, Americans, and maybe trouble. Because I *wasn't* tired.

"Maybe two-thirds of the way through the summer, I realized one day that I hadn't fooled anybody. That everybody knew what I was doing but nobody really cared. And in the end, the only one I was *really* fooling and shortchanging was myself. So I started working because I realized that I had to; I hadn't been 'carrying my weight.' And immediately everything improved—especially my relationship with my peers. In many ways, I grew up that summer. I realized you can usually find shortcuts, and that in the end, they rarely work. You get out what you put in."

It feels like he's told this story before, perhaps to his daughters as a kind of cautionary tale. The success of his company and his punishing schedule over the years are testament to his work ethic. But when I ask if he considers his stick-to-itiveness to be a Jewish trait, he shrugs. "I've always been very determined and ambitious, which has manifested itself on a baseball field or a ski slope, or even the desire to finish reading a book before the other guy starts it." He describes this drive as a "compulsive disorder; I don't know if it relates to my upbringing."

A housekeeper has brought in coffee and cake on white china, but Cole doesn't touch it. The phone on his desk rings intermittently, the cell phone vibrates, his Blackberry moans, the fax purrs, but he ignores them all. I can't help but appreciate that he's decided to keep work out of this meeting, but I'm aware of how persistently it intrudes. Without making too much of it, I do get the feeling that Cole has decided this subject merits his attention.

He continues: "About two months after I came back from the kibbutz, the Yom Kippur War broke out and I wanted to enlist. I felt this sense of connection and obligation. You don't get many opportunities in life to do things that are important. And my kibbutz friends (by far the toughest I had ever known) were all in the military and would be fighting, and I felt I should be with them and not look for another shortcut." Logistics prevented him from joining up. "The realities weren't so simple," he says. "The Israeli army had no interest in taking untrained seventeen-year-old Americans."

It sounds like his radical moment passed like so many youthful phases do, and he's almost dismissive of it now. "In retrospect, that was more a Zionistic thing than it was a Jewish thing for me."

The "Jewish thing" was still dormant as his career took off, and as he drew so much attention in 1985 for his provocative advertising slogans, such as *"What you stand for is more important than what you stand in,"* which didn't show shoes, but a shoelace in the shape of an AIDS ribbon. "The time to do something meaningful is often when others are less inclined to," Cole says. "In my career, that's what I've always done. I made a very public, emphatic commitment to AIDS research nineteen years ago because it was the right thing to do and nobody else was." His ads would go on to address gun control, homelessness, and reproductive rights. For instance: *"We think women should have a choice when it comes to being pregnant. Barefoot is another story."* Or: *"Wearing protection is the new black," "Not voting is so last season," "Gun safety . . . it's all the rage,"* and *"Choice. No woman should be without one."* One ad, *"What's wrong with shoeing the homeless?,"* asked buyers to donate shoes to the homeless in exchange for a discount on a new pair. He donates forty percent of his sales every year to AMFAR on World AIDS Day, and received the Amnesty International Media Spotlight Award in 1998, along with other honorees.

But Cole is wary of suggesting that social activism is specifically a Jewish value. "It's hard to say, 'Jews are this way and gentiles are that way.' And you stand a very real chance of it being misinterpreted." He suggests Jews have been persecuted for centuries, in part because of their perceived smugness: "It's so much a part of the plight of Jews for 3300 years, ever since Moses left the mountain and we said, 'We are the Chosen People.' Even though it is a cornerstone of much of what has driven us, it could be perceived as arrogant and something one probably shouldn't share with others unless you know them to be Jewish. One could certainly make the case (and many do) that we're *all* chosen people. Since most religions trace their roots back to that same moment."

Cole clearly wants to make sure his Jewish pride isn't mistaken for self-importance. That sensitivity has to be born, in part, of having married a non-Jewish woman who is raising their children Catholic. Cole takes care not to undercut non-Jewish faiths, even going so far as to extol the worth of religion, period—no matter what brand. "So many people have improved their lives by finding faith," he says. "It offers moral boundaries they may never have had. It provides a sense of purpose that may never have existed. And it constantly reminds them that they're not alone."

He returned to Israel a second time with his two eldest daughters, then eleven and nine, to give them a slice of his history. "I wanted them to get a sense of the part of them that's Jewish, to understand its richness and at the same time to understand how it relates to other religions—or not—and to be able to put it in perspective."

When he wed Maria in 1987 after a year-long courtship, he joined a family whose Roman Catholicism seems as strong as its Democratic ideology. At their wedding, which took place in the presence of four hundred guests at the New York State governor's mansion in Albany and was covered as a news story by the *New York Times*, both a priest and a rabbi presided. But when it came to raising their children, Cole agreed to defer to Cuomo's religion. It's clear now that he didn't anticipate how difficult that was going to be. "A lot of this journey of mine back to Judaism became more impassioned since," he says. "But this is what we agreed to do. And I felt that this is what we needed to do for the children." He pauses. "And it's hard for me every day."

Clearly he's now navigating his way through conflicting attachments. He celebrates Christmas. He meets privately with a rabbi once a week. ("It's therapeutic," he says. "One hour a week, I close my door and turn off my phone, which I don't do easily. And I try to make sense of who I am, why 'this' has all come to be, and if and how our lives make sense in a world that so often doesn't.") He holds Passover seders—at which some of Maria's family are often present. The "father-daughters trip" to Israel was perhaps another equalizer; he says Israel itself dramatizes the coexistence of faiths. "I wanted to show them the coming together of Christian and Muslim and Jewish beliefs pretty much on one hill, in one place. It was important to me to show them not just what Israel has meant to me, but what it means to the world.

"There's an extraordinary resonance in the journey that the Jewish people have endured. It is prophesied in the Torah that 'The Jews over time will be scattered among nations, will always be few in number,' and our prophets wrote that we will always be 'a light unto nations.' . . . The prophecy as to the breadth of the Jewish nation has so far proven to be true, we know that the Jewish nation is the only one to have experienced and survived in exile twice (the second time for almost two thousand years), and few would doubt that the Jewish world (however small it remains, as dispersed as we know it is) has also had an extraordinarily positive impact on the morality of the entire civilized world.

"We've survived this long despite so much adversity and there is an immense depth in the lessons we have learned along the way. My hope individually is that my daughters can get as much as there is to offer from that. And our hope collectively, Maria and I, is that in the end, they will be thoroughly enriched by both faiths."

I ask him what he thinks his children will say, down the line, if someone asks if they're Jewish: "I hope they'll say . . ." He pauses. "I mean right now they define themselves as being religiously Christian—because the Jews and the Christians all believe that the child is affiliated in the womb from the mother, and so, unless Maria's going to convert, which isn't going to happen . . ." He begins again: "My hope is that they'll make clear that there is a part of them that is Jewish. And there *is*. And to the degree it positively manifests itself in their lives, the more comfortable they will be embracing it."

He is also conscious of steering them away from Jewish stereotypes, which he fears can sometimes be self-inflicted. "I hate the term JAP. Hate it. But I think I know how it's fueled. We tend to want to give our children everything. We want to give everything we had plus everything we didn't have. And in the end, we probably do indulge them and enable them to have a sense of entitlement."

•   •   •

Though Cole has spent the last decade exploring his heritage, he hasn't wanted his Jewishness to classify him. "I rarely accept invitations to speak or make an appearance somewhere because I'm Jewish. I just haven't done that. I've accepted invitations because of what I do and why. And the fact is I'm a Jewish person doing it, for which I'm proud, but I'm reluctant to make the case that the reason I'm doing it is because I'm Jewish."

Is he comfortable being an emblem of success for "The Jews" in general? "I've been uncomfortable doing that," he acknowledges. "I don't know if the success I've had (to the degree you call it that) is because I'm Jewish, or despite the fact. Also, it doesn't feel right for anyone to just assume that mantle. One should keep in mind that if they do choose that course, they might at one point stumble, or even worse, fall (maybe to get up again or maybe not), and then what?" He then qualifies this: "I'm certainly not quiet about being Jewish."

Ever since his third trip to Israel, however, he has been "coming out"—or inching out—as a Zionist. In 2002 he returned with his brother-in-law, Andrew Cuomo. "It was a day after the Passover massacre [when nineteen Israelis were gunned down at a communal seder], and I got a call from Andrew, who was running for governor of New York. He said, 'Let's go to Israel tomorrow.' Just when the State Department was putting out an announcement saying that all unnecessary government officials should return home and a warning to all Americans to stay away."

Cole says the people close to him told him not to go. "*Nobody* was supportive of this trip," he says. "They said, 'Andrew has to go, it's good for him politically, but you're a lunatic, you're out of your mind, who do you think you are?' But I thought this was an important time and that the effort we could make at that moment would have so much more significance than the same gesture made at another time. Israel's existence seemed as much in jeopardy as it had ever been; there was this little island of about five million Jews amongst a nation of six million people, surrounded by over a billion Muslims in the world, many of whom were united by a single common goal: the annihilation of the state of Israel and the Jewish people.

"What is frighteningly noteworthy is that somehow over the last several years, Israel, in the world's eye, has gone from being viewed as the vulnerable David to the intrusive and aggressive Goliath. Upon our arrival in Tel Aviv, I should add, beyond even our greatest expectations, we were embraced and given access typically reserved for heads of state."

It appears Cole has gone from dipping a toe into Israeli politics to an ankle-high commitment. "It can't be just about writing checks," he clarifies. "I wouldn't join a club once because part of the ritual was that every year you had to make a contribution to the UJA. Not that I didn't support them, I did, but I didn't feel that it should be an obligation. And I believe sometimes that just writing a check (although often necessary) is too easy, and is often the course of least resistance. There are so many resources we all have that can yield much more value.

"I do believe strongly in many fundamental Jewish principles: the importance of *tzedakah* [charity], for instance, which we are taught is an obligation and a responsibility, and learn later is actually a blessing and a privilege. And *tikkun olam* [healing or repairing the world], which means that our job on this planet is to finish the process of creation; God gave us what's here and our job is to finish it in a morally just way. But I don't necessarily believe that one has to do it with a yarmulke on."

He uses his fashion ads instead. A fall 2002 campaign, for instance, featured a newsstand scene with a man holding a newspaper whose headline trumpeted "Holy War." The ad copy: *"Mideast peace is the must-have for fall."*

I close our discussion by probing a little further into how he feels about raising his children in his wife's faith. "Under the circumstances, it is the right thing to do," he reiterates. "But it's probably the hardest thing in my life that I have had to come to terms with and it just doesn't seem to get any easier. As hard as it is for me today, however, I believe more than I ever did how important it is for them. To have a sense of faith, so that when they put their heads on their pillows at night, they never feel alone. I have accepted the responsibility that I have to teach them more about that special side of them that is Jewish. And as a result, I've learned more myself over the years and probably taught them more than I was taught more formally when I was their age."

As Cole escorts me out, the dog, Bernie, runs up in a good-bye of sorts. "I should add that a significant concession was made in this house." Cole smiles. "Maria, after much consideration, agreed to allow me to at least raise the dog Jewish."

Beverly Sills

BEVERLY SILLS PHOTOGRAPHED IN 1974 BY JILL KREMENTZ

BEVERLY SILLS, possibly the most famous soprano in the world, has dropped crumbs of ruggelach on the front of her dress and it's my fault. I brought the small Jewish pastries to get us in the mood. "Oh God," she says, taking another bite, "no self-control."

Sills's office at the Metropolitan Opera, where she was chairwoman when we met, is not especially large or personally appointed, but when she starts to talk about her Jewish past, I feel immediately like I'm in my Great Aunt Belle's home (in fact, Sills's real name *is* Belle). Sills is so unaffected and warm, there are no airs of the diva. As we talk, I forget that she's the woman who was once dubbed "America's Queen of Opera"—the highest-paid opera singer of her day—who received the Presidential Medal of Freedom and who has famous friends like the Kissingers, who she says often invite her to their Sunday hot dog suppers. Her smile is big, her laugh is deep, and she's eating a Zabar's ruggelach with proper appreciation.

"My mother's father was a political refugee." Sills explains he had been sent, as a young man, from Russia to Paris to study electrical engineering, and was radicalized there by the writings of Eugene V. Debs. "He returned home a Socialist—a great embarrassment to the family—and was asked to leave. He was very hotheaded, spoke seven languages, a very attractive man. And he left behind my grandmother with three little girls and pregnant with a fourth. The oldest of the three little girls was my mother." Debs helped bring her grandfather to Brooklyn, and months later, the rest of the family followed.

On her father's side, her Grandma Fanny was born in Romania and was widowed three times. "She had *fifteen* children," she marvels, "and she came here with all fifteen. The next to the youngest was my dad." Grandma Fanny was wealthy and also lived in Brooklyn, albeit in a bigger house on Eastern Parkway. "She wore a black dress all her life," Sills says with a chuckle. "We'd say to her, 'Why do you always wear black, Grandma?' And she said, 'I'm in mourning.' And we'd say, 'For whom?' And she'd say, 'Whatever.' " Another deep laugh.

Fanny created massive Passover seders, which Sills recalls as wonderfully chaotic. "There could be sixty people and she did all the cooking. She made all these doughy things and a lot of us kids would eat under the table—there were no chairs for us." Other foods stand out in her memory. "*Teglach*—the honey things with nuts and fruit—oh, I loved those. Macaroons. My grandmother made a lot of knishes. And chicken, chicken, chicken."

Sills, seventy-four when we met, stopped being a Silverman when she began her professional career at age seven. She debuted in a movie for Twentieth Century Fox, for which the producer, Walter Wanger, renamed her "Beverly Sills." "They decided that Belle Miriam Silverman was the wrong name to put on a marquee," she says. Her family, however, has never called her either Beverly or Belle. "My family has always called me 'Bubbles,' " she says. "My mother and brothers always call me 'Bubbly.' "

For someone called Bubbly, her life has been anything but. She married a man thirteen years her senior, Peter Buckley Greenough, who wasn't Jewish, which dismayed her mother and caused her relatives to boycott the wedding: "They didn't want to come," she says. When I remark that that must have been hard, she shakes her head: "It was terrible, not just hard. *Terrible.*"

She started caring for Greenough's three children, one of whom was handicapped, and when she and Greenough had two children of their own, each was born with disabilities—a daughter, Meredith ("Muffy"), who was deaf, and a son, Peter Jr. ("Bucky"), so severely retarded that today he lives in an "adult village" for the handicapped.

Sills says religion didn't help her handle these trials. "I drew on my mother," she says, and describes Mrs. Silverman in terms so over-the-top, they sound operatic. "My mother was one of the strongest, most intelligent, brilliant women I ever met. It's deceptive, because all my life, I've always called her 'Mama,' and people always had the impression she was one of these chubby little ladies, and then when they saw her, she was one of the most breathtakingly beautiful women I've ever laid eyes on. She wasn't just a pretty little hausfrau; she was breathtaking. I'm telling you, she would walk down the street and people turned to look. She was incredible. She was also, you know, one of those women who had dreams for her children and made them all happen."

But it wasn't her dream for her daughter to marry out of the faith. Sills describes dropping the bomb when she told her mother about her new beau: "I said he was married, had three children, his divorce was going to take a little while, and he wasn't Jewish. And she burst into tears and said, quote, 'Why does everything happen to my baby?' So it was not well-received. My father was already dead—I think she was grateful that he was. And yet we both agreed that Peter was my father's kind of man."

By that she means, Greenough was accomplished and impressive—a successful newspaper owner in Cleveland. "And he was very difficult," she adds; "I would not have liked to have worked for him. He was very arrogant. His saving grace to my mother was that he was very handsome. I mean, he was a knockout. When he walked into our one-bedroom apartment in Stuyvesant Town [in New York City], she said, 'Well you're certainly handsome enough.' I guess she couldn't think of anything else to say that was nice. But what really impressed her was how well-educated he was: multilingual, sophisticated, flew his own plane, an officer in the air force, decorated. Very self-assured—he's thirteen years older than I, so my mother knew she couldn't push him around."

I ask Sills how painful it was that her marriage hurt her mother. "I'm ashamed to tell you it wasn't," she answers, "because I knew my mother was a powerhouse. I never worried about her." Greenough also worked hard to win her mother over. "He was very clever because he didn't just court me; he courted my mother. He brought her books, and I remember a lovely little silver pen that was very ornate and Russian. And whenever he flew in to visit me in New York, he would take the two of us to dinner Friday. Mama used to love it: There was a restaurant, I think it was called Le Veau d'Or, and she just loved it when he ordered in French.

"You know, they never fully accepted one another," Sills continues. "They had something in common and that was me. And my mother wanted nothing more than for me to be happy and that was what he wanted too, and so, with this common goal, they overcame all their prejudices."

They were married in her singing teacher's studio by a justice of the peace. Peter's father refused to meet Sills until the wedding day. "Later I asked him," Sills recalls, " 'What was your reaction when Peter told you he was going to marry a Jewish opera singer?' He said, 'Well, I was on my boat fishing and I had two choices: I could have thrown myself overboard or gone right on fishing, and being the intelligent man that I am, I went right on fishing.' We later became best friends. I could never have survived the many things that happened to me—to Peter and me—without the support of Peter's father."

Sills and Greenough agreed to honor one of each other's holidays. "We made a deal at the beginning," says Sills, "that he would do Passover and I would do Christmas." Her brother ran the seders until he died. "He was the catalyst for bringing us all together and went through all the rituals. I see now that unless I do it, it's not going to happen."

She describes her early years in her husband's Cleveland mansion like she was Little Orphan Annie moving into Daddy Warbucks's palace. "I'd never seen a house like that—never mind living in one," she says. "There were a lot of ladies running around keeping it clean and it was a culture shock. I'd left Stuyvesant Town, where my bed went into the closet during the day, into this incredible—I mean, it was a chateau." She never got comfortable with it. "If today someone said, 'You've got to go back to Cleveland and that house is waiting, I'd say, 'Find me a nice condominium where I can call the super.' " The Cleveland social set didn't make things easier. "It was a totally non-Jewish five years," she says. "Totally non-Jewish. And I found it quite anti-Semitic and not terribly friendly."

How did that manifest itself? "Just remarks dropped in my home. A man who worked for my husband on the paper [the *Cleveland Plain Dealer*] in a quite high position, said to me after drinking a nice bit of very good wine, which I regret having served to him, 'You know, if Peter's mother were alive, she'd die all over again; if she knew he had married a Jew.' And I said, 'Don't worry; *my* family went into mourning, too.' "

But when it came to her stage persona, her ethnicity was meaningless. "In the operatic world," she says, "in the final analysis, in the first act of *Traviata*, when the chorus leaves you all alone, it really doesn't matter what you are." That belly laugh again. "You're on your own and it's the loneliest moment of your life! Jew, gentile, white, black, purple, orange, it doesn't matter. Fortunately I was in a profession where no one ever said, 'We're not going to let her sing Violeta: she's a Jew.' The word 'talent' was the primary word. I was never referred to as 'a talented Jew.' I was referred to as 'a talented soprano.' "

Despite the fact that Sills's career defines her in the eyes of the world, it was not central to her husband, who became neither her manager nor her groupie. "I always tease that he thinks all operas end happily," she says, "because he never stays till the end of them." When she talks about her husband, it's with a distinct combination of reverence and candor. "I won't use the word 'arrogance' [although she already did previously], but he has a self-assurance that makes him a little bit less than lovable to other people. And I know that he could antagonize people and he antagonized a lot of my friends who decided that either they loved me enough that they were going to put up with him and they did . . ."—that sentence ends there. "Peter's a powerhouse," she continues (a psychologist might note that she used the same adjective to describe her mother). "He's very sick now, but up until six years ago, when he was eighty, he was one of the most extraordinary men I've ever known—one of the most difficult. I marvel at my strength—I really do—in terms of maintaining my sense of self. Because he's overwhelming."

He was also her stalwart supporter, encouraging her career despite keeping a distance from it. She says he made it possible for her to continue singing despite the many burdens at home. "It would not have happened without him," she insists. "Because when I had this problem with both our children, he gave me fifty-two round-trip tickets from Boston [they were living in Milton, Massachusetts, when the children were young] to go into

New York every week, take a singing lesson, visit my mother, have lunch with a friend, and come back in time for a late dinner with him. That's the way he did things."

She refers to her children's disabilities as a "horror": "I had stopped singing when all this horror happened, and he thought I should go back to singing for therapy. He thought it was a lot better than sitting in some doctor's office bemoaning my fate."

Her children's health issues made any question of a Jewish upbringing moot. "I probably would have been much more aggressive about it," she says, "had my daughter not been born with such problems." She even had to swallow hard and put her daughter in a convent school in Boston because it was the best facility for the deaf at that time. Even her mother was in favor of it. "There was my mother saying, 'It doesn't matter; we've got to get Muffy using a hearing aid and you've got to get this child *educated, educated.*' It's *all* she talked about. We were ten minutes away from the Boston School for the Deaf, which is run by the Sisters of Saint Joseph, who are probably the finest teachers of deaf children in the world. Even my mother didn't hesitate one bit. So my daughter, for the first seven or eight years of her life, was a *Catholic.*" Sills seems to marvel at this even now. "She went through all the rituals along with the other students."

Sills says she was persuaded that Muffy should participate in the full menu of Catholic rites. "The sister called me in and said, 'Do you want her to be the only kid sitting out in the hall? What is going to hurt her? This will teach her that religion exists, it will teach her that *God* exists.' I said, 'It will teach her that *Jesus* exists! I'm not sure that this is what I want.' But then I talked to my mother about it and she said, 'Look, let's get the child educated first. And then we can always introduce her to other choices.' So we all agreed."

But the reality of a Christian daughter was jarring in the beginning. "On the first Christmas that I gave, with the grandparents and all, we hung up the stockings, we did the whole thing for all the kids. And when I went to pick Muffy up from school, Sister Dionyses—six feet tall—said, 'Be sure you ask Mama who is coming to see you on Christmas Eve.' I thought, 'Good, they taught her about Santa Claus.' So after the celebration, we were all just about ready to put the kids down to bed—there's champagne and my old father in law is there—the Bostonian. And I thought, 'Oh, this is the perfect time.' I said, 'Muffy,' and we had to lip-read, 'tell Grandma and Grandpa who's coming to see you tonight on Christmas Eve!' " Sills is already laughing so hard she can barely tell the story. "And Muffy gets down on her knees, crosses herself, and she says, 'Mother, Mary, Joseph, and *Baby God*!' Well, my father-in-law's champagne went halfway across the room. My mother sat there and suddenly these two gloppy tears came down her face; and there's this little fat child with these little blond ringlets—I mean, Muffy couldn't have been more WASPy!—with these big blue eyes, with her hands put together, so pleased with herself that she's speaking! She expected a totally different reaction—applause or something. But there's Grandma crying, Grandpa spitting the champagne across the room, Mama too stunned to speak, and Peter laughing so hard. She was bewildered."

As Muffy grew up, she began to be more curious about her mother's heritage and started asking questions. Sills says it was difficult to answer them. "You know," Sills sighs, "Peter's ancestors came here on the *Mayflower*: it can't be worse in terms of trying to explain to her what being Jewish is."

Sills comforts herself with the thought that some faith was better than none. "I was grateful to the nuns for at least explaining to her that there was a religion. This might not be the one for her, but there was a God, and whatever his or her name is, she's got to know it exists.

"Then the boy was born with worse problems than Muffy's, and so there isn't any question about whether he's Jewish. I mean, he can't speak, he doesn't hear; there's no need to talk about religion."

Though she let her Jewish traditions fall away, nevertheless, a core identity remains unshakable. "Like it or not, who I am is because of my Jewish parents and grandparents," she states. "There is an innate culture that has come to me because of them. And I will tell you this: Peter and I and our children are going to be buried in a Jewish cemetery in Martha's Vineyard next to my mother and father." She says this with great solemnity. "I offered Peter the choice—I said, 'We can go someplace that is nonsectarian and I don't want you to feel obliged to be buried in the Jewish cemetery.' He said, 'I don't feel obliged; I loved your mother, and she and I can continue our discussions.' So he's going to be buried in a Jewish cemetery." (Some do permit burial of non-Jewish spouses.)

I ask why this mattered so much. "It was important to me as his wife that he be with me. And I'm not quite sure that, had it been the other way around, if he'd asked me to be buried in his family plot, that I would have agreed. I'm just not sure I could have done that. And I think he understood that. I don't think I could have gone into a non-Jewish cemetery. I can't explain it."

James P. Rubin

I DIDN'T REALLY EXPECT James Rubin to confide in me—to describe in intimate detail the religious dynamics at play in his marriage to CNN correspondent Christiane Amanpour. Once described as "a Jewish John-John," this former State Department spokesman for the Clinton Administration, who is as press savvy—or should I say "wary"—as they come, isn't leaping to reveal the hurdles that arise when a Jewish boy from Larchmont, whose parents want him to marry in the faith, marries an Iranian Catholic girl who happens to be one of the world's most accomplished war correspondents. So I start slowly: "Did your parents want you to date Jewish girls?"

"Yes," he replies, without elaboration.

Another attempt: "How did that play out?"

"I didn't assign a lot of value to my parents' preferences," Rubin says with a smile, then adds my editorial comment for me: " 'he said, diplomatically.' " He continues: "My parents preferred that I marry someone Jewish, they made a point of preferring it. But I very rarely dated Jewish women, it so happened. Of my three long-term relationships, the two before my wife were not with Jews. I don't have any explanation for that.

I'm sure all sorts of people could imagine an explanation, but it's just the way it is."

Rubin doesn't leave it at that. "But I want to say this, because this is important to me about this subject: My wife and I shared a moral passion and intensity for the Balkans and the oppression and murder of Muslims, primarily in Bosnia. And that to me is the ultimate reflection of the Jewish intellectual and cultural experience that I grew up with. And my wife's passion for that—and her important role in that—is far more important to me than whether she happens to have been born a Catholic or a Muslim. That is, to me, living up to the ideals and values that I understood, coming from Jewish teachings."

It's not that he was seeking a non-Jew; he just fell in love with one. "I once said something to a Jewish newspaper that my wife has never forgiven me for, but I thought it was very accurate and nice—but she didn't. And what I said was that, 'All else being equal, I would prefer to be married to a Jewish woman; but all else *wasn't* equal and I met someone who was not Jewish whom I wanted to be with.' So end of story. And all else is rarely equal in this world."

They had two marriage ceremonies on the same day in a town near Rome in August 1998. The Catholic ceremony took place in the chapel of a fifteenth-century castle; the Jewish ceremony was held at the Odescalchi palace nearby. Guests included Secretary of State Madeleine Albright, Ambassador Richard Holbrooke, and the late John Kennedy Jr., who shared a house with Amanpour when he was at Brown and she was attending the University of Rhode Island. "We had a rabbi whom, I must confess, it wasn't easy to find because my wife's not Jewish," Rubin says.

"I will tell you something personal that's sort of interesting: When we decided to do the separate ceremonies and we had to find a rabbi who would do this, I knew it would be someone who didn't know me." So he asked someone who did know him to give a homily. "One of my close friends is Leon Wieseltier," he says, referring to the literary editor of *The New Republic*, "who I think qualifies as a super-Jew. And he gave the sermon at our wedding. His way of reflecting Jewish ideals and values in our lives was something very meaningful to me; I remember thinking, 'That's what Judaism means to me.' Not the breaking of the glass and whether it's under a *chuppah* or not, but the things he said about us and reflecting back through the history of Jews."

Rubin later sends me the speech, in which Wieseltier doesn't emphasize the bride and groom's differing faiths, but what binds them, instead: *"Jamie, my old friend, you are marrying a woman of nobility: I mean the kind of nobility that lives in interior castles, and displays the unflappable, unbought grace of a natural pursuer of truth . . . She is an angel of the actual; lucid and fearless and with a heart that does not tire. Long before I met her, I learned from Christiane that objectivity is not the enemy of passion, it is the condition of passion. I think of it as Christiane's Principle: If you are going to feel strongly, you had better get it right. And it turns out that she feels sweetly as she feels strongly; that the magnitude of your bride's sweetness is like the magnitude of your bride's strength.*

"Christiane, when you chose to feel strongly about this man, you got it right. He is a cunning man, and he is a worldly man, but his cunning and his worldliness spring from a great tenderness. That is his secret. He, too, has a heart that does not tire. Jamie is a conscience in a sharp suit. His friends and his colleagues have known this for a long time. Outwardly he is as cool as inwardly he is hot with conviction and with devotion. He is a prince of restlessness, a prince of wakefulness; in those qualities, too, and in the quick disabused quality of his mind, you are marrying your match."

Rubin and Amanpour now have a son, Darius John Rubin. When I inquire how they're planning to raise him religiously, the personal conversation comes to a halt. "No comment," Rubin says with a smile. "He's three years old. In government we call that 'TBD.' "

To be determined?

"There you go."

We're sitting in Manhattan's Mark Hotel, where Rubin has only recently checked in after landing from London, where he resides with his family. A partner at Brunswick Group, a London-based financial public relations company, Rubin is in New York to tape two segments of his PBS series, *Wide Angle,* a program that covers international affairs.

He answers the door in freshly showered hair, a red long-sleeve button-down shirt, jeans, and bare feet. Jim Lehrer is on mute and Rubin has ordered coffee from room service. He takes a Marlboro Light. "I never liked matzo ball soup," he says, as we veer back to childhood. "Still don't. Never liked gefilte fish; still don't. The Passover wine was awful. I liked my grandmother's potato pancakes." He has fond memories of singing "Echad Mi Yodaya?" ["Who Knows One?"] at seders. "The one where you would sing up from one to thirteen and everybody would take a different part, and the fun was in how fast you could do it and who would make a mistake.

"We also had a weird tradition with the grandparents where, instead of the kids having to find the matzo, the kids would hide it and then negotiate with my grandfather the return of it, without which you couldn't continue the dinner. And that would involve a negotiation about money and what charity it would go to. It always went to a charity, but you'd still try to negotiate it up because that was the challenge. I remember the whole charity thing as important; nobody ever thought you were going to get that money."

I feel a stab of guilt: In our family, the kids eagerly pocketed those silver dollars every year.

He's never fasted on Yom Kippur. "I know this sounds awful, but I can't fast. I have a metabolism that requires me to eat often, and I get extremely weak if I don't eat. But even if that weren't true, I don't think I would have fasted, because for whatever reason, I tended to not take those rituals as seriously as other members of my family."

It's clear his Jewish identity was forged more in a political atmosphere than a religious one. "My breakfast, lunch, and dinner table tended to be a place where politics were discussed extensively and intensively from the moment I can remember," says Rubin. "The *New York Times* was the newspaper that was discussed. Israel and the Jews were on the table from the moment I became politically aware. Being me, I tended to take the other side of the issue when I was at home; and when I was with other people who I didn't think appreciated the unique feelings Jews have about the Holocaust, and thus Israel, I tended to be more supportive. So depending on which group I was in, I tended to argue the other side, just because that's my style."

His parents dragged him to Israel in the heat of August when he was thirteen: not a great introduction to the Holy Land. "I remember it as one of the most awful trips," he says. "Mostly because my parents wanted to do sightseeing things and I wanted to go swimming at the beach and play sports and do boy things at thirteen, and I was being forced to go to museums and it was hot; we were in hot cars.

"And then I returned again in 1982—a college summer—during the war in Lebanon, and I traveled around more by myself." He was struck by the fact that everyone—from janitor to surgeon—was Jewish. "Seeing

Jewish soldiers, Jewish athletes, people who prided themselves on physical characteristics rather than mental characteristics in Israel was significant to me. Because in America, the Jews I tended to come into contact with were measuring themselves more in science class or whether they were going to be doctors. And it had a real impact on me—at age twenty or so—to see my contemporaries in uniform, who were going to be fighter pilots, I remember that had a real impact on me."

I wonder, as he talks about the ambitious Jewish kids with whom he grew up, whether he felt the stereotypical Jewish pressure to achieve. "My favorite story about this is when I first got out of graduate school [Columbia University—M.A. in international relations]. I remember I was at my first job at a think tank, and I published my first opinion piece in a national newspaper—the *Christian Science Monitor*. And I was very excited because it was the first thing I published—I was maybe twenty-four or twenty-five—and I called my parents to tell them; and almost instinctively and without any bad intent, my father said, 'So why wasn't it in the *New York Times*?'" Rubin lets the question hang in the air a moment. "And I remember it deflating me a little bit, but it also demonstrated the high standards that I grew up with."

He still makes a point of going home for Passover, and for at least one of the High Holy Days. "Two times a year is what I sort of set as a goal. Given my job, there were years when I didn't do that, but I try most years." He says there were many times, during his tenure in Washington, when he had to work on Yom Kippur, but managed to squeeze in a temple visit here and there. "I remember going to Yom Kippur services with Sandy Berger, the national security adviser. We've done that a couple of times, once in London this past year."

I tell him that the majority of the people I've spoken to share his experience: letting go of most of the Jewish practices with which they were raised. Does he worry at all about how Judaism will sustain itself if Jews keep abandoning it? "I have to be honest and say that most of the issues that I struggle with in my life involve Liberia and Bosnia and Afghanistan and terrible, horrible things in the world. And those are the ones that I spend the vast majority of my time contemplating. And I'm aware of—conscious of—the question of the assimilation of Jews and what that all means, but I don't spend a lot of time thinking about it. And when I do think about it, I tend to avoid it. Not because I don't recognize it as a problem, it's just not my highest priority as a human being.

"When I think big thoughts about the meaning of life and the planet, it tends to be about big problems: nuclear proliferation, terrorism, Saddam Hussein, peace in the Middle East—and I see that as separated from its religious context. Now I believe that my passion and intensity for helping the Bosnian people was partially and substantially a reflection of being Jewish and learning about the context of 'Never Again' and Holocaust and ethnic cleansing and slaughter of a people for who they are and not what they've done.

"Bosnia was a very powerful issue because it didn't affect American national interests directly, and so how people responded to it was very interesting. I found a correlation between Jewish people and caring about Muslims in Bosnia. That's the part of being Jewish that means a lot to me: the values, the significance of helping the underdog, the oppressed, the one who is being discriminated against, more than remembering Rabbi Hillel's sayings."

I ask if he ever felt conscious of being a Jew in the State Department. "My religion, and whether I had one leg or two eyes or one nostril, had no impact whatsoever on my ability to tell the foreign service that, 'This is what the president of the United States wants you to do.' Period.

"Now, I will acknowledge that the Clinton Administration happened to have had a very large number of Jews in the national security area, working especially on the subject of Israel. And that was the subject of a lot of written commentaries in the Arab world, and perhaps here as well . . . Arguably and objectively, the Clinton Administration had a tougher love policy towards Israel than the Bush Administration, which has few prominent Jewish-Americans involved in policy at all. So I don't think one's religion had any impact on one's policy prescriptions or presumptions or proclivities. And I don't feel in any way that my being Jewish affected how the foreign service responded to the Secretary of State."

But surely he felt heightened scrutiny when he dealt with Israel and issues surrounding the conflict there. "Yeah, I felt the self-hating Jew accusation if we were being tough on Israel, and I felt the Arabs using my being Jewish against me, but I didn't have any guilt about the whole thing. I believed that one could believe strongly in the security of the state of Israel and occasionally disagree with the government there. And could disagree about what was best for Israel, let alone what was best for the United States. And I was also very clear that my priority was what was best for the United States." In other words, the typical suspicion of dual loyalty was immaterial. "I never felt it, I never experienced it, I never saw it. I mean I was aware of that perception floating around often, but for me, it was always quite clear: I was there to protect, pursue, advance American interests, and ninety-nine percent of the time that was consistent with Israeli interests; and if it wasn't, it wasn't a close call."

Despite his unsentimental attitude toward Israel, he says its reason for being remains clear. "My whole life, the Holocaust has colored my understanding of world history. It's been high up on the list of things that I understood from a very young age as the ultimate in evil. I did my share of reading and moviegoing about the subject and I've been to Yad Vashem half a dozen times. I have complicated views on exactly what one should and shouldn't do between Israelis and the Palestinians; but one thing I do believe is that until Palestinians and Arabs appreciate the magnitude of the suffering of the Holocaust, and *believe* it, that it will be very hard to have peace in the Middle East. So I believe that is extremely important to Jews and to humanity.

"It came into play for me as a government official when I was in office and Bosnia was happening and I remember saying, 'What am I doing? Should I leave the State Department if we don't do anything to intervene?' And then, I hope, I played a small role in helping the president and others come to the conclusion that they should do something about it. Because that was the modern-day version of the Holocaust in Europe. Not that it was the same in magnitude, or even in conception, but it was a people being destroyed in the heart of Europe. And we could do something about it. And ultimately we did—far too late—but we did. So that's how the Holocaust has affected me."

He does not, however, live with the feeling that "it could happen again," and is disdainful of those who say it could. "I've never felt ever that the world which we inhabit—meaning social and material world—is one in which I feel threatened. I've never felt that way. Do I believe that anti-Semitism still exists? Yes. In a variety of forms, it exists. But look: I climbed fairly high in government, and I had no sponsors, no family connections, I had nothing. I made it on merit, I hope. And my last name is about as Jewish a last name as you can have. So I don't feel that my religion interfered with my ability to climb very high—relatively speaking—on the ladder of government and power in America."

It's getting late, and I know Rubin has dinner plans at Centolire, an Italian restaurant in the neighborhood, but I can't let him go without hearing his take on the brouhaha over his former boss and close friend, Madeleine Albright. In 2001, it was revealed that her father was Jewish and her grandparents perished in the Holocaust; many Jews accused her of lying about the fact that she was learning this for the first time. "I have very strong views on that," Rubin says, leaning forward on the couch, "because I was a participant; I observed her become aware of it. I'm continually amazed at the cruelty with which people who don't know anything about the story, who've never looked into it, assumed that she knew and was lying. That lack of thoughtfulness I find offensive. Because anyone who looks into it will immediately realize it's a very complex story that involves her father changing the religion, her growing up with her father having told her she was not Jewish her whole life.

"I know her very, very well; she's never been a secretive, manipulative person. But I remember the reaction of many Jews—particularly Jews who fancied themselves as somehow connected to those terrible moments in twentieth-century Europe when great decisions were made by individuals who had real crises in their lives, whose lives were threatened. And most of those people who had the temerity to comment were living comfortable lives, and weren't in Czechoslovakia when the Nazis took over, or other places like that.

"I think she has said this: Knowing what she now knows, are there things she could have done differently, found out earlier, known at all? Yes. But I think that people who judge her without knowing the facts are not doing the facts or their religion any favors."

Natalie Portman

ON A COOL OCTOBER MORNING, actress Natalie Portman is wearing a jean jacket and dangling beaded earrings, sipping Earl Grey tea in Schiller's Liquor Bar, a favorite café of hers tucked into Manhattan's Lower East Side.

Leaning on a white marble table that sits on a black and white checkered floor, ceiling fans overhead, Portman talks about the difference between Jews in Israel and Jews in Long Island. "I definitely know what being Jewish in Israel means and what being Jewish in America means," says this twenty-four-year-old, who was born in Israel to an Israeli father, fertility specialist Dr. Avner Hershlag, and an American mother, artist Shelley Hershlag.

They moved to the United States when she was three, and they return to Israel every year to visit family. Portman, who uses her grandmother's maiden name professionally, attended Jewish day schools until eighth grade—mostly, she says, because her parents wanted her to keep up her Hebrew. But the Hershlags were not a religious family, nor involved in the local synagogue. "I grew up in the classic American Jewish suburbia, which has a whole different sense of what it means to be Jewish than anywhere else in the world."

I ask her to elaborate. "The people I grew up with on Long Island are wonderful people. But I have friends who grew up in five-million-dollar homes, they all drive BMWs, and the only places they've been to outside the United States are the islands in the Caribbean. Which is fine, it's a choice, and I don't want to be critical of that. But I am. I think it can definitely be a problem, especially since American Jews are the ones who are in a position—politically and financially—to help other Jews around the world who are facing problems that we can't conceive of."

Folding her bobbed hair behind her ears, Portman explains why she never felt a pull to be a part of Jewish life in her Syosset neighborhood. "I never liked going to temple on Long Island because it just had that aura of someone's fake party to me, which always made me uncomfortable. So I never went to temple at home, I never got bat mitzvahed, I just sort of rejected that whole thing; it seemed so tied up with values that I hated. But on the other hand, when I go to Israel, I always want to go to temple on the High Holy Days even if no one in my family is going with me. I'll fast. One year in Israel, my family went to Jaffa to get pizza on Pesach and I would not do that. [No flour is to be eaten during Passover week.] You know, I get much more Jewish in Israel because I *like* the way that religion is done there. Not all the time; I would never step foot in Orthodox temples. But in Israel, it's about what it's about."

She says it wasn't a big deal in her family when she decided to forgo a bat mitzvah. "All my friends were doing it," she recalls. "But people were having hundred-thousand-dollar parties that totally took the meaning out of it."

As she describes some of her Long Island girlfriends, the slur "JAP" pops into my head and I ask how she feels when someone uses the word. "Because it's one of those stereotypes that seems to derive from something that does exist, I don't get offended by it as many people do," she says, sipping her tea. "I mean, I grew up in a Long Island public school that was sixty to seventy percent Jewish and I know what a JAP is. But obviously the word shouldn't be misused. I wouldn't want to have stereotypes used in derogatory ways by people outside the Jewish community, but I think it is something from within the community that we need to examine and be self-critical about, because it's how we're raising our young people. Do they know or care about the outside world? Do they know or care about things other than having a nice car or a nice purse? It's something that we have to be careful of because we are a successful community that doesn't have day-to-day confrontations with poverty, violence, or danger that some of our counterparts in other parts of the world are facing."

She says she was also disappointed by the fact that the American Jewish community, as she watched it growing up, was not focused on giving back. "You see church groups doing community service, but you don't see that as much among Jewish kids in America. Maybe I'm talking about my specific experience, but I also see this among kids from Chicago, L.A. suburbia. Of course there are exceptions, I can't make any sweeping statements. But I don't think it's a value that's instilled early on. The values that you do see instilled are, for example, everyone getting nice cars for their sixteenth birthdays.

"I had a fashion designer tell me that when I wear a dress of his, it sells out across the country because Jewish girls 'look to me,' and Jewish girls are the ones that buy expensive dresses. It made me sort of sad, because I want to be an influence in ways other than by a pretty dress."

Portman is careful to point out that she sees virtues, too, in today's Jewish community. "There's also so much goodness there, and such a value placed on education, which is sort of universal among Jews around the world. I appreciate that obviously; to be a part of that."

But she can't help but return to her obvious frustration with the ideals she saw as a kid. "You belong to a temple and it's totally for social purposes; it's the bar mitzvah–wedding–Rosh Hashanah place where you go and see what everyone's wearing. And it serves its purpose too. But I think the major problem today with American Jews is materialism."

I ask her where she feels more herself as a Jew—in Israel or in America. "It's hard, because I was raised in the Long Island atmosphere, but I *admire* the Israeli atmosphere. So I'm in this strange middle ground." She says starting college at Harvard changed her perspective somewhat, because she found herself feeling pulled toward the Jewish community on campus. "I think you always sort of look for where you belong once you get to school," says Portman. "The first time I felt comfortable in an American religious institution was in college, because campus Hillel was inclusive. And it's nice having Shabbat dinner every week with everyone. Anyone was welcome, so we'd bring all our friends to dinner because the Hillel Shabbat meal was so much better and they served Manischewitz." She laughs. "It was so exciting to get alcohol in the dining hall."

Portman says she's always fasted on Yom Kippur and continued to do so in college. "I think it's a really amazing thing, and I only recently began to appreciate what it's for. I used to just do it as sort of a dare—to see if I could actually handle it because I really have a hard time not eating." She laughs. "I really like eating. But a couple years ago, one of my friends got really mad at me and it happened to be on Yom Kippur. Even though this friend wasn't Jewish, it made me go through the actual atonement list on that day, and the hunger associated with it is really helpful. You see why there are kosher rules and why so many religions have rituals associated with food; because you eat three times a day, so every time you have a restriction on your food, you think about why you're restricting yourself. So whether it's not eating milk and meat together, or not eating at all, you think about how you've wronged your friends and how you should change your behavior in the future. You're made to think. It's pretty powerful. And when you see how difficult it is to go one day without food, it really reminds you of what it is to be hungry."

At Harvard, she took a seminar in Israeli literature (coincidentally, with my former Yale Hebrew professor, Miri Kubovy), and she briefly engaged the Israeli-Palestinian controversy on campus. In the spring of 2003, when a law student named Faisal Chaudhry wrote a column in the *Harvard Crimson* about the racism of Israelis, titled "An Ideology of Oppression," Portman shot off a letter to the editor. "I was reading my student newspaper and the fact that they published something that was such propaganda really upset me and I wrote back. But it ended up bringing more attention to this guy's story than it got initially, so I was angry. I learned my lesson. I helped him get into the *Washington Post*—they gave him a lot more voice than he was due. I'm sure he's a very intelligent and good person, but I think a lot of people don't know what they're necessarily talking about."

I ask her to briefly recap their dispute. "His allegations were that Israel is treating the Palestinians poorly because they're racist and it's a conflict of white people against brown people, which is just so absurd." (Chaudhry wrote, "*White Israeli soldiers destroy refugee camps of the brown people they have dispossessed for decades.*") "My response was that more than half of Israelis are of Sephardic origin: Many of these Jews come from Arab lands and share the same physical skin color. There was a picture on the cover of *Newsweek* that week in which there were two photographs side by side—a female suicide bomber who exploded herself in a supermarket and an Israeli girl who was killed in that attack. The girls were seventeen and eighteen and almost indistinguishable. That was my point." In her response to Chaudhry, she wrote, *"Israelis and Arabs are historically cousins. Until we accept the fact that we are constituents of the same family, we will blunder in believing that a loss for one 'side'—or, as Chaudhry names it, a 'color'—is not a loss for all human kind."*

I ask if she's felt pressure, since she graduated, to use her celebrity on behalf of Israeli causes. "I'm very comfortable with that," she says, "and I'm currently exploring ways to help because I love the country." She's recently become more protective of Israel, in part because people around her have become more impatient with it. "I have a very close friend who lately has this European, anti-Israel way of thinking, and it's very hard for me to have conversations with him. He says, 'Can't you be self-critical?' But it's hard to be publicly critical. It has to be done in a very delicate, well-thought-out manner. These issues come up at parties and dinners with people who don't know a lot, and as someone who was born in Israel, you're put in a position of defending Israel because you know how much is at stake. It's become a much bigger part of my identity in recent years because it's become an issue of survival."

Portman suddenly realizes that she has to put coins in the parking meter and excuses herself to run outside, first asking the waitress to change a dollar. When she returns, rosy-cheeked from the air, I turn the conversation to her career, asking if she feels some Jewish pride in being considered a Hollywood beauty. "Yeah," she replies. "The hard thing is that people often don't associate me with being Jewish. I'm not someone who you look at and say, 'You're Jewish.' People ask me if I'm Spanish, Italian, or even WASPy. So I don't think I can be representative. But in another way, I think I look very Jewish because all the Jewish girls I grew up with, we all look the same: small, short, skinny, dark hair, dark eyes. Little noses." She laughs. "So maybe it is time for a new type. I'd like it if people thought I was Jewish-looking."

I ask if she's ever felt shy about her ethnicity as a public person. "Not at all. But I don't think that any one characteristic should be overemphasized in your real life when you're an actor, because if I play a nun one day, I don't want someone to be thinking when they see me, 'Jew, Jew, Jew.'"

She did play an iconic Jew, Anne Frank, on Broadway at the age of six-teen. "It was an amazing experience," Portman says. The reviews were mixed; *Time* magazine said "Portman's Anne is a little short on stage charisma," while the *New York Times* said she has "an endlessly poignant quality of spontaneity." But some of the criticism was personal. "I got a lot of flack," Portman volunteers. "Cynthia Ozick was awful." (She refers to the prolific author and essayist who specializes in Jewish subjects.)

"She wrote this article in *The New Yorker* without having seen the show," Portman says. (Ozick wrote that Portman's characterization of Anne Frank in a *New York Times* interview was "shallowly upbeat.") "She said the most important line that's been taken out of Anne Frank's diary, *'In spite of everything, I still believe people are good at heart,'* is how Anne Frank has been interpreted, when in fact she was miserable and had this awful life that has sort of been distorted to make her a martyr. [Ozick wrote that Frank's story has been 'kitschified.'] She quoted me out of context from an interview where I was saying that I wanted to bring 'light' to the character.

"But Anne Frank was a twelve-year-old girl; and when I met with Miep [Miep Gies, Anne Frank's father's secretary] and Bernd Elias, her first cousin who is her only living relative, they both told me that she was this hyperactive girl, happy, always running around, they were always yelling at her to slow down and be quiet because they were in hiding; when Miep would come to the house, she would run up to her and always be asking her questions and touching her. So I had this image in my head of the en-ergetic young girl who obviously is put in the most awful situation and cre-ates this world for herself through her writing. It was important for me not to make it The Death-And-Dread Show because everyone knows that even in the most horrific circumstances, there's some sort of life and some sort of humor.

"Anyway, Ozick said I said Anne Frank 'was happy' or something that sounded moronic. [Portman told the *Times* that Anne Frank's diary is "funny, it's hopeful, and she's a happy person."] And then she continued to lecture about it, including at my own university, basically portraying me as this moron and my interpretation of the diaries as completely disrespectful to Anne Frank, which was the last thing I would ever do. None of us know what her life was like or who she was; we can only do as much as we can read, study, and imagine. I don't expect not to be criticized because that's what I do, I put myself out there to be criticized, but I thought it was unfair."

I wonder how personally Portman connected to the character. "Very personally," she says. "Because my grandparents didn't talk about those years much, especially my grandfather. His younger brother, who was fourteen at the time, was in hiding from the Nazis and couldn't take it one more day and ran out and was shot in the streets. And his parents were killed at Auschwitz. He was the one I'd always related to in the family. He was sort of the quiet, brilliant man who led Pesach and I would always imagine him or his father in these horrifying humiliating conditions. The humiliation is almost harder for me to imagine than the physical pain. To think about such dignified people."

She was also surprised to discover how timeless and universal were Anne Frank's fixations. "She talked about crushes and sex and genitals and all of these things that I was thinking about—and embarrassed to be thinking about—when I read the diary for the first time at twelve years old. I thought I was weird and crazy, and then you read this diary and it's not some grown-up's book written for kids, like 'What's Happening to My Body?'; it's another twelve- or thirteen-year-old telling you what they're going through."

When it comes to Portman's own romantic life, it has obviously been a staple of gossip columns (she's been linked to actors Lukas Haas and Hayden Christensen, and to rock star Adam Levine), but she says she's not necessarily looking for a Jewish husband. "A priority for me is definitely that I'd like to raise my kids Jewish, but the ultimate thing is just to have someone who is a good person and who is a partner. It's certainly not my priority." She says her parents don't push her one way or another. "My dad always makes this stupid joke with my new boyfriend, who is not Jewish. He says, 'It's just a simple operation.'" She laughs. "They've always said to me that they mainly want me to be happy and that's the most important thing, but they've also said that if you marry someone with the same religion, it's one less thing to fight about. But according to that argument, I might as well only date vegetarian guys. The term 'intermarry' is sort of a racist term. I don't really believe in purity of blood or anything like that; I think that's awful."

She doesn't think it necessarily takes two Jews to maintain Jewish continuity in a family. "I feel the strength to carry that on myself. It's obviously easier when both parents are in it together, but I don't necessarily think it has to be. I always think that if a guy I date is Jewish, it's a plus, but it's not one of the reasons I would like him."

Portman says she resists any kind of blind tribalism. "I don't believe in going along with anything without questioning. I think that's the basis of Judaism: questioning and skepticism." She says that for her, basic humanity comes before faith. "To me, the most important concept in Judaism is that you can break any law of Judaism to save a human life. I think that's the most important thing. Which means to me that humans are more important than Jews are to me. Or than being Jewish is to me."

Don Hewitt

TO WORK FOR *60 MINUTES* creator and executive producer Don Hewitt, which I did for six years as a producer, was to work alongside an inimitable character who seemed quintessentially Jewish. Don's manic energy—his hopping up and down about stories that grabbed him, his undisguised dismay at stories that didn't, the way he'd yell "Hi honey!" when he charged by you, or repeat the same joke he'd heard to every person he encountered in the hallway, the way he'd exhort you to get an interview or give you a wink when you "did good"; his Brooklyn lilt, his histrionics, his dated fashion sense, his unflashy routine—made him feel familial to me despite his eminence within CBS. He was a cheerleading but demanding Jewish uncle.

But in the strict sense, Don couldn't have been less of a Jew. He observed no holidays (one could always find him at work on Yom Kippur), and he demonstrated zero emotional connection to Jewish identity. "I've always felt more American than Jewish," he says, sitting behind his desk in his trademark camel turtleneck, snug tweed blazer—handkerchief peeking from the pocket. "Let me put it this way: Am I proud to be Jewish? Not particularly. Am I *happy* to be Jewish? Yes! Because I think somewhere somehow it gave me the impetus to be ambitious. I'm proud of what I did at *60 Minutes*, but I'm not proud of being Jewish. I'm *happy* about it. I think being Jewish is *nifty*. And mostly I'm Jewish by temperament." What does he mean by that? (I have my own ideas.) "I like Jewish food, I like Jewish humor, I like Jewish people. But I'm more at home with nonbelieving anybody, including nonbelieving Jews. I've always taken to the nonbelievers."

He grew up in New Rochelle, the child of Frieda, a German Jew, and Ely, a Russian Jew. "I stayed home from school Rosh Hashanah and Yom Kippur, but at Christmas I got Christmas presents. I was confirmed at a Reform temple called Temple Israel mostly because that was the social thing to do in that town. My mother was a little bit snobbish about the people who belonged to the Orthodox or Conservative synagogue. It was not exactly 'feh,' but it approached it." He chuckles.

His phone rings and he answers it. "I think you have the wrong number." (Don often picked up his own line.) He continues: "I never felt really discriminated against, but there was always that undertone that you *could* be. I think that steeled you. I think Jews who have made it in America made it to kind of show their gentile neighbors, 'We're made of pretty steely stuff, and nothing is going to hold us down.' I think my being Jewish probably was a catalyst—it helped me develop the kind of drive that Jews have to be successful. But I never related it to Torahs or yarmulkes or tallises. I always considered those things to be tribal rites. When I used to go to the movies as a kid and I would see people dancing around a fire with gourds in tribal ceremony, I'd think, 'Jesus, that's what they do in synagogue!' I used to sit in temple all the time and listen to these Reform rabbis—" He puts on a Britishy, pretentious accent with great bravado: " 'On this holiest of holies, the Yom Kippur commences . . .' and I'm thinking, 'Where the heck did you learn to talk like that? Who talks that way?' "

Hewitt, eighty-three, orders lunch for us by shouting to his assistant to call up Teriyaki Boy. "Bev!" he bellows to Beverly. "Can we get some sushi?"

He goes on: "My grandfather changed his name from Hurwitz to Hewitt long before I was born. In fact, we used to kid around in the family because they said my grandfather wanted to change his name to Hurley, which is Irish. My aunt tells this great story of being at my confirmation with all the kids' names printed in the program, and overhearing one woman say, 'Donald Shepherd Hewitt? How did *he* get in here?' "

I ask him if there's ever been a time when he turned to some kind of faith. "No. I don't have any faith. As a kid, when it would rain so hard that there'd be a flood, I used to say facetiously, 'How smart can God be? *I* know enough to turn the water off in the shower. *Turn the water off!!* What's the big deal?'

"I used to go out with a Catholic girl when I was a kid. And we used to argue about religion, because I had none. And one day she said to me, 'You've got to admit that the Easter service at St. Patrick's Cathedral is beautiful.' And I said, 'I will admit that Easter service at St. Patrick's Cathedral is beautiful, if *you* will admit that Radio City Music Hall does it better.' " He laughs. "It's *theater*. The chanting, the cantors; it's a performance. And I don't fault anybody who gets something out of it. I don't. The only thing I ever prayed for was a parking space.

"Let me put it this way: If there is a God, a supreme being who created the universe, that's got to be a pretty magnificent entity; I can't believe that anyone so great as to have created life could give a damn whether I worship him or not. Wanting to be worshipped is a human failing. I can't ascribe that to a supreme being. If there is one, why would he care whether I paid homage to him? He's bigger than that. Do you think he's sitting around all day, thinking, 'Don didn't pray today'? I think the last time I was in a synagogue was for [violinist] Itzhak Perlman's kid's bar mitzvah."

Hewitt says his three kids (by his second marriage) weren't raised with religion, but most of their friends happen to be Jews. He chalks that up to childhood summers spent in Fair Harbor, Fire Island. "They just fell in with a bunch of Jewish kids from Fair Harbor," he says. Would his children call themselves Jewish? "I don't think they call themselves anything. *I* don't call myself anything."

He concedes that his third and current wife, Marilyn Berger, whom he married in 1979, might be more observant if it weren't for the man she chose. "I have a feeling that if Marilyn were married to a religious Jew, she would be more involved," Hewitt muses. Marilyn still lights candles for her sisters—the *yartzeit* candles. I look at them and to me, it's like tribal rites again."

Does it give him pause at all that the Jewish line might have stopped with him? "No, no. I have to believe that the world would probably be better—" He's interrupted by lunch arriving. "Thank you, darling," he tells another assistant. (Bev's stepped out.) "Did you tip the guy?" When he looks at the tuna rolls, it's clear they've combined our orders in one plastic container. "We'll eat from the same plate," he announces, pushing the sushi my way so I can reach it. "Here's some napkins." As he chews and talks, he keeps encouraging me, like a Jewish mother, to eat. "Here, there's more here, honey."

Back to continuity: "I think it's a better world if everybody's integrated," he says, mouth full. "There are Jews who get horrified because a Jew marries out of their religion, and a lot of them are very liberal people who think it's great when there are inter*racial* marriages."

Since Hewitt covered World War II as a London-based war correspondent for *Stars and Stripes*, I wonder how he relates to what happened to Jews during that time. "It's terrible," he says. "I don't think you have to be Jewish to be horrified at the Holocaust. You don't have to be black to be horrified by lynching."

He feels that Jewish interests have been hurt by Jews who say their suffering surpasses all others'. "I once said to Steven Spielberg, 'You would do your cause a lot better if you would acknowledge that the Jews weren't the only ones who ever suffered a holocaust. And then he did that movie about the slave ship [*Amistad*]. Which was lousy, but he did it right after we had that conversation. We cannot go on believing that nobody else had *tsuris* but us. There are a lot of people. There are a lot of blacks who say 'Holocaust, shmolocaust; we got lynched!' And they're right!"

Does he think he brings any of his Jewishness to his news judgment? "Yeah, but not consciously. I think what I bring Jewish is called *seckel* [a Yiddishism for "brains, savvy"]. Jews have got *seckel*. I think that's what I bring."

Hewitt's Jewish credentials were harshly called into question when *60 Minutes* did several stories in the seventies and eighties that were perceived as overly sympathetic to the Arab point of view. There was a deluge of protest in 1975, for example, when Mike Wallace reported that Syrian Jews weren't as oppressed as had been previously believed. The criticism from some in the Jewish community culminated in Rabbi Arthur Hertzberg, then president of the American Jewish Congress, requesting a face-to-face meeting with Hewitt and Wallace in their CBS offices. Hewitt says

Hertzberg went after him subtly but personally. "The son of a bitch," Hewitt recalls, "he came over here to see me and he sat in my office and he said, 'Hewitt . . . Hewitt . . . ; there's got to be a *Horowitz* under there somewhere.' " Hewitt smiles. "I said to myself, 'You son of a bitch; you come here for a peace meeting and you make trouble.'

"Now the other hysteria was when we did the Temple Mount massacre." He's referring to Wallace's 1990 story recounting the killing and wounding of Palestinians by Israeli soldiers at Jerusalem's sacred Temple Mount. The Anti-Defamation League was up in arms, charging that the broadcast "failed to meet acceptable journalistic standards" and that Wallace "gave the false impression that Israel is engaged in a deliberate cover-up." Then–CBS president Larry Tisch, a prominent Jewish figure in New York society, got involved. "Larry went ape about this story," Hewitt says. "I was portrayed as a self-hating Jew and I said to him, 'You've never met a more self-loving Jew in your life! I don't hate myself! Secondly, if I did, it would not be because I was Jewish.' " But the personal attacks clearly left their mark. "I remembered that for a long time," Hewitt says.

There were other slights. "I remember going to a cocktail party given for the new chairman of RCA—I can't remember his name—and when Larry Tisch came in, I said, 'Hey boss, how are you?' And he said, 'Don't you *Hey boss* me,' and he walked away. And I left and got in a taxi—it was at the River House—and I came here to CBS and went into David Burke's office [then president of CBS News], and I said, 'David, I resign.' He said, 'What do you mean?' I said, 'I don't want to work here anymore. I just got cut off at the knees by Tisch because of a story we did.' And Burke calmed it all down . . . But it was a tough time."

Another snub: "I went to a party once at Werner LeRoy's [the flamboyant restaurateur], and I got attacked by Mort Zuckerman [real estate and publishing magnate] and Barbara Walters, who said, 'How could you do that story at this terrible time in Israel's history?' And I said, 'How about the stories we did at the terrible time in America's history in Vietnam? Were you worried about *that*?' I was shocked. And I said, 'I get accused of being a self-hating Jew because I'm critical of Menachem Begin. Nobody ever called me a self-hating American because I was critical of Richard Nixon.' There's a *thing* about Jewishness . . .'" He trails off. "Right now the Jews are too big and too smart to cave in to this feeling that we are victims in the Middle East. They're not really victims in the Middle East."

Hewitt heralds the fact that Abraham Foxman, National Director of the Anti-Defamation League, ultimately wrote him a letter apologizing for the ADL's outcry over the Temple Mount story. "He said—I'm just paraphrasing here—'Now the verdict is in: It looks like it happened a lot closer to the way you guys said it happened than the government said it happened, and we owe you an apology and I invite you to use this letter any way you want.'"

Hewitt is even prouder of another letter—one that used to sit framed on his office bookshelf. "It's wrapped up somewhere—I can't find it," Hewitt apologizes as he hastily leafs through his memoir, *Tell Me a Story: Fifty Years and 60 Minutes in Television*, looking for the place where he quotes the letter, sent in honor of his seventieth birthday. Hewitt reads part of it aloud, in a hushed tone. It's perhaps his most compelling piece of evidence that he wasn't such a skimpy Jew after all:

> ". . . As you know, your program is critically acclaimed through-
> out the world and is held in high esteem by many of us in Israel. I
> would also like to take this opportunity to express my personal
> gratitude to you for dedicating one of your *60 Minutes* segments—
> the tragic story of our Israeli Air Force navigator, Ron Arad. Both
> as a Jew and a human being, I was touched by your coverage of his
> plight. I am deeply grateful to you and *60 Minutes* for all your ef-
> forts. As you enter your 25th year at *60 Minutes,* I wish you the
> best of luck and continued success in the future. Sincerely, Yitzhak
> Rabin; Prime Minister of Israel."

Hewitt reads the signature with solemnity. "That letter is one of the proudest things I've got," he says. "I think the terrorist who did the most harm in this world—more than Al Qaeda—was the Jewish terrorist who killed Rabin."

The phone rings and he picks it up. "Hello? Honey—" It's his wife, Marilyn. "I'm sitting here right now with Abby Pogrebin talking about being Jewish and reading her my letter from Yitzhak Rabin." He relates Marilyn's reaction: "Marilyn says, '*You're* talking about being Jewish?'" He laughs. "Yes!" he tells her. "I'll call you back in a few minutes."

Back to Israel: "I always admired Israelis. They were the gunslingers. They were great! Before it was politically incorrect to think about it that way, it was like the cowboys and Indians—Israel were the cowboys and the Arabs were the Indians and it was simplistic; I never knew anybody who rooted for the Indians. I always thought the Israelis were arrogant as hell, but I admired them. But I never understood why the smartest people on earth plunked themselves down in the most hostile place on earth. They could have found a better place. They could have gone to Madagascar or something. But they say, 'It's the land that God gave them.' *Who the heck knows what God gave anybody?!* How do they know that? I think it would be a big loss to civilization if Israel disappeared. I just wish they'd get off all this jazz about 'God gave us this land'; God didn't give you the land—you *took* the land and you made it great! And I love you for doing that, but don't tell me that God gave you this land and he doesn't want anybody else here.

"I'll tell you my favorite phone call: One time, a woman called after we aired a story on Israel. And she said, 'I'm getting sick and tired of you people.' I said, 'Okay lady, what now?' She said, 'You're all pro-Israel, and you're all a bunch of kikes.' I said, 'On your first point, you couldn't be more wrong; on your second point, you could be right.' And I hung up on her."

Mike Nichols

DUSTIN HOFFMAN TOLD ME that when he auditioned for *The Gradu-ate* (1967), the director, Mike Nichols, told him that the WASPy character of Benjamin Braddock was "Jewish inside." When I ask Nichols what he might have meant by this, he says his answer can be found in a Thomas Mann story. "Did you ever read *Tonio Kröger?*" he asks me. (I didn't.) "It took place in Germany one hundred years ago and it was about the blond, blue-eyed people and the dark people. The dark people were the artists and the outcasts. And the blond, blue-eyed people were at the heart of the group and were the desired objects." I see where he's going: Benjamin's an outsider, so he's metaphorically Jewish.

"There would have been two ways to cast and direct *The Graduate,*" Nichols continues. "One is to have Benjamin be a sort of a walking surf-board, which is the way the novel is written, roughly. And the other is to express his difference from his Californiate family and their friends. And only semiconsciously, I think, did I pick the latter. At the time, it was just that no actor—I saw hundreds, if not thousands—of young actors, and no-body was quite there, nobody was quite right, and it was getting desperate;

not only had we seen every young actor, but we'd seen every young *janitor* by that point.

"I said, 'There is a very talented young actor that I saw in an off-Broadway play in which he played a Russian transvestite'—I still remember him cutting up fish on a butcher block wearing a dress. And I said, 'I'd like to see that guy; let's see if we can get him to come out to L.A.' " Needless to say, Hoffman got the part. "Of course, when we saw the film it was clear that this was Benjamin, nose and all," Nichols says with a smile. "And it's not that the piece was transformed, it was that the piece was *achieved*, but in a way that we would never have guessed." In other words, the un-Redford Jew clinched the disaffected WASP.

We're sitting in the airy, book-lined living room Nichols shares with his wife, ABC News anchor Diane Sawyer, on Martha's Vineyard. We've retired to this room with tall glasses of ice water after a generous four-course lunch that included taro tuna rolls, gazpacho, and strawberry lemonade. It's August, and a gentle breeze glides in off the bay through open doors. Nichols is tan but not dressed for this season—he's in long tan pants, long-sleeved black shirt, and loafers. It's too facile to draw a metaphor from his attire, but I can't help it: This comedic director is darkly dressed for a sunny summer day and it reflects something he's alluded to often in old interviews, a sense of being a fish out of water, the way he described Benjamin Braddock. I ask whether he relates this outcast feeling to his Jewishness—to his childhood experience of escaping Nazi Berlin in 1939 as a seven-year-old (he traveled alone with his four-year-old brother, with a "stewardess" looking after them).

"This is tricky," he begins, taking a sip of water, "because I think there are two different things: One is Jewishness and one is refugee-ness. The second one being something you might call the 'Sebold Syndrome,' if you read *The Emigrants*. Did you?" (No; I'm a shamed English major.) "You remember the theme—the Sebold experience: namely that your guilt about the Six Million finally comes and gets you . . . That was what that book was about. Everyone in it in a different way finally couldn't bear having survived. And if you're a refugee, and if things came that close, that's something you push away and push away and push away until it comes and gets you. There's just no question about it. And after that ton of bricks hits you, then you've got to do a lot of work, both inner and active, in the sense of doing something *for* other people, in order to go on. By definition, whether you are a refugee or not, you are a member of a group that has been hated by a large number of people through all history. It's impossible not to be aware of that hatred. And puzzled by it and amazed by it and appalled by it, sometimes joining it—to your own horror—and jumping out again as fast as you can."

He offers an example of when he momentarily "joined" the scorn for his own people: "I once said to Jerry Robbins [the director and choreographer of *Fiddler on the Roof* and *West Side Story*], 'I'm worried that all the great monsters of narcissism in show business are Jewish.' And I named some names, which I won't do now. And there was a long silence, and he said, 'Yes, well: Mickey Rooney.'" Nichols laughs heartily. "I said, 'Oh, thank you; thank you. That feels better.'"

Nichols laments the fact that Jews can't give themselves a poke in the ribs every once in a while. "You know what the problem is, among many other things? Correctness. Correctness was such a blight on humor and the truth. One of the joys of *The Producers* was that every possible correct position was exploded, and you just sat there howling and grateful. It was the death of correctness in a way."

Nichols's outsiderness was seeded when he was still Michael Igor Peschkowsky in Berlin, attending a segregated Jewish school; he doesn't remember being given any explanation for it. "I'm pretty sure I was simply told that Jews were required to attend school separately from Aryans," he says. As Berlin became more acutely inhospitable to Jews, his family knew they had an escape hatch. "The reason that we got out is that my father was Russian and we had Russian passports, and it was during the two-year Stalin-Hitler Pact. That's what saved our lives."

Still, getting the paperwork was arduous. "A long time was spent sitting in consulates hoping for a visa," Nichols recalls. "Very few people seem to know this, but do you know what you needed financially to get into this country?" I shake my head. "Every individual had to have someone guarantee them financially *for the rest of their lives*. We were a family of four; each one of us had to have a specific financial guarantee for our lifetimes. And luckily—to put it mildly—my mother had a cousin with money, who was already in the United States. And he did it. But without that, you couldn't get a visa. It's not exactly '*your huddled masses.*' But nobody knows this. Some people know about Roosevelt turning the *St. Louis* back. But very few people know this."

He's referring to the incident in May 1939 when the S.S. *St. Louis*, filled with 937 Jews fleeing Germany bound for Cuba, was not permitted to land on American shores. F.D.R.'s Secretary of the Treasury, Henry Morgenthau, Jr., who was Jewish, argued to the president that the ship should be welcomed, but Roosevelt refused, and the *St. Louis* turned back to Europe with its passengers, many of whom went on to perish in the Holocaust. "I was talking to Spielberg about this," Nichols continues (in fact, Spielberg had flown to the Vineyard for a visit just the day before), "and saying to him that people keep making not-very-good movies about the *St. Louis*, but that the *real* movie, it seemed to me, is about Morgenthau. The only Jew in Roosevelt's administration who presumably started out saying, 'Mr. President, you have a chance to do something wonderful; we have a chance to do something really important,' must have gone close to insane at the end of the week when the *St. Louis* was sent back, realizing that Roosevelt didn't care at all."

Nichols remembers his own arrival at New York City's shores, at the age of seven. "When we got off the boat in New York, there was a delicatessen right near the dock and it had a neon sign with some Hebrew letters in it, and I said, 'Is that allowed?' So at seven, I had some sense of what that would have meant back in Germany." Despite his childhood English lessons, Nichols could barely communicate. "I only had two sentences: 'I don't speak English' and 'Please don't kiss me.' "

Nichols's father, a physician, had come to New York ahead of his family to take the American medical exams and start his practice. "My father changed our name the week he became a citizen. Because his name was Peschkowsky and he said that by the time he would spell his name, the patient was in the hospital," Nichols smiles. " 'Nicholas' was his patronymic [the name derived from one's father, in this case, Nikolayevich Peschkowsky]. I've been accused often of changing my name, but I didn't." Only five years after Nichols arrived, his father succumbed to leukemia. His mother, who had stayed in Germany after they left because she was ill, joined her boys in America a few years before her husband died. "She, who had never had a job, learned English and supported my brother and me," Nichols says.

All this time, they observed no Jewish rituals whatsoever. "No one in my family would have known *how* to have a Jewish holiday," he says with a laugh. "Nobody in my family knew anything about it, and yet you could hardly say they weren't Jewish."

He explains that his mother's parents were well-known German writers whose Jewishness was not based in synagogue at all. "My grandmother [Hedwig Lachmann] wrote the libretto for *Salomé* with Richard Strauss, which she translated from Oscar Wilde's French. And so she was a pretty well-known poet. And my grandfather [Gustav Landauer] was a writer who had written many books, and along with Martin Buber, was one of the first people to work toward creating a Palestine. But they were a kind of Jewish that didn't exist after that in Germany. That is to say, ideologically they were very Jewish, but they did not speak Yiddish, they didn't observe any of the holidays. They were not Jewish in any perceptible way."

Still, Nichols is surprised that he didn't pick up any Yiddish in his childhood, since it was so close to his native German. "Elaine May and I used to speak Yiddish in our show. We used to improvise stuff based on suggestions from the audience—we'd ask for a first line and a last line and a style. And one night an audience member gave us 'Yiddish theater.' Now, Elaine was raised in the Yiddish theater; her father was at the time a very famous Yiddish actor. So she did a very sophisticated sort of Yiddish thing. She came in with a cigarette and said 'Tata!,' sort of like Bette Davis. She was very hip. And I was beside myself. Finally I just gave up and I spoke Yiddish. Because under pressure, you can do strange things. And it came out. It wasn't exactly a miracle, because I spoke and speak German. I didn't know Yiddish, but I had to, so I spoke it. But that's as far as I ever got with Yiddish or any Jewish holidays."

Just as there were no Jewish rituals in his family, there was no Jewish pressure to marry a Jewish girl. Nichols's four marriages have been interfaith. "My mother was not Jewish in any of those senses," Nichols says. "She was very guilt-provoking, but I don't know that that counts." It certainly paid off in one of the most famous Nichols and May skits, "Mother and Son," where May played the neglected mother and Nichols the guilty son. "When Elaine and I were a comedy team, we had a very central and successful sketch that was about a Jewish mother. And the way it came about was that we were already working in New York, and one day my real mother called me and said, 'Hello Michael, this is your mother; do you remember me?' And I said, 'Mom, can I call you right back?' and I hung up and I called Elaine and I said, 'I have a new piece for tonight,' and I told her my mother's line, and she said, 'Great.' And we *never* said any more about it, but we did the piece that night and it started that way.

"The Jewish mother that Elaine played was so horrifyingly recognizable, so familiar, and so hilariously guilt-provoking." He offers an example: "She [Elaine, playing the mother] was complaining that I never called. She said she hadn't eaten because she didn't want to take the chance that her mouth might be full when her son finally called. I would say, 'I was busy sending up the *Vanguard*, mother'—which was a rocket at the time—'I didn't have a second'; she said, 'Well it's always something.' And then finally, she said, 'I hope I haven't made you feel bad.' I said, 'Are you kidding? I feel awful.' And she said, 'Oh, honey, if I could believe that, I'd be the happiest mother in the world.' She said, 'Someday, Arthur, someday you'll have children of your own. And when you do, I only pray that they make you *suffer the way you've made me suffer.* That's all I pray. That's a mother's prayer.'

"When my mother saw that sketch, she thought it was Elaine's mother we were doing and Elaine's mother thought it was my mother we were doing, but we were free at last. It was really a very big deal for us. Because if you can get a whole audience laughing their ass off at what has made you miserable, you have freed yourself to some extent. And all of that process was being Jewish."

I read Nichols a quote of his from an old *New Yorker* interview: *"The refugee ear is sort of a seismograph for how one is doing . . . A thousand tiny victories and defeats in an ordinary conversation."* "I remember saying it," he says with a nod. "You come to this country and you're seven. You don't speak English. In two weeks, you do speak English, because you're a kid. And from that point on, your ear is tuned forever to 'How are they doing it? What's the way to do it?' And you can't turn it off; that's your central point of concentration—'How do I get to be *one of them* as fast as possible, as convincingly as possible?' "

The only American anti-Semitism he recalls was when he went to the Cherry Lane boarding school in Connecticut. "What I remember was Mrs. MacDonald, the mother of one of my friends with whom I rode horses, saying, 'Now, we'd love *you* at the hunt club—there would be nothing wrong with that—because you're the *right kind of Jew*; it's those others that we really don't want.' And that confused me enormously. Even without that, there was no way *not* to know what anti-Semitism was, because Darien, Connecticut—at that time anyway—was sort of *based* on anti-Semitism."

He says his college friendships made him feel more Jewish. "Because we made immigrant jokes and because what interested the bunch of us was music, which leads you back to Germany, God knows. And through all of that was the sense that we were all Jewish and I guess, to put it briefly, lucky to be at the University of Chicago and alive."

I wonder if Nichols thinks any generalization can be made about why so many comedians and comedy writers are Jewish. "Jewish introspection and Jewish humor is a way of surviving," he says. "Not only as a group, but as individuals. If you're not handsome and you're not athletic and you're not rich, there's still one last hope with girls, which is being funny. Girls like funny guys.

"When I was in this group in Chicago, we all improvised, and this beautiful TV star/jazz singer came to see us all; and out of all the guys, she picked me. That was my first wife, in fact. And I said to her after some time, 'Why did you pick me out of all those guys?' And she said, 'Funny is sexy.' So just when things look bleakest, there's an advantage. Humor is a way of helping you to survive if something awful happens. And all these things Jews are practiced in; all these things Jews have had to pull out of their hats when things got tough. And I guess that's the best explanation I can find. It's not the only kind of humor: Steve Martin is hilarious, and it's not possible to be less Jewish than Steve."

What does he think about the fact that Jews—however funny—are never the all-American ideal in movies? "But in any representative group of Americans, the Jews are there. Jewish characters are very often the people the audience can identify with, can enjoy. In army pictures, the Jew is the funny one, the schlemiel—you *do* identify."

When I ask him whether the unexpected blockbuster *My Big Fat Greek Wedding* could have been made about a Jewish family, his answer differs from the other Hollywood pros I've asked. He doesn't say it wouldn't work with a Jewish family because Jews aren't commercial; he says it wouldn't work because it wouldn't be accurate to a Jewish family. "*My Big Fat Greek Wedding* is about what Greeks have, really more than anyone else, which is a kind of overwhelming sense of vitality, an utterly sustaining love of family. I have a very dear friend who's my line producer and she's Greek, and most weeks there are new cousins visiting her—maybe I've met fifteen cousins. And they're all sexy like she is and they're all full of life. So we don't associate that with being Jewish; we don't associate *joy* and family. If there is an exception, where there is a Jewish family for whom family supersedes everything, then there's a lot of pain in it; there's a lot of guilt; there's a difficult mother, there's a father who's not so easy either, who's also easily hurt."

So what kind of Jewish identity results from being raised with Jewish guilt but no Jewish customs? Does Nichols connect in any spiritual way to being Jewish or is it heritage that moves him? "Certainly heritage," he answers. "Religion? I would have to say, no. In an intellectual way, I'm glad that the Jewish religion doesn't contain things that I find really difficult, like *eating* God. That's not one of the things that I would want to do with God. I've tried and tried to understand it, but I can't. And when Catholic friends explained to me that transubstantiation is *literal*, that it is *not* a metaphor, I gave up. I said, 'Well, I respect it, but I will never understand it.' "

What about Orthodox Judaism? "I have an emotional reaction against some aspects of Hasidic scholars and their absolute concentration and disinterest in anything but their studies . . . it looks like arrogance."

His family—namely his three grown children—were not raised in any faith. "But there was a time when there were various tensions in my family and we were all under pressure and my son said, 'Dad, could we celebrate the Jewish holidays next year?' I said, 'Yes, sure. Let's get a book; let's educate ourselves. God knows it's late for me.' And we have a friend, Lorne Michaels [creator of *Saturday Night Live*], who often invited us to his seder. I said, 'We can study with Lorne and learn how to do it.' And somehow, by the time it came up again, my son said, 'No, I don't want to anymore.' I said, 'Are you sure? It would be interesting, it would be fun.' But he said, 'No.' And I had the feeling that it had to do with the inner workings in the family and the difficult time that we had entered. But he never asked again. Although all three children did go through the stages: first, 'I'm not Jewish because my mother isn't Jewish' and then 'I *am* Jewish.'

"My youngest daughter, Jennifer, once said to me, 'In the end you pick Jewish because it's harder.' " How did he feel when he heard that? "Proud. And impressed. I think it was also accurate. If you get a choice, you do pick it because it's harder. You don't like yourself if you pick the other one and always feel that you're full of shit."

I find myself looking at this famous director, who dines regularly with Spielberg and "Harrison" [Ford], who has a staff at home, and a pool outside, and an equally accomplished wife upstairs on a conference call, and I find myself asking the old chestnut: Does he ever think about how far he's come from that seven-year-old on a boat from Berlin? Nichols pauses. "I do think about that. What I think mainly is that I'm ridiculously lucky. I mean, indescribably lucky. Frighteningly lucky. Sometimes I think, 'Oh please, don't let some spiritual bill be piling up somewhere.' And I'm relieved to remember that the first part of my life was not wonderful by any stretch of the imagination. Maybe, maybe, *maybe* I've paid my dues in that tough, painful first part, which was, after all, very long. We'll see. If not, then I'll be sorry. Of course the gag is that the luck was there to begin with. As I'm always telling my children and they're now always telling it back to me: 'You can never tell the good thing from the bad thing. Sometimes not for years, and sometimes never, because they become each other.' "

Ronald O. Perelman

WHEN I MENTION to Revlon Chairman Ronald O. Perelman that in 2003 an article cited that nineteen of the Forbes 400's twenty-five New York City billionaires were Jewish (including him), he doesn't look surprised. "Look, I think Jews are very aggressive," he says, leaning back in a loden green armchair in his spacious office off Madison Avenue. "I think that by nature we're high achievers. And I think by nature we're smart. I don't think we're *smarter* than anybody else. I think we have to try harder than anybody else."

Why harder?

"Because I think people expect more from us than from anybody else. And I think that we've got to deliver that or else we're viewed negatively."

This compact sixty-one-year-old, who appears thick in photographs but is actually trim in person, has over the years been portrayed negatively, and doggedly, by the New York tabloids; it seems they can't get enough of his marriages, divorces, remarriages, and dustups in the courts—be it the 1997 custody battle with his ex-wife Patricia Duff over their four-year-old, Caleigh, or a 2004 noise dispute with a café across from his East Side townhouse. I ask him whether his religion helps him keep things in perspective.

"A lot," he says with a nod. "I believe that a large part of how we all get to where we are is not entirely our own doing. I am a great believer in that." In other words, moments of adversity are meant to be? "I think you've got to learn from them, deal with them, grow from them." He nods. "That's easy to say; it's more problematic when you're going through them."

I tell him that many of the people I interviewed don't feel that Judaism offers the tools for coping with crisis. "Oh I think it does," he says. "At least for me."

Perelman doesn't just turn to Judaism in the rough patches; he's incorporated it deeply into his daily life. He davens every morning with tefillin (the leather cubes containing scripture that are worn on the head and arm during morning prayers), keeps kosher, goes to synagogue every Shabbat morning, and imports a minyan when he's in the Caribbean. I ask if he finds that it takes work to make time for observance. "No, it's just the opposite, I think," he says. "Take shabbos, for instance: It becomes this great island that transforms the whole family for that period of time." (In addition to Caleigh, Perelman has five other children—four grown kids by first wife Faith Golding and a daughter, Samantha, twelve when we meet, by ex-wife Claudia Cohen. He is currently married to actress Ellen Barkin, fifty, who is also Jewish and has two children by her marriage to actor Gabriel Byrne.)

"On Friday nights, whenever the kids are around, we'll have dinner together," Perelman explains. "The girls will light the candles. We'll say the blessings over the wine and the bread. And then we'll have dinner and just hang around. And then Saturday, I let them do a lot of stuff, but there's a whole bunch of stuff that they *can't* do and they know that. For me, I go to synagogue every Saturday morning, I finish up around noontime, and then we'll just hang around; read, watch a movie. It's this great block of time that's so peaceful and so spiritual for me and so different that I just love it."

I wonder if he understands why many Jews I spoke to say that they don't feel moved in synagogue. "Really?" he asks. "I feel moved every time I go." Is he stirred by the prayer text itself, which I've heard some describe as fairly lifeless? "I think if you've got a great *chazzan* [cantor], it can make it alive," he says. "Like Joseph Malovany, who we have at Fifth Avenue Synagogue—he's unbelievable. But it could be just a kid who is energetic.

You go to a Hasidic Saturday morning service: It is fabulous. It's so full of energy and spirit and joy."

So he wouldn't call it somber? "No, that's a Reform service," he says with a smile.

He keeps kosher at home, and his children have followed. "They're very aware of what they're eating. They'll ask a waiter what's in it. If they're having pasta at a restaurant, they'll ask, 'Is there any fish stock?' Even my nine-year-old [Caleigh] will ask questions as to what's in it. After school, I'll say, 'What did you have for lunch?' She'll say, 'Well they served meatloaf, but I wasn't sure what was in it, so I didn't eat it.' Same with my twelve-year-old. Very aware. And aware of being respectful on shabbos."

When the family travels, Perelman always finds the nearest Chabad House (a Lubavitch shul) within walking distance; or rather, his office finds it for him. "I was in South Beach with my kids this past weekend," he says. "Ellen, my wife, wanted to go to Canyon Ranch for two days. So rather than stay home with the kids, I said, 'Let's go away someplace.' I asked my kids, 'Where do you want to stay?' And my eldest daughter wanted to go to South Beach. She said, 'I hear the Shore Club is the hippest place to stay.' There was this Chabad House like a mile and a half away from the hotel. So on Saturday, I walked over there."

Perelman hasn't always been this devout. "My turning point came when I was eighteen years old; we took a family trip to Israel. It was the first and only time I've been there. It just had this strong impact on me. I felt not only this enormous pride at being a Jew; I felt this enormous void at not being a *better* Jew. So I decided then to begin being a better Jew. As soon as I got married, we kept a kosher house, we became much more observant. We moved to New York shortly thereafter and joined an Orthodox synagogue and the kids grew up with much more Judaism surrounding them than I ever did."

I ask why the Israel trip was so pivotal. "It was seeing a country where everybody was proud of being a Jew, where everybody had the Jewish traditions and religious aspects of their life blended into the social and environmental aspects of their lives. Even when they were not terribly observant they were observant. And they were the happiest, most content, focused, proudest people I'd ever met.

"I went from there—I'll never forget this—to Austria, which I just hated. I wanted to leave after the cab drive to the hotel and go right back to Israel." Why was he so turned off? "Too Germanic. Going from this proud, energetic young country to this very staid, institutionalized, pompous, strict, harsh environment."

He says he hasn't returned to Israel in forty-eight years, mostly out of "laziness" and security concerns. "I always think it's two hours too far," he says. "I'm not a great traveler. I've never been to most parts of the world."

He prefers to stay closer to home—or homes; he has mansions in New York, East Hampton, and Palm Beach. Despite his wealth and stature, Perelman belongs to none of the tony private clubs that he characterizes as anti-Semitic. "New York, which is probably the most open society in America because it's so big and achievement oriented, is probably still one of the most restricted," he says. "You go to the Hamptons or Palm Beach, which are probably sixty percent Jewish now, and you'll see private clubs that are restricted. But none of them will acknowledge that. They'll say, 'We have Jews here.' "

He seems genuinely blasé about this vestige of prejudice almost proud to be excluded. "There was never a time that I wanted to be where I wasn't wanted," he insists. "And I was never bothered. If someone doesn't want you around, why be around them?"

He doesn't feel the same gentile exclusivity in the country as a whole. "I think this is the greatest place for Jews ever in the history of the world," he enthuses. We happen to be talking just a few weeks after the 2004 election, and many Jews I know feel wary about an Evangelical groundswell. Perelman is unperturbed: "I think George Bush has been a fabulous president for Jews—far better than any president in my lifetime. As long as you don't get the nuts—the Jerry Falwells—driving the truck, then the world is a fine place. You start getting them with too much power and you could be in a little bit of danger, but I think the country is too centrist to give too much power to those kinds of people.

"I think Bush has been the best president for Israel in history. He's allowed us to defend ourselves! He hasn't held us back. No other president would have let us do this. Every other president said 'no retaliation for terrorism.' He's the first one that said, 'Okay, you do what you have to do to protect yourselves.' "

Obviously Perelman embodies not only the unapologetic Jew, but the visible, prosperous one. When I ask him if he bristles at the persistent stereotype that rich Jews control the media and Wall Street, he scoffs. "The truth is that we rely on the gentile establishment for our lifeblood: both the banking and advisory world, and to a large extent, the media, which everybody says is Jewish controlled, but that's nonsense. Jews still today are heavily reliant on the gentile establishment. Who are the big banks in the world? Barclays, JP Morgan, Deutsche Bank, Merrill Lynch, Morgan Stanley. They're all predominantly gentile institutions."

So when he still hears the "Jews-run-the-world" adage, it doesn't ruffle his feathers? "No. I mean, if someone called me a 'Jew bastard,' that would ruffle my feathers. I was at a restaurant two years ago and at the table next to us were these Germans; I think they had just come from seeing *The Producers* on Broadway and they were talking derisively about Jews—'Jews this and Jews that, Jews this and Jews that.' Finally I got up and said, 'I have never seen such a bunch of fucking assholes as you people.' And I very rarely do that. I said, 'You guys don't know what the fuck you're talking about, and if you don't like it, you should get the fuck out of here.' "

Perelman is bullish not only about his personal Judaism but about the religion's long-range survival. "Jews have a certain value system that has been the platform for a big part of the world for four thousand years," he asserts. "I think it is important for an individual to have the stability that comes from the belief there is a God and that that God has a great impact on his destiny. I happen to be a big supporter of Lubavitch [a Hasidic sect] primarily because of the continuity issue. I think Lubavitch has been probably the best organization in supporting pure traditional Judaism around the world and getting more young people oriented to that. More young people are realizing the importance of their Jewish heritage and they're leaning more toward the purer aspects of it in Orthodoxy than the Reform aspects of it. If you look at the strength of the two movements, you'll see that Reform strength has declined and Orthodoxy is increasing. I think it's in large part because Reform doesn't give you much to believe in. I mean, you may as well not be Jewish because they rationalize away everything that is the essence of Judaism."

For instance?

"Well, you don't have to be kosher because of refrigeration. You don't have to celebrate Yom Kippur all day because they can start eating in another time zone fifteen minutes earlier. When you get all done, there's nothing there. And I think that kids today—what is it, the fourth or fifth generation here?—are looking for something that is more real, more established, and more substantial. I think that's what is orienting them back."

He also prefers his Judaism the old-fashioned way: adhering to strictures of Orthodoxy. I ask how he reconciles the division between men and women; for example the requirement to sit separately in shul, or with women upstairs. "I think it's great," he says. "For me, it allows for more concentration, more focus on what we're there for. There's less socializing and social requirements than would exist if both sexes were together. And it's not like we put the women in the basement; we put them above us. That's significant, I think, in terms of how Jewish women are thought of; they are really the head of the household."

But not the heads of congregations. Perelman sighs when I ask how he feels about women rabbis. "You know, you start getting into real issues there, because you get into who can read the Torah. And I, for one, am a purist." In other words, women shouldn't. "I feel most comfortable that way."

An avowed traditionalist, he wasn't thrilled at the bar mitzvah of Ellen Barkin's son, when the customary rites were relaxed. "When my stepson was bar mitzvah at Central Synagogue," he explains, "he read from the Torah, his mother got an *aliyah* [the blessing over the Torah], and his *father* got an *aliyah*. His father [Gabriel Byrne] is not Jewish! True, they didn't give him a *bruchah*—they gave him just a "come up to the *bimah*." But here you have a non-Jew standing on the *bimah*! Which I thought wasn't—" He looks for the right word. "That kind of thing bothers me. I think that's one of the reasons that you see the Reform movement waning and the Orthodox movement growing. I think the Jewish youth of America looks at it and says, 'What is this? It's so diluted that it's meaningless.' "

Since intermarriage is considered another dilution by many Jews, I figure I'll ask a veteran: Does Perelman, who was once married to a Catholic, think differing faiths can be negotiated in a marriage? He's more forthcoming than I expected. "I'll give you my point of view." He leans forward. "I happen to have been married four times: three to Jewish girls and one to a gentile girl who converted to Judaism in an Orthodox conversion, prior to our getting married and to our child being born." He's speaking of Patricia Duff, the striking former Bill Clinton fund-raiser who was married to Hollywood producer Mike Medavoy before Perelman. "What I can tell you is that the difference in orientation was very significant," Perelman says, "as was the view of family and kids and life. I'm not saying one's right and one's wrong because there's no right and wrong in this—but it's different. It's like being an electrician or being a plumber; they're both good things, but they're different. I think it makes it very, very difficult for the couple." He pauses. "And I think it makes it very, very difficult for the kids of that couple to know who they are and what they are. There's enough that we all have to deal with. That's not a burden that should be put on a relationship. This is a very personal point of view."

He's shared his perspective with his older children. "I've constantly said how important it is to me and to them to marry a Jewish spouse. And they sort of get it. I don't think they think differently." Although they don't let him forget he once broke his own rule. "Once in a while, jokingly, they'll say, 'But what about *you*?' I'll say, 'Well, she converted!' But they saw the problems too."

The "problems" boiled over when Perelman and Duff split. Newspapers obsessively chronicled their custody battle over Caleigh, a standoff Perelman ultimately won. There was the tidbit that Duff sought $1.3 million a year in child support, Perelman's stipulation that Caleigh be raised as a Jew, and reports that Duff had baked cookies with Caleigh during Passover week, a period when no leavened food, such as flour, is to be touched.

Today, Perelman describes Caleigh as a conscientious Jew who will likely be bat mitzvah, although he says he won't insist upon it the way he did for his older boys. "For the Orthodox, it's not required for girls," he says. "In fact in Orthodox observance, there's not really a service."

Though Perelman's standard of Jewishness is high, he is surprisingly forgiving of those Jews who don't practice at all. "I'd like it to be different because I think it does them and their families—particularly their children—a disservice. It bothers me when you see Jews go out of their way to be so assimilated. But they're still Jewish because they're born Jewish and they feel the pride of being a Jew."

And he thinks that counts? "It doesn't count for me," he acknowledges. "Because I need more than that. I actually think if they were exposed to it, they'd want more than that too." But Perelman acknowledges that he's an exception among his friends. "They're not like me," he says. "But some of them are. And when I go to synagogue, they *all* are. And they look at *me* and say, 'You're not religious *enough.*' "

And when he sees a Hasid on the street, does he feel connected or alienated? "I feel neither," he replies. "I say to myself, 'There's another Jew.' " He gestures toward me. "Just like you; you're another Jew. I just say, 'There's another Jew.' "

Gene Wilder

HE MENTIONS GILDA right away. I thought it was a subject I'd have to work up to, but I haven't been inside his eighteenth-century Connecticut home for ten minutes before he tells me it was hers. She bought it to escape show business. It's also where she was planning to recover. "Gilda and I moved back from California thinking that she was cancer-free," Wilder says with his famously soft voice, "and then three weeks later she found out it had come back." Despite the fact that he's happily remarried for the fourth time to a hearing specialist named Karen, whom I hear him call "Shug"—as in "Sugar"—Gilda seems to accompany him like a spirit. "She's buried out here," he says, gesturing vaguely to the grounds.

It's an undeniable thrill to meet Willy Wonka in the flesh. I spent so many childhood hours watching him in his purple velvet coat and top hat, sipping from an edible flower, entreating Augustus not to drink from the chocolate stream; to this day I know his every inflection. And here he is before me, the man who was at one time the highest-paid film actor in America, the famous flyaway hair even more wispy, blue eyes just as blue, that small smile that barely curls the lips upward. In person, however, it's clear he's not just "The Candy Man"; his face reveals the Comic with a

Requisite Life of Sorrows. Despite his current good health and good marriage, despite all the laughter he's engendered in classics such as *The Producers, Young Frankenstein*, and *Stir Crazy*, the sadness or weariness is evident, and for good reason.

His mother died when he was fourteen. His second wife's daughter, whom Wilder adopted, is estranged from him. His great love, Gilda Radner, died only five years after their wedding in 1984. Ten years later, he was diagnosed with non-Hodgkins lymphoma, which he's managed to fend off. When we meet, he's nursing Karen's mother through her dying days under their roof. I ask him whether Judaism has helped him through any of these hard times and he shakes his head. "I think Freud got me through," he says. "When I was in desperate trouble for maybe eight or nine years, I went to a neuropsychiatrist."

We're sitting on a weathered orange-red leather sofa in his office—a haphazard but inviting room that looks like it has accumulated things over the years without any real plan. There's an upright piano, a quilt draped over the piano seat, purplish wall-to-wall carpeting, a Macintosh computer on a wooden desk, videotapes on a shelf, and one or two of Wilder's own watercolors—surprisingly skilled—on the walls.

"I'm going to tell you what my religion is," Wilder announces, leaping to the point. "Do unto others as you would have them do unto you. Period. Terminato. *Finito*." (I can't help hearing Wonka's voice in the factory: "*Finito!*") "I have no other religion. I feel very Jewish and I feel very grateful to be Jewish. But I don't believe in God or anything to do with the Jewish religion."

Wilder—formerly Jerome Silberman—says his Jewish background consisted of attending an Orthodox temple where his grandfather was president. His sister and mother had to sit separately—"not being equal to men," he jokes sardonically. His father was born in Russia, his mother in Chicago, of Polish descent, and neither was particularly observant. But he was bar mitzvahed—"I don't know to please whom," he says. "I practiced singing the *maftir* a year before my bar mitzvah," he says, referring to his designated Torah portion. "And I was so distraught—because I had a high soprano voice and no one could hear me in the temple when I started to sing. So I said, 'I'm not going to be bar mitzvah if you don't have microphones next year!' And they put the microphones in. And then, of course, my voice changed."

His father switched the family to a Conservative synagogue when they moved to a new neighborhood in Milwaukee, but Wilder jettisoned the temple visits altogether when he was offended by the rabbi. "I went back to visit Milwaukee, Wisconsin, and heard the ignorant rabbi giving his views on the Vietnam War, and I wanted to get up and start hollering at him. But I thought, 'My mother and father will be embarrassed and their friends will say, *Why did he do that?*' So I didn't. But that's the last time I went to a temple."

When I ask whether Wilder was conscious of being in a minority growing up, he tells a doleful story. "My mother was very ill and she had heard from distant relatives that there was a military academy in Los Angeles [the Black-Foxe Military Institute]. And she talked my father into sending me to the military academy to stay there for a year. And I got so excited—I thought we'd be playing war games. I got there and I was the only Jew—I was thirteen—and they beat me up or insulted me every day that I was there."

He tells me he fought back only once. I ask what happened. "I got beat up," he replies flatly. "They didn't hit my face: They'd make my arms black and blue, so when I came home for Christmas vacation, I was wearing long sleeves and my mother didn't know right away. My mother had thought I was going to learn about sex, and how to play the piano, and bridge, and how to dance. I think she'd seen Tyrone Power in *Diplomatic Courier*. She asked me to play something on the piano and I played 'Nobody Knows the Troubles I've Seen' very badly. It was so bad and she was so disappointed, she walked out of the room, which was a cruel thing for her to do. And when I changed for dinner, I took off my uniform shirt and she walked in and saw all the bruises all over my body. And I started to cry. She'd had no idea. I'd written to my father, but he hadn't told her. And she just held me." Wilder's voice has gotten quieter. His parents pulled him out of the school.

That wasn't the last of the childhood hazing. He was mocked in junior high school, and he reproduces the jeering so quickly, I realize it's at the tip of his memory. " 'Hey, Jew Boy! Why don't you ask the Jew Boy?' "

I remark that this experience must have had some kind of impact. "I don't know how it could *not* have," Wilder allows. "But again, I didn't associate it with any religious philosophy; only the fact that I was something called 'Jewish' and why did they hate me just because of it? I was always afraid to talk about the teasing at home because my mother was so ill."

He felt no anti-Semitism once he started doing theater, but he changed his name anyway, when he was twenty-eight, as so many actors did. "It was 1961; I'd just been admitted to the Actor's Studio. I'd been studying with Lee Strasberg in private classes using my name, Jerry Silberman, and I didn't want to be introduced to Elia Kazan, Paul Newman, and Shelley Winters as 'Jerry Silberman.' " He consulted a friend on possible alternatives and seized on "Wilder" because Thornton Wilder's *Our Town* is his favorite play. "Gene" was chosen because he loved the lead character of Eugene in Thomas Wolfe's play *Look Homeward, Angel*. He didn't connect that it echoed his mother's name until he was in therapy years later. "I was telling my analyst and she said, 'Uh huh . . . By the way, what was your mother's name again?' Dot dot dot . . . And I said, 'Jeanne.' [He spells it.] J-E-A-N-N-E. I'd never thought of that."

The only one who still calls him Jerry occasionally is his sister. I ask him if that name feels like him anymore. "When she says it, yes. But if someone hollered out 'Jerry,' I probably wouldn't turn around."

I ask him how it felt to play two classic Jewish film roles and he holds up one finger: "You mean one," he corrects me: "In *The Frisco Kid*." But what about Leo Bloom in *The Producers*? I ask. "Oh! Oh!" Wilder says with a smile, "I never thought of that. I suppose so. I never thought of it. Of course, Leo. Well, because Zero and Mel *made* it Jewish. But there was nothing overtly Jewish in the writing. Well actually, I can't say that either because the way Mel writes, it *is* Jewishy, but not filled with Jewishisms."

Leo Bloom in *The Producers* (1968) is the uptight accountant who conspires with a failing Broadway producer (Zero Mostel) to produce a guaranteed flop. In *The Frisco Kid* (1979), Wilder played on Orthodox Polish rabbi in the 1850s, Avram Belinski. Complete with long black coat, thick beard, and black hat, Belinski schleps his prized Torah across the plains on a grueling journey to his new congregation in San Francisco. The naive rabbi undergoes myriad hardships, several of which involve being mercilessly assaulted, until he hooks up with a tough cowboy, played by Harrison Ford.

Wilder needed to supplement his scant Jewish education to prepare for the role, so he hired two rabbis and a cantor. "The cantor recorded prayers for me on the tape recorder," Wilder explains, "and I had to study to be able to sing them. Everywhere I went I had that recorder. Then for technical advice, I consulted one Conservative rabbi and one Reform rabbi. Just to answer questions for me. But the cantor was the most helpful. The idea of singing in Hebrew on-screen was something I would have instinctively rejected—'How am I going to do *that*?' But when I heard it on the tape recorder and I could repeat it and I knew what the words meant and the phrasing, and I could make it my own, then I could do it."

I ask him if that role made him think about being Jewish. "A lot of it did come easily," he answers. "I wrote a lot of that movie. Not the prayers, I mean," he says with a chuckle, "but the dialogue. When I was writing I was thinking, 'What would be funny for a rabbi to do?' I didn't think, 'What would be funny for a *Jew* to do?' I know I'm saying the same thing, but in my mind, it wasn't. I am Jewish, so I don't have to wonder, 'What would a Jew do?' "

In one hilarious scene in the film, Rabbi Belinski has just been beaten, robbed, and abandoned by bandits in the desert when he spots a happily familiar sight in the distance: men in long black coats and black hats. He rushes toward them, assuming they're Hasidim, frantically talking in Yiddish about his ordeal, when he realizes they're not fellow Jews: They're Amish. I ask him how he learned the Yiddish that he jabbered in the scene. "Oh that was from Mel," he says with a laugh. "I told him, 'I want to get all excited when the Amish come; what can I say when I'm trying to talk to them and I think that they're *Jews* and I want to tell them I was beaten up—" Suddenly he's in character, accent and all. " 'They nearly killed me, they chopped me, they kicked my kishkes!' And I asked Mel, 'How would I say that in Yiddish?' And Mel said, 'You say, *G-gyhagen machin dyhuda yhiddina . . . !!*' " (It's a rant of makeshift Yiddish that sounds like vintage Mel Brooks.) "I told Mel, 'Wait! Wait!' And I wrote it down. I got it all from Mel. Whether it makes any sense, I don't know."

Before Harrison Ford took the cowboy role, it was offered to John Wayne. "Wayne wouldn't read it until we agreed to the usual price: one million dollars, ten percent of the gross," Wilder says. "The studio stalled, haggled, finally said 'Okay.' Wayne read it, he said, 'I'll do it. It's a funny script.' He was in Long Beach. I said, 'Give him anything he wants—billing, or whatever. If he does this movie, then it won't be perceived as a Jewish film; it will be a Western!' And then one of the guys from Warner Bros. went out to Long Beach and tried to *Jew him down*"—he clearly uses the slur to make a point—"to $750,000, and Wayne quit. And so we lost John Wayne."

I ask him if Harrison Ford ever mentioned being Jewish himself. "He probably said it." Wilder seems foggy as to when, then remembers. "I think when we were in Greeley, Colorado. Harrison and I would go to dinner in a little pub that had a dartboard and we'd eat and then play darts afterwards. And at one point during some conversation, Harrison said, 'Why do you say that? I'm half-Jewish.' He certainly didn't seem Jewish."

Wilder met Gilda Radner doing *Hanky Panky*, directed by Sidney Poitier (1982). "I married a Catholic, then I married another Catholic, and then I married Gilda—she's as Jewish as they come," he says with a mischievous smile. Did he feel more Jewish while he was married to her? "Yeah, because she was *so* Jewish." He laughs. "She was pretty young, but she talked like an old Jew. And her jokes and her kvetching—it would have been easier to take, but it was so *Jewish* when it came out. I used to say, 'Do I have to listen to you kvetch in Jewish?' "

Her illness made him seek healing from wherever it might possibly come. "I went to a Buddhist master," Wilder recalls. "He said, 'If Gilda gets in trouble with pain, call me, and just put the phone wherever it hurts.' " Wilder's tone suggests he believed in the touchy-feely ritual, but—"It's bullshit," he states abruptly. "Still, I did it. His telephone number was 322-U-GOD—something like that. Meaning: 'The god is within you' or 'You are god.' And I said, 'Well, I'm a Jewish-Buddhist-Atheist, I guess.' "

As someone who fears a cancer diagnosis is inevitable, I pay special attention to those who have managed to slog through it. So I can't help wondering aloud if Wilder ever asked the proverbial question: How could God let this happen? "That ignorant question—and I say 'ignorant,' not 'stupid'—never crosses my mind," he says. "I would never have dreamed that God would favor you if you did this, and piss on you if you did that. If you pray for help, he or she or it will help you, and if you don't pray, 'I'm not going to help you.' There couldn't be any God that cruel or dumb or uncompassionate. So I don't think, 'How could that be?'

"In *Unforgiven*, when Clint Eastwood shoots Gene Hackman, Hackman says, 'I'm building a house; this isn't fair.' Eastwood answers, 'Fairness has nothing to do with it.' " (The film's dialogue actually has Hackman saying, "I don't deserve this. To die like this. I was building a house." Eastwood replies, "Deserve's got nothing to do with it.") Wilder continues: "*Fairness has nothing to do with it*," he quotes. "*That's* the answer to your question. The world is not based on fairness. Human beings can *rise* to fairness, can administer something that *makes* it fair or just. But that's not God. When I was being radiated twice a day at Sloan-Kettering, they'd wheel me down there and I'd see these little kids—five, six years old—bald from the chemotherapy. I'm supposed to think that if their mothers had prayed to God, asking, 'Please help my child,' then they wouldn't be here? Nonsense." Wilder shakes his head.

"You asked me at the beginning, 'Why do I feel Jewish?'" he says, "and I said, 'because of my parents' love and embracing, because they gave me confidence.' If my mother hadn't laughed at the funny things I did, I probably wouldn't be a comic actor. After she had her first heart attack, the doctor said, 'Try to make her laugh.' And that was the first time I tried to make anyone laugh. [Wilder was just six at the time.] It seems to me you either have an optimistic outlook on life, or you have a Jewish pessimist's outlook." All of a sudden Wilder's playing an Old Jew: " 'Oy—my luck, it would happen to me! Of course they'd be closed! Of course the car would break down!' " Back to himself: "I always hate it when I hear that. They don't know what trouble is till they've seen real suffering."

Old Jew again: 'They're out of cabbage; of course. No more orange juice in the whole shop. They haven't got *one* chicken left.' "

I can't help laughing and feeling relieved to see a flash of Wilder-the-performer again.

I ask him at what moment in his life has he felt the most Jewish? He pauses for a full thirty seconds before answering: "I think when I was with Zero Mostel and Mel Brooks," he says finally. "Not while the camera was rolling, but while they were talking. I identified with *something* that was Jewish. They weren't talking about Jewish subjects. But I said to myself, 'Yes, I'm part of that; I'm part of what they're doing, and how they sound, and how they're thinking.' That's *in* me." I don't know where I got it from. My mother wasn't at all like that. She didn't have any Jewish expressions or typically Jewish intonations or even a Jewish outlook—she wouldn't have talked about God. The closest I ever heard my father talk about God was when it had been raining and I had an umbrella and I came in out of the rain and opened the umbrella in the living room. And he said, 'Jerry, close the umbrella; you're opening an umbrella in the house.' I said, 'Daddy, are you superstitious?' He said, 'Not in the least, but why take a chance?' Now, that's Jewish."

Dr. Laura
Schlessinger

DR. LAURA SCHLESSINGER—with over twelve million listeners daily, the fourth most popular radio personality in America after Rush Limbaugh, Sean Hannity, and Howard Stern—decided in 1998 to convert to Judaism. She was already half-Jewish, having been born to a Jewish father, but she decided to embrace the faith fully and formally as an adult. She says the last thing she expected, when she discussed her conversion on the radio and in speeches, was to be "reamed" by other Jews. "The primary anger I've experienced is from Jews," says Schlessinger, sitting in her Los Angeles office in a powder blue warm-up suit, with coral nail polish and diamond earrings. "The Orthodox community has really embraced me. But the rest, like the Federation folks, have been horrible—really *brutal*."

She's referring to the Jewish Federation, namely the Dallas women's chapter, which invited her to be the keynote speaker at a fund-raiser in March 1997 and then apparently regretted it. "When I did my presentation, it was a *horror* story," Schlessinger says. "I was talking about my spiritual journey, and the room got more and more hostile. You see, nobody had told me."

She was unprepared for what she describes as the tacit understanding among Jews that a Jewish speaker shouldn't extol Orthodoxy when talking to non-observant Jews. She tells a joke to illustrate. "The rabbi asks a Jewish person to come and speak to his congregation, and the Jewish person says, 'What should I talk about?'

" 'You know,' the rabbi answers, 'Judaism.'

" 'Okay, I'll talk about the beauty of shabbos, and observing.'

" 'No, no, no: You can't talk about shabbos!' says the rabbi. 'That's unacceptable.'

" 'Okay, well then I'll talk about being kosher and the beauties of holiness.'

" 'Oh no, you can't talk about being kosher!' the rabbi says.

" 'Well what should I talk about?'

" 'You know: being *Jewish*.' "

Schlessinger throws up her hands. "I didn't know that when you go into your basic non-Orthodox Jewish audience that there's going to be defensiveness and rage when you say that these rituals—shabbos and kashrut—are part of Judaism; they're prescribed to us as holiness, they're commandments. When you're a convert, you're in the middle of all this enthusiasm, you're embracing it all, and I was trying to put that context in my speech.

"I also commented on a videotape that the Federation showed before I spoke—because they were raising money, and the tape talked about how good you feel when you give money. And I said, 'It's not about how good you feel; it's how good you make *other* people feel.' In Jewish law, it doesn't matter what you're going through; you're supposed to give anyway."

The reaction in the banquet hall was unreceptive, to say the least. "I was stunned," says Schlessinger. "I thought if there was a group in the world—" She pauses. "I'm going to try to tell you this without crying because this is one of the more painful things I've experienced in my entire life. I thought that I had joined a family. I come from a really bad family; for me, this was joining a family. And I expected, when I walked in that room, that I was going to have that dream met. Instead, it turned into my original dysfunctional family." She laughs at the irony. "During the Q & A, it was so nasty and so noisy in the room. And at one point, you know what

I did? I picked myself up and I said, 'Thank you very much,' and I walked out. They had raised more money than they'd ever raised. But I left and I cried.

"The next day, I go on air; I decide I'm not going to say a word about it because I don't want to embarrass anybody, right? But then somebody faxes me an e-mail that went racing around to rabbis all over the country: It said how horrible I was at the Federation dinner, how disgusting I was up there. Now mind you, I've been talking for twenty years: I had never gotten a report card like that, reaming me that I should never be asked to talk to a Jewish group again. I had just seen this fax that was circulating and I made the mistake of going on air. And I said, 'When I first started talk-ing on my show about being Jewish, I was warned that anti-Semitism would come out of the Christian community. From day one that has never happened; I've gotten calls from ministers, pastors, priests, and nuns unbe-lievably supportive that I was standing up for communal values, right? And here I am, blindsided *by my own people.*' And I was choked up on the air. This turned into something that was in *Newsweek, Time, USA Today,* CNN, every news station. The *Forward* did a cover story on me."

I venture that maybe the Federation audience was reacting to her pol-itics, which have been such a lightning rod. "It wasn't my politics because those weren't an issue yet," Schlessinger says, shaking her head. "It was just that I was upholding traditional Jewish rituals and values. That's all it was about. And this is an audience—at the Federation event—which perceives that, if it does charity work, that is sufficient. I didn't know that there were these political subdivisions within Judaism. Nobody had clued me in. And I got mowed over."

Did that event change her behavior at all? "I only spoke to Orthodox groups after that. Because the Federation folks went after my reputation, which is against Jewish law . . . That's considered *lashon harah* (the evil tongue); you're not allowed to do that."

Her son is the reason she converted—or embraced her patrilineal her-itage. "Derrick was about five or six years old," she recalls. "It was a rainy Saturday, we were watching television, I was clicking through the chan-nels, and up comes PBS and Nazi footage of the naked Jewish mothers holding their infants and being machine-gunned into graves. And my finger froze on the channel turner, because I had never seen that myself. I'm frozen and my son gets hysterical: 'What is that?'

" 'That was a long time ago,' I told him, 'and those are German Nazi soldiers.'

" 'Well, what are they doing?'

" 'They're murdering those women with their babies.'

" 'Well who are the women with their babies?'

" 'They're Jews.'

" 'What's a Jew?' "

She sighs. "I said, ''They're our people.' He said, 'But what is a Jew?' I said, 'I don't know, but I'm going to find out.'

"So I started reading and I read the part in Torah where it says *you are a nation of priests and you are a light unto the nations.* Suddenly a lightbulb went on. I suddenly felt, 'That's what I'm supposed to be doing.' It all clicked together with what I was doing on radio: trying to help people do the right thing." As she became more absorbed in Jewish study, she changed her radio show's tagline: "It evolved from 'Now go take on the day,' which was what I said at the end of each hour, to, 'Now go do the right thing.' My mission solidified. I had to help people *do* better; not *feel* better; *be* better."

She was brought up with no religion, despite having a Jewish father and an Italian-Catholic mother. "My father's family was cruel to my mother because she wasn't Jewish; evidently my father's mother would call the house when my father was out and wish my mother dead on the phone. So you wouldn't think that would make me feel warm about Judaism, would you? And my father was hostile toward Judaism—I remember him saying," she bellows, dramatizing his voice, " 'Passover: what a disgusting holiday! Imagine celebrating the *death* of newborn children!' " Schlessinger is referring to the point in the Passover story when God sends the worst of ten plagues to the Egyptian people: the death of their firstborn. "And I said to myself, when I was a little kid hearing that, 'Oh my God, you mean to tell me that this religion celebrates dead kids?' "

She was stunned to learn as an adult that her father had missed the sadness and regret of the Jewish people over this horrific punishment. "We went to a seder at our neighborhood temple, and it got to the point in the service where you take the wine and drip ten times for the plagues. I heard the rabbi explain that they were the tears. And I started sobbing in the middle of this room and had to run out of the building. My father had *lied to me*. We're not celebrating these children's death at Passover, we're *crying for them*." She gets teary. "I was so angry and so struck."

It's strange to be sitting in a quiet room with this startlingly petite, soft-spoken, fifty-six-year-old woman with platinum hair, and to think how many people revile her. "The Jewish Anti-Defamation League went after me on the issues of homosexuality," she recounts. "And Orthodox rabbis wrote to them saying, 'How could you condemn her for the same things we say in the pulpit every Saturday?' They had no answer. So I've been targeted by that political position or mentality; it's been unbelievably ugly."

I ask her what made her publicly apologize—or "atone," as she put it— to the gay community three years ago on Yom Kippur. She bought a full-page ad in a special "Gay Hollywood" edition of the trade paper *Daily Variety* to say:

> While I express my opinions from the perspective of an Orthodox Jew and a staunch defender of the traditional family, in talking about gays and lesbians some of my words were poorly chosen. Many people perceive them as hate speech. This fact has been personally and professionally devastating to me as well as to many others . . . On the Day of Atonement, Jews are commanded to seek forgiveness from people we have hurt . . . I deeply regret the hurt this situation has caused the gay and lesbian community.

But Schlessinger still stresses the Torah forbids homosexuality. "The Jewish line is that homosexuality is an unacceptable behavior; not that a homosexual is an unacceptable person. In Leviticus, there's a long list of things you're not supposed to do. Basically it asks you to be the master over your impulses. And God said certain behaviors are unacceptable. Period. That's the position. It's as simple as that. So I did not apologize for the content because that's like saying, 'God's wrong'; I can't do that. But what I did say was distorted for political reasons, and the distortion hurt many people—devastated many people. That has been probably the biggest pain: That the homosexual activist groups were willing to lie about what I said . . . But if people are hurt by what comes of what I do, I am sorry."

After a deep breath, she adds one personal note: "You need to know that my closest male friend is homosexual—but he doesn't have homosexual relationships. Four out of my five dearest girlfriends are all lesbians."

So how does she advise a caller who has a gay son or daughter? "You tell them that the behaviors are unacceptable but you love them to pieces and they should come to dinner Sunday and don't bring their laundry. I've never said other than that."

I mention the fact that her critics have often suggested she's trying to couch far-right ideas in the cloak of a religious Jewish persona. "It's Jewish *law*," she exclaims. "I have not—and I want this quoted—I have not said anything that the pope hasn't said. But I haven't seen a stopthepope.com! Christianity, Judaism, Islam—all have the same rules about certain behaviors. And they're supposed to be God-given. They're not mine—I didn't make them up; I would *not* have left out bacon." She laughs. "If you left it to me, we'd be eating cheeseburgers."

She's kept kosher since her conversion, though occasionally she asks to smell a friend's food. "I went out to dinner last night, everybody else is Christian, we're at a nice pizza place, and I had to make my own stuff. And somebody ordered prosciutto on her pizza and I said, 'Can I smell it?' " She inhales deeply, demonstrating.

Keeping kosher has been easier than keeping the Sabbath. "For the first couple weeks, I stayed in bed most of the day—I was so miserable. I couldn't go *shopping*. So it was wonderful for the family when we finally embraced it. Now I will say that over the years, we have modified it, because we're not willing to just stay in the house with the lights off. So now I go sailing. I find that sailing, frankly, has helped with prayer and spirituality. And it's legal because you don't turn on the motor and you don't use electricity!"

Though she's comfortable with rules of observance, she's less certain about her spiritual connection. "I wish, during the times when I was hurting or scared or confused or feeling emptied out, that I could turn to God and get something back. But I feel it's a one-way street." In other words, there's no spiritual payoff, no sign that God's listening. "I've joked on the

air that every day I go outside and look at my backyard; I have a ton of
bushes and none of them is burning. I don't know what it is I'm looking
for or that I need to hear."

It was a stranger who recently brought her up short, she says, on a call-
in show on MSNBC: "Suddenly someone asks, 'Do you feel that God
loves you?' And I was stopped. I had many things going through my mind:
*Do I tell the truth? Do I get that personal? Do I deal with the struggles that I'm
having with my own religion?* I couldn't lie, but I didn't want to tell the truth
either. So I said, 'No, that's not something I spend a lot of time thinking
about,' because it hadn't been."

But more and more she thinks Jewish rituals disappoint when it comes
to inspiration. "I spoke once to some western association of Conservative
rabbis and they asked me, 'Why is it easier for the Christian churches to get
people to keep coming to church?' I said, 'I can tell you why easily.' I
picked up the mike, I came around, I stood in front of them, I put my arms
up and I yelled at the top of my lungs"—she whispers it now—"'Jesus
loves me!' We Jews don't have that—that passion, that emotion. We have
intellect. Rabbis are scholarly people who sometimes don't know how to
connect emotionally. Of course, when I did that, some of the rabbis in the
room were immediately offended. I said, 'Well, you asked me the question.'

"I see my Christian friends: When they go and hear the beautiful music and singing, they are elevated. There are testimonies to how one's belief has helped one cope with alcoholism, for instance; they are permeated
with this positive, uplifting feeling. I said, 'We don't seem to have a parallel; at least one that I've experienced.' "

The lack of divine feedback clearly has made it harder for her to
weather the anti–Dr. Laura onslaught. "Many days I want to throw it all
away and never come to work again, and then I read a fax that says, 'Because of you . . .' And they tell you what they've accomplished because of
listening to me. And I realize that God gave me a job and I have to do it,
and if it costs me a price, I have to be willing to pay it. Because you don't
live for yourself. You live to perfect the world—*tikkun olam*. So when I
think of the political stuff that tries to silence me—the Susan Sarandons and
StopDrLaura.com's of the world—I realize that there has never ever been
a time in history, nor has there ever been a person trying to do something
positive, who hasn't been attacked. And you should forgive this from a Jew:
It's my cross to bear."

She says her son, Derrick, feels more spiritual than she does. "He went to an Orthodox high school—he's now graduated—where he davened every morning for an hour. And he loved it. For that hour, he goes into this other place, and it must be something about having started it younger."

She says Derrick will be starting a predominantly Christian college in the fall, which she realizes is going to create a challenge. "We've already arranged to have a kosher butcher from Detroit send meat twice a week, because he can't go without meat; he's an athlete. And we've worked out driving him to synagogue on Saturdays—as many Saturdays as he can or will go. He also understands that he's going to have to write and study on Saturdays—he has no choice, because he has to get through school. I said, 'If you're in the military, you shoot people on Saturdays. And rabbis walk around with guns in Jerusalem; so you do what has to be done.' "

She's realistic about whether Derrick will remain observant. "My guess is that some of it will go by the wayside pretty quickly and then he will get it back, because he'll miss it. So I'm not one of these mothers who is going insane. You know, every few months I'll send him a few new *kipot* [yarmulkes], just in case he loses them, but I'm letting him find his way because I think he'll embrace it better if it's his decision and not 'Mommy's pissed' or 'I have to fake it in front of Mommy.' "

I ask her how important it is to her that he find someone Jewish to spend his life with. "There's no question in my mind that he'll marry somebody Jewish. No question. This is something he loves and wants in his life, for his children, for his home. He probably won't marry an Orthodox Jewish girl—I don't think he's crazy about the long skirts and the wigs—but he'll probably marry a girl for whom Judaism is serious."

Postscript

Three months after I interviewed Dr. Laura, she announced to her radio audience that she was no longer going to practice Judaism. "I have envied all my Christian friends who really, universally, deeply feel loved by God," she told listeners.

Referring to the mail she's received over the years, she said, "By and large, the faxes from Christians have been very loving, very supportive. But from my own religion, I have either gotten nothing, which is ninety-nine percent of it, or two of the nastiest letters I have gotten in a long time. I guess that's my point—I don't get much back. Not much warmth coming back."

Though she said she still "considered" herself Jewish, she said, "My identifying with this entity and my fulfilling the rituals, etcetera, of the entity—that has ended."

Jason Alexander

"IT SPECIFICALLY SAYS in the Torah that you can eat shrimp and bacon in a Chinese restaurant," pronounces actor Jason Alexander—formerly Jay Greenspan—as he sits in a maroon sweater in a corner banquette of a New York restaurant near Lincoln Center.

While he was growing up, the Greenspan family of New Jersey did Jewish rituals "by the book"—separate dishes, never mixing meat and dairy, celebrating every holiday, a perfect Jewish report card—except, that is, when they ate Chinese out. He recalls seizing on this hypocrisy to argue his parents out of forcing him to attend Hebrew school. "I mean, it was a *pig parade* in these Chinese restaurants!" he protests. "So my logic with Mom and Dad was that, 'If these traditions have that little significance ultimately for you—the big, grown-up enforcers of this Judaic world— why the hell am *I* going through all this?"

Does he recall his parents' response? "Oh sure. They said, '*There are people in this world who would kill you just because you're a Jew, and you have to know what you're dying for.*'" He laughs. "This was a real incentive program." He eventually gave up trying to enlighten his folks. "These were very brief conversations because they were pointless, and even in my eleven-year-old mind I knew they were pointless. So I just toughed it out until the bar mitzvah."

Though he dreaded Sunday school, he always looked forward to "lovely" Passover seders. "Just like most of the Jewish families I know, getting through the Haggadah meant," he nudges an imaginary cousin, " 'Skip a bit, brother.' God forbid you should suffer through the entire book!" His mother cooked most of the multiple-course meal. "There was just *abundance*," Alexander recalls. "You have to have a brisket, of course, in case somebody doesn't like chicken."

When Alexander, now forty-six, was finally bar mitzvah, he washed his hands of observance for a while. "I was finished to the point that I don't think I ever did a Yom Kippur fast again. I was pretty done."

He says part of his disengagement was his discomfort with the concept of one supreme deity. "I just could never muster the ego to believe that when I speak, Paine Webber listens. I kind of think about it this way: 'I think there's an ultimate spirituality and morality that keeps the universe balanced and in harmony. But I don't know if any of that requires reading the Torah, or growing my sideburns really long.' "

So, despite a somewhat observant childhood, he felt almost no qualms about giving it all up. "It was fairly simple," he says. "Except I remember the first time I ate on Yom Kippur and I went, 'You know, *if I'm wrong*, then this is probably a *death* sentence right now.' " He laughs. "So I took the Woody Allen approach of 'I don't believe in an afterlife, but I'm taking a change of underwear just in case.' It was always, 'Oh, God, I'm not showing up to temple today—but no offense!' "

He says he married a Jewish woman by accident; he hadn't been looking for one. "I was very attracted to blond hair, blue eyes, high cheekbones, very Aryan, Nordic, which is not your average, typical Jewish girl. And amazingly, my wife looks nothing like that and I found her very attractive." His parents were relieved—"It was very important to them," he concedes, adding that both his brother and sister had already married non-Jews. Still, he says he didn't choose a Jewish wife for the sake of his parents. "I was not a good enough son to worry about it."

Now that he's been married to Daena Title for twenty-four years, Alexander says that sharing a similar background helps. "The more common your mutual knowledge is to each other, the easier it becomes. Not that it isn't fascinating to have your eyes opened to all new things by some-

one you're in love with, but on that particular level of religious background, there is nothing that divides us. So there was no question about
who's going to marry us, or 'If we have children, what will they be?' Daena
and I both grew up with twenty-seven Yiddish tunes that we can reference
when needed."

Their traditional Jewish wedding vows were modified a bit to accommodate Daena's egalitarian sensibility. "There's a ritual where the husband
basically says, 'With this ring I consecrate you unto me,' " Alexander explains. "So Daena asks the rabbi, 'And then what do I say?' And the rabbi
said, 'Well, you don't say anything; once the man says that, it's done.' Daena
went, 'Hold the phone: he'll be consecrating himself unto me as well.' The
rabbi said, 'Well, he can say it, but it doesn't mean anything,' and Daena
said, 'It will mean something to me.' "

Their two boys—Gabe, born in 1991, and Noah, born in 1996—were
both circumcised, but not without their parents' hesitation. "It was a real
decision with Gabie for many reasons, not the least of which was that Gabie was born sick—he was born with a pneumonia-like infection, and he
was in intensive care for ten days before going home. This whole notion
that a perfect little baby comes out and then he's sick and we put him
through this living hell for the first ten days of his life and then we say, 'And
now we're going whack the tip of his dick off'—just didn't feel right.

"We went back and forth on it. Apparently many couples do it because
there's a desire on the father's part to have his son look like him, but I had
none of that, at least that I was conscious of. We did it only because we
said, 'Look, we're probably going to give them a Jewish education of some
kind and it is possible—unlikely, but possible—that our sons will have more
of a feeling for this than we do and want to be more religious than we are.
In which case, they're going to be ostracized for not being circumcised. So
why don't we just get it over with while there's no memory of it, and no
stigma on it.' And that's what we opted to do. But it was not a slam-dunk.
It was a real hard decision."

Despite Alexander's dreary memories of Hebrew school, he's already
enrolled his young boys. "Part of it is the same dopey reason my parents
gave to me," he says sheepishly. "I've even used the same line with them:
'Somebody's going to kill you one day because you're a Jew. You might as well know
what you're dying for.' "

Though Daena also likes the idea of their sons getting Jewish history, she worries about the brand of indoctrination. "Daena feels that Judaism is a sexist religion," Alexander says with a smile. "She thinks most religions are sexist religions. So Gabe comes home and she'll say things like"—he puts on a detective's suspecting voice—" *'What did they tell you today?'* " He laughs. "So she can de-program him."

Alexander confesses he has a secret fantasy that motivates him to keep his kids in Jewish school. "When I was twenty-nine, I had a life-changing experience by going to Israel," he says. "Not the religious Judaism, but the cultural connection. It became important to me. And my fantasy is that my kids will, individually, as they prepare for their bar mitzvahs, learn this history and this journey that their people have taken, and I will take them by the hand to Israel and say, '*Here's where it all happened.* The history is real.' That to me is worth four years of going through some hard Sundays."

Alexander has become very involved in peace efforts in Israel, but he is often reluctant to agree to front a Jewish cause. "You know I'm the first one to say, 'If I can, I will, but you really got the wrong Jew.' " He says it's because he won't proselytize. "I don't think it's important to be part of the Jewish Federation. I like service groups that don't have a religious mission."

I ask whether he knows who his fellow Jews are in Hollywood—if there's a special camaraderie among them. "I can tell you that project to project it's profound. I mean, on *Seinfeld*, the poor goyim who came to work on our show were walking into the Land of Canaan. Our director for the first four and a half years was a guy named Tom Cherones—not a Jew. Never really got what was going on there—and was an outsider because he couldn't riff with us. That being said, Julia [Louis-Dreyfus] and Michael [Richards] aren't Jewish, and Jerry was no more connected than I am; but between Larry [David, creator] and Jerry, and their writing staff, and the network guys, it just became a Jewish show. It's *not* a Jewish show, but it was a *very* Jewish show."

And yet *Seinfeld* wasn't usually discussed in terms of its Jewishness. "Well, that's because Jerry and Larry would have absolutely rejected it as a notion. They would tell you, if anything, it's a New York show. So many times people would say to me, 'George and his parents are Jewish, so what's with the Costanza name?' But Jerry and Larry in fact would shy away from anything Jewish, with the exception of one episode, which I think is the worst episode we ever did: the mohel episode." (A mohel is a person or-dained to do ritual circumcisions.)

"We had a character who was a child-hating, neurotic mohel. I said, 'Here is a Jewish figure that you're taking head-on, and to a non-Jew, a mohel is already shrouded in voodoo and evil-doing, and you're making him into a child-hating neurotic!' " He said he tried to get them to make a few changes to make the character less awful, "but I don't think they ever fixed it." I confess that I don't recall that particular episode. "It's very forgettable," Alexander says. "The mohel was a very nervous guy, and he would say things about the baby like, 'All right, bring the little bastard in.' "

The restaurant keeps sending out extra courses; a celebrity is in the house. "This is evil," Alexander remarks as we're plied with panna cotta.

Though Alexander has held on to the Greenspan name on all legal documents (he points out that his children are also Greenspans), he says it's occurred to him since 9/11 that perhaps a Jewish name on a passport may not be prudent. "Of late, I have wondered if I am being foolish not to get a passport that says 'Jason Alexander.' That has crossed my mind. Because I do have that fear of"—he puts on a German accent—" 'Passports!!! Hand over your passports!' 'Greenshpan?' Oh, well. Dead man. And I'll tell ya, and this is a horrible thing to say, but I know it's true, so I'll put it out there: If I'm on a plane and I'm being held hostage and they yell out, 'All the Jews step forward,' I'm not stepping forward."

Though he might disown his Jewishness in a hostage situation, he resents those who do so at Christmastime. Put simply: He judges Jews with trees. "It absolutely bothers me," he confesses. "I always make a joke about this: I say, 'You know, I got nothing against homosexuals. But I have a little problem with *bi*sexuals. *Make a goddamn choice.* What is it, 'I'll fuck anything'?" He laughs. "You're a Jew or you're not a Jew." He puts on a whiny voice: " 'I'm a Jew, but, you know, I like candy canes.' Either get out or get in. One or the other."

I assume he feels the pressure so many Jewish parents feel to make Hanukkah as great and enticing as Christmas so the kids don't feel cheated? "Yes," he nods. "You already get into the pissing match: 'We have *eight* nights, kids! Your poor non-Jewish friends? One night and it's all over.' "

As our dinner winds down, I ask him how important is being Jewish to him? "The true answer is, I don't think I could have accomplished what I've accomplished without being a Jew," he replies. "I think that my essence is *supremely* Jewish. It oozes out of every pore. And since most of my acceptance as a celebrity or as an actor has been as a *comedic* actor, the sensibilities of Jewish humor, culture, and background are so much the ba-sis for what I think is funny, that without that grounding, I don't think—" He pauses a moment. "In a strange way, I lead with my Jewishness." Which means what? "There are two kinds of Jews: There's the alter-ego Jew who says, 'I'm a Jew and everyone else is dirt'—that tends to be the more Orthodox variety. But take that away, Jews are the most self-deprecating people I've ever met. A lot of that is me.

"I was incredibly shy as a kid, and compensated for it by developing this sort of public persona that has become what people think of me. But the way to do that is to walk into the room and say, 'It's all right. I'm a short, bald person; nobody has to look at me. I'm nobody. Keep going about your business.' It's a very Jewish entrance.

"The whole key to playing George for me, which became my calling card to the world, was that this guy, who's full of piss and vinegar and bravura, is, in the next second, asking, 'Too much? Did I overdo it?' A guy so fully aware of his own limitations, and self-critical, that it took the onus off of all his selfishness and bad behavior.

"The only way I can function in life as Jason Alexander instead of Jay Greenspan is because if Jason Alexander fucks up, I can go, 'Hey, I'm only a Jew from Jersey. What do you want from me? I'm playing with big kids out here and it's not me. I don't know how to act, I don't know how to behave, I'm just a Jew. I'm a little, unsophisticated Jew.' I actually carry that everywhere I go."

Richard Holbrooke

THE PHONE RINGS NONSTOP in Richard Holbrooke's home. It's difficult for him to complete a thought. "Hello? Hey, Claire. What's going on tonight? Is Colin going to be there or not?" We're sitting, on an April afternoon, in Holbrooke's muted study in his apartment on Central Park West—one of three homes he shares with his wife, Kati Marton. Married since 1995, they're a high-profile New York couple: Holbrooke, pictured above with his son, David, was Assistant Secretary of State for East Asian and Pacific Affairs in the Carter Administration, managing editor of *Foreign Policy*, U.S. Ambassador to Germany from 1993 to 1994, credited for brokering the 1995 peace agreement that ended the war in the Balkans (nominated for a Nobel Peace Prize for his efforts), and then U.S. Ambassador to the United Nations from 1999 to 2001. At sixty-four he is now vice chairman of a private equity firm, Perseus.

Marton, fifty-seven, is a well-respected journalist and former ABC News foreign correspondent who has written five books, including a biography of Raoul Wallenberg, who saved Jews during World War II, and an investigation into the murder of CBS reporter George Polk. She serves on the board of the International Rescue Committee, whose focus is on refugees, and she used to head the Committee to Protect Journalists.

Both are tall and striking, they host star-studded parties with guest lists that include everyone from Bill Clinton to Robert DeNiro, and both have high-profile exes: Holbrooke dated Diane Sawyer for seven years and Marton was married for fourteen years to ABC anchor Peter Jennings, with whom she has two grown children, Christopher and Elizabeth. (Holbrooke has two sons, Anthony and David, from his first marriage.)

Both are also Jewish, though Holbrooke was raised by his German mother as a Quaker, and Marton didn't learn of her lineage until she was an adult. "She was brought up Catholic in Budapest," Holbrooke says, putting his bare feet up on the coffee table and sipping a can of caffeine-free Diet Coke, "and didn't discover her Jewish background until she was in her thirties. You don't know Kati, do you?" I shake my head. "She's the one you should be talking to for this book; she's got the real Jewish story."

It's not easy to get Holbrooke's story, because the phone keeps ringing and he keeps picking it up. "Hello?" He starts chatting with someone on the line, deconstructing what sounds like the latest issue of *Foreign Affairs*. "I also thought Les's piece was very good," Holbrooke says. "I thought Paula's defense was pathetic and Judith's piece was really good. The Milosevic piece said nothing. That was a lost opportunity."

When he's off the phone, I ask about Slobodan Milosevic—whether comparisons to Hitler ran through his mind as he sat at the negotiating table with the man considered to be the architect of ethnic cleansing. "Milosevic himself was certainly aware of my Jewish background," Holbrooke allows, "because as a Serb, ethnicity would be exceedingly important. In that screwed-up part of the world—you might call it Southeastern Europe—where the Austro-Hungarian and Ottoman empires and the Russian Empire all met and mixed, ethnic identity was a very important thing. And so Milosevic was certainly aware of it."

Again the phone. "Hello? Yeah, put him on." Holbrooke stands up from the couch and leaves the room for about ten minutes. When he returns, I make the mistake of asking a question with the wrong information: How meaningful was it to him to be the first Jewish ambassador to Germany? "I wasn't," Holbrooke corrects me. "Arthur Burns was." I apologize—my research had led me astray. "I don't think you can find a single statement that I was the first," he scolds me. Great start.

"Well of course it was significant," he goes on. "I had expected to be named ambassador to Japan, and then [Walter] Mondale wanted to go to Japan. So when I got the call from Christopher [Warren Christopher, Clinton's secretary of state], I was totally unprepared for it. Never ever had anyone hinted at the possibility of Germany."

Another call. His assistant patches him through to his stepdaughter, Elizabeth Jennings, in her early twenties. They make a lunch date. "Why don't we go to Michael's?" Holbrooke says to her, suggesting the watering hole for the city's media elite. "I can show you off . . . Or are you ashamed of me? . . . Are you paying or am I paying? I'll pay for all our meals together until you get married . . . One o'clock at Michael's . . ."

Back to the ambassadorship: "The administration asked me to reply in twenty-four hours. My first call was to Les Gelb—this was like seven in the morning." Leslie H. Gelb, at the time Holbrooke and I meet, is president of the Council on Foreign Relations and an old friend of Holbrooke's. "So Les correctly said, 'This opportunity is *better* than Japan. It puts you in a new area of the world, it's more challenging, there are more issues.' And he of course was right. And then I called my mother and I said, 'I've got bad news and good news. The bad news is I'm not going to Japan; the good news is I'm going to be the American ambassador to Germany.' And there was this kind of long pause," he recalls. "She had not set foot in Germany since 1933." Trudi Kearl escaped Nazi Germany when she was a young girl. "And here I was, sixty years later to the year, going to Germany. I think she was completely stunned. But she ended up visiting me three times."

I tell him I read that his mother created quite a stir when she came back to the country she'd fled. "That was a great drama—my mother's return trips," Holbrooke says with a nod. "She was very ambivalent about it. But she liked the house, she loved the service, she liked the butler—she *loved* the butler; she wanted to take the butler home with us. Who wouldn't? She began to remember things. When the butler served us, she said, 'We had a butler like that.' For the first time, I got a much deeper sense of the kind of life she lived in Hamburg as a girl, which was much wealthier than I'd realized."

He says his mother resisted at first getting too relaxed in her home country. "She speaks perfect, accentless German, of course, but at first she didn't want to talk German. Then she started talking *only* German. Then the press did stories on her and she got quite upset because they kept describing her as 'German-Jewish'—or 'Jewish-German,' I don't remember exactly—but they kept describing her as Jewish. Felix Rohaytn told me the same thing happened to him." He's referring to the former financier and ambassador to France. "Felix says that French articles about him always referred to him as Jewish, where American articles never mention it."

I ask why it bothered his mother to be referred to by her religion. "Felix and my mother, they feel that the reference to being Jewish is subliminal or latent anti-Semitism. They are very clear on this point. They are separated in age by maybe ten years, grew up in the same environment, and they're much more sensitive to these issues than we are. At least than I am."

So it didn't bother him at all? "I didn't care. It didn't seem to me to be a big deal. In Europe, cultural and ethnic identity seem more important, and I don't believe there is overt anti-Semitism in either country, other than the kind of residual anti-Semitism which exists in so many parts of the world, including parts of the United States. In Germany, the real issue isn't anti-Semitism today, it's antagonism towards Turks. And I repeatedly told the Germans, who are dealing with their responsibility for the Holocaust quite responsibly, that they can be proud of the fact that they faced up to the Holocaust in retrospect, but they ought to not ignore the fact that there are only one hundred thousand Jews in Germany today, but there are four million Turks, and they ought to face up to the Turkish problem that is real and present."

Holbrooke says he never felt—either in Germany or in the Balkans—that anyone made an issue of his religion. "Never noticed it," he says. "When I joined the foreign service in 1962, my grandmother was still alive; she was Swiss-Jewish, not German-Jewish, and she said, 'How can you be a diplomat? Jews can't possibly succeed in the diplomatic world; it's not possible.' I said to my grandmother something like, 'I don't understand what you're talking about.' It never occurred to me."

A *New York Times* profile of Holbrooke during his tenure in Germany described how he displayed, in his elegant ambassador's residence, a photograph of his grandfather in a World War I uniform: "I show it to German visitors as a symbol of what they lost," Holbrooke told the *Times*. When I ask him about it now, he shows me the very picture. "Every German family has a photograph like that. And so I just kept it in the living room. Some people would ignore it; others would stop and stare at it. Some would demand to know why it was there—what was the message I was sending? I said, 'This is an existential fact; this is my grandfather. You may read anything you wish into this photograph.' And I also said, 'If history had turned out differently, maybe I'd be Germany's ambassador to the United States instead of America's ambassador to Germany.' My mother didn't like it at all. She said it was a militaristic picture and there are a lot of nicer pictures; she's not into symbolism at all. And it's true; I could have had an ordinary picture of my grandfather. But don't you find that picture—the original, with his handwriting—extraordinary?"

The phone again—his assistant calling. ". . . very much so, but not now. Tell him when I start up to Columbia in about ten minutes, I'll talk to him . . ."

Holbrooke takes another sip of Diet Coke. "I think the most memorable day I ever spent in Germany was the opening in Frankfurt of *Schindler's List.* About fifteen members of Schindler's list—I think they were called 'Schindler's children'—came to it. And Schindler, as you know, had died a broken-down man in Frankfurt sometime in the 1960s or '70s [1974]. And these were the people who had taken care of Schindler and brought him dinner and watched over him as he declined, after his wife left him. Spielberg and Liam Neeson and some of the cast came. And beforehand, Spielberg went around and talked very quietly with the survivors— some of whom he had interviewed for the movie for research. And then we watched the movie in this large auditorium in Frankfurt—there must have been fourteen hundred people there. Hearing the movie dubbed into German, with the harsh, guttural accents of people saying these grotesque anti-Semitic things in their original native language, was very powerful.

"At the end of the movie, there was complete, dead silence, except for a few people who were crying. Spielberg said, 'I want to dedicate the show to the survivors who owed their lives to Schindler.' And then Richard von Weizsacker, who was then president of Germany, said, 'It took an American to make this movie. Only an American could have made this for us.'

"Then Spielberg went around to these survivors again and asked, 'Is that the way you remembered it?' I heard one old lady say, 'Of course I remember Goeth—[Amon Goeth, played by Ralph Fiennes, was the commandant of the Plaszow Concentration Camp]—on his white horse, just as you have it, but it was much worse than the film.' Spielberg very gently said, 'I know; that was the most I could manage to put in a movie.'

"Then Spielberg told a very interesting story about how, two or three nights earlier, the film had opened in Vienna, and the Austrians had applauded wildly at the end, and how offensive Spielberg had found that, because, of course, the applause suggested that the Austrians didn't feel connected to these events. If memory serves, the Führer was an Austrian himself."

Holbrooke said the Holocaust pervades modern Germany. "In Germany, unlike Japan, the Second World War and the Holocaust are *daily* events. You can't move through the job as ambassador—at least not if you have any cultural sensitivity whatsoever—without being constantly reminded of the past. Whereas, had I gone to Tokyo, the Japanese would never bring it up unless you do. But in Germany, it always comes up implicitly or explicitly."

I ask if, when he visited Auschwitz, he felt connected personally at all. "Well, two of Kati's grandparents perished in the first transports out of Hungary and she only discovered that relatively recently. Did you read her article in the *New York Times*?" I did; Marton wrote stirringly in 2002 about her journey to her ancestral village, which she said hadn't confronted its Nazi history. "I was there with her on that trip."

So has Kati's exploration of her lineage caused him to look back at his own? "Yeah, I think it has. It's something we talk about a lot. She is kind of the anti-Madeleine in a sense," he refers to Clinton's second secretary of state, Madeleine Albright, who learned about her Jewish roots when she was in her sixties. "Some people confronted with a midlife discovery of their origins push it away," Holbrooke says. "Others want to know more and more and more. And Kati is in the latter group; Madeleine was in the former group."

Holbrooke's parents chose Quakerism instead of Judaism and I ask if he knows why his mother decided not to raise him as a Jew. (His father, a physician, died of colon cancer when Holbrooke was fifteen.) "You have to ask her that. But remember that she was assimilated; she wasn't raised Jewish. Hungarian and German Jews were very assimilated, much more than Eastern European Jews. And so, as I understand the story, when Hitler came to power, my grandfather called his four children in and said, 'We're

Jewish; time to go. We've got to get out of here.' He was very smart and he'd read *Mein Kampf* as a literal document, not as some kind of fantasy. And he had enough money to get the family out immediately. But when he said to them, 'We're Jewish,' they said, 'But Poppy, we're not Jewish; we're Catholic!'—or Lutheran, or whatever they thought they were. He said, 'No, you're Jewish.' "

So where does that leave Holbrooke and his identity? Would he call himself Jewish? Holbrooke says with a laugh, "I don't call myself anything."

But if someone asked him what he was?

"It depends what they ask. I'm very literal-minded. If they say, 'What religion are you?' I say, 'I don't go to church much—to put it mildly.' If they say, 'What's your background?' I say, 'Jewish.' It's no big deal. I read an article or two a long time ago that said I was trying to deny it or suppress it; that wasn't true. I never had any doubt about my background, my parents never disguised it. But I didn't go to synagogue or shul, I didn't have a bar mitzvah. My parents didn't believe in organized religion; that's why they chose Quakerism. They loved the values of Quakerism. They were humanists in the best sense of the word, which the conservatives now consider a dirty word. There was this wonderful joke, because so many of the Quakers were Jewish in background. You know the Quaker faith is called 'The Society of Friends'? So the line was—I can't remember the setup—but the punch line was: 'Some of my best Jews are Friends.' It's a great line."

Although his parents did not identify as Jews, Holbrooke says their experience as refugees—his mother's escape from Nazi Germany, his father's from Stalinist Russia—informed his professional focus. "There's absolutely no question in my own mind that my involvement with refugees, starting in 1978, is related to the fact that my parents were refugees. Although my mother refuses to agree that she was a refugee; she was 'an immigrant.' " He smiles.

"There isn't any question that people like Mort Abramowitz, who was ambassador to Thailand in the seventies, and myself, were driven in part by the fact that the U.S. had failed in its responsibilities vis-à-vis refugees in the thirties and could have saved an enormous amount of people if the State Department itself had not been as bad a bureaucracy as imaginable in dragging its feet on permitting entry into the U.S. for refugees. The then—assistant secretary of state was a virulently anti-Semitic man named Breckenridge Long. He was a terrible man. I ended up in his job, so my photograph's on the corridor along with this dreadful Breckenridge Long. So for all of us, refugees were key."

Not just key, but formative—more so, it seems, than Holbrooke lets on to me. In June 1999, when Holbrooke testified before the Senate Foreign Relations Committee at his confirmation hearings for the U.N. ambassadorship, CNN reported that *"an emotional Holbrooke teared up when describing his father's background as a European refugee and, unable to read the rest, he submitted that part of his statement into the record."*

"What you want to know"—Holbrooke points a finger toward me— "is whether the fact that I came out of a Jewish background was a factor or not in who I am or what I do, and you know what? *I don't know.* It's your book. You decide. If you think it did, you can say it, and I won't disagree with you. If you think it didn't, you can say it, and I won't disagree with you. All I can say is that every single person is the combination of his or her experiences subliminally submerged and accumulated, and combined with one's DNA when one comes into a problem."

However he feels about his Jewish DNA, Holbrooke is held up as a compassionate Jew by countless Jewish organizations that have hailed his peace efforts. He has received prizes from the World Jewish Congress, the Anti-Defamation League, Jerusalem's Hebrew University, and Yeshiva University. "Les Gelb has this great joke that they're inventing Jewish organizations to give me awards," he says with a laugh. "Don't ask me. They invite me; I'm very proud to do it.

"But I just want to go back to my core point," he says to me. "I've often said to people that my background made no difference to my positions. But that really is a tautological issue. You don't sit in a room and say, 'Gee, my mother was a refugee from Hitler and my father a refugee from Stalin, two societies where anti-Semitism ran rampant, therefore I have to take a certain position on Israel or refugees.' That isn't the way it works."

In the foyer, we can hear his wife arriving home. "I'll tell you something: Kati's story is more interesting than mine." Kati Marton walks in, somehow managing to look modish in a track suit, clearly busy, but offering a hospitable smile as I'm introduced. "I was just saying how much more interesting you are than me," Holbrooke tells her. "I'm going to change my clothes, but tell Kati what you're doing," he says to me, and he urges her to relate her life story on the spot. Marton has to feel somewhat ambushed, but she's polite. "Can I just make a cup of tea first?" she asks her husband. They have an easy banter about their evening plans, and then she encourages me to follow her into the kitchen, where she puts up a kettle as her husband grabs the ringing telephone.

Kati Marton

KATI MARTON, fifty-seven, speaks perfect English but doesn't sound exactly American. The lilt in her voice, the precise intonation—even her manner of delivery—hint at her old-school European origins.

But even more classically European, she tells me, was her parents' reaction twenty years ago when she confronted them with the secret they'd kept from her for thirty years: that they were born Jewish, and that her maternal grandparents had perished in Auschwitz.

"I called my father in Washington," the Hungarian-born journalist and author recalls (the family had emigrated there in 1957), "and I said, 'Why didn't you tell me?' And his voice was quite *cool*. He said, 'We came to this country determined to start new and to give you (there are three of us) a new start. We didn't see any reason to burden you with our past. Besides, Kati, you wouldn't understand.'"

Her mother, a French teacher and former United Press reporter, was even less forthcoming. "The subject made her well up and retreat from the room," Marton says. "It was not possible to have a conversation on this subject. I could never say, 'Mom, we need to talk.' That was not our language. I said, 'Can't you tell me something about them?' More imploring than demanding. And she would just tear up.'"

The story begins in 1978, when Marton stumbled on her staggering discovery in the course of reporting a story. She was thirty, a rising foreign correspondent for ABC News, and living in London with her then-husband, anchorman Peter Jennings, and their two small children, Elizabeth and Christopher. She returned to her home country on assignment. "I went to do a five-part series called 'Budapest Revisited,' " says Marton as we sip tea. "That began my reclamation of my personal history, because in the two decades prior to that time, I had hardly ever looked back. I was so busy becoming the all-American girl and fulfilling my parents' highest expectations. I'd been very forward-looking and focused."

Marton's family barely escaped Hungary's Communist crackdown in 1957, when she was eight years old. She had previously lived through two harrowing years while her parents, Endre and Ilona Nyilas Marton, were imprisoned by their government for alleged Communist activity. When they were taken away, she and her sister were sent to live with a guardian they'd never met. Once the family started anew in America, there was little talk of the past.

"It was during that trip to Budapest for ABC that I picked up the story of Wallenberg," Marton continues. She's speaking of Raoul Wallenberg, the Swedish diplomat who, despite incalculable risk, saved thousands of Hungarian Jews from Adolph Eichmann's scourge in 1944. "I passed a street named Wallenberg Street and I just had this vague recollection of hearing something about Wallenberg, so I called my father in Washington and said, 'Tell me everything you know about him.' He said, 'Well, I don't know too much—your mother and I were underground during the war—but here are three names of people who would.' "

Marton began to track down Wallenberg intimates all over Europe and Russia. "One day, I was doing this interview with this woman in Budapest—a friend of my father's—who had been saved by Wallenberg, and she just very matter-of-factly said, 'Of course, Wallenberg arrived too late for your grandparents.' " Marton knew at once that this woman was talking about her maternal grandparents, about whom she'd been told very little. "I had never seen a picture of my maternal grandparents and knew nothing about them, except that they were killed during the siege of

Budapest in 1945—the last stand between the advancing Soviets and the re-treating Nazis. The city was reduced to rubble by these two forces and a lot of people died, so the story that was told to me of my mother's parents' deaths was entirely plausible; I never had reason to question it. So when this woman said, 'Wallenberg arrived too late for your grandparents,' I was dumbstruck. But I thought if I said, 'What do you mean?' I would be dis-loyal to my parents; because clearly they had not seen fit to share this with me. So I didn't ask."

Marton had been raised Roman Catholic and pious. "I never missed Mass on Sundays as a little girl, and in fact, I had a very special relationship with the Virgin Mary after my parents' arrest because my godmother taught me a prayer for political prisoners that I used to mutter during class and between classes. When they were released—my father after two years, my mother after one—I was sure it was because of my fervent interven-tion." I tell her I read somewhere that a Madonna hung in her childhood home. "Oh yes," she affirms. "It's on my parents' wall to this day."

When she confronted her father in 1978, Marton was angry. "I was young and very judgmental," she says. "And rather harsh in expecting them to just put everything on the table for me, which they really couldn't do. I now understand why it was very difficult for them to talk about this, be-cause I've since experienced this reluctance so many times with other peo-ple who also lived through this almost unprecedented hell: the last six months of the war in Budapest. Budapest had gotten off pretty lightly un-til then; everybody knew the war was over and thought they had survived the worst, but then Eichmann came in. It happened with such breathtak-ing speed that it left those people really in permanent posttraumatic shock. They lost their identity, they lost their status in a country where they had all of those things heretofore, particularly in Budapest.

"The middle class of Budapest was Jewish but entirely assimilated. My parents were already Christians; I don't think my father had ever been in-side a synagogue. They were already the second generation of non-observant Jews. They really thought of Judaism as a religion, not as a race. And for a while, so did the Hungarian nation and government. No ques-tion there had always been elements of anti-Semitism, but it was contained. But now suddenly it was unleashed."

Marton stresses what an upheaval it was, for her father especially, to be suddenly stripped of his prestige, let alone his humanity. "My father was very much part of the Budapest upper-middle-class establishment. He was a fencer, graduate of the University of Budapest, Ph.D. in economics. And suddenly he was nobody: couldn't sit on a bench or date a non-Jewish woman. And he was in his twenties and thirties when all this happened. Of course, to this day, he does not consider himself Jewish."

These revelations left Marton feeling unmoored—and bitter that such essential information had been kept from her. "So what did I do? I wrote a novel using large chunks of my own childhood and fragments from theirs. Because this is how a writer resolves this kind of identity crisis."

The novel, *An American Woman*, published in 1987, centered on a foreign news correspondent named Anna who, in the course of reporting a story, stumbles upon her Jewish past. At one point the character says, *"This must be like finding out at age thirty-six that your parents aren't your real parents."* And about her father: *"He had lived a lie for her . . . He had sculpted himself into the embodiment of everything Anna thought Jews were not: aloof and indifferent to the past and to any God."*

Marton says that one of Anna's fictional conversations with her father was taken almost verbatim from one she had with her own. The father asks, *" 'Aren't you being a little bit of a voyeur? All this vicarious dramatizing? Claiming your right to this . . . this history,' he hissed the word at her, 'without ever having paid a price for any of it.' "*

"That was a conversation that I had with him," she says with a nod, "and he had a point. But on the other hand, I also have a right to grandparents. I think my parents made a mistake and I think they know that."

How did her parents react to the book? "Oh, not well at all," Marton replies. "Not well." I ask her to explain that feeling of being "duped," as she described it in the novel—denied something she was entitled to. "But now I understand why," she replies, "which I didn't then. As incredible as it is to think that a person like me could be persecuted or that my children could be marked, that's the world my parents wanted to shield us from and that's the world that formed them. And they will never get over that. They're in their nineties now—this was fifty years ago; but these people are scarred for life. No matter how successful they were here in America. What they went through in those six months . . ." She doesn't finish.

I ask if she's ever seen her mother mourn her parents. "No. I only saw her trauma, and her inability to talk about any of this and her resentment at *my* need to talk about it—as if this were not my business. This was hers.

And this was hers to carry with her and grieve. I think she has guilt at having survived in Budapest, though clearly there was nothing she could have done for her parents because by this time she was in danger too. But I know for a fact that she has not slept a single night without a sleeping pill."

Despite Marton's distress at learning her true biography so late in life, she regrets putting it in writing. "I think if I had it to do over again, I wouldn't have done the novel," she confesses. "I didn't expect the novel to upset them so much . . . But at the time, I was so full of the story, so full of my past. I felt that there was a discrepancy between the person I was conveying to the world and the person inside me. There was just a big, yawning gap between this successful network correspondent married to 'The Anchor Monster' and the mother of beautiful children, and this person who was me, who wasn't quite sure who she was. Everyone else seemed more defined than I was, and I wanted some of that definition."

Part of finding it was to write *Wallenberg: Missing Hero*—her first nonfiction book—which was the culmination of those years of following Wallenberg's trail from Sweden to Hungary to Russia, where the man considered the quintessential savior of Jews was ultimately incarcerated, never to be heard from again. The book was well reviewed and even her parents kvelled. "They were very proud of *Wallenberg*," she says, "but there was a drama associated with that book too: I had dedicated it to my grandparents. I wrote, 'To the memory of my grandparents, for whom Raoul Wallenberg arrived too late.' And my parents said, 'Kati, we've never asked you to do anything for us, but we're going to ask you to change that dedication because it is an infringement of our privacy.' And so I changed it: 'To the memory of those Hungarians for whom Raoul Wallenberg arrived too late,' meaning my grandparents. I hated to give that up because it was going to be my very modest memorial to my grandparents."

She said at one point that excavating her past became an obsession. "Yeah, I was pretty riled up," she says. "I wanted details; I wanted to fill in. I had, by then, given up my childhood Catholicism, and I loved the historic aspects of Judaism and the association with so many people I admired. Although I was married to a high WASP, I always had Jewish friends. They seemed so familiar to me because Hungarian humor, culture, cuisine is all very close to me."

She said she could celebrate her newfound heritage because she had the luxury of being safe. "I felt entirely secure in my new country, my new identity, my position here, and therefore I embraced all this. I think that for older immigrants—let's say Madeleine Albright—it's more threatening, because it's not so secure here. They have to pass for something other than what they are. I remember having this conversation with Madeleine, who is, I guess, almost a generation older than me and she didn't want to talk about it. But I couldn't get enough of it."

Marton's siblings felt she was going too far. "My brother and sister were worried that I was upsetting my parents too much. 'Why can't we just let them be?' You know, 'They've earned their peace.' But I've always been the family truth-teller. It's not always a fun role to play," she says with a smile, "nor is it fun for the family to have such a person."

I ask if the rift with her parents had lasted. "Yes," she replies. "I don't think things were ever the same, because things can't be. You love and need each other too much not to resume relations, but once you've gone through something like this, it's the end of innocence in a way. I know that they're not exactly what I thought they were and they realize that I wasn't quite the ever-compliant, eager-to-please daughter who was just almost entirely invested in making them happy and proud. This was my first real act of rebellion. I was claiming my own right to something which was not in their interest. And that was a first. They were not used to me being particularly feisty."

She says she's been calmed by time passing and by her continuing probe into events that in many ways defined her parents' experience. "I have since spent so much time reading and studying and talking about this whole issue, that I am infinitely more understanding and tolerant of them. Because the Hungarian Holocaust was unique, and it was uniquely terrible."

Her relationship with her parents has shifted in the last few years because of their age and infirmity. "It's fine now. Because I'm looking after them. I'm the caretaker. They depend on me for many things now." (Ilona Marton died six months after we spoke—at age ninety-two.)

I find myself asking her if her parents ever said they erred in withholding the truth. "Yes," she replies. "My mother has. She said, 'We were wrong. Our motives were good. But we were wrong.' You see, when my family came here in the late fifties, people couldn't imagine that decades later, you'd go to Budapest for the weekend. The world was really divided then and we got out by the skin of our teeth. And they never wanted to look back."

But she learned lessons from their choices that she vows not to repeat with her own children. Just the same way that her novel's Anna doesn't want her daughter "*to fall between cultures, the way she had*," Marton has made sure her children understand theirs. They were raised as Christians—"When the kids were little and Peter cared more than I did, we used to go to the Episcopal Church"—but they know every corner of her past. "I didn't want there to be any mysteries," she says. "Because it's very damaging to children to learn things late. I have taken both my children to Budapest and shown them all the sort of stations of my cross: where I lived, where my sister and I lived when my parents were arrested, where we hid during the revolution, which was the American Embassy." (It's where she and her husband, Richard Holbrooke, were later wed.)

I assume that when Marton hears or reads about Auschwitz, there's a special resonance now. "It feels personal," she affirms. "I tried watching *The Pianist* the other night and I just couldn't. It's beautiful, but it's very, very painful in a very personal way because I'm always thinking, 'At what point did they know what was happening to them?' And my grandparents did push one of those postcards out from the train, which my mother got." She's describing one of the desperate acts Jews made in the attempt to contact family as they were deported in cattle cars. "My mother's younger sister still lives in Budapest and she told me that they got this postcard saying, 'We're on our way, and the important thing is that you are safe.' "

I wonder if, when she first learned of her true bloodlines, she suddenly looked at her then-small children and thought—Marton finishes my question: " 'They're half-Jewish'? Yes. And you know, Peter was really great about that. He thought it was wonderful and exotic. He'd not only married this Hungarian refugee, but he'd married a child of the Holocaust. I remember he went to the Middle East shortly thereafter and brought me back a ring, which I still have. It's a coin that was minted by the first Jewish state."

Marton did not focus her career entirely on subjects surrounding her heritage. She went on to write *The Polk Conspiracy—Murder and Cover-up in the Case of CBS News Correspondent George Polk, A Death in Jerusalem: The Assassination by Jewish Extremists of the First Arab/Israeli Peacemaker*, and *Hidden Power: Presidential Marriages That Shaped Our Recent History*. She hosted a weekly broadcast on international affairs on National Public Radio and became chairperson of the Committee to Protect Journalists.

But the fixation still lingers. As recently as the summer of 2002, she went to visit her grandparents' hometown of Miskolc, and wrote a forceful op-ed piece in the *New York Times*. *"I have come to this place in search of the grandparents I never knew—or some memory of their world,"* she wrote, going on to describe her frustration at not meeting any townspeople who could direct her to the old synagogue—even those who worked across the street. Finally she manages to find it.

> The interior wall of the courtyard is crowded with marble plaques honoring "the innocent people" who were "deported in the most brutal and dehumanizing manner." The language is strong, even moving. But who sees these plaques behind locked gates? Not the people in the pub across the street, not those at the McDonald's a few blocks away, certainly not young Hungarians.
>
> As I walk the bleak streets of Miskolc, I scan the faces of passersby. Where were you, where were your parents, what did you do before, during or after the disappearance of one quarter of your town's population? Were your parents my grandparents' neighbors? I feel slightly ashamed for thinking that these people share a collective guilt. But I cannot help it. The town of Miskolc has buried its past and so cannot expect redemption.

"I'm wondering if my parents wouldn't sleep better if we would have dealt with it early," says Marton. "But they are sort of pre-Freudian, pre-analysis; their way of dealing with pain is not to touch it. And of course we always have to remind ourselves that being who they were was life-threatening. And therefore I am much less pious and judgmental today than I was twenty years ago."

Part of the credit for that, she says, goes to her husband, Holbrooke, whom she married in 1994. "Richard was very calming when he came into my life," says Marton. "I was still somewhat distanced from my parents and he was then—and is now—extraordinarily respectful of them and what they stand for, and always appeals to my most generous nature in forming judgments about them. Because he thinks they're such remarkable people who lived through the worst nightmares of the twentieth century and who emerged with grace and dignity and started new lives here. He just thought I was being too tough on them. In some ways, he's a much less judgmental person than I am."

I remark that it's ironic, in a way, that she and Holbrooke are actually technically a Jewish couple. "Yes," she says, as if the thought had never occurred to her. "Yes. If there's such a thing as Jewish genes, we have them."

Does she feel Jewish now? "I certainly feel that who I am has definitely been shaped by these historic experiences; I'm only one generation from that. I see things in myself: my drive, my need to keep doing good works, the fact that I can never relax. I'm very happy, I love my life, but I can never say, 'Okay, I'll take a year off now and have lunch with my friends and go skiing.' I'll never be able to do that. I think that was born of these genes. And the need to eternally prove myself worthy of my good fortune. I'm so damn lucky, and I want to—without sounding pious—I think I have a need to earn that good fortune. And whenever something really great happens to me—a good book review, or getting on the *New York Times* best-seller list with the last book—there's always a little voice in me that says"—she whispers—" 'That's for you, Grandma.' "

Joan Rivers

I HEAR JOAN RIVERS before I see her. "I'm coming! I'm coming!" she bellows from the elevator as she rides up to her private floor, where I'm waiting in her showily ornate Upper East Side town house. She's running late, but her assistant, Jocelyn, a friendly, no-nonsense type, has made me feel at home in an extremely formal parlor. It is stuffed with fancy things that hover between chic and gaudy: leopard carpet, dog statues flanking a fireplace, large tufted leather sofa, and embroidered pillow emblazoned with the adage, *"I need a man to spoil me or I don't need a man at all."*

A butler—an actual white-jacketed *butler* named Kevin—has already brought me mineral water and pastel-colored cookies on a silver tray. I could get used to this. Jocelyn explains that her boss is rushing back from the annual Central Park Conservancy luncheon, which is known for its at-tendees' extravagant hats. "I hope she's still wearing hers," I tell Jocelyn. "Oh, she'll keep it on," she assures me, "because you don't want to see her hair underneath."

Soon Rivers, seventy-two, appears in all her riotous finery—a hot pink satin suit with ruffled black chiffon blouse, black hose and matching fuchsia hat whose brim barely gets through the door. It's a loud entrance befitting the arbiter of awards show taste. "I'm sorry I'm late," Rivers apologizes, as her three dogs—Veronica, Yorky, and Max—yap at her arrival.

She doesn't take the time to change into something more comfortable, and I worry that she can barely sit down in that tight pink skirt. Despite the surfeit of inviting furniture in the parlor, Rivers perches on a tiny ottoman opposite me (Jocelyn set it up ahead of time, knowing, I suppose, that's her preferred interview seat), and takes off her hat. "Please excuse my hair," she says, "this is *really* hat hair."

She actually seems human all of a sudden, despite her getup, despite the surgically taut face, despite decades of studied celebrity. And I'm surprised, frankly, at how bluntly, tribally Jewish she is. "The Jews take care of everything and everyone hates the Jews," she says. "The blacks hate the Jews. You fools! Who marched with you? *Who marched with you?* Not the WASPS. Trust me; not the WASPS."

She's fanatically watchful of anti-Semitism being more barefaced recently. "Oh, it definitely is. Look around," she insists. "Queen Noor's book is number one on the *New York Times* best-seller list!" She's referring to the former first lady of Jordan, an American-born, half-Lebanese Princeton graduate who married King Hussein and wrote a book about her life in the Arab world. "Jewish people—Jewish *friends of mine*—went to her book signing!" Rivers moans. "Her book has *overt* anti-Semitism! I had a Jewish doctor of mine say, 'No, no, no; she's my patient; she's not anti-Semitic.' I got so upset on the examination table. 'Read the fucking book!' I yelled at him. 'Read the *New York Times* review—you don't even have to *buy* the fucking book!'

"I did something at a dinner party." Rivers isn't done with Noor. "I got her back. For the Jews. She was on one side of this host, who is a very famous person—I don't want to give names—and I was on the other side. And the host was supposed to talk to me for the hors d'oeuvres because I was the lesser guest, and then talk to her for the main course. And the gentleman spoke to me for the first course, and then I thought, 'I'm going to keep him so amused, he's not going to talk to that bitch for the main course.' And I kept him talking to me for the *whole dinner*. And I thought to myself, '*That's for the Jews.*' I'll fix you, Queen Noor, you anti-Semite! Number one on the best-seller list! And who buys the books? Jews!"

Her loyalty is rabid and Israel has become her litmus test. "Let me tell you something: I left Clinton because he left Israel, and if Bush is in there defending Israel, I'll defend Bush. That's where my allegiance is. I'm the reverse of the Dixie Chicks." She laughs. "Because Israel is not going to go down the tubes with Bush—we hope." She thinks the Holy Land is truly in peril. "I worry that they're going to wipe it off the earth. I only hope that they'll take us all with them. Because Jews shouldn't go quietly this time. If they're going to kill us, we'll kill you right back."

Rivers—formerly Joan Molinsky—grew up in Brooklyn on a street known as "Doctors' Row," since so many physicians lived there. She remembers that during the war children were being sent from Europe to safety in New York. "There was always some doctor who had a niece or a cousin from Prague coming to live with them. And that's because these were kids that were being snuck out. I remember we lost relatives in France. I was old enough, in 1945, to hear all the Holocaust stories. The one that stays with me was one of the good Holocaust stories: An uncle was hidden through the whole war in one of his patient's cellars. And we had another uncle whom my mother was sending clothes to, who wrote us about a jacket he received: 'When I put my hand in the pocket and I found gloves, I felt like a gentleman again.' "

When the Molinskys moved from Brooklyn to Larchmont—a New York City suburb—Rivers's father founded the temple there. The congregation met in the firehouse in its early days "because there were so few Jewish families," Rivers explains, and her dad was the cantor until they found a professional. She is still proud of her father's gifted voice. "He sang to the end," she says wistfully.

Two anti-Semitic incidents stand out from childhood. "I was having my teeth cleaned at our dentist, and he said, 'You'll never make a good college because you're a Jew.' I was twelve. But see, that was good for me, because even then I thought, 'Oh yeah? Want to bet?' It was almost like an impetus: 'I'll show you, Doctor.'

"The second one was when I got a summer job in the junior department at Wanamaker's; I was fifteen and I worked all summer with another girl. And the last week she turned to me and looked at something on the clothing rack and said, 'Ech, only Jews would buy this.' And I was in shock. We'd worked all summer together."

Rivers attributes much of her moxie to her ethnic constitution: "Maybe it's that Jewish immigrant ethic of 'I will do it' that I still have to this day." Her fists go up. "Don't you dare tell me I can't do it. I always say to [daughter] Melissa, 'Jews are smarter, we're brighter, and we can do it better.' "

We discuss Jews' reluctance to be viewed as *too Jewish*. "That's about class," she asserts. "It goes back to all of us who are now a little more educated, polished, assimilated; you don't want to be that stereotyped, big-mouthed lady with too many diamonds." (This is said without any discernible self-irony.) "There are certain clubs I know I can't get into even now. All my friends belong. I don't even want to be in them. No matter what—I could stand on my head—I'll never be in the Everglades Club. Across the street," she gestures outside, "if there's ever a problem, I can never go into the Metropolitan Club."

Did she ever feel she looked too Jewish? "Oh, I know I do!" She laughs heartily. "I look at pictures of myself and I look like what I am: a middle-aged or old Jewish matron. There it is. You are what you are. But I'm also so proud when it's a Jew that wins the Pulitzer Prize or the Nobel Prize. And conversely, I'm always so glad when the serial killer isn't Jewish."

She concedes there are times she wishes she had a different religion: "Every time I see a good-looking German guy in leather." She laughs again. "Show me a blond blue-eyed guy in leather and I'll say, 'Oh, what a pity I'm Jewish!' "

But her parents instilled an unshakable self-respect and urged her to marry within the faith. "It was important to me, too," she adds. "First of all we're the chosen people, and I like that we're continuing; I don't want it to stop. If these people have struggled thousands and thousands of years, it should not stop with me. Who am I to say, 'You buried your candles during the Inquisition and now I've decided not to continue'? And I love going to temple—I love Rosh Hashanah, Yom Kippur, Hanukkah. And then when Hanukkah's over, I do the biggest Christmas tree you can imagine! But I love the Jewish tradition. On Passover, I look forward to doing my meal. I love when you break the fast on Yom Kippur." She fasts? "No. Never have. I don't think God cares."

She says she feels moved in temple when she hears prayers like the Shema. "At those moments, I'm in the right place and I'm doing something I've done every year of my life and it's a tremendous landmark for me. And if I don't go to synagogue on Yom Kippur night, I'm devastated. I missed *one* once." It was eighteen years ago, Kol Nidre night, when she and Melissa walked into their usual synagogue on Fifth Avenue, Temple Emanu-El. "My husband, Edgar, had just killed himself in August, and we went into the service here in New York and it was pouring rain and we were ten minutes late—*with tickets!*—*assigned seats!* And some smart-ass said, 'You can't come in.' And we said, 'We'll sit in the back.' And he said, 'You can't come in.' "

Distraught, she decided to salvage the holiest day of the year by going shopping. "I took Melissa and we went to Ralph Lauren. Polo. And we *bought*. I said, 'We're going to do something to make this better.' And then the next year on Yom Kippur, we were walking into temple, and that bastard came to me and said, 'Surprise! I'm the one that didn't let you in last year.' And I said to him, 'I only hope it happens to your family.' And he said to me, 'It's Yom Kippur! How can you say a thing like that?' And I said, 'Look what you did to *me* on Yom Kippur!' "

When Edgar Rosenberg died, Rivers found the Jewish ritual of sitting shivah for a week—receiving friends and family at home—to be curative. "Oh, I think it's wonderful," she says. "It makes sense! Seven days of eating and talking and laughing and crying and being in the house is so great because you're so happy to be quiet finally when everybody goes home. It's so brilliant: Then you're so happy to be able to go out of your house again. And meanwhile they've kept you going. Shivah's wonderful."

She says she also drew strength from a heritage of pluck and perseverance. "It's all about survival. My husband's *entire* family was killed in the Holocaust; I have a little pillbox upstairs that's all that's left of his German family. So I'm not here to fall apart."

The Holocaust seems to be at the forefront of her consciousness. Even when she watched Melissa costar in the ludicrous ABC reality show *I'm a Celebrity, Get Me Out of Here!* (2003), she connected it to Auschwitz: "When Melissa came back, I said to her, 'I watched you on that program and thought to myself, 'You could have survived the death camps.' That's where the mind of the Jew goes, watching someone go through what Melissa was doing. I said to her, 'You were strong enough; maybe you would have gotten through.' "

After her husband's suicide in 1987, she eventually started dating again. "I was going out for a while with a man who was very Jewish. And I loved that; he lit the candles and cut the challah, and I loved that. I loved everything but this man."

Was it important to her that Melissa marry someone Jewish? "Not as important," Rivers says as she shakes her head. "Because I could see the handwriting on the wall, and I don't know why." In other words, she could see Melissa gravitated toward non-Jewish men, despite her upbringing. "She came from a Jewish family, we had the traditions, she went to Sunday school, but she's never connected with Jewish boys. And it makes me terribly sad, because I still believe all the clichés: They still make the best husbands." How so? "I think they're more for home and hearth. I think they're really into their work. They don't drink as much. Everything they laugh about is absolutely true. And so I was quite disappointed.

"Melissa was going out with him [John Endicott] for seven years, so it's not like, when they decided to get married, I fell against the door and clutched my heart. Obviously this was what was coming down the pike. But it made me very sad. I always had the fantasy that he would see how great Judaism is, how logical and ethical it is, and he would end up saying, 'This is what I want.' But we never got to that." Endicott and Melissa divorced five years after the wedding—an interfaith ceremony that still makes Rivers shudder. "We had a rabbi and a minister—you know, one of those terrible marriages. I mean, what's the baby going to be?"

Indeed: What is the baby? Edgar Cooper Endicott, according to his grandmother, is absorbing the traditions of the parent he's with most: mom. "He's with her now, and the mother's Jewish, and so it's whatever you come out of," Rivers says. In other words, custody is destiny. Before the separation, Melissa did not welcome her mother's questions about how her grandchild would be raised. "It was always, 'We'll make the decision,'" Rivers recalls. "I pushed because I just didn't want him to be *nothing*. But then I thought to myself, 'Don't worry: I'll get him in New York for Passover, Hanukkah, Yom Kippur. He'll know what he is.'"

Though Rivers clearly has a clannish instinct, she says she wasn't conscious—during most of her career—of who the other Jews were in show business. "But now, I *am* more aware and I've started to use it." She explains that there was a "new regime" of executives at the E! Channel, where she was a host, and she couldn't break the ice with them. "I finally turned to one of them and began to talk about Sunday school. And we now talk to each other as Jews! I just got flowers from them with a note that said, 'The *mishpucheh* [family] loves you.' I said to Melissa, 'I don't know if I'm shitting them or they're shitting me.' Cause we're all connecting on this big Jewish level now. But generally, I don't think that helps at all in the business—the way AA [Alcoholics Anonymous] members have each other or gays have each other. I don't think that's there for Jews. It's never been there for me."

And despite the fact that she is in many ways the archetypal Jewish celebrity, she says that she's not the one Jews put up as the famous face of Judaism. "Oh, I only wish I were! Are you kidding? Oh, how wonderful to say, 'She's the one we look to.' I think they look to Barbara Walters, this age group. Which is stupid. Come over here! It's more fun over here!"

Jerome Groopman

JEROME GROOPMAN, M.D.—an expert in AIDS, cancer, and rare blood diseases who helped discover the drugs that made AIDS survivable— is a hugger. "I was kissed from the time that I was a little boy," says this broad-shouldered, six-foot-five-inch oncologist, pictured above in a tallis, who is folded into his office chair on a cold day in Boston. "It was natural for my uncles to kiss me, for neighborhood men, who were Eastern European Jews, to embrace me. It was a different sort of cultural expression— perfectly natural." He says the affection he grew up with in his Bayside, Queens, neighborhood informs the way he administers to his patients. "I just can't imagine not touching someone," he says. "It's sort of a recognition of another person's humanity."

I tell him that when I read his book *The Measure of Our Days*, I noticed how many times he described hugging a patient or holding his or her hand. Groopman, fifty-five, with a bald pate, white beard, and wire-rimmed glasses, acknowledges that his physicality is connected to the affection he received from the Jewish community growing up. "Absolutely," he says. "It's very strong." He notes there was a reaction to his article in *The New Yorker* magazine—where Groopman has been a staff writer since 1998—

when he wrote about Christopher Reeve and his miraculous spinal cord regeneration. "Someone who knew Reeve quite well said to me, 'You touched him when you met him? No one touches him.' But how could I not?"

He refers to his professional ethos as "the medicine of friendship"—a phrase he first heard from a Protestant patient. "In Judaism, when you say a prayer for someone to get better, it says you should heal the spirit and heal the body. I thought to myself, 'These prayers are always constructed for a reason, in smart ways: So why does it say heal the spirit—the soul—*before* you heal the body?' It's too simple to say, 'That's because there's a mind/body connection,' because there are plenty of people who have positive thinking but die anyway. So this sort of glib *mishigas* where some guru says, 'If you just think right, your breast cancer will go away,' or Norman Cousins says, 'Laugh and your lupus will go in remission,' just doesn't work. Ultimately for all of us there will come a time when asking for the body to be healed won't work: because we're mortal beings. But until the very last breath, you can always heal the spirit, reconcile yourself with people in your life, with yourself.

"And that's where the medicine of friendship comes in. I think embodied in the prayer for healing [*tefillat mi sheberach l'refuah*] is the imperative to the doctor that when he or she no longer has the drug to give or the surgery to perform, that they are still there. They're there to try to help that person arrive at a place where they can heal their spirit." Groopman folds his hands around a lanky knee. "I think it's what *I* want in a doctor," he continues. "I want someone to know who I am. I realized this while working in oncology and in AIDS—especially before the drugs were developed. How much could I really give someone sometimes? But I was *there*. That's what you give them."

Groopman has groupies; chiefly, it seems, because he flouts the paradigm of the dispassionate scientist. He writes about his cases often in spiritual, hopeful terms, always careful never to whitewash the callous realities of disease. But Groopman's fans, drawn to his humility and candor, don't necessarily know about the intensity of his religion. "There's no corner of my life where it doesn't somehow inform or influence me," Groopman says. "I mean, I definitely grew up with an identity which was informed by strains of paranoia and distrust and fear about the gentile world. My grandmother had witnessed pogroms in Lithuania and my mother's extended family had been largely exterminated in the Holocaust. So this fear wasn't fantasy; it was the real thing. But I think the wonderful thing about Judaism is it makes you a fuller human being. I mean that's really what the Talmud is—this undertaking to say, 'Let's describe the whole human experience.' So there is no separation for me."

He was tutored in Yiddish as a boy because it was the language of his relatives, chose to write his thesis for Columbia University (class of '72) on Marx's impact on the kibbutz movement, and spent a college summer studying at the Weizmann Institute in Israel. He keeps up with the weekly Torah portion (he once described Talmud as a "compendium of second opinions and opinions on opinion itself"), visits shul on Saturdays (at one point, he belonged to five temples), and davens with tefillin. "At times I wondered if I should become a rabbi," Groopman says, "but I didn't think my faith was unalloyed. There were times of doubt or times when the ritual felt contrived. I certainly couldn't imagine dealing with a board of trustees at a shul," he says with a laugh.

The Jewish pride with which he was raised was insisted upon by his father. "He had made a decision, which was communicated to me, that he would not try to pass or assimilate," Groopman explains. "In terms of who we were and how we represented ourselves to the gentile world, there was no compromise. No name changing, no nose jobs; none of that."

Groopman says he has tried to relate that same religious dignity to his own three children, albeit without heavy-handedness. "I'm not the kosher police," he says. "Everyone has to be kosher in the house, and then they decide what they want to do when they're eighteen." Similarly with ritual: "I want synagogue to be a positive experience," he says. "I don't want it to be suffocating or rammed down their throats."

When it comes to teaching his kids about Jewish values, Groopman says, "It involves tremendous respect for others—remembering the idea of having been the persecuted minority. And because of the work I do with AIDS, my kids are very conscious of gay civil rights, very conscious of not being anti-Arab, anti-anything. There's even a rabbinic concept—*Kiddush hashem*—which means that Jews should act in such a way that they reflect positively on Jewish values and on the community."

Groopman's wife, Pamela Hartzband—an endocrinologist who is also Jewish—did not share his devout upbringing. "The woman I married grew up completely assimilated with almost no background in Judaism," Groopman says. "I'd always thought I was going to marry the *rebbetzin* [rabbi's wife]. I didn't. I fell in love with someone who I would say embodies all of what is marvelous and important in the tradition. She had grown up in London—her father was a chemical engineer who worked for Esso. They didn't keep kosher, hardly did the holidays. They thought I was the Lubavitch rebbe when they first met me," he says with a chuckle. I can't help but notice that he could easily pass for one.

I ask if he and Hartzband had to reconcile their Jewish ground rules before they were married. "Yeah, we did," he replies. "We had a big negotiation. And the deal was that she would agree to keep a strictly kosher house if I learned to ski." He smiles. "My answer to her was, 'Jews don't ski.' "

Groopman marvels even today at how two Jews could be so different. "Her family was everything we weren't," he says. "They were cosmopolitan, living in Europe, integrated into the gentile world—she hadn't grown up in a ghetto like I did. And they were avid skiers." Ultimately, however, they bridged the gap. "I learned to ski and we have a kosher home," Groopman says, looking pleased.

One of his sons is an "Arabist" at Columbia who developed his interest, in part, because of his father's friendship with Jordanian King Hussein's nephew, Prince Talal. Groopman treated Talal for cancer and they stayed in touch. "We're extremely close," Groopman says, gesturing to a photograph on his desk. "And that's his wife, who comes from a very prominent Lebanese family; my son stayed at the royal palace with them. They are direct descendants of Muhammad—the Hashemites. No kidding around. It's not like when you find fifty Hasidic rabbis who tell you they're the direct descendants of King David, but it's bullshit. These guys are for real."

In addition to family photos, Groopman has on his wall an enlarged rendering of his book jacket for *The Biology of Hope*, which he says asks "whether you should ever relinquish the right to hope, and if there is an authentic biology of hope." The book is being considered for a television series, which will mark Groopman's second foray into pop culture: the 2000 ABC drama *Gideon's Crossing* was based on his first two books, with the main character modeled after Groopman himself—the humanistic doctor.

The creators decided to cast Andre Braugher, a formidable actor who is black, for the role. "I wasn't against it per se," Groopman says now.

"They wanted Andre Braugher because he was such a great actor, and the character was supposed to transcend the fact that he was black. They wanted the audience, ultimately, not to care. Whether that was accomplished or not, who knows?" I ask him whether he sensed any hesitation to center a series around an explicity spiritual Jewish character. "You don't have any control of these things," he replies diplomatically. "I think it would have been interesting and maybe even sociologically challenging to try to have the spiritual overtones that my book, *Measure of Our Days*, has. So I think that part was missing."

The "spiritual overtones" of Groopman's life are revealed just by visiting his modest office. "It's not subtle," he says with a laugh, gesturing around him. The array of Judaica is mostly gifts, he explains, from appreciative patients. Groopman gives me the audio tour. "That was given to me by someone whose mother I helped with breast cancer," he says, gesturing to a candelabra. "That was from the wife of an Episcopalian priest whom I took care of," Groopman says, pointing to a stone etched with a psalm. *"Teach us to remember our days."*

Maimonides' prayer hangs on the wall: *"Let me look at a patient neither as a rich man or a poor man, as a friend or a foe, but let me see only the person within."* "To me, that captures what you aspire to as a physician," Groopman says enthusiastically. I notice a beautiful print with the well-known phrase *tikkun olam:* "to repair the world." Groopman has a chuckle about this one. "You'll never guess who gave me that," he says. "Cornell West!" he guffaws, referring to the famed Princeton professor of African-American studies. "I was his doctor when he got prostate cancer, before he left Harvard and he was in the middle of the blowup with Larry Summers. [Harvard president Summers offended West in 2002 when he questioned aspects of his scholarship.] Cornell calls me 'Brother Jerome.' This gift shows that he is a very acute observer of who I am—my identity and my roots."

There's a Talmudic line quoted on this same print, *"You are not obligated to complete the work, but neither are you free to abandon it,"* which Groopman says he relates to in his chosen trade. "It's that wonderful tension between feeling that it might be overwhelming when you look at the level of suffering, the complexity of biology and medicine, but that you continue to persevere." He writes often about this friction: the frustrations of illness versus the optimism of medicine, the realities of mortality versus the sustenance of faith. "The way I see religion informing my work is not that it's magical," Groopman explains. "It's that I'm part of creation—we all are—and we are given certain divinely inspired, wonderful gifts which give us the opportunity to prevail. Not necessarily even to survive sometimes—because we die, we're all mortal. But to endure."

Sarah Jessica Parker

© PETER LINDBERGH

SARAH JESSICA PARKER, whose father was Jewish, is eight months pregnant when I meet her, dressed in denim overalls and a black leotard, sitting in a Greenwich Village café near her brownstone. She says that she and her husband, actor Matthew Broderick—whose mother was Jewish—are still not quite sure how they're going to raise their impending baby. "We happen to live next to a temple and I think it's really nice, and I wonder, 'What should we do?' " says Parker. " 'Should this child of ours have more religious education than *we* had?' Sometimes I think there's something attractive about Unitarianism. It's a little bit more progressive and philosophical. If I could apply that kind of approach—what I understand it to be—to being a Jew, that might feel right. I would like our child to have choices and know more than I've ever known about his or her religion. But Matthew doesn't know what he wants for this child and it's important to me that he feels comfortable."

It also gives Parker pause to realize how little she knows about Judaism. "I said to Matthew, 'If we went to this temple next door, where would we begin? We're so behind.' In temple, it seems like you have to know what you're doing. And it intimidates people; it certainly intimidates me. And I keep saying, 'I'm not a religious person,' but I know that's not true; I know that I believe that there's somebody who watches over us and he or she takes care or not, or teaches us. I really do—strangely enough—kind of cling to that. And I think that Matthew is as deeply religious as I am, but he's cynical about it because he's seen that it can be so harmful and hurtful and destructive."

She says Broderick's ambivalence was evident when they were preparing the baby's room. "A dear friend of mine named Bettianne, who is Jewish, gave me a beautiful mezuzah; she got it at West Side Judaica. It has three little children on it and they're playing, sledding. I said, 'When we move into the new house, we'll put it up.' And I thought I'd told Matthew—I'm almost sure that I told him at one point—but when he heard me saying on the phone to Bettianne, 'When Matthew's home next week, we'll put the mezuzah up,' he said, 'What? We're not practicing Jews—we can't have a mezuzah in our home.' It seemed wrong to him. I said, 'It's not wrong. It's a really nice thought. It's just a gift to say, 'Safekeeping to you.'

"So Bettianne and I put it up ourselves on the door to the baby's bedroom. And I love it. I walk up the steps every day and I see it in our new house on the door to the baby's bedroom and I feel like it's yet one more person keeping an eye on the baby. It doesn't bother me; doesn't seem to bother Matthew." She said it feels like the mezuzah is in the right place. "It's not on the door to our home because that's too big—too much," she says. "Frankly, if someone had given me a tiny cross that meant something—" She cuts herself off. "There's this man that I see in the neighborhood all the time. He gave me this card for the saint of fertility and the saint of babies and this tiny little medal. And I was very touched by it and I've kept it next to me for my whole pregnancy because I thought, 'For him that means something and it's a nice thought.' It doesn't mean I'm converting to the Catholic Church. This is a nice man; he wishes me well, he wishes my child well. I wouldn't hang it, but it's nice to have."

The baby will have a Christmas tree. "Matthew and I get one every year, but it has no religious content. Growing up, it wasn't religious at all. My Mom and Dad loved the smell in the house—I mean my stepfather, who raised me. We love the tradition of it—we've had the same ornaments from the time before my oldest brother was born. It's about family and ritual—the same things that I respond to in being a Jew."

Parker, born in Cincinnati, says her biological father's parents were "from that part of Eastern Europe that would go back and forth between being Russian and Polish." According to family lore, the name "Parker" was created by a series of miscommunications. "My great-grandfather on my father's side came over to Ellis Island. His name was Bar-Kahn, which means 'son of Kohen,' and the immigration officer thought he said 'Parken.' He wrote his N's like R's, so 'Parken' became 'Parker' and he was so happy to be in America and to have a business that was fairly thriving, that he never corrected his customers and he became Parker. So there's also great pride attached to this idea that we're Kohens," she says with a smile, referring to the fact that Kohens—or Kohanim—were the ancient line of high priests. "You know, the great tribe of Israel."

Parker believes her mother has Jewish blood as well, but that lineage is hard to trace. "According to Matthew, Hitler would have been perfectly happy to call me a Jew because there was enough Jewish blood in me that I was not a desirable. And I have, frankly, always just considered myself a Jew. Maybe I feel Jewish because my mother is very skeptical of organized religion in general and being a Jew felt more cultural to me. I was always responding to things that were Jewish.

"I think also because New York was this great jewel to us and it was such a Jewish city that I was so thrilled to identify with anybody from there, to be part of it."

Parker's Jewishness, she says, is rooted in large part in nostalgia. "My father was raised on Ocean Avenue in Brooklyn—he was on the Brighton Beach line. It's a very Jewish community. And every year on our summer visits, the people we spent time with were Jews. Whenever we came to New York on Sundays we always went to Chinatown. To us that was a very Jewish thing.

"A lot of the literature that my mother read, including *The New Yorker*, had a lot of Jewish writers. I was always very aware of that. My mother always said that when she met my father, he reminded her of Philip Roth. They were both Jewish writers from blue-collar families. So from an early age, I had some idea about Jews being cultured intellectuals, Jews being on the correct side politically. I learned later on that Jews can be very right

wing and very different from what I understood a Jew to be, and that being Jewish wasn't just about food and culture and art."

Adding to the religious amalgam is Matthew's sister, who is an Episcopal priest, and Parker's older sister, who is an observant Jew. "My sister is
Modern Orthodox. She didn't shave her head—you don't have to. She's
one of my best friends. And I've learned more from her about the actual
practice and ritual of being a Jew than I've ever known before." Parker says
her other teacher has been her husband. "Matthew not *only* identifies as a
Jew. I mean, he *really* is. He knows more about the Bible and the Jewish
story. He really sees things through the eyes of a Jew and it's fascinating to
me. His perspective in life has very much to do with Hitler and the persecution of Jews. He identifies as a Jew, but it's much more political for him.
He's not curious about any other religions. It's not like he's thinking, 'Let's
explore Unitarianism, let's explore Buddhism, and let's also explore Judaism as a choice for our child.' He would only think about being a practicing Jew. We're always looking for a seder. This year we drove four and
a half hours to go to a Rosh Hashanah dinner. Matthew likes a lot of the
rituals—when he sees them, it's very moving to him. But I don't know that
he wants to be an active, religious Jew because I think he finds fault, as we
all do, with a lot of religion. For instance, the separation of men and
women in services, and some archaic ways of living your life.

"And frankly, for us—traveling gypsies that we are—nothing that requires that kind of commitment is appealing. Or sometimes it is and some
times it isn't. But you can't dabble in it. It's not like being into sushi or
something. It's a real thing; you can't belittle it. It's too meaningful to
people."

She says the crisis in Israel makes them both feel more Jewish. "It
makes you identify. I feel much more strongly about the situation there and
I feel foolish about it too because I don't know the history. But I do know
that I feel defensive when people say, 'How can Israel go in with tanks?'
What are they supposed to do? Children are being killed by people willing
to strap bombs to their bodies and walk into the public market. So Israel's
response to this is to protect its people. I am not an Ariel Sharon fan, but
what are the Israelis supposed to do? Just be decent? When you think of
Rabin and all these remarkable people who have died, it makes you really
much more of a Jew."

She says she has trouble hearing people question Israel's conduct. "To me it's like trying to have a logical argument with a pro-lifer. I can't have the conversation because there's no logic that applies. If you don't understand why Israel has to defend itself . . . The extremists want the Jews gone. So why should the Jews feel safe?"

I ask for her reaction to writer Nat Hentoff's comment, made a few months after 9/11, that he can imagine one day hearing over a loudspeaker, "All Jews gather in Times Square." "I live with someone who can imagine that, I think," Parker says. "So I'm inclined to be able to imagine it myself. You often become the person you're married to or you live with; you just do. And I'm pretty influenced by his thinking often anyway. It wasn't so long ago that the Holocaust happened. It really did happen very recently. And so many denied it and couldn't bear the thought of it or were'nt interested in the plight. So, yes; it's not beyond imagining."

I ask her if she notices which of her friends are Jewish. "If Matthew and I are with friends who are Jewish, you just feel something you can't describe—like trying to describe a color; you can't. It's just commonality—like, 'Oh yeah, we're with our people.' But I have a lot of non-Jewish friends. Many of them seem to think of being Jewish as slightly exotic."

I ask Parker if she cared about marrying a Jew. "No, but when I met Matthew, I was like, 'Well this is that guy!' " She exhibits a kind of *aha*! " 'This is the type of guy my mother always liked: the cultured, well-read Jew from Greenwich Village in New York City!' "

Parker says she and Matthew share similar reference points, despite the fact that they grew up so differently. "There's a lot about the aesthetics of our childhood that were extremely similar. And I honestly feel it's because when my mother was raising us in Cincinnati, she was thinking: 'How do cultured Jews in New York City raise their children?' " Parker says her mother emulated an ideal she had implanted in her mind. "The goal was a combination of how cultured Jews in New York City raise their children and how Rose Kennedy raised her children. She was sort of hoping to get the best of both."

I ask her if she's been asked to talk publicly about her Jewish half. "A couple of times newspapers have called—the *Forward*, for example—and I've said, 'I can't do this because I would do a disservice to your faith; I don't know enough about it. I'm a Jew because my father is, and that's what we feel we are. But I think sometimes people would like anybody who has a public face at all to be part of it. I wouldn't call myself a famous Jew, but my experience over the years has been that if someone wants me to talk at length about being Jewish in a Jewish paper or publication, I feel I couldn't be further from an authority and I don't want to say things that are uneducated. There are people who are more of note who know more about being a Jew than I do. So I've never done it."

Though ethnic publications may look to her as a role model, I wonder if, in the early days of her career, she was viewed as an ethnic type? Parker nods. "I was offered a movie and it was rescinded because they decided I was too Jewish." She won't say who rejected her. "I shouldn't because they probably wouldn't want—" She chuckles. "Because they're Jews! That's what I thought was so ironic. It's like, 'Oh, you're a Jew calling me *too Jewish*!' I think they said I was just 'too Jewish looking.' I think for a long time, people who had curly hair and features that weren't traditionally accepted as pretty were just considered ethnic and still are. I think there's a place for those types more now, but it's not as if we've come so far that it's the new standard. It's not gone the way of the hula hoop."

One could say that, thanks to Carrie Bradshaw—her character on *Sex and the City*—she created a new archetype. "I don't know that anything's changed," she disagrees. "I think I've had luck because I've found parts and obviously more recently, specifically *a* part. But Carrie Bradshaw is clearly not a Jew. So that character didn't disprove the bias that beauty is incompatible with ethnicity. I don't know if there's a ripple effect for me professionally or not. And I don't pay too much attention to it because, frankly, there was a period in my career years ago when it stopped mattering to me that a studio executive didn't think I was pretty. Because I couldn't let it. I hadn't started off with a career in which that mattered and I knew that that wasn't what my career was going to be."

Didn't she have a moment of wishing she was the classic American beauty? "Yes, I did have a moment. I remember pretty vividly—because I actually articulated it at the time—I said, 'This is really frustrating because I'm always playing the cerebral best friend of the pretty girl.' Now, what I didn't mind about that was those were generally the more interesting parts. But it's frustrating to not be considered attractive by men who make decisions. That's what's hurtful. It's not the quality, necessarily, of the role; it's the personal ego stab that is hurtful. And you just figure out whether you have the constitution to continue. That's why I think my parents were very against me working in television and film. I think they thought that in the theater, beauty has broader parameters. My parents saw that it was when I got involved in movies that my feelings were hurt."

But did she view those slights as related to her being Jewish? "I saw it as an ethnicity issue," Parker replies. "I thought if I had straight hair and a perfect nose, my whole career would be different. And I *still* feel like, when I walk on the set of a movie or a television show, and my hair is straight and all the guys say to me, 'Wow, you look so pretty,' I always joke—if I know them really well—'You're an anti-Semite!' Because I just feel it's a little stab at the Jews. I always feel that people think that straight hair is pretty and curly hair is unruly and Jewish. I think it's anti-ethnic."

I'm talking to Parker before she starts taping the last season of *Sex and the City*, and I'm curious about the show's explicitly Jewish character, Harry Goldenblatt—Charlotte's paramour. (At the time we spoke, Harry had told Charlotte he couldn't marry someone who wasn't Jewish and she was considering conversion.) "We live in a city that's full of Jews," says Parker, who is also the show's executive producer. "The fact that we haven't dealt with it more and also didn't do better fleshed-out Jewish characters bothered me," Parker says. "And I still worry that Harry Goldenblatt is too clichéd. That's the problem with being a man on our show. It takes time for dimension to come. We have this great actor, Evan Handler, and he's really sexy and smart and I'm excited about the potential of that. But I think we have to be careful that he doesn't become the false cliché of the loud, boorish Jewish lawyer who's aggressive; that he is dignified and interesting and smart and sexy and witty and flawed and all the things that make any guy interesting. I'm excited about it, but I hope we do it well."

In other words, if they do it poorly, it could be bad for the Jews. "If I watch a television show about somebody and there's a Jew on there—I don't mean fiction, I mean reality—and there's a guy on there named Goldfarb and he's a jackass, I'm like, 'You're bad for the Jews.' It's one more excuse for bigots to say, 'Look at the Jews.' And I'm very protective that way. I'm very ashamed of stereotyping and one person doing a great disservice to millions."

A couple pass our table wheeling their newborn in a carriage, and Parker comments on how cute the baby is. She chats easily with these strangers—they clearly recognize her despite her pulled-back hair and lack of makeup—and it's an unremarkable conversation, like any other between new parents and a mother-to-be from around the neighborhood. It occurs to me that Parker is not just on the cusp of childbirth but of all the child-rearing issues that follow; she realizes it will be up to her to shape this new Broderick's identity, when she's still not quite sure of her own. "If there was a temple I could go to," Parker says, "to get guidance—counsel of some kind, or just a place to sit and contemplate, whatever that means for me . . . If there was a place where you could come in and they say, 'This is what we're going to talk about today and let me put it in context for you and see whether it applies to you or not,' and hear great music and be with people who are like-minded, I think you'd have a much more growing population of people who practice the Jewish faith."

Leon Wieseltier

LEON WIESELTIER PHOTOGRAPHED IN 2005 BY JILL KREMENTZ

ONE OUT OF EVERY FIVE PEOPLE I talked to about this book said, "I assume you're talking to Leon Wieseltier." One prominent magazine editor referred to him as "The Grand Poobah of Judaism"; others called him simply "Super Jew."

The literary editor of *The New Republic* for the last twenty-one years, Wieseltier is, in his spare time, a rumpled encyclopedia of Torah commentary, Jewish philosophy, and Talmudic law. He is fluent not just in Hebrew, but in libraries of obscure Jewish texts. His book *Kaddish* was a chronicle of the year—1996—that he spent going to synagogue the required three times daily to say kaddish for his father. He excavated, it seems, every conceivable discussion from every imaginable rabbi who ever had an opinion, all in the effort to make sense of this one prayer for the dead. A fifty-three-year-old graduate of Columbia, Harvard, and Oxford, Wieseltier is also the author of *Nuclear War, Nuclear Peace,* and *Against Identity*, and has written more essays and sat on more panels than it would be possible to enumerate.

I meet him in his Washington office at *The New Republic*—a sterile space which he's managed to make a little scruffier thanks to haphazard stacks of books on the carpet, couch, and bookshelf and careening heaps of papers on his desk. He's wearing jeans and cowboy boots; his trademark Einstein-like thatches of white hair are appropriately unkempt. He turns off his Mahalia Jackson CD so that it's quiet enough for my tape recorder, and he seems genuinely startled that I actually finished *Kaddish*, which even he refers to cheerily as "my turgid tome."

Some warned me that Wieseltier would be disdainful of my ignorance in Judaic matters, but I didn't find that to be true: rather, he's disdainful of Jewish ignorance in general. Nothing personal. "I think the great historical failing of American Jewry is not its rate of intermarriage but its rate of illiteracy," he says. "I can go on for many long hours about this. The amount of Judaism and the Jewish tradition that is slipping through the fingers of American Jewry in times of peace and security and prosperity is greater than anything that has ever happened in the modern period anywhere. It is a *scandal.* Now what I'm not saying is that there should be more believing Jews or more belonging Jews; this is a free country. We believe in freedom; people can think and do what they want. The problem is that most American Jews make their decisions about their Jewish identity knowing nothing or next to nothing about the tradition that they are accepting or rejecting. And a lot of American Jews *accept* things out of ignorance, too. The magnitude of American Jewish ignorance is so staggering that they don't even *know* that they're ignorant."

I tell him he sounds judgmental. "I judge it very harshly," he agrees. "I loathe it. Because we have no right to allow our passivity to destroy this tradition that miraculously has made it across two thousand years of hardship right into our laps. I think we have no right to do that. Like it or not, we are stewards of something precious; we are custodians, trustees, guarantors. We inherit the language in which we think, we inherit most of the concepts that we use, we inherit all kinds of habits, and one of the things we inherited is this thing called the Jewish tradition."

He brings to mind two lines in his book, *Kaddish*, which stuck with me: *"Do not overthrow the customs that have made it all the way to you."* Also, *"Sooner or later you will cherish something so much that you will seek to preserve it."*

But many of the people I've spoken to say they're turned off by the amount of time observance requires, the rigors of ritual. "Come on," he interrupts me. "That is a miserable excuse. We're talking about people who can make a million dollars in a morning, learn a backhand in a month, learn a foreign language in a summer, and build a summer house in a winter. Time has nothing to do with it. Desire, or the lack of it, has everything to do with it. It's about what's important to people. We're talking about intelligent, energetic individuals who master many things when they wish to."

That said, he has capacious sympathy for someone who engages the tradition, but then decides to forgo it. "I don't mind when Jews tell me it's not important to them. I feel sad, but they have a right to decide it's not important to them. That is the risk you run in living freely, and we should be happy to run that risk. Who would not prefer the danger of ignorance to the danger of extermination? But I would much rather people say, 'I don't care to be Jewish anymore.' The bad faith of the noisily faithful makes me crazy."

He derides a kind of Jewish identity that might be described as Judaism Lite—an identity tied to ethnicity, not education. In other words, Jews who "feel" Jewish because of a tune they remember, a cheese blintz, or a visit to shul twice a year. "Owing to the ethnic definition of Jewish life, there has occurred a kind of internal relativism among all things Jewish," he says. "If we're just a tribe, if we're just an ethnic group, then all of our expressions are equally valuable, they all delightfully express what we are. 'I like Maimonides, you like knishes, but we're Jews together!' Right? The philosophy, the food, it's all different ways of being Jewish. But if you invoke the old Jewish standard, the traditional standard, all this falls apart."

And that standard is? "The standard is *competence*," he answers. "The standards by which Jews should be judged are not *American* standards; they are *Jewish* standards. That is to say, if one is making judgments about the quality of Jewish identity of individuals or groups, that the criterion has to be taken not from the society in which we live but from the tradition that we have inherited. And that's where I think Jews are going to be found to have been criminally negligent."

But why? How does he explain why so many people essentially dropped the rituals that used to define being Jewish? "Whereas American society does require the thing we call 'identity,' it doesn't require that the identity be religious and it doesn't require that the identity be thoughtful," Wieseltier answers. "More so than it's ever been before, the ethnic or tribal dimension of Jewishness has been brought to the fore in this country. Especially since the ethnicization of American life since the late 1960s. So it is very possible in this country, where you are expected to be a hyphenated individual, for the non-American side of the hyphen—in this case the Jewish side—to be entirely an ethnic or tribal or biological sensation of belonging. That's enough for Jewish identity, American style.

"American Jews, like Americans, have a very consumerist attitude toward their identity: They pick and choose the bits of this and that they like. They ornament themselves with these things, they want to bask in the light of these things . . . Most American Jews don't see identity as an enterprise of labor, a matter of toil. It's something automatic that confers upon you a certain status. As I say, a form of luck.

"So in America now it is possible to be a Jew with a Jewish identity that one can defend and that gives one pleasure—and for that identity to have painfully little Jewish substance. The Jewish substance of Jewish identity is not necessary, or it is minimally necessary."

I tell him that many of the people I'm talking to feel great pride in being Jewish, whether or not they're students of Judaism. "Generally in American Jewry, pride exists in inverse proportion to knowledge. So you will often find that the more learned or knowledgeable Jewish individuals are, the less strident and hoarse with self-admiration they tend to be. And the ones who know very little are looking for anti-Semites everywhere, because they need enmity to sustain their Jewishness. (It doesn't matter that sometimes they find it. We were never Jews because there were anti-Semites.) They think that the best way to express Jewishness is by fighting for it. And so in this way pride does the work of knowledge, sentimentality does the work of knowledge."

So when he says that Judaism has failed— "No—" he stops me. "Judaism hasn't failed. The Jews have failed Judaism." But those who taught Judaism failed somewhere along the way, too, it seems, if there are so many disaffected people. "Yeah, I think that's true," Wieseltier concedes. I venture that if all the bored temple-goers had had someone to turn them on to Jewish traditions and texts, they might— "But you know what?" Wieseltier breaks in. "You have to want to be turned on. That's like saying, 'There's no point in going into the record store, because almost all the records in there are terrible.' But you go into the record store because there's one record you really really dig. I mean, nobody ever didn't walk into a record store to buy a Charlie Mingus record because there was a Keith Jarrett record for sale, too. Again, it's all about what's important to you. It's about motivation and will; about one's expectations of oneself, about what makes the world tingle for you. It's about the tingle."

Wieseltier certainly hasn't lost the tingle, even though he did lose the Orthodoxy with which he was raised. (The son of Orthodox Eastern European parents, he attended Yeshiva of Flatbush.) One day, he walked away from all of it. "I was alienated from shul for lots of reasons," he says, "and I had philosophical problems with my picture of the world and I resolved that I would not go through my life without food, wine, or women."

He explains why those pleasures were off limits: "I was an Orthodox boy. I wasn't allowed to put my hands on girls or have a good bottle of red. I decided for reasons of personal hunger and philosophical perplexity and real alienation from the synagogue that I had to wander."

Was there literally one precise day when he stopped living by the rules? "There was a day I took my yarmulke off in my senior year of Columbia College," he answers. "And then my first violation of the shabbos was a phone call to Lionel Trilling. And my first cheeseburger was at a Patti Davis show at CBGB's. And my first cheese pizza was at V & T's. I remember that Art Garfunkel was sitting at the next table."

How guilty did he feel? "It depends when and where. There's also enormous pleasure associated with sin, as you may have heard."

But his internal religious clock was unshakable. "Even when I was allegedly gone, I always knew that Friday night was shabbos. I always knew that, when I was eating something I shouldn't eat, something I shouldn't eat was what I was eating. I was never indifferent to it; I was never dead to it."

He said his parents were not dismayed. "My parents knew how much I loved the tradition and they saw that I was devoted to it intellectually. They saw that the whole way. They were a little perplexed about how one could be so ardent a Jew and still live at such a distance from religious practice. They were perplexed. But it would have been harder for them if I had started my literary life with essays about, say, Mallarmé, and not with essays on Jewish subjects. So even if they were perplexed, they knew their son's Jewish heart, they had confidence in it, and they were right. I may have been a weird or troubling case, but I never left. I could never leave. It was a matter of honor, but also it was a matter of love."

Love?

"I have an erotic relationship with Judaism. I really do. Judaism is the instrument that opens up the world for me. The world doesn't open up Judaism for me. The history of the Jewish people is one of the greatest human stories, obviously. So if you go and study Jewish history, you can't do it just to study about the story of how this magnificent people finally climaxed in the birth of yourself. It's not about, 'How did I get to be me?' It's about what human experience is like and what are the extremes of human experience, internal and external. That's what Jewish history is about because of what happened to Jews.

"And similarly, philosophically, this tradition gives me the words and the instruments to break into the universal questions. And that's one of the things I tried to show in my turgid tome. You take this highly specific, highly particular thing, this concrete tradition, and you use it to break open the universal questions. That's what our tradition is for. It's not there to be smugly particular or to keep one in love with oneself. If the Jewish tradition is beautiful, it's not because it's *my* tradition. It's a great human tool. And everyone needs a tool."

One crucial implement, Wieseltier believes, is the Hebrew language. "On the question of Jewish literacy, of the need for—and the beauty of—Jewish languages, of Hebrew, I'm an evangelist. I speak to American Jews about Hebrew till I'm hoarse. The first words my little son heard were Hebrew and I sing Hebrew songs to him and he got his first Hebrew books with his first English books." Wieseltier's son is fifteen months old at the time of our meeting.

Why is the language itself so important? "Because I think to be a Jew is not to be an American or a Westerner or a New Yorker," he replies. "To be a Jew is to be a Jew. It is its own thing. Its own category, its own autonomous way of moving through the world. It's ancient and thick and vast and it's one specific thing that is not like anything else. And though it converges with other identities and other traditions and other ways of going through the world, it's not them. And one of the ways Jews should go through the world is in the Jewish language. You cannot really know what Judaism is if you drop the Hebrew; it just can't be done. And the joke is: We have Jews who couldn't care less about this but would be absolutely scandalized if you suggested that they go to a performance of *Die Walküre* in English. They'd think you're accusing them of loving kitsch. They'd be absolutely outraged. And if you suggest that the drawing that hangs over their sofa is a reproduction, they'd get really offended. But their Judaism, at least from the standpoint of literacy, is a reproduction. And that's okay with them. It would be comic if it weren't tragic."

It's implicit in our discussion that most of the accomplished Jews I'm talking to for this book wouldn't meet Wieseltier's standard of Jewish "competence." I suggest that maybe it's because the most successful are kind of hyper-assimilated, and for various reasons dispensed with rituals along the way. "The question is does their assimilation have any integrity?" he asks. "I don't mind assimilation—we're all assimilated. In fact, assimilation is a good thing. It's about, what are the grounds for their Jewishness? What have they decided to be and not to be? What are their reasons? And the scandal is, they often don't have reasons. It's very lazy. They just don't care. And this is not worthy of respect.

"I can respect heresy, I can respect alienation, I can respect Karamazovian rebellion, even Oedipal rebellion (up to a certain age, when the statute of limitations on childhood rage runs out); there's some grandeur to all of that. Say you hate it. Say you hate your parents so much, you can only eat pork. Or deny that there is a God. Or say the Jews are stealing the air from your lungs and if you don't get out, you're going to die. Just say it and then we can talk about it . . . I don't mind renegades or apostates. Again, I really have a lot of respect for the renegades and the apostates and the angry ones and the bitter ones. Jewish history is full of such people. And there are good reasons to be angry and alienated. Sometimes I think that the synagogue is Judaism's lead bulwark against spiritual life. There are many reasons to be angry. And Hebrew school is a halfhearted effort that led to a halfway house that alienated more people than would have . . . but we're not talking about that. My point is that most American Jews are not renegades; they are slackers."

So if someone says, *I go to High Holy Day services; I sit there, but the words mean nothing to me?* "I say: Then don't go," Wieseltier replies, "or learn the words. But what you just described is what I can't stand. If the words mean nothing to them, they shouldn't go. They don't go to Chinese opera either. But they're not prepared not to go, because that would involve accepting the responsibility for their tradition. Instead they want to inherit something passively, like all inheritance. So I say to them: Don't go, and deal with the paltriness of your Judaism. Or, if you're sincere in your complaints, take two weeks out of your busy and sophisticated year and *learn the words.* That's all. And then come back and tell me that it's still so boring.

"The truth is that anger is a form of connection. So anger's fine. The great freethinkers in modern Jewish history were people with whom believers always talked and debated. Because they *knew* what it was that they turned away from. You can spend hours arguing with someone who completely rejects what you completely accept because you both know what you're talking about and it's a primary discussion."

But if someone who values their Jewish identity yet doesn't practice its traditions says, *My Jewishness is just a part of me—it's who I am, it's in my blood,* why doesn't that count for something?

"Then I would say to them, 'That's fine; but you have just admitted that your Jewishness is a trivial fact about you. And you won't be insulted if I consider it a trivial fact about you.' "

Wieseltier's bottom line is clear: His disappointment is not that Jews are marrying out of the faith or assimilating beyond recognition, but that their Jewishness is flimsy. "Basically there are two questions," he says. "The survival of the Jews and the survival of Judaism. I don't worry too much about the former."

Why not? "Partly because history gives me a paradoxical hope, and partly because I have a mystical confidence in the eternity of our people. When I regard all the things that have happened to Jews and to Judaism in all of Jewish history, I come away bitter, of course, and angry, of course, but also astounded by our perdurability. And we've been in much worse shape than we are now. Many, many times. I don't like Jewish hysteria. In fact, I think hysteria is sometimes used as a way to avoid having the toil of Jewishness. Some American Jews think if you want to be a good Jew, all you have to do is worry. Worry will do the work of your Jewishness. There's this game that Jews play: Who worries most? And whoever worries most wins. Whoever is the most hysterical is the most faithful. It's stupid."

But even if he's not himself worried about Jewish survival, does he understand the obsession with Jewish continuity? "Of course. There should be an obsession about continuity. But there's something even about the word 'continuity' that's so cold and formalistic. It's sort of a kind of real estate term or something. Continuity of what? The fashion for klezmer: That's continuity, too. But as far as I'm concerned, that's also discontinuity. Because the Jewish tradition is essentially a verbal tradition, and no amount of clarinet playing—or Carlebach singing, or John Zorn screeching—is going to disguise that fact.

So the question remains: continuity of what, exactly? What matters more and what matters less? In American Jewry, what matters more tends to be the aspects of the tradition that are less intellectually taxing and more emotionally immediate. I understand why our leaders and rabbis worry about the rate of intermarriage. But let's say that more Jews start marrying more Jews. Then what? There's still the question of the happy couples' relationships to the tradition. Is it enough that Epstein married Rosenblatt? I guess that's something. But then what do Epstein and Rosenblatt do next as Jews? I don't like tribalism. I don't like tribal definitions of identity. Jews should not think the way Serbs do. The sick joke about tribes is that all tribes think that they are chosen people. Too much of our talk about continuity and too much of our anxiety is tribal anxiety."

Wieseltier also bemoans a phenomenon he calls "Jewish self-love."

Which means?

"The smugness that Jews feel about themselves as Jews. They're in love with themselves."

I propose that maybe this self-congratulation has something to do with Jewish survival—the fact that Jews had to build themselves up over the centuries because they were in danger of being wiped out.

"Yes, but it has to be earned. The love has to be earned. We're taught that the highest form of love is unconditional love, but that's wrong. The highest form of love is conditional love, because if you're still being loved, that means you're earning it. It has a foundation in what you really are. I don't want to be loved no matter what I'm like. Such love is insulting, except from parents. Which is to say that unconditional love is a form of infantilization. No one should ever want to be loved the way their parents loved them. Except by their parents. That's a working rule of adulthood. So do Jews want to love themselves? Fine, but it has to be a conditional love."

I wonder if Wieseltier thinks anti-Semitism has, in part, been born of that perceived smugness and what he labels self-love?

"No. I don't think that one seeks the cause of anti-Semitism in anything that Jews are like or not like. I think that's a basic mistake. I think if you want to understand anti-Semitism, you study the non-Jews, not the Jews. If you want to understand racism, you study whites, not blacks. The idea that you study Jews or blacks is itself an expression of prejudice."

But he must have encountered Jews—most of us have—who felt ashamed of other Jews.

"I know. I understand it psychologically, though of course I don't take kindly to it (except in certain cases: We have our villains, too). It has to do with immigrant communities, it has to do with the memory of immigrant parents. There was a writer in New York in the 1950s called Harvey Swados. He has a story—you should find it; it's so painful—about a young Jewish man whose father is a peddler and has a pushcart on the Lower East Side. I forget the story exactly, but the young man finally convinces this really swell chick from a well-to-do Jewish family to go out with him; and they have dinner and it's all fine, and they go for a walk, and suddenly, to his increasing horror, the young man sees that at the end of the street where they're walking is his father with his pushcart. And he doesn't know what he's going to do. And when they get to the pushcart, he walks right by his father and doesn't acknowledge him. It's excruciating to read. But I understand it psychologically; status anxiety is not an exclusively Jewish phenomenon. The status anxiety of the children of immigrants we know a lot about. The Muslim communities in America are about to start experiencing this, and good luck to them."

This reminds me that he was married to a Muslim—a Pakistani woman—for eight years; not an obvious match for someone whose Judaism has been so central. For the last three years, he has been married to a Catholic woman, Jennifer. "My wife's a convert," he explains. "Orthodox. The advanced degree. Often I'm envious of converts because they made a decision; the rest of us were just born Jewish. A lucky accident, a lucky honor. But when you make a decision, you must have reasons, and when you think about your reasons, they deepen. Kierkegaard somewhere said that it is harder for a Christian to become a Christian than for a non-Christian to become a Christian. The same may be said of Jews."

So, despite what he describes as his "erotic relationship with Judaism," he never married a Jew?

"No. Jennifer converted. So I guess I never did." Isn't that surprising? "Well, my mother once said, 'Don't you feel that you have to marry a Jewish woman?' and without being at all ironic and without missing a beat, I looked at her and said, 'If I hadn't been given the finest Jewish education in the world, I might have had to marry a Jewish woman.' I don't need anyone to be Jewish *with*, and I have no interest in making love to myself, if you see what I mean. I don't need two of everything. And so I tell all my Jewish friends looking for love and marriage, 'If you can't find a Jew, make a Jew.' I mean, it's a big, wide world. Conversion is a very beautiful thing. And I take personal freedom and democratic life very seriously. (Anyway, I never hold myself up as a model of how to live.) It happens that you fall in love with someone you're not 'supposed' to marry. That's called living in an open society. I understand why the Jewish community and the Jewish tradition want me not to marry such a person, and when I married such a person, I never told my parents that I was right. I always said to them that I recognized that by the standard of our tradition, of our law, I was wrong. But that is not the only standard by which a rational and democratic person lives. So what was by their lights a betrayal was by my lights a collision of principles. It's a very complicated thing."

But he didn't fret about it?

"No. I didn't fret about it because if I was the only Jew on the planet, Judaism would still survive. I mean, it would survive as long as I survived. And any child I would have made would have been taught to know Jewish words and ideas and customs well. I don't have any doubt about my competence as a Jew. I have a princely confidence as a Jew. This is not vanity—I know how much I don't know and I know who knows a lot more than I do and I know where they are and I ask them questions all the time. But I took the trouble of acquiring the knowledge I would require to live thickly as a Jew in the entirety of my tradition. And I do so not least because I wanted to acquire this confidence, this authority."

And his and Jennifer's plans for this new Wieseltier?

"He will go to a Jewish day school. No question about it. Many years ago a wise and lively man, a liberal judge in Boston named Charles Wyzanski Jr., remarked to me over a lot of brandy that the only people who have freedom in matters religious are people who were indoctrinated in one as a child. And I think he's right. So I want my son to be completely fluent in Hebrew, in Judaism. And when he grows up he can decide for himself what he believes and how he wishes to live. If he leaves, it won't be ignorantly. If he stays, it won't be dilettantishly."

Talking about Wieseltier's parenting, I wonder about his father; it struck me, as I finished *Kaddish,* that I had little grasp of who his father was. "That's right," he says with a nod. "I wasn't writing a memoir. And it's none of my reader's business who my father was." But wasn't it part of the process of saying kaddish—to reflect on his father and their relationship? "It was to a certain extent, but that's not something that would be of interest to other people as far as I'm concerned. That strikes me as a private matter. And again, one of the reasons I wanted my readers to know almost nothing about my father is that I did not want my religious life to be reduced to my filial life. That's why I did no promotion for the book. No book tour, no radio, no author's photograph, no blurbs; nothing, *nada*, *niente*. My publishers thought I was mad. But I said to them that I did not want to travel the land being asked psychological or soap-operatic questions about a father and a son. I was writing about religion and philosophy and life and death, not about Mark Wieseltier and Leon Wieseltier. There had to be enough about me as a son to make it clear that all these texts of mourning were being lived and not just studied. But not so much that the study of mourning in Judaism could be reduced to this son's experience of it. It was tricky."

If he doesn't want to tell me about his father, can he at least tell me whether the year spent saying kaddish for him was a kind of reckoning? "Of course it was. And the reckoning I made with him turned out to be unexpectedly free and candid precisely because I was doing my duty. I squandered no energy on guilt or delinquence. I simply made myself into an instrument of my obligations and proceeded to think my thoughts. My thoughts about my tradition I recorded; my thoughts about my father I did not."

Does he concede that those few times in the book where he describes his father as difficult do beg the question of what this man was to him? "Sure, but discretion is a large part of dignity. It is perfectly clear in my book that the author loved his father and was wounded by the death of his father. Also that he was a Polish Jew who came to the States after the war, the sort now known as a Holocaust survivor, and a troublesome man. That seemed enough."

I ask him to flesh out the story he tells in the book about the time a friend of the family offered to say kaddish for his father in his place. "I just went to that man's funeral," Wieseltier says with a dose of irony. Why did this man make that offer to be his surrogate? "Because he didn't trust me," Wieseltier answers. "Because I was heterodox in many ways and the family knew it. And you know, the kaddish, like a lot of contemporary

Orthodoxy, has been absorbed into a folk-religious view of things, and so basically he was worried about the fate of my father's soul and so the kaddish, three times a day, was absolutely essential to get my father a good verdict."

In the book, Wieseltier is less sanguine about the incident: *"I was furious,"* he writes. *"I do not deny that I live undevoutly, or that the fulfillment of this obligation will be arduous for me. But it is my obligation. Only I can fulfill it."*

This responsibility clearly brought him back to the fold, so to speak. *"I was a pariah until I became a mourner,"* he writes. *"Then I was faced with a duty that I refused to shirk, and I was brought near."*

I remind him of another passage: *"All my life I went to shul with my father, that is, I went to shul as a son. It was because I found it almost impossible to stop going to shul as a son that I stopped going to shul. I came to conflate religion with childhood. But childhood is over."* It's the notion we discussed earlier, of leaving the childhood "trauma" of Jewish indoctrination behind and reclaiming it. "I wanted to be a Jew on my own," Wieseltier emphasizes. "I didn't want to be just an heir. I knew that I was an heir and in my ways I lived all my life as an heir; but I wanted to be an autonomous individual as a Jew also. And then I could consent again to being an heir. If you're just an heir, then you're still a child, merely a son, forever a passive receptacle. I wanted to be an active receptacle. And so I had to break out of the tyranny of the family over my spiritual and intellectual life. And out of the tyranny of the people and its politics, too. On some level I keep my Jewishness private from other Jews as well; I don't want them to ruin it either."

I personally relate to this idea of one's religion being tied up in—and muddied by—family expectations or obligations. I read Wieseltier his line, *"Religion is not the work of guilty or sentimental children."* He nods. "Look, in the matter of religion Freud was philosophically wrong and empirically right. He was philosophically wrong that religion is simply an expression of reverence for the father. It is not—which is one of the reasons I've never liked the concept of God the Father, the way I don't like God the King. One has to be very careful about the metaphors that one imports into one's beliefs about the world. But he was empirically right in that for most people religion is simply an enlargement of their attitude towards their parents. And that's a terrible thing. It means in the matter of religion most people are permanently children. And so religious life to them becomes a process of endless re-infantilization. Over and over again. It's insulting to the soul.

"Religion is about the fate of every individual soul. Religion is not even primarily a collective thing. The practices, the rituals, the gathering—that's for the people, that's for the family. But family life is not the same thing as spiritual life. (And often it's the polar opposite.)"

I tell him that, for many of the people I've interviewed—not to mention many people close to me—religion *is* primarily about family. "That's because people cannot disassociate their religious life from their parents because they think that being religious is a way of being good little boys and girls. And of compensating for the distance that they've traveled from their origins, of making up for all the other ways in their life where they refuse to be good little boys and girls. It's the peace offering that they bring to their living or dead ancestors. And they are encouraged in this reduced sense of religion by many Jewish institutions, which give the impression that all that matters to Judaism is the children. But Judaism is not for children. I mean, there are children who have to be raised as Jews, but this is not essentially about the children. This is about the spiritual existence of mature souls and moral agents."

Wieseltier gets a phone call from his wife: She wants to know if he's ready for her to swing by and pick him up at the office. Before he goes, I want to know what Wieseltier would advise someone if they came to him asking what it means today to be Jewish. "The one-word answer is 'Judaism,' " he says. "That's the only answer there is or ever will be. Everything else is a corollary of that. I mean, the Jews are a people, the Jews are a nation, the Jews are a civilization—but they're all of that because they are first and foremost a religion. That's the source of the whole blessed thing. Except for our religion, we would not be a people. When Jews come to me with perplexities about the meaning of Jewishness, I say to them: Judaism. Just go to it; check it out, study this, study that, try this, try that, humble yourself for a while before it, insist upon the importance of having a worldview, develop reasons for what you like and what you don't like, *get into the fight.* Get into the fight. That's the one-word answer: Judaism."

Nora Ephron

NORA EPHRON PHOTOGRAPHED BY BRIAN HAMILL

NORA EPHRON CAN'T DEFINE Jewish humor and doesn't seem interested in trying. "I don't know what that means," she says over the din at an overpriced café on Madison Avenue. "I just know that there is a tradition of humor that I think of—for example, in what Woody Allen used to do in his stand-up comedy routine. He would get up and talk about all the women who rejected him, and by the time he was five minutes into it, every woman in the place wanted to go home with him. So I'm certainly very conscious that I think of stand-up comedy as being fundamentally Jewish. That kind of personal approach—'If I can make you laugh, you'll like me'—that seems to me to be some sort of distant cousin to whatever one might think was a Jewish tradition or humor. But I don't think of myself as a Jewish humorist or a Jewish writer in any real way, even though in some way I think of myself as a Jew. Or as *Jewish*, but not a *Jew*; or as a *Jew*, but not *Jewish*."

Ephron feels like she's been categorized as more Jewish than she actually is, because other people make an issue out of it, even if she doesn't. Raised without any Jewish education by atheist parents who had "contempt" for religion—("My mother believed that organized religion had in one way or another been responsible for almost everything bad that had ever happened")—she doesn't exactly exult in her Jewish identity. "At this point, it doesn't make the top five of what I would say about myself," she says. "And it probably never did."

Nevertheless, she believes it's an undeniable part of her makeup—a realization she made at Wellesley College, when she found herself gravitating toward other Jewish women. "It was clear to me that we were very interesting. There was nothing bland about us in a college filled with many bland young women—many of whom didn't know what they thought, what they believed politically. Whereas the Jewish girls were very opinionated and vital and fun and funny. It was sort of interesting to me to discover that I was drawn to this group. I definitely had a sense that there was some kind of . . . *thing* about Jewishness that was not what I had grown up with—which had been a delicatessen Jewish, a well-read-parents Jewish. It became clear to me that some of what *I* was was Jewish, in some way or other, even though it had nothing whatsoever to do with religion, which continued not to interest me at all."

She was fascinated, however, by Wellesley's required Bible-reading course. " 'Bible' was fantastic. But I got the only D that I ever got in college when I wrote a paper saying that Jesus had never really meant to start anything new, he was just objecting to some of the things about Judaism. Which I still believe is true, by they way, but my bible teacher did not like my theory."

In pearls and a black sweater, her brown hair neatly framing her face, Ephron speaks with her unmistakable drone: a combination of dry humor and imminent irritation. I ask her, for instance, if she still has a copy of the college paper about Jesus. "No, of course not," she says dismissively.

"One of the questions you asked in your e-mail," she moves on, referring to my interview request, "was whether it had ever been an advantage to be Jewish. It was definitely an advantage to be Jewish at Wellesley because there were so many Jewish guys at Harvard and Harvard Law School. And a lot of them were under strict orders to date Jewish girls. The Jewish girls at Wellesley and Radcliffe had, I think, a much more active social life than anyone." Did she seek out a Jewish husband? "I don't think I necessarily wanted to find a Jewish guy, but I wanted to find a *funny* guy."

It's unclear how funny her first two husbands were, but they did happen to share her background. "I did marry two Jewish guys. The first was

Reconstructionist." The second, well-known journalist Carl Bernstein, is the father of her two sons. Her current marriage to journalist Nick Pileggi (not Jewish) is seventeen years old.

Her boys grew up going to Passover seder at the home of Bernstein's parents. "Neither of my boys asked to be bar mitzvahed, which was a gigantic relief to me," says Ephron. "First of all, because of my feelings about religion, and second of all because they're so expensive, and third of all, because nothing is more awful than a divorced bar mitzvah. But they didn't ask for it, despite the fact that they were in the height of the bar mitzvah madness; they both went to Dalton [a top private school in Manhattan] and attended bar mitzvahs that cost more than I made until I was about fifty-six years old."

She doesn't care who her sons end up with, or how they choose to raise their children, if they have them. "I believe that it makes it hard on the marriage if someone is religious and the other one isn't. But that would be *their* problem, not mine. My husband is not Jewish and it's definitely my happiest marriage and sometimes I think that that's one of the reasons. Given that almost everyone I know was raised in some religion or other and they don't observe it in any way, it seems to me fairly idiotic to get worried about what one's grandchildren are subjected to."

Her parents—both Hollywood writers—told her as a child that they had no interest in religion, but that she was welcome to it. "They said to me that they were not sending me to Sunday school or anything because they didn't believe, but that, if I ever wanted to be any religion, it was fine with them. So when I was about twelve years old, I went to camp in the summer, and I was a voracious reader and I read *Charles and Mary Lamb's Bible Tales*. And I came home from camp and said to my parents, 'You know you always said I could be any religion I wanted?' And they said, 'Yes?' And I said, 'Well, I've decided I want to be a religion.' And they said, 'What religion is that?' And I said, 'Presbyterian.' And they said, 'Why?' And I said, 'Because I believe in Our Lord Jesus Christ.' And they both— I'm not kidding—laughed so hard, they fell on the floor. And that was the absolute end of my brush with Christianity. I cared way too much about their opinion to survive an episode like that."

She recalls that her parents' Jewish friends were casually connected to their religion, "some of which was manifested by conversations about whether there were any Jews playing in the Rose Bowl," she says deadpan, "and if there were, shouldn't we be backing that team as opposed to others?"

Her Beverly Hills neighborhood has changed demographically from her youth. "When we moved there, I was five and there were still Christians in the Beverly Hills school district; but by the time I graduated from college, you had to drive to the San Fernando Valley to see a house with Christmas decorations." Unless of course you drove by the Ephrons' home. "We celebrated Christmas and it was *mild* compared to the way I celebrate it now," she says. "I *love* Christmas. And you know, I always went to school on the Jewish holidays, because my mother said, 'What are you going to do if you stay home?' "

But it was Wellesley, in 1958, where she had an epiphany: being Jewish marked her in some inevitable way. "That was the most interesting moment for me in terms of realizing this was something I'd better think about," she says. "After I was admitted, they sent me a little housing form where I was supposed to put down my religious preference. It was the first time I was asked if I had a religious preference. I had, for example, not wanted to go to Mt. Holyoke because it had compulsory chapel. But anyway, I got this thing from Wellesley and I didn't know what to put: I didn't think that 'atheist' was a religious preference. So I thought that leaving it blank was sort of the right response. And I got a letter back saying I wouldn't be given a room assignment till I told them my religious preference. So I wrote them a letter saying that I was an atheist but I had been born a Jew. And then I went off to Wellesley and it was absolutely clear to a *blind* person that Wellesley's housing department worked in the following way: Catholic girls roomed with Catholic girls, Jewish girls were put with Jewish girls, and Protestant girls were put with Protestant girls.

"When I was working on the school newspaper, we exposed this policy. And I went to interview the 'dean of housing,' as she was called, and she justified it by saying [Ephron dons a perfect schoolmarm voice] 'Well we wouldn't want a Christian Scientist to room with a doctor's daughter, would we now?' And I said, 'Well, why not?' So the policy was ultimately changed. But at Wellesley I suddenly realized that whether I thought of myself as a Jew or not, *other* people thought of me as a Jew, and I had to come to terms with what that meant.

"And then my best friend my freshman year was from someplace like Cincinnati or someplace like that and she had never been friends with a

Jew. She told me there was such a thing as 'Jewish legs,' but that I didn't have them." What are Jewish legs? "Well, I can draw them for you," Ephron says, though she doesn't. "I know what she meant," Ephron says.

As soon as Ephron graduated, she went directly to New York City, instead of home to Beverly Hills. "You could substitute the word 'Jewish' for New York," she states. "From the time we moved to California till the time I moved back to New York at twenty-one, I was truly in some horrible Diaspora. I couldn't believe we had moved to California when I was five; one of my earliest memories is thinking, 'What am I doing here?' And couldn't wait to get back to the place where I felt like myself."

Fans think of Ephron as a die-hard New York enthusiast; her films— *When Harry Met Sally, You've Got Mail,* and *Sleepless in Seattle*, with its Empire State Building finale—bear this out. But though many Jewish publications and even Amazon.com reviews have described Ephron as a Jewish humorist in the tradition of Woody Allen, she reiterates that she doesn't see herself as a Jewish writer. "It's like being interviewed as a 'woman writer,' " she says. "Obviously I'm a woman writer, obviously I'm Jewish. But it just seems like a narrow way of looking at what I do. When someone says, 'Oh, you're a woman writer' or 'You're a woman director,' then you kind of say, 'Really? Is that what you think I am? Don't I make *movies*?' " But she's not so bothered that she calls people on it. "I'm not that interested in making—as a Jew would say—a megillah out of it.' "

Though Ephron doesn't write explicitly Jewish movies, I'm curious about whether she thinks an overtly Jewish story is marketable today. "I don't think there's any question but that if you write something that is Jewish, you're going to have trouble getting it made," she says. "Because they're not going to go see it in Athens, Georgia. There's lots of stuff they aren't going to go see in Athens, Georgia, and that's one of the things they're not going to go see. By the way, they didn't go see *When Harry Met Sally* either: I just remembered hearing what our grosses were in Athens, Georgia, that first weekend and it was the only place not doing any business. The point is that there are big-city movies, there are movies that play in L.A. and New York. If you're doing a movie *about being Jewish*, it's not going to be a big-city movie."

She seems struck by the paradox that many Hollywood pioneers were Jews and yet explicitly Jewish movies don't usually get made. "Jews basically started the movie business, which is responsible for all the American dreams—their immigrant dreams—the dream of the happy family and the perfect farm. But movies are a mass medium, and these days, when it costs sixty or seventy million dollars, you want it to be a movie that everybody is interested in."

Ephron has neglected her beverage. "They don't have good coffee here," she states. I'd brought chocolates. "Just one," she allows. Ephron's not one of those celebrities who makes her slim figure seem effortless—"I diet constantly," she says.

The topic of Israel brings on the same bluntness. "When I visited for the first time, I did not think, 'These people are me.' " She was there during the 1973 Yom Kippur War. "I was actually shocked by the number of people who were violently anti-Arab in the way I associated with how Southerners once talked about blacks. It was racist at its core and I had grown up believing that Jews were on the front lines against racism, so to hear that so explicitly . . ." She drifts off.

On a lighter note, she compares Jewish humor in Israel and New York. "When I went to Israel, one of the things that seemed very clear to me was that this thing that you call Jewish humor, whatever it is, partly comes from being in a minority. In my stereotype of Jews, one thing I love is how funny they are—how funny *at their own expense* they are. You don't see a whole lot of that in Israel. So I began to wonder whether being in a majority was bad for their sense of humor."

Ephron drew on her ethnicity for the punch line in a May 2003 *New York Times* op-ed piece about President Kennedy's newly uncovered tryst with an intern: "Now that I have read the articles about Mimi Fahnestock, it has become horribly clear to me that I am probably the only young woman who ever worked in the Kennedy White House whom the president did not make a pass at," Ephron wrote. "Perhaps it was my permanent wave, which was a truly unfortunate mistake. Perhaps it was my wardrobe, which mostly consisted of multicolored Dynel dresses that looked like distilled Velveeta cheese. Perhaps it's because I'm Jewish—don't laugh, think about it, think about that long, long list of women JFK slept with. Were any Jewish? I don't think so."

Aaron Brown

"THIS WILL COME OUT WRONG, but I'll say it anyway," says anchor Aaron Brown, wearing pancake TV makeup, sitting in his office at CNN. "It never occurred to me that I wouldn't be successful. I never thought about that. Ever. I thought it might take me a little longer than it should, but I knew in the end that I'd sit in this chair, I'd have this job, I'd do this work. I think there was a peculiar sense that we—we Jews—would be successful. Now, did I think that 'we' were smarter? No; I didn't actually think that. I just think that God, for whatever reason, I guess, was going to make us successful and funny—and short. And that being short was okay if you were funny and successful."

It's clear that his conviction that things would turn out auspiciously—however haughty it may sound on first hearing—buoyed him along when people doubted him or told him he couldn't cut it. "I've just hung in there," says Brown, fifty-seven. "I hung in there and hung in there and never stopped believing and never gave up, even when people at ABC News were saying, 'This will never happen.' I said, 'Okay, thank you for your opinion.' It never occurred to me that it wouldn't. And I don't know why I think of that as Jewish. As I say it, it sounds incredibly stupid and I hate sounding incredibly stupid, but for some reason I just believed, from a very young age, that I come from a history of very successful people. But, I mean, my father was a junk dealer; we're not talking about Einstein here, he was a scrap metal dealer. It's just that somewhere in me, that lives."

I ask if Brown has thought much about the fact that he's the first Jewish network anchor. He shrugs. "Of course, sure. But honestly, I mean, there's a lot of other things that make me unlikely in this job, too. I'm the first one that's not classically handsome, I'm the first one that doesn't have a really deep voice, I'm the first one—well, I'm not the first one that doesn't have a college education." (Peter Jennings does not.)

"I don't think being Jewish was especially *helpful* along the way. But it wouldn't be fair or correct to say that the reason I didn't get this job earlier, at age forty-four or thirty-four, is because I'm Jewish. But you know, being Jewish certainly didn't help." I'm trying to get at whether it actually got in the way. "Well, I don't know: You'd have to ask all those people who didn't hire me. That's the point. It's an unknowable in some respects. They look at you as a sort of package and they say, 'Okay, what's the package here?' And I don't know that they went, 'Well the package is five-foot-nine, Jewish, midwestern, nasal voice, kind of smart, a little quirky, funny sense of humor'—I don't know that they ever broke it down that way. I just assume it was one of those things that was out there and wasn't determinative, but was part of the equation. My sense is that being Jewish wasn't helpful, but in the end, my sense is also that for 99.9 percent of viewers, it's completely irrelevant. Whether those people like me or not depended on a lot of other things before we get to that one."

For those who *are* paying attention to his religion, does he take some pride in being a role model for other Jews? "I'm just a little anchor on a cable network; let's not go nuts here. Maybe someday it will mean a little more when CBS, NBC, or ABC has a Jewish anchor; I don't know. To the extent that I want to be seen as a role model, I want it to be for the way I've lived my life, and the way I've done my work. I've worked really hard, and I worked against incredible odds and I believed in me and what I do and the way I do it. And the lesson there is 'Don't give up.' There are a million obstacles. And maybe one of them is you're fat and maybe one of them is you're Jewish and it doesn't matter: Deal with it. And the way you deal with it is you outlast them. That's certainly, professionally, the way I've dealt with it."

His obstinacy was bred in a small town outside of Minneapolis, where he grew up as one of just a handful of non-Christians. "There weren't Jews there," Brown says matter-of-factly. "I mean this is the fifties and early sixties, so there was certainly an institutional—I don't know if I'd call it anti-Semitism—but I would call it *aggressive Christianity*.

"In the second grade, I had an issue with the teacher who insisted I sing 'Silent Night, Holy Night,' which I would not do. I said, 'This is not my song.' It really had to do with my maternal grandparents: I just didn't want to do anything that would dishonor them. It became a big deal, but it shouldn't have been. And then there were blatant anti-Semitic moments, and you just deal with them." Do any particular episodes stand out? "You know, they all stand out and they all mean nothing in a way," Brown replies.

So he never wished he were "one of them"? "No. I wished that I didn't have confrontations at eight or nine years old with teachers singing 'Silent Night.' But it never occurred to me to sing it to get along. But I wasn't exactly out there with *payess* either. We were 1950s American Jews. My parents neither tried to assimilate nor avoided assimilation. They were Diaspora Jews and they lived their lives. They had more things to worry about than what people thought of them."

At the same time that he plays down the impact of childhood ridicule, he concedes that the experience informs him to this day. "I understand better than most people what it means to be the outsider. One of the things that I wondered about as a kid is how different our history would be if, in all of the generations—all the hundreds of years—when we didn't have a voice, people had heard us. And in the application of my work, I keep that in mind: that there are truly voiceless people out there. And sometimes those voiceless people are Palestinians. And it seems to me that it is in the great and important tradition of my upbringing, religion, and history that we not make the mistake of denying voice to people who have no voice.

"It's in that same tradition, by the way, that American Jews were hugely important in the American civil rights movement of the sixties. It's one of the great tragedies of modern history that that relationship has been lost—it's a great sorrow, I think, for which both sides share some blame. But it came out of that Jewish tradition—an exquisite understanding of what it meant to be denied."

The young Jewish activists who went down to Mississippi and Alabama had a keen impact on Brown. "I was twelve, thirteen years old, and the fact that there were guys named Goodman and Schwerner who were involved in that struggle made me pay some considerable attention to it. I was proud that people down there had my background. I thought they were doing important and courageous work."

The capture of Adolf Eichmann, mastermind of Hitler's "Final Solution," was the other news event which proved indelible. "I remember vividly the day," he says. "And how that became the defining question of whether you support or oppose capital punishment." For Brown, Eichmann's capture brought home the Holocaust more than any history lesson had. "Here was a real player in all of it—someone who was alive who was *responsible*."

When it comes to observance, Brown says unequivocally, "I don't do organized religion." Ironically, his wife, Charlotte, does. She converted from being Presbyterian and is now more strictly Jewish than her husband ever was. Why did she decide to convert? "Honestly, you should ask her," he says. "I just remember that she came home one day and said this was something she wanted to do. I don't believe we ever talked about it. I didn't care at all. I *did* care how we raised our kid; *that* I did care about. But not for theological reasons. I found that if Gabby, our daughter, was going to experience any of the prejudices of being Jewish, she also ought to be aware of a proud and joyful history. But I just think Charlotte was looking for something she hadn't found as a Presbyterian. And she found that, and she's happy with that. It works for me."

I try to get at why his wife made the considerable commitment to adopt his religion and all its rites—including an adult bat mitzvah—when he is unmoved by its rituals. "That was a major undertaking for her," I submit. "Yes," says Brown. "She worked at the conversion, and Friday night dinner is a big deal for her—that it's done a certain way. And it makes her feel good and that's terrific." It's not awkward that his wife does so much more than he does? "If she said to me, 'You must go to temple,' I would say, 'We have an issue.' But she doesn't. She says, 'This is what I want to do.' It's important to her. I mean, she's not walking three steps behind me in a wig, either," he adds. "It works fine. For one thing, we've loved each other a long time, through different incarnations, I suppose. I mean, I loved her when she was Presbyterian and put up a Christmas tree. She loved me when she was a Presbyterian and put up a Christmas tree."

But Brown makes it clear that his wife's passion for observance hasn't rubbed off on him. "I look at Judaism in two parts," Brown explains. "There's a theological component, which I don't spend a lot of time with. And then I think there is a cultural, historical part which I clearly embrace, which is an important part of my life, my child's life, my family's life, my upbringing; all of that. I would argue one can be an atheist and a Jew; they're not mutually exclusive. I don't actually see myself that way, but one could be that. So I see it as an act in two parts and I choose the second, not the first."

His daughter seems somewhat caught in between. Gabby, a teenager, was bat mitzvahed, but there were days where she questioned why she had to go to temple if her dad didn't. "We told her, 'You don't have to go; you made a choice to go,' " Brown recounts. " 'And having made the choice, there is a family rule: Once you commit, then you commit. Browns don't quit. But after that point, you can do what you want.' And she's chosen— again for reasons that are hers—to continue on and be confirmed."

I ask him what he thinks constitutes being Jewish if Jews drop the rituals. "What matters to me is that I live my life in a way consistent with an extraordinary history of my people. And part of that history—not an unimportant part—is theological. But only a fool would say that it's the *only* part of our history, and I think I could make a persuasive argument that it is not the most important part. I think what ought to matter is not whether we light a candle, because the biggest hypocrite on the planet can light a candle. I'm more interested in how they live their lives the other six days and how they treat people and what they care about.

"That's my issue with organized religion: I don't think it tells us anything, honestly. It doesn't tell me anything about the people who are there [in temple or church], other than they are there. *They showed up.* But it doesn't tell me the size of their heart, it doesn't tell me their spirit or generosity, how they see their place in the world, it doesn't tell me anything that I actually think is important. Now maybe that's my excuse. But it is the way I view the world. I give you no points for showing up. I give you points for how you live your life, how you treat people."

Does Brown take the anchor seat on Yom Kippur? "I don't, actually. I worked this year on Rosh Hashanah, but I won't next year because I don't want to answer the mail. There are people who got very upset by that. It's not worth it. I'll take the day off. There was a reason why I felt I had to work on Rosh Hashanah. But Yom Kippur, no, I wouldn't do it, because it would almost be an aggressive action—trying to make a statement—and that's not how I feel. I'm just trying to live my life by a set of rules that make sense to me and one of them is don't be a hypocrite if you can avoid it."

I tell him it's hard to believe that the hate mail he occasionally receives doesn't rattle him at all. "No, it doesn't," Brown says. "Because I've been doing this a while, I know that the people to whom your religion matters—good or bad—know your religion. For example, long ago, I had just gotten out of the service and was working at a little radio station in a little city in western Pennsylvania trying to earn enough money to get a car. And one of the first calls I got was from *the* Jewish family in town. *How did they know?*" he says with a smile.

"My whole deal in life is I'm pretty calm about it all, whatever it is. I try not to get too terribly worked up over people who I think of as idiots. I've never met a *smart* anti-Semite."

How does he approach Israel as a journalist? "I'm pretty careful about how I report the story," he says. "One of the things I know better than almost anyone on the planet, I think, is that no matter what I do on that story, both sides will find fault with it. We did a program one night, and my normal routine is to come down and take a quick glance at the e-mails that came in that day, and there were back-to-back e-mails—I mean, they literally came in within the same minute: The first one was from someone very upset at our pro-Israeli slant on the story and the next note was from a guy in Colorado who was incredibly nasty, referring to the exact same story on the exact same show, describing me as the modern-day equivalent of the concentration camp kapo who would turn on his own people for money. So it doesn't matter because fundamentally—and this is harsh, but I believe it—the partisans on both sides really don't believe the other side has a story. So I've just come to accept the fact that I'm not going to make everybody happy; I might as well make *me* happy. And I'll report and edit the story the way I think we ought to do it. And some days we do it pretty well and some days we don't, but we never don't do it well because we're Jewish."

Does he find himself cringing when he reports on wrongdoing by Jews? "It's funny: When President Kennedy died, the first thing I remember my mother saying was 'Oh, my God, I hope the assassin wasn't Jewish.'

And I said, 'Whoa. Wow.' No, I think in an odd way it's kind of nice that we have evolved to a point in our history when we can have, comfortably, Jewish bad guys, Jewish villains. When I was growing up, the big mobster in Minnesota was a Jewish guy: Isadore 'Kid Cann' Blumenfeld. I'm pretty sure he was Jewish. So it never occurred to me that we were somehow perfect; nor did I think we had to be. I just thought, if you were going to be a gangster, then you had to be really good at it; I think that's what God's always expected of us. So I was a little disappointed that he got caught."

I'm curious about those who want Brown to be more publicly Jewish than he is—who ask him, for instance, to speak to their Jewish organizations. He usually declines because he's supposed to maintain a reporter's distance, but recently made an exception. "I went back to Minnesota a year ago; I'd promised I would do it a long time before and in retrospect, I probably shouldn't have done it. But I went to talk to a [Jewish] Federation dinner. It was a big deal. And I didn't talk about the Middle East until we got to the questions, even though I knew that's what they wanted me to talk to them about. I couldn't do that, it would have been highly inappropriate—it was a fund-raiser, for God's sakes. But one of the things I said to them then and have said before, is that this is a really important distinction I want people to understand: *I'm not the Jewish anchor.* I'm an anchor who happens to be Jewish.

"If they want me to be the Jewish anchor, then they're disappointed because I don't make judgments with that in mind. But I think they get a lot out of my being Jewish, nonetheless, because I bring to my life, my work, to the decisions I make, a sense of who we are; what history has required of us. I think those sensitivities—even when they make people uncomfortable at a given moment—are really important. They're a huge part of who I am. I embrace them, I rejoice in them. I can't convey to people in terms more strongly than that, that it's a source of considerable joy and pride to me. I think I come from a culture of exquisite values and I think I bring those values to what I do. And that ought to be enough."

Fran Drescher

FRAN DRESCHER PHOTOGRAPHED BY FIROOZ ZAHEDI

SYLVIA AND MORTY DRESCHER happen to be staying with their daughter, Fran, when I come to interview her in Los Angeles. Sylvia wanders downstairs during our meeting, looking every bit the coiffed Brooklyn Jewish mother from central casting. Their conversation seems plucked right out of an old *Nanny* script:

FRAN: This is my mother!

SYLVIA: Guess what I came down for? Daddy wants candy.

FRAN: [To me] Mom and Dad came into town because I got a Woman of Achievement award last week.

MOM: Let me tell you something: I can't stand these people that stay skinny and eat all day!

FRAN: What's with Dad and all the candy?

MOM: He likes candy.

FRAN: Maybe he'd rather have the pineapple sorbet.

MOM: He wants chocolate.

FRAN: Okay, okay. Are you comfortable? Are you resting?

MOM: I may never leave.

FRAN:	I wish you wouldn't. Have you gone into the bathroom upstairs?
MOM:	To make a sissy? No.
FRAN:	You have to go in there; it's paradise in there.

Fran Drescher laughs in person just the way she does on TV. It's that unmistakable, nasal, unrestrained heh-heh-heh-heh. "I'm Jew up the wazoo," she says. "I have Jewish moments every day." We're sitting in her white-on-white living room, which overlooks the Pacific Ocean. Her home is in a nondescript building on the Pacific Coast Highway (I drove past it twice, searching for the address), but inside it feels like a spa, with white wood floors, white furniture, white cushions, and white flowers. There's a shock of blue in the large fish tank built into one kitchen wall, and the smell of the sea, which is frankly less fragrant than fishy.

I can't help but feel that this environment was fashioned deliberately as an antidote to the upheaval Drescher's experienced in the last few years. First she divorced her husband of twenty years—Peter Jacobson, the cocreator of their hit show, *The Nanny*; then she spent three years fighting off uterine cancer. "I felt in touch with my spirituality in a deeper way than I had ever experienced before," she says, her bare legs ending in trendy Ugg boots, propped on the coffee table. "I saw God everywhere doing small favors for me—allowing me to see the beauty that's life and the love that surrounded me." She devotes much of her time these days to increasing medical awareness for cancer victims. "I feel like I have a purpose now. I became famous, and then I had the cancer, and now I lived to talk about it, and now I feel like this was destiny."

It's a much more New Age outlook than I would have expected from a no-nonsense loudmouth from Flushing, but it's clear that Drescher, forty-eight, is still the "pretty Jewish girl with a voice that could call the cows home," as she once described herself.

Drescher grew up in a heavily Jewish Queens neighborhood that, she says, basically shut down on Yom Kippur "out of respect"; even her gentile neighbors dressed up for the occasion. She idolized Barbra Streisand—"God's gift to all little Jewish girls in need of a leader," she once wrote—and grew up intensely close to her sister, Nadine, and parents, Morty and Sylvia, who were always looking for a discount and didn't waste a scrap of food.

In her 1995 autobiography, *Enter Whining*, she refers to her mother as "The Kishkila," which she defines as "someone who really enjoys their food." Sylvia always encouraged her to eat more. "I was fed when I was sad, I was fed when I was good," she writes. "We ate to celebrate, we ate to mourn and in between, we'd describe what we were going to eat later."

Back in 1993, when Drescher and Jacobson created *The Nanny*, the network and advertisers worried that it would be too Jewish. "CBS said, 'We can get Procter & Gamble to buy the show if we make your character Italian,' " she recalls. "And I said, 'I don't want to be Italian'—not that I couldn't play Italian as an actress—but television is too fast a medium to play something that's not really close to who you are. And the whole essence of my humor comes from my background. So I said, 'This is it: what you see is what you get.' And as it turns out, everybody sponsored us anyway. You can't analyze it too much. It was the Midwest and the Sunbelt that embraced *The Nanny* before New York and L.A."

I was surprised to hear that Procter & Gamble, in the mid-nineties, would worry about a Jewish character in a sitcom. "Actually I'm the first person in I don't know how long who was a *Jew playing a Jew*," Drescher informs me. "It really didn't happen before. You know Valerie Harper is not Jewish. She played Rhoda Morgenstern, but she is not Jewish. So, for advertisers, it just must have seemed like a double whammy." She laughs. Indeed, *The Nanny* went on to run six seasons and trounced the competition. "*Who would have believed that a nice Jewish girl from Queens would beat* Star Trek: Voyager, Melrose Place, Coach *and* The Fresh Prince of Bel-Air?" wrote *USA Today* in 1995.

I ask Drescher if she knew her sense of humor would connect with the rest of America or if she felt she had to Americanize the nanny. "I Americanized my character by pitting her against a Brit," she explains, referring to her "boss" on the show—a British widower with three blond kids. "That's how I did it. And it was a very contrived choice. I am a blue-collar, American, working-class girl—red, white, and blue all the way. He was *Upstairs, Downstairs*. Who could relate to *him*?" So she'd be the character audiences would connect to? "Right. Even though I'm a funny New Yorker, it made me American. Because he *wasn't*. And he didn't have the heart that I had. Now it didn't hurt to have her in short skirts—don't get me wrong. But she was a good person. She brought love into a home that was loveless. And everybody could relate to that."

As the show took off, some Jewish commentators held up Drescher's character, Fran Fine, as breaking new ground for Jewish images on television. "*Who would have thought,*" wrote the *Forward* in 1997, "*you could fashion a Hollywood starlet—who made* People*'s '50 Most Beautiful' list—out of real-life, bridge-and-tunnel Yiddishkeit? Many actresses in Ms. Drescher's place would have tried to lose their accents, suppress their big hair and play to Middle America by conforming. Not Ms. Drescher, who is the only reigning Jewish actress on television with the chutzpah to celebrate her ethnic 'otherness.'* "

But there were others who denounced both the character and her creator. "*Executive producer and star Fran Drescher is a whiny, manipulative clothes-horse, hunting rich (non-Jewish) men by projecting a non-threatening ditziness,*" wrote Nora Lee Mandel in the Jewish feminist magazine *Lilith* the same year. "*A hit for CBS,* The Nanny *has the whole world laughing at her.*"

One episode in particular raised Jewish brows: The Nanny goes into a tailspin to create a picture-perfect Christmas for her boss's family. "I'm the one who teaches these people how to have a real Christmas," Drescher told *The Jerusalem Report* in 1994. "I'm the one that shows them that family and togetherness are what's important. This was a show about a Jew who is having a Christmas every Jew dreams of. To deny the fact that growing up, it always seemed like Christmas was a more fun holiday—if anybody isn't honest about that, they're bullshitting themselves."

Drescher wasn't bruised by the critics. "There were people that wrote editorials and things putting me down because they didn't feel that I represented the Jews well. For many different reasons: the fact that I was in love with my boss who was gentile. The fact that I didn't speak the King's English or look refined or act refined. It never rattled me. First of all, every loudmouth is going to try to take a position just to get a platform. So that's the first thing, and I'm hip to that. The bottom line is, anyone that would put me down for doing what I was doing is insane. I had such a likable character. I was loved by people in Egypt and Jordan and Saudi Arabia. On a trip to Israel, I climbed Masada and when I got to the top, there was a girl who worked there who said, 'Oh we love you much!' And the Israelis honored me at the Knesset."

In 1997, the Jerusalem Fund of Aish Ha Torah bestowed Drescher, John Kluge, Sanford Weill, and others with the Theodor Herzl Award, which is, according to the Web site, "designed to highlight the achievements of individuals remarkable for their strength of will and commitment to realizing their dreams." "It was fantastic," Drescher gushes. "My parents came."

When she spoke, she says, she commended the Jews for believing "so wholeheartedly" that they are the Chosen People: " 'Whether it's true or not,' I said, 'it is the smartest *brainwash* known to civilized man. Because it doesn't matter how many people kick sand in our face, how many countries we're thrown out of, how many places don't want us, how many people don't like us; we still feel *great* about ourselves.' " That laugh again. "You can't really break our spirit in that way. I thought, 'If only other minorities could subscribe to the same kind of ego-booster!' Most people who get knocked feel downtrodden; but when someone knocks us, we say, 'Ach, what do *they* know?' "

When it comes to Jewish ritual, however, she's less gung-ho. "I feel like I'm not comfortable with a lot of organized structure. I like to subscribe to the positive things that make me spiritually a good human being, a caring, understanding, altruistic person. I defend and protect my roots, my family, and my friends. And in so being, I feel like I am a good Jew."

The doorbell rings and Drescher answers it. "Hi, dahling!" she greets a young woman whom she introduces as her manicurist/pedicurist. "She's been doing me for years," Drescher tells me. We move into the white bedroom, where Drescher settles herself in a rocking chair, and we continue talking while Drescher gets filed and buffed.

"I would say that a great majority of my close friends are Jewish, but some of my closest friends are not Jewish," she says. "I just came out of a four-year relationship with a gentile—actually he was half-Arab. We had a wonderful, loving, and very deep and meaningful friendship, and we were very respectful of each other's heritage. When you stop looking at the differences, you start to see how similar we all are. For many years, I've been very, very close friends to Danny and Donna Aykroyd. She's Christian, he's Catholic, I'm the legal guardian of all three of their children, if God forbid, something happens to them. And we are a family; we love each other."

Her first marriage, to Jacobson—her high school boyfriend—lasted twenty years (they served matzo ball soup at their wedding in 1978). "I think, growing up, we were conditioned to thinking that it's easier to marry one of your own kind; then you don't have to decide what you're going to do with the kids." (She hasn't had children, but says she still wants to.) "You have this ethnicity that's bonding. People who didn't grow up being haunted by tales of the Holocaust don't really know what that's like. Even my last boyfriend, he could not get over how paranoid Jews can be."

The afternoon light has dimmed the whiteness in the bedroom, and with Drescher's feet now soaking in a small tub, I feel like I'm intruding on an intimate toilette. Before I leave, I ask her very simply, what it means to her to be Jewish. "It means to be a member of a tribe—a very warm-blooded tribe, full of life and tenacity and ideals. And it makes me proud. It's not always easy. But what is?"

Edgar Bronfman Sr.

EDGAR BRONFMAN SR. PHOTOGRAPHED BY RICHARD LOBELL

MOST BILLIONAIRE EXECUTIVES don't have a Torah in their corporate office. A Torah under glass, to be precise. But Edgar Bronfman Sr., former president of Seagram's Co. Ltd. (the liquor giant), has one, displayed importantly in its velvet sheath near his massive desk and his tufted black leather sofa. "I don't want to put my religion in anyone's face," he says. "But this way they know who I am."

He also has an ornate shofar—the ram's horn traditionally blown on Rosh Hashanah made of silver and wood, poised in the middle of his black marble conference table. And there's a library no yeshiva would sniff at, including a multivolume set of the Talmud and tomes such as *Jews and Medicine*, *Torah Linguistics*, and *Jewish Law*.

All this Judaica is a fairly recent fascination for the seventy-six-year-old Bronfman. As a kid, he rejected Judaism because he rejected his father, Samuel Bronfman, who was a demanding and detached figure in his life. The senior Bronfman, who built Seagram's from a Canadian distillery into an American empire that made every subsequent Bronfman extremely wealthy, was renowned for being an adroit entrepreneur but an overbearing, volatile man. "I was really rebellious as far as my father was concerned," Bronfman says, "and I just turned my back on the whole Jewish thing. It really started when I found out that he didn't know what he was saying when he was praying. He was just reading Hebrew because he had been taught to read it. I didn't consider that praying: If you don't know what you're saying when you're praying, then I'm outta here. And I left and I didn't go back to it till I was in my fifties."

Samuel didn't care particularly that his son abandoned Judaism after he became a bar mitzvah. "I don't think he gave much of a damn," Bronfman says, his hands folded over his green and yellow Hermès tie. "My father went to synagogue because it was expected of him—because he was a leader in the community. But religious he was not."

Bronfman absorbed his father's indifference. "I was supposed to go to Sunday school and junior congregation on Saturdays. But since my father didn't go to synagogue—he went to the office—I didn't see any reason to go. Sunday school was just dreadful. I'm sure there are seventeen zillion people who will tell you how awful supplemental education is; it's something we really have to take a hard look at because it's awful." It's become one of his personal crusades—to make Jewish learning intriguing to young people. "I'm chairman of the governing board of Hillel," he says. "I love to go to different campuses and see the kids—I get big audiences because they want to meet me—and I just love talking to them about being Jewish and how much fun it is. We do study sessions and they're all blown away—the fact that I can actually discuss the texts with them."

He can spar on Talmud because he's been a dedicated student of it ever since the mid-1980s. That was when, as president of the World Jewish Congress (established to safeguard fair treatment of Jews internationally), he had a clarifying experience during one of his trips to the Soviet Union. He was in Russia to lobby for Jewish freedom—the ability to pray openly and to emigrate. One evening he watched hordes of Jews defy a ban on worship in order to observe one of their holidays in the streets. "On Simchas Torah, they were all milling around outside the synagogue; only three or four blocks from Lubyanka," Bronfman recalls, referring to the location of KGB headquarters. "It's not as if the KGB didn't know what they were doing. But they took a chance. The Jews really wanted to be with other Jews on that day. There they were, thousands of them, talking to each other, saying, 'Hag Sameach' [Happy Holiday]. This, after seventy years of prohibition against religion in the Soviet Union." He raises his untamed eyebrows. "I thought to myself, 'There must be something to this that I've missed.' And that's when I started to look into it."

He relied on his colleague at the World Jewish Congress, Rabbi Israel Singer, to be his informal guide, and started reading the Torah two hours or more every week. "I suddenly discovered this was something *I* was interested in. Not discovering good works—I'd done that, I'm still doing it. But this is just how to be a better Jew. Singer said I'd make a great Talmudist, because I love to argue about these things."

He says that dialogue and debate are the foundation of Judaism and therefore he's made it the organizing principle of the High Holy Days services held in his home every year. "We have a nice service and Arthur Hertzberg [former president of the American Jewish Congress] is there. The rules are that no sermons are allowed; the whole congregation gets involved in the discussion—it's not just that someone is giving a lecture. Synagogue bores me to tears. I don't get any spirituality out of going. Some people like the music, some people like the davening; I can't understand why they like it, but they do. I like the intellectual part. I like to discuss this business of what was Abraham doing taking his son, Isaac, and almost killing him? And what was Isaac doing letting him? There was more to it than obeying God. And there's a passage before, with Sarah throwing out Hagar, the thirteen-year-old, and all sorts of theories about the kid's homosexuality, masturbating, whatever. All nonsense. The fact of the matter is that Sarah was jealous of Hagar because Abraham was having a good time with her. So she threw her out. Until she had a son of her own. I find it fascinating that the Bible lets everything hang out—all our faults. There it is, for everybody to see."

As he eased himself out of Seagram's business two decades ago, he started giving more and more time to this new pursuit. "I fell in love with the Talmud when I first discovered that it had to do with fairness and decency," Bronfman says. "I think God is that little conscience in your head; you know when you're doing something wrong. And I don't think that's only Jewish—I just think it's wonderful that Jews are the ones who brought it. This is not exclusive; we're just the first."

He doesn't buy the fact that the Torah was handed down from God. "Please," he scoffs. "Don't try to give me that stuff. It's all written by men. But I think the beauty of it is that they were trying to teach a people how to behave ethically and decently and morally. And that's how I like to live and that's why I stick with it. I don't need the miracles, so to speak. My own interpretation of God is that God is the creator, created the universe. Because otherwise, why does the universe behave so properly? But a personal God? Don't be silly. Why would kids get cancer? Babies born with AIDS—why would that happen if there was a benevolent God who looks after people?"

So how does he comfort people who are going through some tragedy and ask where God is? "Don't ask me where God is. What about the Holocaust? Where was God then? That's not the kind of God we're talking about." He says Jews are understandably misled by the prayer book, which does extol a protective, all-powerful deity. "The problem is that in synagogue, we talk about this *Avinu Malkeinu* business ["Our Father, Our King"] all the time. I don't do that. I mean, I can sing it, but while I'm singing it, I'm saying, "It's not *my* father, it's not *my* king. I don't talk about God when I'm trying to console somebody. I say, 'Look, life isn't fair. All sorts of terrible things can happen.' "

He has his own way of explaining God to his grandchildren—he now has twenty-two—all of various religious persuasions. "My sixth grandchild—she was four or five years old. We were down in Virginia and it was a gorgeous sunset. And I said, 'Look at the painting God has made for us.' And she said, 'Who's God?' And I said, 'God represents everything that is good on earth. We try to be more like God so we can be good.' " But he also teaches them that God doesn't stop evil. "Man has free choice. But we do know the difference between wrong and right—that's the little God in our head."

He suggests that that "little God" was missing for him during his college years, but he's vague about why. "I was really in bad shape, but that had nothing to do with religion. That had to do with my own personal rebellion. I'd overdone it to the extent that I needed a little help. After I fell off my motorcycle, then I got help. I don't know how the hell I survived that night, but I did."

In his memoir, *The Making of a Jew* (1996), Bronfman says that his father made his school years difficult by sending him, without much choice, to Williams College, where there was a five-percent limit on Jews, and before that, to a preparatory school in Ontario called Trinity College, where there were no other Jews. "I was the first Jew to ever go there," he says. In his book, he writes, *"To this day, I do not know what my parents were try-*

ing to accomplish with this bizarre treatment . . . Perhaps he reasoned that our generation would be rich enough and important enough that we would successfully break down those barriers. But did he have to make it that hard for us to be Jewish?"

I mention my conversation with Leon Wieseltier—specifically his point that one's religion often gets confused with feelings about one's parents. "That's true," Bronfman says. So how did he reconcile that for himself? "It wasn't reconciliation. My father was dead—long dead—when I was in the Soviet Union and discovered Judaism. Obviously there was always the spark in me someplace . . . I began to feel pride in it; that was the key."

Ironically, he tells a story about how he persuaded his father to start putting up Christmas decorations outside the Seagram Building on Park Avenue every season. "I said to my father, 'We really have to do something about Christmas.' My father said, 'But Edgar, we're Jews.' I said, 'I know, but we do forty percent of our business at Christmastime; we should at least acknowledge it.' So I said, 'Can I try something?' He said, 'Okay.' So I got Philip Johnson to design the trees that are in the pools every year. My father said, "That's beautiful! We should get some Christmas cards made!' I said, 'Father! We're *Jews*! Don't get carried away.' " He laughs.

As for his own fatherhood, he wishes he could do one aspect over again. "The only regret I have was that I didn't have a Jewish home for my children. Israel Singer said it very well when he said, 'It's a very Protestant country; if you're a Protestant and you don't practice your religion, you're still Protestant. But if you're a Jew and you're totally secular, then you're nothing.' "

He says he couldn't be disappointed when four of his five children married non-Jews. "I couldn't blame them; I didn't give them any Judaism growing up. How could I suddenly say, 'You can't marry her, she's not a Jew.' They'd say, 'What do you mean, Dad?' No, I'd have to be consistent."

Bronfman has been married three times—first to a Jew, then to a non-Jew who converted, then to Jan Aronson, a Jew and an artist. They opted for an Orthodox ceremony. "I just thought it would be more kosher," he explains. "I think probably because it would be recognized in Israel." Though his wife does not share his zeal for study, they light candles Friday nights and have decided to keep kosher. "One day, I was sitting in the dining room with the then-head of the National Urban League, who is Jewish. And we were eating crab cakes. And suddenly the thought occurred to me, 'What does this guy think of me as the head of the World Jewish Congress and chairman of Hillel eating *treyf*?' So I said, 'No more.' "

I probe for what he thinks has driven him to be so committed to Judaism so late in life? "I don't know. Sometimes, when I've had a couple of drinks on the airplane with Richard Joel [former president of Hillel], I'll say to him, 'I feel I have a calling.' " Bronfman uses the same language to explain his extensive philanthropy and his successful campaign to make the Swiss banks pay retribution to Holocaust survivors. "This is something I have to do. I've done very well in business; no problems there. I'm old enough that I don't have to think about business. And I like to think about the Jewish world and how we can make it better."

These days, he worries more about Jewish ignorance than anti-Semitism. "We live in a racist world," he says, "and I keep telling Abe Foxman [National Director of the Anti-Defamation League, which tracks hate crimes all over the world], 'Relax; it doesn't matter how many pieces of graffiti you count in bathrooms. It's unimportant. The important thing is that being Jewish doesn't keep you from getting a job in this country, that you don't have to go to work on Saturdays. The rest is good for fundraising. What is important is that we're not bringing up our child Jewishly because we have forgotten how. We have to remember that when our forefathers came over here, they didn't come here to be better Jews; they came here to be better Americans.' " He says the focus on education took precedence over maintaining Jewish life. "We lost a few generations of schooling. Nobody cared." He also says we lost Jewish pride. "You can't be proud of something you know nothing about."

Even so, he thinks young people shouldn't be observant for the wrong reasons. "You can't expect Jews in America today, or any place in the Diaspora for that matter, to be Jewish because of the grandmother who's going to turn over in her grave or because of the Holocaust—which is a *lousy* reason to be Jewish—or because of Israel. Why is it good for *you* to be a Jew?

"I have something I say to all the Hillel kids when I go on the road, that I call 'The Mirror Test.' Every day when you look in the mirror—because you have to when you brush your teeth or put powder on or whatever it is you do—look at the person and ask, 'Do I like that person?' And if not, then why not? What have you done that makes you unhappy with yourself? And if you've insulted or hurt somebody, make it well. If you can do that, that's the essence of Judaism."

He also says the essence is community: gravitating toward other Jews. "You go to any room, even in New York, because it's probably the most cosmopolitan city in the world—especially for Jews—and at a party, you'll see the Jews on one side and non-Jews on the other. I think it's an old habit of self-protection; it's also that they have more to talk about with other Jews than non-Jews. It's the herding instinct; you want to be with your own people. As bad as they are sometimes, you know them."

And does he worry about bad Jews giving Jews a bad name? "It used to bother me; I always thought it would create anti-Semitism. But then I learned that anti-Semitism isn't created by Jews; it's created by anti-Semites. We're people just like everyone else; we've got our crooks and our prostitutes. We may be the people of the book, but we're still in training to be the 'light onto nations.' We don't deserve that honor yet."

Leonard Nimoy

" 'JEW BASTARD' was something I heard a lot," says actor Leonard Nimoy, who grew up in an Orthodox family in Boston. We're sitting in his serene, beige and cream living room overlooking the Museum of Natural History, decorated with some of the art photographs he's taken—a hobby that has morphed into an obsession over the years.

Nimoy, wearing black loafers without socks, looks elegant at the age of seventy-four, still utterly recognizable as Mr. Spock. "When I was a little kid, I became enamored with magic tricks," he continues. "Simple little things—card tricks or coin tricks. And there was a shop in downtown Boston which was within walking distance of where we lived where they carried that kind of stuff, and whenever I had a little spare money, I'd go in there and shop around. One day when I came home, having bought something or other, I opened the bag and discovered that, along with my merchandise, the store clerk had slipped in some literature. And the litera-ture was the most crude, primitive kind of mimeographed anti-Semitic, scurrilous stuff, with the terrible caricatures of the hoary Jew—sinister, looking for world conquest—really nasty stuff.

"I was maybe ten. It really shook me. I didn't quite know what to do about it, except I didn't even tell my parents. I just destroyed it, threw it in the garbage. But that was the kind of thing you could run into in Boston. We lived in view of a very large Catholic church—still standing—which, after Sunday school, was a dangerous place for Jews to be around because young Italian kids and Irish kids came out having just been told that we had killed their Christ."

Had his parents prepared him for the bigotry? "My parents were very fearful people," he says. "And their fear was itself an education. Jews were always to keep a low profile so as not to become targets: 'Don't boast about success or brag about it, stay amongst your own people, stay out of the wrong neighborhoods.' They came from a village in Russia that had experienced pogroms. So they were really quite ghettoized."

Because his grandmother spoke only Yiddish, he became fluent. "I still use it whenever I can, and I get the mailings from the National Yiddish Book Center. Aaron Lansky runs it in Massachusetts. Are you familiar?" I'm not. "He started this thing some years ago of rescuing Jewish books. He's done a remarkable job. And I've been somewhat supportive, just sent him a check. They send out a monthly brochure and there are stories in Yiddish, and English translations, and I try to sit down and spend some time reading the stuff in Yiddish and see how far I can get."

He says his family's emphasis on education was not about trying to push their son to do great things but simply to support himself. "Here we were, my grandfather a leather-cutter, my father a barber, and there were six of us living with one bathroom, and they were very, very frugal. My mother taught me, 'You walk into a room and turn on a light, that costs a penny. So if you have to turn it on, turn it off as soon as you're done with it.' It's still a habit of mine—walking out of a room and turning off the lights. But that was their sense of achievement: security."

Nimoy got security and then some. *Star Trek* made him a multimillion-aire. Though only on the air for three seasons—1966 to 1969—it became a cultural phenomenon that spawned ten films (Nimoy acted in the first six and directed the third and fourth), four TV sequels (including a cartoon version), and generations of rabid fans—"Trekkies"—who remain loyal to this day. Nimoy's fame (he says Spock's plastic ear tips have garnered as much as three thousand dollars) created its own burdens for his two children, now adults who have their own families. Not surprisingly, they lack the shtetl perspective with which he was raised. "They have, frankly, a distorted view of how things work in the world, because they have been given so much subsidy from my income, that it's unreal. Their lives are unreal, and they know it. My daughter and her husband, now in their mid-forties, are finally trying to exist in a way where they have some sense of self-sufficiency. My son and his wife are still wrestling with it—responsibility versus entitlement. It's a struggle, and I sympathize with it."

If Nimoy's children have been somewhat crippled by his success, ironically, his parents never seemed to acknowledge it. Not until they saw him play Tevye in a Boston production of *Fiddler on the Roof* in 1971. "When I did *Star Trek*, they knew that something major had happened, but they didn't understand it at all. They couldn't watch *Star Trek* and relate to it in any way. Science fiction, strange makeup, the future—it just wasn't their world. But they knew that something major had shifted; suddenly their phone was ringing—because they were listed in the phone book. People were knocking on their door, and people were coming to my father's barbershop, and he had a picture of me up on the wall, and they would say, 'My kid wants a Spock haircut.'

"But when I went home on tour in Boston doing *Fiddler*, and they came to the theater, and saw twenty-five hundred people pack the house, screaming and cheering, and laughing and crying, they got it. They knew what *Fiddler* was about."

Still, his parents never actually praised his work, a fact that continues to baffle him. "To this day I'm not sure why. Maybe because they didn't like what I did, or because they didn't think it was going to be a very good life for me. They didn't want to encourage it, so they offered no encouraging words."

It's startling to see a famous seventy-three-year-old man still smarting from a parent's disinterest. "I learned to get by with my own sense of confidence," Nimoy says. "There's an old story that applies about the young guy who comes home from the army and the first thing his mother does is offer him some food, and he says, 'Mom, I've got great news, I've been promoted: I'm a captain.' And the mother says, 'Sit down and have something to eat.' And he says, 'Mom, did you hear what I said?' 'Yeah, I heard what you said; have something to eat.' 'Mom, I'm a captain, it's a big deal.' She says, 'To me, you've always been a captain, you'll always *be* a captain.' "

Does he see this as a characteristically Jewish thing? "There's a tradition there somewhere; that's why that joke works: 'Let others praise you. I don't have to praise you, I'm your mother. I love you. To me, you're always wonderful. It's what other people think of you that counts. So don't come to me for praise.' "

Though his family didn't foster Nimoy's career, it did have an unintentional hand in his choosing it. "I became an actor, I'm convinced, because I found a home in a play about a Jewish family just like mine," Nimoy says. "Clifford Odets's *Awake and Sing*. I was seventeen years old, cast in this local production, with some pretty good amateur and semiprofessional actors, playing this teenage kid in this Jewish family that was so much like mine it was amazing. The same dynamics, the same tensions in the household. The family lived with the grandfather, who was a barber, and the dominant mother was the power figure, which was the case in my family— my father was a shadow figure. And there were the same concerns about financial security. I felt like I was in a warm bath in this play; I was saying things that I would have liked to have said to my parents. And I thought if I could do this for the rest of my life I'd be a very happy person."

Nimoy didn't just use his family to connect to roles; he used his childhood Yiddish. "I was put in touch with some of the old Yiddish theater actors who were coming to California to do an occasional weekend of Yiddish productions. Maurice Schwartz sort of took me on; he was the founder of the Yiddish Art Theater in New York, a pretty famous Yiddish theater figure—a great talent. Speaking Yiddish in front of an audience was a great thrill for me."

But Hollywood wasn't exactly champing at the bit for a Yiddish-speaking leading man with Nimoy's looks. "Guys like me were playing all the ethnic roles, usually the heavies—the bad Mexicans, the bad Italians. And those were the jobs that I took and was happy to get for a long time. I played Indians in Westerns many times. The first Indian role that I took was a role that a Native Indian turned down because the Indian character was so unredeemably bad. I was happy to get the work, thank you very much."

Despite the ethnic typecasting, Nimoy says, Hollywood was much more hospitable to Jews than Boston had been. "I came to the realization that anti-Semitism wasn't acceptable in Hollywood. People who were anti-Semitic were extremely covert about it because a lot of very powerful figures in Hollywood were Jewish.

"I distinctly remember, when I was really struggling—before I had my first job—I was with an agent who was Jewish, and he walked me into a casting office to introduce me to the head of casting. And in addition to talking about my acting background, he told him, 'He's a nice Jewish boy.' And I thought, 'Wow, he's trying to help me gain entrance by announcing that I'm Jewish.' It was amazing to me that he would try to make a Jewish connection to help me get work. That was a revelation to me."

But Nimoy pauses when I ask whether he felt he had to play down being Jewish when he became Spock. "It's a valid question," he answers, "and I have to think about it. I think it's fair to say I was kind of neutral on the issue. In playing Spock, I never saw any point of making a big deal about 'I'm Jewish, I'm Jewish!' It would have seemed gratuitous somehow."

Would it surprise him if today people didn't know he was Jewish? "Well, I think a lot of people know what I am. Certainly at *Star Trek* conventions, I've told the story about where this came from," he demonstrates the Vulcan greeting: a raised hand with forked fingers—the pointer and middle fingers sandwiched together and the ring and pinky fingers similarly aligned. "I've always talked about this coming from my Jewish background."

He invented the hand signal based on his memory of seeing the rabbis do it when they said the priestly blessing. Nimoy recites the prayer for me in Hebrew and then translates: "It says, 'May the Lord bless and keep you and may the Lord cause his countenance to shine upon you, may the Lord be gracious unto you and grant you peace.' "

He points to one of his photographs behind me, which depicts an isolated hand shaped in the famed Vulcan salutation. "I was talking to this rabbi cousin of ours about that image one day [Rabbi John Rosove of Temple Israel of Hollywood, a cousin of Nimoy's second wife, Susan Bay], and I told him that my childhood memory was that when these guys did this traditional blessing, it was really theatrical. These men from our synagogue would cover their heads with their prayer shawls, and they were shouters— these were old, Orthodox, shouting guys. About a half a dozen of them would get up and face the congregation, chanting in a magical, mystical kind of way. They would start off by humming." Nimoy hums. "And they're swaying and chanting. And then the guy would yell out: '*Y'varechecha Adonai!*' And then the whole bunch of them would, like a chorus, respond, '*Y'varechecha Adonai!*'—all six of them. It was really spooky.

"So, the congregation was all standing, and my father said to me, 'Don't look.' And in fact, everybody's got their eyes covered with their hands or they've got their heads covered with their prayer shawl, the entire congregation. But I peeked, and I saw these guys doing this. So I introduced it into *Star Trek*. But I said to this rabbi cousin of ours, 'To this day, I'm not really sure why my father said, *Don't look*.' And he explained, 'The traditional belief is that during that blessing, the *Shekhina*—the feminine presence of God—enters the congregation to bless the congregation. And you shouldn't see God, because the light could be fatal to a human. So you close your eyes to protect yourself.' 'Well!' I said. 'I never knew that! My father never said, "Close your eyes because God is coming." He just said "Don't look." ' So that changed my life when John said that—that was only five or six years ago. The impact was enormous on me. Wow, not only was there this whole theatrical thing going on, but here comes God, the *female* version. Whoa. So I thought, 'I'm going to photograph women.' "

He started taking art pictures of women's bodies—some very sensual. "I began to explore the idea of putting together this image with the female figure and it ended up being a book." *Shekinah* was published in 2002. "I love the idea that there is a feminine spiritual presence," says Nimoy. "Because to me, it's nurturing, it's compassionate, it's creative, it's aesthetic, it's warming, it's comforting. And in a strange kind of way, I guess—this is the first time I'm trying to articulate this—I feel less judgmental of that presence than I would of a male presence. To the male God, I say, 'What are you doing, where are you, what are you thinking? Why are you letting these things happen, looking the other way, or saying, *Go ahead, work it out for yourselves, guys?*' But this whole feminine thing, I don't have that kind of expectation, because to me it doesn't present itself as being the all-powerful figure; it's a maternal figure, it's a loving figure, it's even an erotic figure. But it's not a power figure in the sense that it has control of everything. So I'm comfortable with it, and I'm comforted by it. Does that make sense?"

Obviously any project Nimoy does these days generates attention simply because he is still Spock to the world—no matter how accomplished a photographer he is, or how many other movies he's acted in or directed. (He received an Emmy nomination for his portrayal of Golda Meir's

husband, Morris Meyerson, in *A Woman Called Golda* (1982), he directed
Three Men and a Baby (1987) and *The Good Mother* (1988), and in 1991, in
Never Forget, he played an Auschwitz survivor, Mel Mermelstein, who
went to court in 1980 to prove the Holocaust happened.)

Nimoy doesn't fight his *Star Trek* identity as he once did when he
wrote his first of two memoirs, *I Am Not Spock* (1975), but he does try to
make it count for something. "In the mid-nineties, I was invited to go to
a *Star Trek* convention in Germany. I had been invited several times before,
and had always said no. But some people whom I knew and trusted in L.A.
and who had been to these German *Star Trek* conventions encouraged me
to go, and said, 'You'll find that it's an amazing audience, they are fervent,
supportive, perceptive, and you'll have a great experience.' I went to our
rabbi, and I said, 'What do you think? I hated being there ten years ago.'
And he said, 'Do they know you're Jewish?' And I said, 'I don't know,
maybe some do, maybe they don't.' And he said, 'I think you should go,
and identify yourself as a Jew, and let all these people who admire you discover that you're Jewish. And let them examine their own feelings about
liking somebody who's a Jew.' So right then and there I knew I had to go.
I was committed.

"I went trepidatiously; I went with the intention of finding the appropriate moment to say to this audience 'I'm a Jew; how do you feel about
that?' I went somewhat confrontationally. I had two days of presentations
to do to the same audience and I was looking for the appropriate way to
time this thing so it would be a climactic moment. I thought, 'I'll tell a lot
of stories on Saturday, and on Sunday I'll get to it.' So, I get out there on
Saturday and I'm only maybe ten minutes into it, when a hand goes up,
and somebody says to me: 'Mr. Nimoy, you did a television movie about a
Holocaust survivor who went to court against some Holocaust deniers.
Would you tell us how you got involved with that and what was your interest?' And I thought, 'I have underestimated the awareness of this audience correctly.' I sensed that they knew more than I thought they knew,
about me and who I was. So I talked about Mermelstein and immediately
went into the whole story about the Vulcan thing and how the hand sign
came from my Jewish background and so forth . . . When I finished, the
place started applauding and they would not stop. When I tell you they
wouldn't stop, I mean they *would not stop*. They went on and on and on. I

started crying. They were on their feet, and they were cheering. It was in-credible. And there was this message in it that I picked up, that has some-thing to do with: *We are a new generation.*" Nimoy gets choked up. "We are a repairing generation. We are a reconstituting, healing generation . . . It was extraordinary."

Tony Kushner

TONY KUSHNER PHOTOGRAPHED IN 2004 BY JILL KREMENTZ

"I THINK THAT BEING JEWISH was invaluable preparation for being gay."

Tony Kushner is sitting in his cramped office near Union Square in Manhattan. I would have expected a Pulitzer Prize-winning playwright to work in a somewhat larger space—this is the size of many walk-in closets—but its atmosphere feels appropriately artistic. We are surrounded by books climbing the walls on blond wooden shelves (a ladder allows him to get to the high volumes), there are two lamps with fringed lampshades, photographs of his award-winning epic, *Angels in America*, an easy chair, and a desk jammed into the corner. Kushner is wearing gray wool pants, black sweater, black boots, and purple socks. He keeps patting his curly hair when he speaks and it springs back.

"When I came out, my father and I started having these terrible fights because it wasn't easy for him at all," says Kushner. "He would say, 'Okay, it's too bad that you are homosexual, but why do you have to tell anybody about it?' He said, 'I knew homosexuals when I was a kid and they stayed to themselves.' When I'd argue with him, I used Jewishness as a metaphor. I'd ask him, 'Why don't you have your nose cut off and change your name to Brown or White and become a goy?' Hannah Arendt's right: If you're a pariah, your only protection is to embrace the fact. Not to try to pretend that you're accepted, because you can't be. Pretending carries you out of your history—you'll turn against yourself, and when you're found out, you're contemptible not just because society holds you in contempt as a Jew, a black person, or a gay person, but also because you recognize you're a traitor to your own kind and your own self and you're weakened because of it."

I wonder if this argument worked on Kushner's father. "I think to an extent it worked; it may have been useful to him, I'm not entirely sure. It was a long process. I think it helped him." It certainly helped Kushner— the notion that he could take a page from Jewish experience when it came to his sexuality. "I already knew what it was to be a proud member of a minority in a secular, pluralist democracy," he says, sipping coffee. "I had a long history to fall back on. What gay people have had to do in the last thirty or forty years is invent that identity for themselves. And I don't think it's any coincidence that so many of the people who have been immensely important in shaping that identity have been Jewish lesbians and gay men. We sort of arrive knowing how to be unpopular and how to turn that into a source of power for ourselves and not to feel condemned because society condemns us. And we also have a belief that justice triumphs. Pharaoh doesn't win. In the long run, the righteous are triumphant, even if the wicked seem to be winning at the moment."

Kushner's faith that fairness prevails was instilled by liberal parents (ho-mophobia aside) in a small, very old Jewish community in Lake Charles, Louisiana. His parents drummed into him and his siblings that "you didn't have to take shit from people," such as teachers who made them kneel at his Episcopal day school ("We didn't want to kneel," Kushner says) or teachers who said things like, " 'The Jews killed Jesus.' We had a good lib-eral frame of reference," Kushner says with a smile, "we knew our rights." He also knew his ethnic pedigree: his parents regularly held up the usual triumvirate of Jewish achievement—Einstein, Marx, and Freud—and re-joiced when Israelis triumphed in the Six Day War. "A lot of people my age remember our parents saving the newspapers for every day of the war," says Kushner, who was ten at the time. "There was a *Life* magazine picture of an Israeli army jet, with a Mogen David [Jewish star] on each wing; I think the headline was something like 'The Miracle of the Desert.' I remember hearing this idea that the Jewish suffering was at an end because Moshe Dayan and Golda Meir were here—the new Maccabees. There was tremendous pride."

He has discovered over the years that non-Jews who don't share these childhood landmarks will never fathom his fidelity to Israel and will feel free to criticize it. "It's why I think the left is frequently accused of anti-Semitism without actually being anti-Semitic: There is a way in which non-Jewish people who are incredibly well-meaning and not anti-Semitic *just don't get it.* I went to the Occupied Territories this summer with six other people, none of them were Jewish, and they're all very left, very progressive, and very smart, but I found myself feeling very isolated in a lot of moments. Because what they don't get is that no matter how beastly I think Ariel Sharon is, or how appalling I think the behavior of the IDF [Israeli Defense Forces] is, you don't understand what they're doing there unless it's a part of your lived history. I didn't grow up with pogroms, but I grew up with the kind of normal anti-Semitism that you would run into, and that history is with me; people who died in the Holocaust—they're with me."

When I ask if that's made him gravitate toward Jewish friendships, Kushner seems to bristle. "I've never really done the demographics of my friends," he says. "I find that, in general, I get along best with Jews, Irish people, Italians, and black people. There are strong similarities in eloquence and aggressive intelligence. My partner, Mark, had a Polish Catholic mother and a Jewish father."

Kushner, forty-nine, and Mark Harris, forty-two, had a commitment ceremony in April 2003, which was announced in the *New York Times'* "Vows" column and which included guests such as Mike Nichols, who directed Kushner's *Angels in America* for HBO, and his wife, ABC anchor Diane Sawyer. Kushner and Harris stood under a canopy before a rabbi in a favorite Manhattan restaurant, Gabriel's. Kushner told the *Times* that Mark was someone "who needs more hysteria in his life." Harris said, "Now I have plenty."

Kushner says Mark's family has some wonderful, quirky Jewish stories. "The first year that Mark's parents were married, his Catholic mother, Harriet, wanted to impress his Jewish dad's mother, Minnie Moskowitz. So Harriet made this huge seder meal, and at the conclusion of the meal, Minnie made a toast, saying, 'I'm deeply moved that my new daughter-in-law, the enemy of my people, has made such a beautiful seder meal.' "

Though Kushner wanted a Jewish marriage ceremony, he's not opposed to interfaith unions. "Walt Whitman in his poem *A Passage to India* says God's purpose from the start is for races to intermarry and continents to merge, and I really believe that." That said, Kushner has been surprised by his feelings of clannish pride when it comes to his godson. "I have a godchild who was born on my birthday in the same hospital I was born in: Mount Sinai. He's the son of Brian Kulick [who directed Kushner's play *A Dybbuk*] and Naomi Goldberg, and they're both Jews, so Noah's one hundred percent ethnically Jewish. I feel sort of like I shouldn't admit this—you should never feel this way—but *that means something to me*; I feel a certain sort of kvelling, *schep naches* [taking and pride and pleasure]. There is some sense of continuity about that, and I find myself thinking something that I feel very uncomfortable with: that 'this kid is like me.' And I like that because I love Jews and I want to see us continue as a presence in the world.

"But I also believe that there is nobody smarter or more gorgeous in the world than my two nieces, whom I love immensely and who have an Irish mother." He sighs. "I think there's no point in denying the fact that it's human and important to want to see the religion and the culture continue. And yet also nothing should continue preserved in amber."

Kushner says Judaism has in fact proved flexible—enough to accommodate both his sexuality and his taste for old-fashioned worship: "A house so big has a room for you in it somewhere, if you want it," Kushner asserts. "And I've found a couple rooms that I feel comfortable in." Thanks, in part—surprisingly enough—to klezmer music. "Discovering the Klezmatics changed everything for me," Kushner says of the New York–based sextet. "It really did. Because I just fell madly in love with the music. My parents are both musicians—my father was a clarinetist, my mother was a really great bassoonist; she recorded with Stravinsky. Listening to David Krakauer [clarinetist] play had a tremendously powerful effect," he says. "It helped me discover Yiddish again, which was hugely important. And half the Klezmatics are gay. There's this whole gay Jewish movement that has grown up around klezmer, klezmer revival, 'klez camp.' That was incredibly important."

Kushner found another "room" in Daniel Boyarin, head of Talmudic studies at U.C. Berkeley. "I read his book *Carnal Israel* [subtitle: *Reading Sex in Talmudic Culture*] and got to know him. He deals with sexuality and

Judaism in a way that makes you aware of things that you always suspected. You go to an Orthodox shul and you see these guys dancing with each other and the sensuality of davening and the weird kind of privacy of the whole thing—its onanistic quality—and you think, 'This is not a religion of people with no bodies or no sense of the sensual.' And of course, it's true."

Kushner is drawn not only to Judaism's sensuality, but also to its argumentativeness: the constant questioning and disputation. He was a star debater in school, and he says conflict is elemental to his heritage and his DNA. "Struggle and battling is so much a part of what being Jewish is," he says, "even on a family level. You learn that if it's a good fight, that fighting can be constructive and that it's necessary—it's part of life. I look at people like my friend Larry Kramer [the playwright and gay activist who founded Act-Up], and I sort of marvel at his unquenchable appetite for brawling; but then I look at my Aunt Martha and I understand Larry. These are not people who have any expectation that life is ever going to be peaceful. And what is peaceful? Peaceful is boring and dead."

His seders, not surprisingly, are never serene. Kushner took up his father's mantle and sits at the head of his family's table each year. He encourages wide participation, which, when it comes to the subject of Israel, inevitably leads to warfare. "I have a cousin who is a poverty medicine doctor in Santa Fe," he says, "and since the second intifada, both of us have become rabid—just apoplectic. It just turns into a horrendous free-for-all—people yelling and screaming—just terrible."

Clashes aside, he's developed a new appreciation for a quirky family tradition: "I used to think how corny it was that at the end of the seder every year we sang 'America the Beautiful.' But I actually think now, 'What a great thing'—that it's exactly the point. It isn't about Israel; it's about American constitutional democracy. *That's* the promised land. This is what has worked. America is where we—where Jews—have lived better lives.' "

Passover is one of the few holidays Kushner still observes. And for very personal reasons, he has always—and will always—fast on Yom Kippur. "When I was twelve, my mother got breast cancer and they fucked up the operation really terribly and she almost died from being over-radiated. That was the deal I made: I would fast if she could live. The operation was right before Rosh Hashanah and she was out of the hospital in time for that holiday and then, the day before Yom Kippur, she got terribly sick again and she had to be flown to New York for six months. It was horrible. They overdid the radiation so much that they'd actually given her a bone infection. But she survived—for twenty more years. So that's when I started fasting, and I've done it every year since."

He seems suddenly bashful, aware it might sound like utilitarian Judaism: "I don't want to disappoint you." I assure him he needn't apologize— that in fact, most of the people I've interviewed are similarly randomly observant and find piety complicated. "Judaism is really hard and it's intentionally hard. I think the reason we're so smart as a people is that the religion over the centuries is such an imponderably difficult task. It's not masterable. The Talmudic tradition is literally sort of an embrace of the condition of being at sea."

Ed Koch

FORMER THREE-TERM New York City mayor Ed Koch is calling out to his secretary, with yet another request: "JODI!!" he bellows in his pinstriped suit from his office in a Manhattan law firm. "GET THE CORRESPONDENCE WITH ABE FOXMAN!" Koch wants me to see every exchange of letters in which he's bombarded someone with outrage—no matter how long ago. There are the letters, for instance, about Peter Jennings's 1996 documentary on Israel: "I'm very direct and I told him what was wrong. I said, 'You loaded the program with boorish Jews and cultured Arabs, so anyone coming away from it would say, 'Oh, those boorish Jews!' Then I wrote a column—a really good column—you'll see; she'll find it." Jodi does. "She's amazing!" Koch exclaims. "You see how good she is?"

A few minutes later, Koch recounts similar objections he made to a program on Channel 13, the New York public television station. *"I don't send them a nickel anymore,"* he says bitterly. "They did a program with really nice Arabs speaking beautifully and saying all of the right things about wanting to live alongside Jews in Israel, and then they had some atrocious-speaking Jews—some with American Brooklyn accents. I'm going to give you my correspondence with Bill Baker [Channel 13's president]. "JODI!?! GET THE CORRESPONDENCE WITH BILL BAKER!"

Finally there's his tiff with writer Susan Sontag. "She is, in general, just one of those terrible people," Koch says. [Sontag has since died.] "I had a correspondence with her and with Arthur Miller when I was mayor." Naturally, I'm going to hear the story: "I'm a member of PEN [the writer's advocacy group, Poets, Essayists, and Novelists] because I wrote twelve books. And I once said that Israel shouldn't be bringing the press to the front lines to take photographs that are antithetical to Israel. What they end up showing is an Israeli man shooting an adolescent. But they don't show you the adolescent throwing the stone first! And I have been the subject of having the stone thrown at me during the intifada, and I have nine stitches in my head! And if the stone had hit me in the *eye*, it would have blinded me!"

Koch has a photograph on his wall of the time in 1990 when he was hit with a rock while walking with former Jerusalem mayor Teddy Kollek. "My feeling is, if you're a soldier, you don't have to take that stuff. You don't have to expose yourself to being blinded or killed or injured. You say to them, 'Stop throwing stones,' and if they don't stop throwing stones, you shoot 'em! You have a right to self-defense."

Back to why he hated Susan Sontag: "So I gave this advice to Israeli leaders: 'You shouldn't have the press up close taking pictures, because the pictures will be used against you and they're not going to be fairly reflective of what's taking place.' And I get a letter from both Susan Sontag and Arthur Miller, saying, 'If you don't retract this, we're going to seek your removal from PEN. How dare you suggest that the press not take pictures?' So I wrote back, 'When did you become the Thought Police?' How dare they?"

Before we get too far from the rock story, I'm curious how he came to be pelted in Jerusalem. "That incident came about in the following way: I was in Israel, the guest of Teddy Kollek, and he said, 'I'm going to show you the new museum.'" It was located under the Western Wall, and they walked there without any security. "Suddenly there are stones thrown and I'm hit on the head and I bleed like there's no tomorrow because there are a lot of veins up in your scalp. I was in Israel because they'd asked me to come to promote tourism, which was suffering because of the first intifada. And so I'm saying to myself, 'I know that this story is going to go all over the world and make a bad impression—there are so many photographers here.' So I try to make light of it, saying to Teddy, 'Teddy, this was meant for you, not for me; everybody loves *me.*' And Teddy jokes back, 'No, Ed; this was meant for you, not me, and if you had my head of hair, you wouldn't have felt it.' "

Edward Irving Koch, now eighty-one, grew up in Newark, New Jersey, and attended the Hebrew Free School. "The teaching was terrible," he says. His father, Louis, was a furrier, and his mother, Joyce Silpe, was a "terrible cook." "She burned everything," he says with a laugh. "And my father loved everything to be burned. I like rare food. I like it bloody."

He says his mother was determined to assimilate. "She hired a tutor to teach her to lose her Yiddish Central European accent."

In his last year of college, he was drafted into the army, where he "had a fight because I was a Jew." It all started because his platoon, according to Koch, was composed of twenty-five percent Jewish New Yorkers. "It was an unusual number," he says, "and many of them simply couldn't do the obstacle course. I must say, I found it hard, but I practiced. I wanted to look good. What the Jewish kids *did* excel in was asking questions. So when they had seminars, the Jewish kids would put up their hands and ask questions. And one day, this one guy said, 'Which is the next Yid that's going to ask a question?' I knew I couldn't take on a fight because I wasn't strong enough yet—this happened in the first few weeks of basic training. So I said, 'I'm going to build myself up and ultimately I'm going to challenge him.' "

Koch trained hard over the next sixteen weeks. "It didn't help," Koch admits with a smile, "he still beat me up. But I was proud of the mere fact that I challenged him. I went over to him and grabbed him by the throat and I said, 'We're going to have it out.' And he said, 'Why? What did I do?' And I couldn't say to him, 'It's because of what you said.' He looked baffled, but all I could say to him was, '*You* know. *You* know.' "

I wonder if, once Koch got to be the blustery, bigheaded, likable mayor of New York, he became more Jewish on the job than he had been. He nods. "Sure. It made me speak out more. I am very proud of the fact that, as a result of being identified as proud of my faith, I got higher percentages of Catholic votes than I got from the Jews." Like most dyed-in-the-wool candidates, Koch rattles off numbers: "Eighty-one percent of the Italians and the Irish supported me in my elections, whereas with Jews, it was only seventy-three percent, and the reason is very simple: I'm not liberal enough for the West Side Jew. And I'm proud of that! I am a *moderate*! Jews have a very large group that is too radical for me in a host of areas. But the Catholics *love* me. I'm proud of the fact that John Cardinal O'Connor asked me to do a book with him. It was called *His Eminence and Hizzoner*."

Koch makes sure to attend synagogue on the High Holy Days every year, though he never had a seder at Gracie Mansion. "But I put up a mezuzah on the door there," he points out. "Abe Beame had a mezuzah." (He refers to a famous predecessor.) "But I had a better mezuzah. And when my father died, we sat shivah at Gracie Mansion. That was nice."

When I ask him if he feels more Jewish or more American, he winces. "It's not a question that should be asked. Look, I am an American. I happen to be a white male, a senior citizen, and I'm Jewish. If I had to pick the two things I'm proud of, it's being an American and being a Jew. But my overall allegiance is American."

Koch pulls out an anecdote to illustrate: "When I was a congressman, early on, I noted that they had prayer breakfasts in Washington every two weeks, where a group of legislators would meet for breakfast and discuss religious matters. One day, a congressman from Mississippi, Sonny Montgomery, meets me on the House floor and says, 'Ed, next week we want to discuss Judaism. You are a Jew?' 'Yes, I'm a Jew.' 'Would you come and lecture on Judaism?' I said, 'Sure.' At the time, I thought, 'I'm not a scholar; how much do I know? I'll go to the library and figure out what will amuse them.' I took out a couple books, read them, and went to the breakfast. And I told them about Jewish exotica, which they enjoyed, and then they asked questions. At the end, I said, 'What's interesting to me is you are all avoiding a question which I know is on your minds by looking in your eyes. And the question that you're not asking me is, "Do Jews have dual loyalty?" Isn't that what you're wondering?' They all nodded. 'So I want to make you one pledge,' and I raised my right hand. 'I swear to you, that if Israel ever invades the United States, I shall stand with the United States.' And they roared."

But Koch does have a deep fealty to Israel that clearly makes him hyper-aware of when it's the target of condemnation. "It's clear to me that anti-Semitism has re-arisen to an extent even greater than before World War II, without the killings in concentration camps," he says. "I don't want to overstate it, but I mean, it's amazing—the hate and the venom. It's directed at Israel because it wouldn't be acceptable in polite circles to direct it at Jews, but it's intended to be directed at all Jews."

I ask how he would explain this Jewish hatred. "First: anti-Semitism is based, in large part, on actions of the church; and we're very lucky there have been two popes who have changed that to an enormous degree. But take Cardinal Glemp in Poland. I met him; he is a vile anti-Semite. And he's the *primate*—the number one cardinal! So in Europe in particular, you have still the residue of that.

"Second is: We're supposed to be *dead*! *'Why are you still standing?!'* There's a certain resentment: 'How could it be? We've kicked the shit out of them; why are they *still* standing?' "

Barry Levinson

BARRY LEVINSON PHOTOGRAPHED BY YVONNE FERRIS

BARRY LEVINSON, the director of *Diner, Rainman, Good Morning, Vietnam*, and *Wag the Dog*, is unshaven in sweatpants, sitting in his gracefully designed home office on his Connecticut estate, talking about his 1999 film, *Liberty Heights*. "Jews, gentiles, and Colored People," Levinson pronounces. "That's what I wanted to call *Liberty Heights*. The studio had a fit: 'No! My God, are you kidding?' I said, 'Why not? That's who it's about.' In the end, it was decided it was too inflammatory. I had thought, 'At least the title will jump out at you.'"

The semiautobiographical 1999 film chronicled a middle-class Jewish family, the Kurtzmans, in suburban Baltimore. Joe Mantegna is the family man who each year on Yom Kippur skips out of services to go to the Cadillac showroom and view the new model; Adrien Brody plays his older son, who becomes obsessed with the typical shiksa goddess—played by model Carolyn Murphy; and Ben Foster is the younger brother, Ben, who falls for a smart, attractive black classmate.

Early on in the film, there is this exchange between Ben and his buddy, Sheldon, as they discuss the sign at the local pool that says "NO JEWS, DOGS, OR COLOREDS ALLOWED":

BEN: How do you think they decided the order?
SHELDON: What?
BEN: That Jews should be first.
SHELDON: Yeah. I would have thought it would have been "Dogs, Colored, Jews."
BEN: That must have been some meeting to come up with that. Someone had to say, "No, I have to tell you, the Jews bother me more than the dogs."

Levinson, sixty-three, believes to this day that the explicit Jewishness of his script gave Jewish studio executives the jitters. "The reality is that anytime you do a movie where there are Jewish people in it, there is always going to be this situation where they'll think, 'Well, it's too Jewish; no one's going to understand it, no one's going to like it. *I* can love it—I'm Jewish—but no one else will'—that kind of sensibility. Which may be part of the inferiority complex of a Jew who thinks no one can understand them except *them*.

"Studio people are petrified. When I did *Avalon* [his 1990 film about a Jewish family striving to assimilate], they thought, 'Only a Jewish person could enjoy this movie.' The reality is that, over the years, I get letters from Japanese, blacks, Norwegians who say, 'That was just like my family.' That's the amazing thing about film or literature—people can make connections. But when you do these projects, not only do you gamble, but you sort of take your artistic life in your own hands. Because it's a very difficult road to go down. Very.

"Studios are afraid to distribute it; they don't advertise it the same way. It's fraught with a lot of danger zones. Film at the end of the day is a commercial business; they look for the most commercial work to do. Therefore, when you get into certain kinds of movies, they're very nervous about it. It's one thing when you have a certain violence to it; then you can increase your commercial viability."

In other words, if he had scripted some Jews getting killed? "Yes!" Levinson smiles. "If you don't do that, then it's just '*Jews*.' It's interesting that ultimately the most successful movies about Jews are really about dead Jews and not Jews that live and laugh and everything else; because then they're 'just *Jewish*.' But dead Jews: *Then* it's significant. Anytime you do the rest, it's 'Well, they're too Jewish.' Have you ever heard the comment

'They're too Italian'? Do you ever hear 'It was good, but I thought they were too Catholic'? You can only be 'too Jewish.' "

I wonder if he's ever worried that he'll be pegged as a Jewish director. "I don't think you can worry," he replies. "You are what you are. But it's true that, in the world we live in, to be considered a Jewish director is not a great thing to be. That doesn't have great cachet to it."

Why does he say that? "Because I think the way the business views things, that is not important enough."

Levinson obviously decided to proceed on *Liberty Heights* regardless of the skepticism. "There are some ideas that just propel you," he explains. "So you're going to fight studios and fight distribution and ultimately you may end up with a film that may not have the same commercial viability. But you do it because you believe in the work."

The idea for *Liberty Heights* was sparked when Levinson read a critic's review of his 1998 science fiction movie, *Sphere*. Lisa Schwarzbaum of *Entertainment Weekly* called Dustin Hoffman's character a "Jewish psychologist" when his ethnicity was nowhere in the script. Schwarzbaum wrote, *"Okay, so he's not officially Jewish; he's only Hoffman, who arrives at the floating habitat and immediately announces, noodgey and menschlike, 'I'd like to call my family.' You do the math."*

"It jarred me for a number of reasons," Levinson says, putting a leg up on a coffee table piled with scripts. "I don't know her at all; I assume she's Jewish with that name. But the reference that she made, implying that we were either hiding the fact that he was Jewish or that he wants to call home like a nice Jewish boy, I just thought was kind of weird. And some people might say that's an overreaction, but I was thinking about it: I mean, no one would mention that someone is a Protestant in a review. It stayed in my head. And I began to think, 'What is this whole thing about Jews? Why do we somehow have to define who's who and what's the point of it?' I suddenly started to write and there it was. At the end of it, I wanted to be able to show the absurdity, the nonsense of prejudice. And also to show that it wasn't really based on hatred."

The film was not a great success. "To me it was very disappointing," Levinson says, "because we got great reviews, but the studio was petrified of a movie that was going to deal with those issues." He seems bitter that Warner Bros. didn't promote the film. "They didn't bother," he says.

•   •   •

Like so many others in this book, Levinson remembers despising Hebrew school—"I might as well have been on Mars for two hours." His Jewishness is found in the milieu of his movies more than in any spiritual identification. "It is what I am, you know? It's a sense of a big extended family—the traditions when so many of us gathered. And it is made up of the stories of being in Russia or Poland or Latvia—that journey to America. That's where my connection is. How important is it? I don't know. But it affects everything that I do in some way, unconsciously or consciously. Mostly unconsciously."

In *Liberty Heights*, for example, it can be found in the character of the father, Nate Kurtzman, who, like Levinson's own father, Irv, checks out the new Cadillac every Yom Kippur; or the character of sixteen-year-old Ben, who, inspired by Levinson's real cousin Eddie, dresses up as Hitler one Halloween and is forbidden to leave the house. Or the character of Grandma Rose, who always stays on the telephone after she's answered it, even when it's not for her. "Hang up!" her grandson yells.

Levinson idealizes the gentile girl in the film just the way he and his friends did as kids: "In the script, I alluded to Lewis and Clark: 'We found the Northwest Passage and there were all these blond-haired girls and they were all great-looking and they had names that sounded terrific and we thought we'd found the Promised Land.' "

He says when he dated non-Jewish girls as a teenager, they shared one trait in common: They were prompt. "We would go to pick up gentile girls at their houses and we always remarked, 'They're so punctual! You ring their bell, they're ready to go!' But it never occurred to us what that was really about: They wanted to get out of the house before we had a chance to come in and meet the mother and father and say, 'Hi, I'm Barry *Levinson.*' We were thinking the girls were so punctual, when really it was about the fact that they'd otherwise have to introduce this Jewish boy to their Protestant or Catholic family." Levinson says his parents didn't weigh in on whom he should date or marry. "Didn't come up," he says. "My grandmother on the Levinson side was much more religious—she kept kosher—but she said something to me before she died which was extraordinary: 'A Jewish girl, it doesn't matter. You should find someone to make you happy.' "

He did. Diana Rhodes, Levinson's second wife, is a painter and a non-observant Catholic. Their two sons, Sam and Jack, have taken opposite religious paths. "Jack studied and is going to be bar mitzvah and Sam, on the other hand, had no interest in it," Levinson says. His stepdaughter, Michelle, who came into his life when she was seven, decided as an adult to convert to Judaism. "So we've got a family that's all mixed up," he says with a chuckle.

Levinson wrote a line for *Liberty Heights* that captures how he has tried to revisit—or revivify—the atmosphere of his Jewish childhood. The character Ben Foster says at the end of the film, *"Life is made up of a few big moments and a lot of little ones . . . but a lot of images fade, and no matter how hard I try, I can't get them back . . . If I knew things would no longer be, I would've tried to remember better."*

William Kristol

WILLIAM KRISTOL, one of the most influential opinion-shapers on the political right, founding editor of the conservative *Weekly Standard* magazine, former chief of staff to Vice President Dan Quayle, now a ubiquitous television commentator, bristles when people say "Jewish" and "neoconservatives" in the same breath. "That's a polemic attack," he says, sitting in his office, legs crossed, in a gray-striped suit. "Part of that is done by people who are hostile, who want to say, 'They're just apologists for Israel really, distorting American foreign policy to serve Israel's goals,' which really isn't true."

The list of Jewish neoconservatives usually includes Kristol, Richard Perle (resident fellow at the American Enterprise Institute), David Brooks (former *Weekly Standard* senior editor, current *New York Times* columnist), Charles Krauthammer (*Washington Post* columnist), Douglas J. Feith (undersecretary of defense for policy under President George W. Bush), and Paul Wolfowitz (president of the World Bank). "When I was a political theory professor," Kristol says, speaking of his early days teaching at the University of Pennsylvania, "my friends who are neoconservatives—or Straussians, to use another term that's become sort of famous recently—

were not particularly Jewish. No one at the *Weekly Standard* now is Jewish except for me. I mean, I haven't done a census; we don't have a test here. But here I am, at the heart of this famous neoconservative magazine that is supposed to be so Jewish, with Fred Barnes and Terry Eastland—serious Protestants—and other people who are less serious Protestants and Catholics."

In other words, there is no right-wing Jewish cabal at the *Weekly Standard* plotting to commandeer foreign policy for the benefit of Israel. Furthermore, Kristol insists that his ideology is not informed by his religion. "In all honesty, in terms of my political views—pro-Reagan, pro-Bush—I really don't think it has much to do with my being Jewish." And when people assume that his aggressive stance on Iraq was driven by loyalty to Israel? Kristol scoffs, pointing out that his magazine has pushed for intervention in many other hot spots. "We were hawks on China, we were hawks on Bosnia, we were also hawks on getting rid of Saddam. But just because Iraq happens to be in the Middle East doesn't mean that it has much to do with Israel policy. On Israel, I'm actually moderately hawkish, but I'm not a big Likudnik. I'm sort of where [Prime Minister Ariel] Sharon is now: a combination of tough on terror, don't give back every inch of the West Bank, make the security arrangements you need but then don't try to have Greater Israel. Really for me, Israel has always been an important part of the world—you have to think about it—but it has not driven my general views about American politics."

So when his ethnicity and that of his cohorts is constantly mentioned, does he view that as anti-Semitic? "Well, sure. Pat Buchanan invented this, let's not forget, twelve years ago, when he accused the first Bush Administration—not a wildly pro-Israel administration, I might point out—of pursuing the war against Saddam because it was serving Israel's interests. He accused at least me and Krauthammer of supporting that war because of Israel. So it's always lurked out there on the right."

Kristol, fifty-three, was weaned on this kind of controversy. His parents, Irving Kristol and Gertrude Himmelfarb, riled the New York intellectual elite back in the 1950s when they abandoned liberal orthodoxy and embraced—or pioneered—the neoconservative movement. Some Jewish critics viewed neoconservative policies as un-compassionate and therefore un-Jewish. It's still a criticism leveled at pundits like Kristol today. "It's nonsense," Kristol says. "That just assumes that liberal programs work better or are more compassionate than conservative programs. Rudy Giuliani was a more conservative mayor of New York and a supposedly less *compassionate* mayor of New York than David Dinkins. Were poor people better off after Giuliani was mayor or with Dinkins, when crime was out of control and schools were terrible? I'm not going to endorse every conservative idea out there obviously, but I just think a lot of people want to say that liberal policies are better for poor people and then if you're not for liberal policy, you don't care about poor people. And that's not true."

What about the sense that conservatism doesn't further the Jewish premium on social justice and goodwill? "Look, I think people should give to Jewish charities and we do, and people in our synagogue do, and some of the politically conservative Jews I know actually do more of that than some of the liberal Jews I know. Liberal Jews seem to give all their money to the Museum of Modern Art and to Harvard [where Kristol went], which does not really help poor people. So let all these big-shot liberal Jews actually go give some more money to help poor people."

I suspect that Kristol would characterize "Jewish values" very differently than most of the Jews I grew up with, but I ask him for his definition. "I'm sort of hostile to the phrase," he says. "Because to a degree it just becomes another word for liberalism. I just think it's an importing of people's views—which are legitimate views, some of which I even agree with—into the Jewish tradition, which obviously has plenty of support for a whole bunch of alternative political and social views. I think the Jewish tradition, Jewish religion, and Jewish thought are very important. But I've always rebelled a little when people say, 'My Jewish values lead me to really care about the poor.' I know some Christians who care about the poor, too."

Kristol was raised among many of the "big-shot liberal Jews," as he calls them, on the Upper West Side of Manhattan. Educated at private schools—Lycée Français, then Collegiate—he went to Hebrew school in an Orthodox Spanish-Portuguese synagogue three times a week. "Shearith Israel is the grand old Sephardic synagogue in New York," says Kristol. "It's very formal and ornate, as I think the old Sephardic synagogues were in the old country. People wore a top hat to come to the Torah. So as a thirteen-year-old, I wore a top hat for my bar mitzvah."

Though he says his family wasn't devout, his mother studied Jewish thought and religion during her days at the Jewish Theological Seminary (which she attended while a student at Brooklyn College), and his father was similarly drawn to Jewish learning. "So there was more of an identification than probably your average, not-too-observant Manhattan Jews," he says. "It was very much a part of our life, my parents' intellectual careers, their understanding of who they were."

At Harvard, Kristol didn't visit the university Hillel: "It was a little house on the fringe of campus, kind of a pain to get to," he says. "People who went were Orthodox." He attended High Holy Day services at Harvard's Memorial Chapel—"It was kind of amusing, they'd cover up the cross"—but he wasn't immersed. "I was a Scoop Jackson Democrat, I was pro-Israel. But I wasn't Jewishly involved."

Even so, in 1975, when he married Susan Scheinberg at Westchester Reform Temple, he opted for a traditional Jewish wedding ceremony. "We got married with a *kipah* and a chuppah because I wanted it . . . I remember at the time my mother saying that my grandmother wouldn't believe it was a Jewish wedding if it hadn't had those components. Susan wasn't terribly well-educated in Judaism; she went to Reform Sunday school and learned whatever they learn in Reform Sunday school: social justice." He smiles.

The Kristols became more Jewish when they had their three children. "Kids are always the key, of course," he says. "We joined a synagogue and they went to Hebrew school and had a bat and bar mitzvah, and the kids got involved in B'nai Brith Youth [an organization that includes social activities, summer camp, trips abroad, etc.]. So for the last twenty years, I'd say there's much more involvement—more by Susan than me, but me also. I got personally more interested—I won't say 'studying,' that's too fancy a word—but reading about Jewish thought, biblical stuff, going to Israel more; I'm on the board of a think tank over there now. Susan actually is about to become president of the synagogue, which is of course a nightmare. I think it's a pretty significant part of my life and my family's life. And it's not that I'm searching for it. I think it's actually, existentially, a big part of my life."

He says his kids, in some sense, took the lead. "They moved faster in this direction than we did. My daughter, Rebecca, began keeping semi-kosher earlier. Then we adopted some version at home—no pork, no shellfish—partly in response to our kids' slight nudging. I would say that my kids are more Jewish because they live in Northern Virginia rather than New York. Because you have to sort of a make a decision when you live outside New York. Once you make a decision to go to Hebrew school, have a bar mitzvah, join the B'nai Brith Youth, and go to a three-week summer camp, you're involved. In New York, everyone's so Jewish you don't have to try to be Jewish. And I think as a result, when you get to college, you sort of drift away and then some people never come back."

Does he think his children will create Jewish families? "I don't know if they'll marry Jews or not, but I think Judaism is important enough that they would try to get the spouse to convert or to get the kids to be brought up Jewish. I think it matters," he says. "Obviously, since we're a Conservative synagogue, we're pretty strict; you can't have a bar mitzvah unless you're Jewish. Which means either the mother's Jewish, the father has converted, or the kid has converted." And he subscribes to that thinking? "I'm a little ambivalent," he confesses. "But I think you can't just give a bar mitzvah to a kid who's Jewish and then he goes off with the other parent to Catholic Mass the next day. There's something just too weird about that. We don't police it. But I think that you want to have a little more of a sense that this is a choice. You can't be everything."

That said, Kristol doesn't lose sleep over assimilation and intermarriage. "I'm slightly on the optimistic side," he says. "Just based more on my personal observation than any grand theory. I just see in my kids' generation a greater interest in Judaism. I think if you're a smart kid, you don't have to be Orthodox or have been educated in a yeshiva to appreciate this stuff."

In the same way that he's not exercised about assimilation in America, he's not worked up about the Christian right. I read aloud a quote he gave the *Forward* in 1995, when he responded to Jewish fears of a Christian revival: *"[Jews] are right to be slightly concerned that . . . a serious Christian revival would set Jews apart from the mainstream of America . . . and I think that's probably going to happen,"* he told the newspaper. *"It will make people for whom perfect assimilation into America is their goal a little bit uncomfortable. I would argue that's better for everyone."* I ask him to explain that. "If Jews are at all serious about being Jewish, they're going to be in some state of tension with the mainstream non-Jewish culture," he says. "If that mainstream culture is a little more Christian, Jews will feel some tension. I think to some degree that's happening—it's just a fact. And I think ultimately it's healthy."

Put simply: If the mainstream Christian culture becomes more Christian, it will compel Jews to be more Jewish. "My father famously said that the threat to Jews in America is not that Christians want to kill Jews; it's that they want to marry them."

He thinks Jews should choose whether they're going to be in favor of more faith generally in this country, and if so, it's only fair that more religiosity apply to all religions. "Jews can't say, 'We want to have a really vigorous Jewish culture, but the Christians should just continue to become secular and assimilated.' It's just silly. And for the same reasons, those of us who do want a more vigorous, self-conscious, even *separate*, Jewish identity, can't really begrudge the Christians having their own identities. There will be slight tensions around the edges—the occasional *Passion* movie or whatever. But my personal view is that instead of a homogenized, secular, postmodern country that is not terribly attractive to me I'd prefer to have a country in which there are vigorous Jewish *and* Christian communities."

I tell Kristol that I don't see Jewish leaders arguing for a more religious way of American life in the same way the Christian right does, not to mention that Jews will always be outnumbered so dramatically that the country can't be religiously balanced the way he describes it. "Right, no, it's not going to be balanced. But again, it's a little hard to say, 'You guys can't have your own rebirth. We get to rediscover all these Jewish thinkers and you don't get to read C. S. Lewis.' It's not tenable. The same things that are leading a lot of intelligent Jews to want to recapture their tradition are leading a lot of intelligent Christians to say, 'Is this really the best we can do? A modern, secular, reality TV–obsessed way of life?' Like Jews, they decide to go explore their roots. Like Jews, some go a little bit off the deep end. But at the end of the day, I still think it's a little healthier than just saying, 'Well, we can't even look at that stuff because two hundred years ago it led to anti-Semitism, which is sort of the ADL [Anti-Defamation League] position. I'm exaggerating a little. But there's been a certain amount of hysteria about the Christian right somehow."

Doesn't he understand why some people would worry about a more Christian America? He nods. "Look, there are times when I worry, and there are things I would oppose that they want to do. But a lot of this just depends on one's judgments about whether America is ultimately going to be healthier with a little more religion or a little less religion. If your answer is 'a little more religion,' you can't then say 'but it can't be Christian religion!' "

I tell him that most of those I've interviewed don't keep up Jewish rituals, and I wonder if he thinks Jews can be Jewish without them. "I could imagine, two generations from now, people being Jewish who don't light candles. But I think it would be hard, if you didn't do anything at home and didn't go to synagogue; you're really then depending on an ethnic or intellectual identity. I think if you don't have that basic ritual, it's just hard to make the kids see what it's really about and you yourself tend to fall away—things come up, it's inconvenient. So I tend to agree that it's worth preserving some level of ritual. At least seder, but maybe a little more . . . I would say that on the whole, when one looks back, I regret not having done a little more. Of course it's easy to say in hindsight. At the time we were busy doing other things and the kids were doing other things. But if you do more, the kids can always still decide to drift away on their own. Whereas, if you don't give them more, it's hard for them to come back."

Kyra Sedgwick

"THE JOKE ABOUT MY MOTHER was that she was an anti-Semitic Jew," actor Kyra Sedgwick says with a smile, sitting on a large sofa in the Manhattan apartment she shares with her husband, actor Kevin Bacon, and their two children, Sosie, twelve, and Travis, fifteen. Sedgwick, thirty-nine when we meet, is dressed in black leather pants and wears a pocket watch as a necklace. "My mother's first marriage was to a very WASPy guy—my father. My last name is Sedgwick, so I always thought of myself as nothing: neither Episcopalian nor Jewish. When my mother got remarried to my stepfather, Ben Heller [a successful New York art dealer], we started to have Passover. He was very religious in his way. He talked often about what it meant to be a Jew, especially during Passover, and it moved me: It meant being responsible for your actions, for the community, giving back. I felt that way as a child anyway: responsible for the world, solemn in a lot of ways, serious. So his words rang true to me."

Sedgwick grew up in New York City and started acting at the age of sixteen in the soap opera *Another World*. She went on to such roles as Tom Cruise's high school girlfriend in *Born on the Fourth of July*, Paul Newman's daughter in *Mr. and Mrs. Bridge*, and Julia Roberts's sister in *Something to Talk About*.

"I don't know from what age—but I guess it was my early teens on, I really embraced being a Jew," says Sedgwick. "That didn't mean being religious, but it really meant rejecting my father and his religion. He was Episcopalian and every once in a blue moon someone he knew would die and he would ask us to go to church and I thought it was real hypocrisy. The more I learned about it, the more I felt like, all you had to do was ask for God's forgiveness and you could do all sorts of heinous things. And I didn't like what had been done in the name of Christianity. I was really rejecting what I perceived as my father's repression and his 'WASPy' upbringing. So I was sticking it in his face pretty much: 'I'm Jewish; I'm a Jew.' I remember when I first said that to him, it really took him aback and he was sad and offended by it. I remember feeling powerful and strong about it, and knew that he would fight me on it, but I distinctly felt, 'I feel like a Jew inside. I really do. I can't so much put into words what it means to me, except that I feel it very deeply and intensely.'

"When I was seventeen, I did a movie about the Holocaust [*War and Love*]. It was a movie that no one ever saw; it was not very good. We shot a lot in Hungary, but we also went to Poland and actually filmed at Auschwitz. And that was hugely powerful for me. From that moment on, I became obsessed with the Holocaust. It was actually a horrible time for me."

The "obsession" was more than a phase. "I got home from Poland and honestly, I had survivor's guilt. I know that sounds unbelievable, but it really was what it felt like for me. I felt like, 'How could this have happened? How could I be living and eating and happy when all these people—?' " She stops. "I began to track down survivors, and survivors were attracted to me because of the movie and they knew who I was—" Her daughter has just poked her head in. "Hey, baby!" Sedgwick calls to her. Kevin Bacon ambles in behind her. "Hi, honey." Sedgwick smiles. He introduces himself, then goes into the kitchen.

"So I spent a lot of time with these survivors," she continues. "I went over to their houses, and I hung out with them, and I asked them about their experiences. And they wanted to talk—that was the common thread with all of them: They wanted to tell me what happened. My stepfather, Ben, always talked about the Jews being the Chosen People and what that seemed to mean was that they had to be driven out of places where they were living, treated horribly, and yet they still believed in their religion, in God. That had meaning for me—the fact that they were persecuted for it, they had to fight for it, and yet they still embraced their religion and died for it. When I was with these survivors, some of them believed in God, some of them no longer did. I was having a lot of conversations with God, thinking, 'How could you have done this?' I feel like in a way that kind of cemented my relationship with Judaism."

I ask Sedgwick how she managed to link up with survivors in the middle of New York City. She says that was the easy part. "They just gravitated toward me. I mean literally—I'd be on West Seventy-second Street and they're *all there*. I'd get on a bus, and there would be a woman getting on behind me and she'd be having a little trouble, and I'd help her on the bus, and she'd say, 'Thank you,' and she'd have an accent and I knew she was old enough to have been there, and I'd say, 'Where are you from?' 'Oh, I'm from Poland.' And then it would all just start spilling out. Every book I picked up—Elie Wiesel's, for example—I kept trying to find an answer, a reason why it happened; for some reason, I immersed myself in it.

"There was this woman, Isabella Leitner, who has an amazing story. She wrote a book [*Fragments of Isabella: A Memoir of Auschwitz*], and she really fastened on to me. When she wrote a play based on her book, she asked me to do a reading of it, which I did. Survivors want so desperately just to tell their story. And if you're there to listen, and if you're a celebrity of any kind, certainly that makes you even more valuable to them. They want their stories to live on."

I wonder how Sedgwick's mother reacted to her fixation at such a young age. "I'm sure that she felt for me," Sedgwick replies. "I know that she was sad for me. But she didn't minimize it. It's not like she said anything like, 'You're only half-Jewish' or 'What's the matter with you?' I think she knew that I was a deeply sensitive person, and that was part of whatever I was."

It was her Jewish stepfather, Ben, who finally helped her snap out of it. "He was in World War II and had been there at Dachau and freed some of the prisoners. He never talks about it. And he's the one who said to me, 'You just need to suck it up and move on.' To me that's such the Ben Heller Jewish experience: 'Life's tough, suck it up, move on.' "

And that calmed her? "Yes it did. Because he said to me, 'I was there; I know what it was like, too. And it was horrible.' He wasn't invalidating me at all; he was a comrade-in-arms. He said, 'It's horrible, there's no way to ever explain it; it sticks with me for the rest of my life—I can never get away from it, but you have to move on.' "

I wonder if playing Rose White in *Miss Rose White*—made for television in 1992—brought her obsession back to her. In the story, Rose—formerly Reyzel Weiss—escapes Poland before Hitler's invasion but has to leave her mother and sister behind; years later, an Americanized Rose is startled to find that her sister—played by Amanda Plummer—survived. They have a wrenching reunion. "I was in a better place and I could deal with it more," says Sedgwick, who was nominated for a Golden Globe Award for her performance. "And I was very happy I wasn't playing the Amanda Plummer role, because that role would have put me right back there in a really bad way."

Though she never went "back there," she still holds a prejudice against Germany. "It's unfair," she concedes, "but I can't stand the German language. And no, I won't buy a German car, I don't want to go to Germany if I don't have to. That's so ingrained."

Her daughter, Sosie, reappears. "Hey sweetie, I'll be done in a few minutes. Love you."

I ask Sedgwick if she's aware of who is Jewish in her industry. "Very much so. And so often people will say to me, 'Oh my God, you're Jewish! Of course!' And I love saying, 'Yeah' "—Sedgwick dons a heavy New York accent—" 'I'm a New Yawk Jeew! Bawn and raised!' I respond to a familiar openness in other Jews—a willingness to talk, a loud, boisterous, lively quality. A lot of people in Hollywood are Jewish, and I feel so proud to be able to say I am too. Because I look like a WASP. I don't know that I've ever played a really WASPy character yet; that's the thing that's going to scare the shit out of me."

I point out that it's what's made Sedgwick commercial: She can play the pretty, blond, all-American girl. "I think that it's been easier for me in movies that way," she agrees. "And you know what, it's easier for me in the world generally." She says that someone close to her—she prefers not to name him—recently said something with a whiff of prejudice. "He said he wants to marry a Jewish girl, but he doesn't want a girl who looks 'too Jewish.' " She shakes her head.

As for her own wedding to Bacon in 1988, it did not include a Jewish ceremony. "We had a judge marry us. I didn't want God involved in any way because I don't know who God is for me. The thing is, I don't really know how to pass on any kind of feelings of what it means to be a Jew to my children. There are so many great things about it: the fact that we have Yom Kippur where you spend the whole day in atonement, thinking about your mistakes and taking responsibility for them, maybe even doing something about them. I keep coming back to the word 'responsibility,' but I think it's such a big part of being Jewish. It's not getting away with anything. It's knowing in your heart what you do and don't do, about being a good citizen. I'm religious in the way I treat people, the way I expect people to treat others, the way I contribute to the world." Sedgwick is involved in various organizations, including the Children's Hope Foundation, which trains volunteers to work with children affected by HIV, and the Epic Theatre Center, which works with inner-city kids.

As for carrying on the one religious holiday she observed growing up—Passover—her kids go to seder with her every year. "I think that they get some meaning from that. But I would feel hypocritical to suddenly start—it's perhaps shameful in some way—but I would feel that suddenly starting to light the Hanukkah lights or do the Jewish rituals would be irresponsible in some way."

She says her children haven't received any religion from their dad's side, either. "I wish that I had had a faith," says Sedgwick, "and I wish that I really believed that there was something other than ourselves that we could count on and listen to for guidance."

I ask if she's ever been drawn to any other religions—particularly the ones in vogue, such as Buddhism or kabbalah. "Yoga," she says. "But that's pretty much it. I'm in the process of trying to open myself to spirituality a little bit and asking for some guidance in that, because I feel like I need it. I want to at least be able to hear something."

Max Frankel

MAX FRANKEL PHOTOGRAPHED BY BILL CUNNINGHAM/NY TIMES

DESPITE THE FACT that Max Frankel, former executive editor of the *New York Times*, barely escaped Hitler's Germany at the age of eight; despite his clear recollection of Nazi guards terrorizing his father's dry goods store and preventing his family—and so many others—from going to the movies, sitting in a coffeehouse, or swimming at the public beach, Frankel, now seventy-five, harbors no bitterness. "The only explanation I have for that is that it's a survival mechanism," he says, sitting in the Upper West Side apartment he shares with his wife of sixteen years, *Times* Metro columnist Joyce Purnick. "My survival mechanism is a kind of cockeyed optimism. It's not a lack of caring; it's 'I'm bigger than they. I can outlast this.'" He traces his lack of vengeance to his mother, Mary. "My father was more the angry type." But he wasn't around to influence young Max. "He was gone for a long time."

Eight years, to be exact. Frankel's family was arrested—along with other Jews of Polish origin—in late October 1938, and they were taken to Poland. Max and his mother got permission to return to Germany to pick up visas for the United States, but Max's father, Jakob, who was supposed to join them two months later, was arrested in Poland by the Soviets. He ended up being sent to a Siberian labor camp, where he almost died. After the war, in 1946—eight years after he'd last seen his wife and son—he managed to join his family in New York.

During the interim, the young Max endeavored to become an American as quickly and completely as possible. "Assimilation as a refugee kid was a total escape from the unpleasantness of the past," Frankel says, "and total immersion in the uncritical acceptance of everything American. This was a great country: You could breathe, you had total opportunity. I remember fiercely debating my elders in the neighborhood up in Washington Heights who were complaining about this or that in this country, and I just wouldn't hear of it. I never even realized how far my assimilationist tendencies went; I mean, I wouldn't speak German back to my mother, even though she would talk to me in German because she wanted me to be able to communicate with my father when he eventually joined us. And I never even dated a German girl—a refugee girl. I was hell-bent to get out of the neighborhood—to go to a different school than all the neighborhood kids. Now that's assimilation with a vengeance."

Frankel sits in an easy chair with his arms folded and the remains of yesterday's February blizzard visible behind him between wooden Venetian blinds. His carpeted study is muted except for the computer's hum and its occasional chime signaling an incoming e-mail. Frankel is wearing Mephisto sandals over gray socks.

I wonder if his mother felt wounded by his hunger to assimilate. "I think my father found it harder to accept," he says. "My lack of dependence on his counsel."

Still, he had made a pact with his mother that when his father finally joined them, they would let him reassume his role as head of the family. "It rankled," Frankel recalls. "He and I had our blowups." But the son sympathized with the father's displacement. "I understood why my mother wanted it that way, how hard it was to reinsert him into the family."

Frankel's childhood—absorbing hatred so young, being without siblings and for years without his father—clearly accounts for his early independence and his lack of sentimentality. "I not only learned to be alone as a very young kid, but in one sense, I invented my own cheering section. I'm sure it made me fiercely competitive. My form of retribution and vengeance was the feeling I had when I finally returned to my hometown in Germany with an American passport: 'Take that, you bastards.' "

Still, there was never generalized hatred. "To me there were no such things as 'Germans': There were Bad Germans and Good Germans. I only saw them as people, trapped in a ghastly system." When Frankel hears people write off an entire population because of the Holocaust, he has no patience for it. "I consider it stupid and unthinking and ultimately a lack of experience," he says in a clipped tone. "You see it repeated in people now thinking that there's something unique or special about Muslims or Arabs."

"I have a Hobbesian view of humanity," he goes on. "I think our worst instincts are terrible and the beauty of our Jewish ancestry is that they invented the concept of law to inhibit the worst human instincts." It is that contribution that moves Frankel. "Jews codified a set of values and laws, synthesized in the Ten Commandments, that form the roots of our culture as I see it," he says. "There is ultimately no way of explaining the American Declaration of Independence, the Bill of Rights, and the concept of the Constitution—no way of divorcing that from the ethical precepts that are embodied in ancient Jewish religion. They were *preserved* in Christianity. But it is the concept of *law*, as opposed to *love*—which is the Christian contribution, in my view—which permits the peace. It's romantic and it's lovely to love one another, but my observation is that we don't. And so we better just restrain those other instincts with laws. And that's an incredible contribution to thought. So if I have pride as a Jew, it's because of that contribution. But our own people have betrayed it so often that I cannot claim any other kind of superiority."

When have Jews betrayed it? "Most obviously in Israel today. I think we're tone-deaf to the needs of other people for law, order, stability, and equal rights. I just don't think Jews are any better than any other group; that's all I'm saying."

Frankel knows firsthand why Jews needed Israel as a refuge, but finds great fault with the country's end result. "I'm beginning to wonder now whether the imperative of those years, and of that generation—of those survivors of Hitler—whether it was ultimately wise to have yielded to that need and to create this artificial state and implant it in the midst of such hostility. I was all for it, because these people had no place to go. And the whole notion that we could finally write our own passport and have our own flag and our own jails for our own criminals I thought was crucial. In this horrible world, I guess it is still crucial and still important. But nationalism is also the curse of our time. And the Israelis are proving the two-sidedness of that proposition.

"So yes, I have an emotional feeling toward Israel, the extreme of which I felt when that business was going on in the U.N. about defining Zionism as racism. I personally stopped—even broke off—relations with a couple of diplomats that I knew whom I had fond relations with, and who, out of a sense of loyalty to their own governments, were supporting that movement. But I really felt it so offensive, that if they insisted on defending it in private to me, I said, 'I don't want to have anything to do with it anymore.' Not because I was a Zionist, but because I felt they were just defining the people who had found a haven in Israel as inhuman."

I want to clarify his comments, because readers may take from them that he fundamentally questions whether the establishment of the state of Israel was a mistake. "History is history," he says. "Maybe Texas shouldn't belong to the United States either and maybe the Mexicans have a right to keep on complaining about it. And maybe half of Poland shouldn't have been moved into Russia and half of Germany back into Germany; no, I don't play those games. I'm a hardheaded realist. What is, is, and every people has to deal with the hand they're dealt. I just think that Israel happened as an accidental response to Hitler. It would have never become what it became and Zionism would have never succeeded if it hadn't been for the guilt of the rest of the world. I understand that. So in that purely emotional sense, I understand the resentment of some of the Palestinians and other Arabs. But, tough. They have enough territory in which to make do. And maybe Puerto Rico should have been, like Cuba, independent. But it isn't. I have no patience for people who want to undo history; it can't be done."

Frankel's opinions on Israel roiled some readers when he wrote for the *Times* editorial page and later became its editor. "The attacks didn't sting," he says, "I just felt, 'How stupid these people were,' saying that I didn't know who Hitler was, that I was a self-hating Jew. That just proved the total incoherence and the stupidity." He corrects himself: "It's wrong to call people stupid; they weren't stupid, they were just unthinking."

I tell him that Mike Wallace and Don Hewitt related a similar story: They were assailed as being lesser Jews when their *60 Minutes* reports were perceived as anti-Israel. He explains why those journalists and he as well were considered traitors. "The first rule of the shtetl is you don't let the goyim see you divided," Frankel says. "You fight like hell among your-selves, but you must present a united front to the rest of the world."

I ask him if his willingness to be a Jew who criticized Israel affected his Jewish friendships. "I wouldn't say that, no. But it's probably kept me away from certain circles. You know, we sent our kids to Hebrew school, but I protested vigorously when the school was being corralled into protest marches downtown on various political issues. I not only wouldn't let the kids go, but I really argued strenuously at the synagogue. Because it was 'Is-rael all for one; they can do no wrong.' It was propagandizing the kids in a way that I thought harmful. It made them unthinking Jews, which I used to think was something of a contradiction, but it isn't. Regarding my friendships, I guess it's fair to say that I was never attracted to the all-out Zionist circles. So it's not only that it disrupted friendships, I never gave myself the opportunity for friendship."

Would he say his closest friends are Jewish? Frankel pauses, clearly run-ning the names through his head. "Yeah, they are," he replies. He doesn't see that as significant. "I think it's just a function of New York and the media."

Frankel's dispassion when it comes to Israel and to German guilt car-ries over to his lack of spirituality. "I can't pray," he says simply. "After my bar mitzvah, I went to synagogue for my parents' sake," he says, "and then I went for my first wife's sake [Tobi Frankel died of brain cancer in 1987], and then for my children's sake, because I did want them to be exposed." His son David is a film and television director; his daughter, Margot, a graphic designer; and his son Jon a former network correspondent who now has his own business making video biographies; all three have children of their own. "I couldn't very well push my kids—I was a bad enough ex-ample at home for being unreligious and got hell for that—so I went along with it and tolerated it. I'd go to temple once a year, and we'd have good seders. We did these things out of kind of a feel-good emotional sense of identification; 'keep the candle in the window' kind of thing. But at syna-gogue per se, I do not find it psychologically important. So I don't pray."

He did, however, give his children a Jewish education, and hopes they do the same for theirs. "I wanted my kids to be able to feel emotionally that they belong to this diverse group of people known as Jews. And if I sud-denly had to, God forbid, care for my grandchildren, I would do the same thing. I think it gives them a sense of belonging and the knowledge to understand what it is they're rejecting, without hating themselves.

"I still think they need that feeling of 'where do I come from and what is it that I'm saying *no* to in this society'? *I* at least know what I'm *not* doing. The fact that I can walk into any synagogue anywhere in the world and open the book and know where they are and what they're doing and why they're doing it, even though it doesn't touch me emotionally at all, I think that makes me a better rejecter of religion than if I were somehow on the outside looking in."

Would it be important to him that his grandchildren call themselves Jews? "I don't go through life saying 'I'm a Jew,' and I don't think the most devout Jew does. Our own sense of our own uniqueness goes much deeper than that. We only need these labels for the sake of relations with others. It's a way of saying what we're not."

But what makes a Jew Jewish if the rituals are abandoned in the end? "What makes us anything?" Frankel asks. "What makes us American? I don't go around saluting the flag or wearing a flag. It is a set of beliefs, emotional attachments, comforts. I'm much more a journalist than I am a Jew," Frankel continues. "A journalist that stands apart and feels a need to observe others and not ultimately get swept up in all their passions because I want to write about them accurately and I want to understand them—that part of me is much stronger than any sense of affiliation with anything."

I realize each individual Jew isn't responsible for the sustenance of his or her people, but if indeed it is true, as I'm finding, that many high-achieving Jews—our country's role models in many instances—are less and less religious, what will be the outcome? Does Frankel think the Jewish people need the Jewish religion—at least to some degree—in order to carry on? "I don't know," Frankel replies. "What is it that is oozing the religion out of us? I think it's education: learning to question. That's only the half of it. The other is that the great American colleges are melting pots and that's where Jews and Christians and others begin to treat each other as equals and the distinctions begin to disappear. And that's why all this intermarriage and the cultural bonds that are formed among educated Americans are so much stronger than wherever they happened to be dragged to church when they were kids. So I think religion will continue to erode as an experience, and I don't think that church attendance or even holiday observances will be anything but a remnant of another era."

So despite his personal brush with a train to the concentration camp—
or perhaps because of it—Frankel is not anxious about Jewish survival, nor
haunted by the sense that the worst could happen again? "I find myself reacting very profoundly and emotionally to things like *Schindler's List* and
The Pianist," Frankel says. "Because I was literally there until a month before the gates closed. And so the notion of having escaped by a hair—and
if Mother had turned left instead of right, I wouldn't be here—in the one
sense, that's a very liberating feeling; it makes you very cocky. It makes you
feel that you're walking with some lucky star over your head. And on the
other hand, you realize how precarious life really is."

Alan and Marilyn Bergman

MARILYN AND ALAN BERGMAN PHOTOGRAPHED BY TERRY O'NEILL

ALAN AND MARILYN BERGMAN, who have written most of Barbra Streisand's most famous lyrics—from "The Way We Were" to "You Don't Bring Me Flowers"—are sitting with me in the attic level office of their re-laxed Beverly Hills home (on a high shelf, three Oscars, three Emmys, two Grammys), and somehow this couple has made me cry.

Alan, eighty, was just telling a simple anecdote: how he started a ritual, years ago at the Jewish weddings he attended. "I always pick up the bro-ken glass," he says. "No matter whose wedding it is—"

"He's done this for years—" Marilyn interjects.

"—and I put it in a glass box and we give it to the couple on their first anniversary. And it means so much to them. That connection—with each other, with history, with tradition. It's so meaningful."

In an instant I'm aware that I'm unaccountably choked up. I tell my-self it would be ridiculous to show it, and then the next moment, my head is in my hands. "I'm sorry," Alan says, "I didn't mean to—"

"Oh dear," says Marilyn, seventy-six, who sounds teary now, too. "What is this about? Do you know why you're crying?"

I'm not sure I do. It has something to do with a flash of recognition—of being linked to them and to anyone else Jewish: It's about doing the things that for centuries have been done. That's all. Those small acts, in and of themselves, bind and extend us. Stamping the glass under the *chuppah* is just one custom—most people don't even know what it symbolizes—but it makes a wedding Jewish, one couple to the next. As I imagined Alan bending over those shards, I suddenly wished someone had done that for me and my husband—and realized at the same time how that particular moment was irretrievable.

I have since learned that Alan's gesture has become a cottage industry: one Web site after another—yidworld.com, judaism.com, jewishbazaar.com, etc.—sells keepsakes for your crushed wedding glass: candlestick holders or mezuzot filled with the shavings you send in. When Marilyn mentions that she's seen similar souvenirs advertised in *The New Yorker*, Alan seems mildly nonplussed. But that's all beside the point. Something has been triggered for me, and the Bergmans are immediately parental, proffering Kleenex and nodding their heads empathetically.

I have to remind myself that these are people who hang out with "Barbra"—who, when I'd first arrived, told me they were exhausted from a late-night recording session with Streisand the night before. These two decidedly *haimish* grandparents are the songwriting team that became the first ever to receive three out of five Oscar nominations for best song in the same year, who penned the themes for *The Summer of '42, Same Time, Next Year, Tootsie*, the television series *Maude, Alice*, and *Good Times*. Marilyn leans back with her feet up in her leather recliner—a casual throne of sorts—with her upswept hair and black turtleneck, looking majestic and earthy at the same time. Alan's lanky frame is in an upright chair, catty-corner to his wife; his eyeglasses are too large for his face, but he's worn the same-size frames for decades.

The only time they've confronted their Judaism in their work was when they wrote the lyrics for *Yentl*, Streisand's 1983 star turn as the Jewish girl so eager for a yeshiva education that she goes undercover as a boy.

"When we did *Yentl*, we did a lot of research," Alan explains. They studied with two rabbis—one Reform, one Orthodox. "And as a result of that," Alan continues, "a lot of waters were stirred in you," he gestures to his wife, who nods. "It was the first time that there was ever some kind of historical context for me," she says. "We met once a week for a year—Barbra, Alan, and I and a few other friends."

"Laura put the Bible in a context of dreams," Marilyn recalls, speaking of Laura Geller, senior rabbi at Temple Emmanuel in Beverly Hills. "Laura said, 'When you have a dream, you don't demand of it that it be linear, logical, literal, sequential—you don't demand that of it.' She said, 'That is the way the Bible should be read: It is a dream of a people.' I never had heard anything like that and it really clicked. It suddenly became such a personal way to view the heart and soul of Judaism."

I'm curious as to whether they were worried about the movie being too Jewish; that had to be a concern. Marilyn says it was embraced more readily by non-Jewish audiences. "It was interesting; the picture wasn't wildly successful in the places where we thought it would be—the Jewish enclaves like parts of Florida and New York. The most successful places were in the hinterland, the Midwest."

"I can tell you a very interesting story about that," Alan chimes in, with an anecdote that illustrates the reluctance of Jewish audiences to openly embrace the film. "*Yentl* opened here for some hospital charity—a very rich, affluent group, mostly Jewish. And they *sat on their hands*. Because what was clearly going on in their minds was, 'What are the goyim going to think?' "

"Yes," says Marilyn, "That's the important point: Jewish self-hatred and shame and paranoia. Everything is focused through 'Oh, how does this look to gentile eyes?' "

"Three days later," Alan continues, "Barbra, Marilyn, and I sneaked into a theater in Westwood—nobody noticed us. We sat in the back. And it was, I would say, maybe thirty-five percent black."

"Young—" Marilyn adds.

"Yeah, young," Alan agrees. "And when the character, Yentl, gets accepted to the yeshiva, they stood up and they cheered, 'Yay!! Go!!' It was a completely different reception."

"In *Yentl*," Alan continues, "the emphasis, so to speak, was a feminist approach to that story, more than the Jewish background. And maybe we didn't think about the Jewishness—"

"Sure we did," Marilyn scoffs. "Of course we did."

"About worrying how it would sell—" Alan finishes his thought.

"Well, we knew that, by definition, it was going to be a niche kind of movie," Marilyn says. "That it wasn't going to be a hugely popular kind of movie."

And how conscious were they of their songs—the music—having a Jewish feel and sound?

"It doesn't," Alan says definitively. "That's why we chose Michel Legrand." (French composer Legrand wrote over two hundred film scores, including *Wuthering Heights* and *Lady Sings the Blues*.) "When the three of us were talking about a composer," Marilyn adds, "we didn't want, you know, *The Yiddle with a Fiddle* music."

"Or even the Broadway conception of *Fiddler [on the Roof]*," Alan cuts in, "which is terrific, but we didn't want that either." Marilyn explains: "We felt that *Yentl* was a story of Middle Europe at a particular time. They happened to be Jews—but really it was an interior monologue of this young woman, and a great deal of it was very romantic, and I think we decided that what would make it maybe more accessible—we probably did have accessibility in mind—was a composer who wrote European, romantic music."

"And a love song, who would write for the instrument that Barbra has," Alan says.

Judaism has not figured into their work since. In fact, the Bergmans have written Christmas songs, such as "Christmas Memories," with lyrics such as "*Singing carols, stringing popcorn, making footprints in the snow/Memories, Christmas memories, they're the sweetest ones I know.*" "I felt so deprived of that as a child," Marilyn admits, "and I thought, 'I can divorce it from any religious significance.' Of course, hanging a wreath on my door, I would never do that."

But her own daughter, Julie, did. That is, until Julie's husband took it down. "It was only *firs*," Julie says with a laugh (she's stopped by with her five-year-old daughter, Emily). "Not a green ribbon or anything. It was just like a harvest thing. And my husband took it off and he put a note in its place on the front door that said, 'The only wreath that will ever hang here is Aretha Franklin.'" They all laugh.

Julie describes her parents' Judaism as more political than spiritual (Malcolm X's daughter was at their seders, and their rabbi would often deliver provocative sermons). But she'll never forget her father's annual, dependable comment about generational ties, which he imparted every year in temple on the High Holy Days. "I remember him always leaning over to me and whispering, 'You know, Jews all over the world are doing *exactly this* right now.' " Julie says. "And I'd always roll my eyes—'Yeah, yeah, yeah, you told me that already.' But you get the importance of that when you're older."

We're eating rye bread. I haven't mentioned the rye bread—which is almost as memorable as my imprudent tears. When I'd first arrived, I mentioned that I'd been to L.A.'s Jewish deli, Langer's, and the Bergmans insisted I sample Langer's rye bread. Before I can stop him, Alan has disappeared to fetch two slices because I simply must try both the regular and the thin. Not toasted—"This kind you don't toast," Alan says solemnly (it would mar the bread's integrity?)—and a schmear of cream cheese is required.

Maybe it was the setting, the topic, the familiarity of a Jewish family pushing food on me, but it was the freshest rye bread I'd ever tasted. (Alan says it's "twice baked," whatever that means.)

While I'm chewing, Julie describes how she happened to end up marrying a Jewish man even though it never mattered much to her parents. After she leaves, however, her father says it did. "It would have driven me . . ." He pauses to find the right words. "I would not have been happy about it."

Alan and Marilyn were coincidentally born in the same hospital—Brooklyn Jewish—and they both describe childhood bouts with prejudice. "I remember feeling such gentile envy," says Marilyn. "Seeing these girls on Sunday morning in their white dresses and their veils like brides, going to communion—oh, I wanted it so badly. And I made my mother buy me a cotton slip with lace on the bottom—she didn't know why she was buying it for me—and one Sunday morning, I put on this slip and I put a sweater over it, because it was, after all, a slip, and I went out thinking I was going to be able to join in this beautiful tradition. And the girls laughed at me and said, 'Oh, Marilyn's out in her underwear!' I must have been about five or six at the most."

Alan was older when he felt shut out. "I was a pretty good Ping-Pong player, and I wanted to learn how to play tennis. The Nationals, which were the predecessor of the U.S. Open, took place in Forest Hills, in a white-glove club which was restricted. I went there—from Brooklyn, you had to take a bus and a trolley—and asked, 'Who hires the ball boys?' I figured if I was a ball boy, I could learn how to play. And the man in charge said, 'What's your name?' I said, 'Alan Bergman.' He said, 'Go home.' Well, I had chutzpah in those days and I said, 'Well, I'm a pretty good Ping-Pong player, I've won a couple championships; I'm going to go to the *Brooklyn Daily Eagle* and tell them you won't let me in because I'm Jewish.' He said, 'You come back tomorrow.' I said, 'I can't come back tomorrow; it's too expensive.' And he finally relented and I was a ball boy for two years and that's how I learned how to play tennis."

"He's a very good player," Marilyn interjects.

"Well . . ." Alan demurs.

Marilyn's grandmother was a Russian immigrant who was firmly Orthodox. "All I remember about religion was that it was inconvenient and unpleasant," Marilyn says. "God forbid you should put the wrong fork in the wrong drawer or use the can of kosher soap with the red on it, when I should have been using the blue. I just remember it was rigid."

But when she went to Israel for the first time, she was overcome. "I remember being on the airplane with the Israelis—when they sighted land, they started singing 'Hatikva.' Well . . ." Her eyes fill. "We stepped off the plane and you saw Jewish soldiers and Jewish policemen and Jewish everything: It was overwhelming. But look what they did, how they fucked it up.

"I always talk about this," she continues, "but George Steiner—the philosopher—wrote a piece in 1948 about his fears about the creation of the state of Israel. And he said the reason that Jews all over the world have made contributions in all kinds of disciplines—way in excess of their population—is because they were outsiders. They couldn't own land, couldn't go into business, couldn't be soldiers. They didn't have a flag or an anthem or a boundary. Being on the outside, they were observers, commentators—through art or whatever else. And he warned the Jews of Israel that this could be the beginning of the end. And oh boy, I think about that piece more often than I care to. Very prescient and true."

For the Bergmans, longtime progressives, politics and religion seem inextricable. "If you take the Jews out of it, the liberal movement is a very lonely place," Marilyn says. "That's true everywhere. Which is one of the reasons I think we're a politically endangered species . . . I don't understand how a black woman like Condoleezza Rice—how can somebody who comes from an oppressed minority, whether they be Jewish or black—can identify with the very forces that suppress their people? It's a contradiction in terms. I think if this administration should be elected again [we met before the 2004 election], I don't think we will recognize this country. I don't think anybody of any political persuasion that *I* can identify with will be safe. And I don't think that's paranoid.

"The larger question you're getting at is deeper, though: What does it mean to feel Jewish? I don't know. It's such a rich soup."

"I'm sure if you would ask people," Alan says, " 'Would you rather be something other than Jewish?' you would get the answer, 'No.' "

"Oh, it's inconceivable," says Marilyn. "It's essential."

Alan Dershowitz

TREKKING ACROSS HARVARD SQUARE in the driving rain to visit law professor Alan Dershowitz, I can't help but feel I'm braving the elements to get to America's Über Jew.

Dershowitz's celebrity derives not just from having been appointed to Harvard Law School's faculty at a mere twenty-five-year-old in 1963—he's now sixty-seven—nor from defending such notorious figures as O. J. Simpson, Michael Milken, Mike Tyson, Leona Helmsley, and Claus Von Bulow. His renown was also cultivated from his big mouth—the nation's reliable megaphone for Jewish interests, showing no hesitation to cry anti-Semitism when he sees it (even when others don't), and defining—even embracing—the prototype of the brilliant, pushy Jew.

When I enter his disheveled office, he announces that he can give me only a half hour because he has to leave for the annual reunion of his oldest childhood friends—all Jewish—from Brooklyn. "This year we're going to Foxwoods," he says with a smile, referring to the hotel and casino in Connecticut. (Other years they've gathered at his summer home on Martha's Vineyard.) Dershowitz is rushed, but he doesn't seem as manic as usual. His hair is tamer than I remember it from his countless media appearances or from Ron Silver's portrayal of him in *Reversal of Fortune* in 1990. He looks downright suburban-conventional, wearing a blue V-neck sweater and tilting back in his black office chair.

"I'm a kind of anti-theological Jew," he says, rocking. "I don't buy into the theology. On the other hand, I have enormous respect for Judaism as a civilization. I look to Jewish sources. For example, I have a very large collection of responsa. What is responsa? It's the Jewish common law. I don't care what the rabbis say about whether you can mix milk with meat, but I'm fascinated by the way they answer deep moral questions. So, when I have a complex philosophical question, I'm likely to look to Jefferson *and* Maimonides without any feeling of inconsistency; they're both brilliant men. In fact, I even look to Jesus, who was a great Jewish rabbi—not Christ, but the rabbinical Jesus. I teach a course in scriptural sources of justice. Students ask me all the time how come I'm always quoting the Torah and the Talmud in my classes, and I throw back at them, 'How come you're always quoting Blackstone?' [Sir William Blackstone was the eighteenth-century British jurist whose writings greatly influenced American law.] We look to what sources we find meaningful or relevant."

Dershowitz had an Orthodox upbringing in Brooklyn and a tight group of buddies who were determined to succeed not by joining the crowd but by beating them. "We were out to prove a point," he wrote in his 1991 book, *Chutzpah.* "Not to become assimilated."

They created the Knight House in high school—a sports team made up entirely of Orthodox schoolmates. "Let me tell you, the greatest thrill in my life was when Knight House won the athletic championships at Brooklyn College." Dershowitz beams. "When us nerdy Orthodox Jews beat all those kids . . ." He shakes his head, still marveling today. "Of course, I considered the people we were beating to be the WASPs of the world, when in fact they were only Conservative and Reform Jews, a couple of Italians, and a few Irish kids. But when we became the athletic champs, it was like Israel winning the Six Day War. We were defying all the stereotypes."

He never felt like he was missing out on the popular clique or the prettiest girls. "I think our attitude was more, 'Why don't we run one of our—quote—"girls" as homecoming queen?' We thought that the young women we were going out with were as beautiful as anyone else. We never said, 'You look too Jewish.' And it's interesting that all the eight couples—all sixteen of us—have very different views of the world, different views on Democrats, Republicans, different levels of wealth, but we all are deeply Jewish in different ways."

Dershowitz's Jewishness is no longer by the book. He abandoned morning davening, he says, because of his children. "All the ritual was for *other* people. In the beginning of my life, the 'other people' in my life were my parents, so I did it for them. Then, when the more important people in my life became my children, I stopped doing the ritual for them. I couldn't justify it, I couldn't give them my parents' answer: 'Because that's the way we did it.' I wanted to bring my children up with a rational view of Judaism, a view which I could explain: 'Judaism is community.' And so I held on to the traditions that create community: The Shabbat dinner is a very important part of our life, for instance. Also the Passover seder, synagogue membership. But the tallis and tefillin were not an important part of my life."

He didn't want his kids to be trained in ritual he no longer practiced himself. "I didn't want to tell them, 'I'm doing this, even though I don't believe it.' I wanted to explain how everything I was doing was integrated into my life. If I have one core in my life, it's that I must be an integrated being. I tell my students all the time, 'I can't stand the idea of being a Friday, Saturday, or Sunday religious person, and then Monday through Friday at university you're a secularist, an atheist, an agnostic. You must integrate your worldviews.' My life has a theme . . . And I wanted to give that to my children—an integrated view.

"And of course it produced, as you might imagine, three very different children. One of my sons (Jamin), is virulently anti-religious, one (Elon) is moderately traditional and loves the ritual, and I have a daughter (Ella) who is too young to make judgments about it but who goes to a Jewish school—Reform." (Ella, by his second marriage to Carolyn Cohen, is thirteen at the time of our conversation, recently a bat mitzvah.)

Jamin is married to a non-Jewish woman. "The departure wasn't so important to me," he insists. "What I wanted, if I could have my preference about my children, was for my son's Jewishness to be so important to him that it would be natural for him to want to marry someone who he shared that Jewishness with. That's the way it was with me: I didn't marry my wife because I went out and picked somebody who was Jewish. I went out to pick a wife with whom I have a lot in common. I happened to meet her at a Jewish event and we have a tremendous amount in common because we had common approaches toward our Judaism. The fact that my son married someone who wasn't Jewish was a natural result of him being a rebel and rebelling particularly against the religion."

But Dershowitz points out that Jamin is still a Jew, whether he chooses to embrace Judaism or not. "His name is Dershowitz, his kids go to the Horace Mann School [which has traditionally had a large proportion of Jewish students], they live on the Upper West Side [heavily Jewish], and everybody else assumes that they're Jewish. And the kids, with the name Dershowitz, are identified as Jews whether halachically [according to Jewish law] they are or they aren't."

I try to get at whether his son's rejection of Judaism was painful at all. "I wouldn't use that description," Dershowitz replies. "I would say that it made me understand the consequences of giving children freedom. My mother is almost ninety years old. She comes with me every time I speak in New York and everybody comes over to her and says, 'You must be *schepping* [taking in] such *naches* [pride].' And she says, 'No, no, no; it's all my fault that he's not Orthodox. I let him go to Brooklyn College.' And of course she's one hundred percent right. I grew up in a very strictly Orthodox background, and if she had kept me there, I would have not known my alternatives. I wanted to give my kids the maximum alternatives and let them choose. I'm not in control of their lives."

But in his book *The Vanishing American Jew*, he writes in stronger terms about the issues raised by Jamin's marriage:

> I do not want my grandchildren and great-grandchildren to break our link with Judaism. I do not want them to become the first non-Jews in our family history . . . I want them to stay Jewish, not because Jewish is better but because Jewish is what we have been for thousands of years . . . I would not be as troubled as I obviously am about the prospect of having grandchildren who are not Jewish or who are of mixed religious heritage. But the empirical evidence suggests that the children and grandchildren of mixed marriages in which neither party converts tend to abandon their Jewish heritage.

Is he concerned with continuity in his own family—keeping the tradition alive? "I don't believe in the life-support theory of Judaism," he says, rocking again. "I don't want to keep it going just to deny Hitler a posthumous victory, as a rabbi in Canada said. If Judaism has enough that's positive to offer coming generations, then it should thrive. The theory I raise in my book *The Vanishing American Jew* is: Is it possible that Judaism can thrive only in a context of persecution? Is it possible that Judaism has never developed the tools for living in a free and open society of choice? We may never know that, because just as we thought anti-Semitism was over in the late nineties, it's coming back. And we have a lot of Jews now returning to Judaism because of French anti-Semitism. But that's not a good reason for being a Jew."

He tells a story to illustrate how Jews end up feeling more solidarity when threatened than when they're simply encouraged to embrace their heritage. "Columbia University asked me a few years ago to come and speak because the Jews were not identifying as Jews at Columbia—of all places. I said, 'I can't do it in the next month, but call me back in two months.' They called me back and said, 'We don't need you anymore; we got somebody better who came and really organized the Jewish community together: Louis Farrakhan.' When he came to speak, everybody remembered they were Jewish. That tells a very important story: Farrakhan, who preaches negatives—anti-Semitism—does a better job in bringing the Jews together than I, who preach a very positive Judaism—not a defensive or persecution-oriented Judaism."

I comment that "positive Judaism" seems to be a harder sell; many of the Jews I'm talking to feel pride in being Jewish but don't prioritize Judaism. Dershowitz nods. "In *The Vanishing American Jew*, I propose 'The Candle Theory' of Judaism: The closer you get to the flame of Judaism, the less likely you are to be a productive, successful, creative person. The great successes in Judaism are people who moved away from the flame. But the problem with that is that the further you move away from the flame, the less likely you are to have Jewish children and grandchildren. It's a great paradox. There's no answer. You need to be the right distance away. If you look at almost all the great people that Judaism has produced over time, you find that many of them do not have Jewish grandchildren. Particularly in this century."

And he doesn't perceive that as a loss? "I don't make a moral judgment about it. If it's a loss, it says something about the imperfections of Judaism. It says something about Judaism being a culture, a civilization that has proved its adaptability to crisis and persecution more than it has to openness."

Dershowitz also believes those who aspire to high achievement—and its attendant visibility—are reluctant to be pegged as overtly Jewish. "I think a lot of people want to transcend their Judaism," he says. "They want to show they're bigger and better than that. If my only—quote, unquote—'success' came as a Jew, I would think that I was limited. I didn't want to be a rabbi, after all. I wanted to be a lawyer who has influence around the world. But a very important part of me is being a *Jewish* lawyer."

He stands up. "I gave a talk the other day in New York about what it means to be a 'Jewish lawyer.' I said, 'Sandy Koufax wasn't a Jewish pitcher. Nothing about his curve ball was Jewish. He was a Jewish pitcher because of something he *didn't* do: pitch on Yom Kippur.' I'm a Jewish lawyer because of what I *do* do: My teaching is very Jewish oriented. I know the Talmud; I use it all the time. I'm a well-educated Jew, which is another distinction. I don't feel uncomfortable with my Jewishness, because I know it." And how would he describe it? The voluble professor actually pauses for a moment. "I've never found the right way of describing my Judaism," he says simply. "It's very hard. I'm not a cultural Jew and I'm not a spiritual Jew. I'm Jewish the way my friends who are black are black. When I'm in the synagogue, I don't believe a word of it and I'm totally irreligious. When I'm sitting on the beach under the stars in Martha's Vineyard, I get a leap of faith."

Wendy Wasserstein

WENDY WASSERSTEIN PHOTOGRAPHED IN 1997 BY JILL KREMENTZ

"THE ONLY CONTACT I HAD with people who were not Jews was on the Coney Island bus." Playwright Wendy Wasserstein is talking to me in her crowded neighborhood Starbucks on the Upper West Side. "There were girls in parochial school uniforms who had plaid skirts rolled up, and I thought they were fantastic. They looked great."

Wasserstein, the Pulitzer Prize–winning author of *The Heidi Chronicles* and *The Sisters Rosensweig*, is a graduate not just of Mount Holyoke College, but Brooklyn's Yeshiva of Flatbush. "For Bruce and me," she's referring to her brother, Bruce Wasserstein, head of the investment bank Lazard LLC, "the yeshiva looms large. Even my brother, who is not prone to exaggeration or hyperbole like I am, tells me that he still has nightmares about the Kitchen Ladies at the Yeshiva Flatbush." The Kitchen Ladies, she says, were dissemblers. "As you know, keeping kosher means you can't have milk with meat; so we used to have mock hamburgers, mock frankfurters. I may be eight years old, but I'm smart and I *know* that's not a hamburger and I *know* it's not a hot dog; *don't tell me that it is.*"

She says that, at the age of fifty-five, she still encounters fellow yeshiva alumni around New York City. "The estate lawyer my parents use at Simpson, Thatcher went to the yeshiva. When I was at Holyoke, I would meet people who went nearby to Yale who I remembered from yeshiva who had changed their names. I won't give you their exact names but, for example, suddenly you'd meet a guy at a dance and his name was something like Stanley Stone, and you'd think, 'Wait a minute; aren't you Shmuel Starkhas?' "

Her childhood alma mater is now called Joel Braverman High School—named after a rabbi who haunted Wasserstein as a child. "I can remember from second grade, Joel Braverman coming around on Sunday mornings—terrifying—saying, *'Did you go to shul yesterday?'* And I hadn't gone because my mother made me go to the Judy Taylor School of the Dance every Saturday instead. And I begged her, I said, 'Please, if you're going to send me to this yeshiva, let me at least go to temple!' I really thought burning bushes were going to come through the window to punish me; I thought the whole family was going to blow up. But she made me go to dancing school instead. My mother had me lying in second grade to that man. Maybe if I had gone to temple I would have become a nice doctor like the rest of the graduates."

Her mother wasn't religious but harped on Jewish pride. "I remember my mother knocking on the television when someone came on and saying, 'He's one of us.' She told me Barry Goldwater was one of us, and I thought, 'No, he's not.' But she thought his name was Goldwasser and that he was from a department store."

Wasserstein's father, Morris, a textile manufacturer, made regular contributions to Israel, and Wasserstein remembers being told that the quarters and pennies she sent there would get her name on a tree. Despite her youth, she was skeptical. "Even then I thought, 'There isn't my name on a tree somewhere. There just isn't.' "

But she did absorb her parents' lesson that true altruism was anonymous. "It wasn't about saying, 'I want my name on a plaque'; it had nothing to do with that. In fact, we knew there were pish-pish people out there—or as my mother would say, 'the hoo-hah people,' but we were not them. Definitely not them."

The "pish-pish" people still seem to piss her off: She's eager to remind them that all Jews are equal in the eyes of an anti-Semite. "The ones who pretend they're Episcopalians because they're chicer than you are, because they're classy—the fanciest Jews whose children are named 'Brooke'—to those people, I want to say, 'Listen, honey: When push comes to shove, you're Jewish and so am I, and that's the bottom line, kid.' "

When there's a Jew in the eye of a scandal, she doesn't wince for The Jews. "With Monica Lewinsky, there was a part of me that thought, 'Finally! A chubby Jewish girl is looked at as a sex object!' "

How much Jewishness would she say is in her work? A critic in London once implied there's too much. *The Heidi Chronicles* was called "too New York," Wasserstein told the *London Times*, *"The only thing 'too New York' about Heidi is maybe my last name."*

But Wasserstein is unquestionably held up as a quintessential Jewish voice in the American theater. In her early play, *Uncommon Women and Others*, the main character, Holly Kaplan, was the only Jew in her clique at WASP-heavy Mount Holyoke. The main character in *Isn't It Romantic*, Janie Blumberg, rejects the Jewish doctor her parents want her to marry. And Wasserstein has described the three siblings in *The Sisters Rosensweig* as "a self-loathing Jew, a practicing Jew, and a wandering Jew."

Wasserstein acknowledges that her characters are products of her childhood. "You know, after my friend [playwright] Martin Sherman saw *The Sisters Rosensweig*, he said, 'This is about people you knew when you were eight years old!' And I thought, 'He's correct! Like the character of Merv, the faux-furrier, for instance: I actually don't hang out with a lot of furriers, but my father was in the garment business, and that guy and the world of that guy, the warmth of that guy, the decency of him, comes from a different time to me."

I ask if she associates Jews with that kind of warmth or feels an intuitive connection with other Jews. "It depends," she responds. "When I'm around people who clearly think, 'I'm Jewier than you are because I separate the milk from the meat and I have a better sukkah than you,' I can't bear that." Wasserstein refers to the makeshift outdoor shelter constructed in honor of Sukkot, a harvest holiday. "On the other hand, yes, I do think there's a warmth, there's an irony, and there's that ability in some ways— in the good tribal way—to look at others as family. So there's an inclusiveness. I sent my daughter to the Y for a reason." The 92nd Street Y nursery school, which her daughter, Lucy Jane, attends at the time we talk, offers a kind of preparatory Jewish education. "I thought Lucy might as well know this heritage, and later she can choose whatever.' "

Wasserstein gave birth when she was forty-eight and is raising Lucy Jane as a single mother.

She's also upholding the family tradition of "taking in a show." "Not all religions or societies actually have the respect for the arts that the Jewish culture does," she says, sipping her hot drink. "On Saturdays, my parents would take me to the theater. That's what you did. And my parents gave me dancing lessons. And these were not pretentious people in any way, it was just their values."

Those values also included marriage at a young age, which Wasserstein has defied every year she's stayed single. Wasserstein told the *Los Angeles Jewish Journal* that "I am a walking *shanda*"—a disgrace—and that, when she graduated from Holyoke and the Yale School of Drama without a marriage prospect, her parents called her on the phone to sing "Sunrise, Sunset."

How important is her Jewishness? "I guess it does define my character," she says. "I'm not a religious Jew, but my sister died recently, and you do, at those times, look for spiritual love. My daughter was born premature and was in the NICU [neonatal intensive care unit] at Mount Sinai. When Lucy was in the hospital, I called all my Catholic friends, all my New Age friends, I went to Temple Emanu-El, I just thought, 'Wendy, you've just got to hit all the bases here.' I called Chris Durang [a fellow playwright whom she met at Yale Drama School]—he's in touch with all the New Age crazies—and I said, 'Call them. Get the crystals buried in the ground, whatever they do, just tell them to help.' "

While Lucy's first days felt so precarious, did being Jewish matter? "Well, yes it did because I was at *Mount Sinai Hospital* during the *High Holy Days*. I had Jane Rosenthal [who runs a film company with Robert DeNiro] bringing me her mother's brisket in the hospital room. So in some ways yes, because that was a Jewish hospital and it was the Jewish New Year and there was my friend Jane with brisket."

Lucy survived and thrived and Wasserstein has carted her to Broadway shows ever since. I ask if she's talked to Lucy about being Jewish. "I've brought it up," she says with a nod. "We celebrate everything—Hanukkah, Christmas, Valentine's Day. Just recently, we celebrated the cleaning lady getting married."

She has no problem celebrating Christmas even though her family never did ("We went to Miami instead"), but then she recoils when I ask if she gets a tree. "That I couldn't do, no," she says with a shudder. "I would think flying hams would come into my house if a tree was there."

One of Wasserstein's most successful plays, *The Sisters Rosensweig*, features perhaps her most overtly Jewish characters. Sara, the oldest—originally played by Jane Alexander—is living in London (as Wasserstein did for a while) and downplays her Jewishness; the middle sister, Gorgeous Teitelbaum—played originally by Madeline Kahn—is a gregarious president of the Jewish Sisterhood in Newton, Massachusetts, who lusts after Ferragamo shoes and constantly quotes her temple rabbi; and Pfeni, played by Frances McDormand, is a single, socially conscious travel writer. When the oldest sister, Sara, rebuffs the advances of Merv Kant—the visiting Jewish furrier from Brooklyn—he challenges her:

MERV: I don't understand what's so wrong with you, Sara. I like you.

SARA: Your world is very different from mine.

MERV: No, it's not. I changed my name from Kantlowitz, and my daughter, the Israeli captain, went to St. Paul's. And where did you come from, Sara?

SARA: Don't proselytize me, Merv.

MERV: Sara, you're an American Jewish woman living in London, working for a Chinese Hong Kong bank, and taking weekends at a Polish resort with a daughter who's running off to Lithuania!

SARA: And who are you? My knight in shining armor? The furrier who came to dinner. Why won't you give up, Merv? I'm a cold, bitter woman who's turned her back on her family, her religion, and her country! And I held so much in. I harbored so much guilt that it all made me ill and capsized in my ovaries. Isn't that the way the old assimilated story goes?

Wasserstein says *Rosensweig* played very differently in Israel than it did in New York. "It was performed in Hebrew, and I actually remembered enough Hebrew that I could tell it wasn't such a great production," she says. "Because the central issue in the *Sisters Rosensweig* was about identity, and in Israel they *know* they're Jewish."

She does worry about Israel and whether "the world really cares" that it survives. "I think that part of the world believes that if we could just move the country to Iceland or Pluto, it would be a lot easier. Or to Martha's Vineyard. That would be really nice because all the Jews would be happy and a lot of them have homes there because they're pretending that they're actually Episcopalian, so it would work out nicely. And Bill Clinton could come and play golf and everyone could shop."

Barney Frank

BARNEY FRANK, who has represented Massachusetts in the U.S. House of Representatives since 1981, told the *New York Times* back in 1996 that he's never been in the majority: "I'm a left-handed, gay Jew."

We meet over his large desk in his congressional office with its cranberry-colored carpeting. "Being Jewish made me feel like an outsider," Frank says, "but so did being gay. In my case, remember, you can't really separate out the two; and in fact, by being gay, it made me even more of an outsider, because I was an outsider even among Jews. But I think it left me better prepared to be a minority than a lot of people. I was used to it."

At sixty-five, Frank has a bit of a paunch and a little more salt in his salt-and-pepper hair, but he still retains his trademark machine gun delivery and doesn't spend a lot of time on questions he deems unworthy of reflection.

For instance, how has he reconciled Judaism and being gay? "There's nothing to reconcile," Frank shoots back. "They are both facts of my life. What's to reconcile?" Well, for example, the fact that he's a homosexual and that the Torah—in Leviticus—calls homosexuality an "abhorrence." "Well, I don't keep kosher. I eat lobster. I eat shrimp. They're all in Leviticus. I don't have a strong theological sense. I do not observe Shabbat. I don't sit around worrying about how I reconcile driving on Saturday afternoon."

Frank grew up in a "very Jewish" family that was loosely observant. "If I were ever eating bacon when my grandmother came, out of respect, we would put it away."

His parents talked to him about identity. "My father, especially, was wary of Christian society," says Frank. "I was born in 1940, so I can remember in 1947, 1948, we had a little box for the Jewish National Fund and a 'Boycott Britain' bumper sticker on the car."

Frank associates altruism and tolerance with his Jewish upbringing. "My father had a truck stop, and it was the only one in the forties and fifties where blacks were allowed to sleep overnight. I was very proud of that."

Today, Frank doesn't fast on Yom Kippur, but he doesn't go to the office either. "On Rosh Hashanah and Yom Kippur, I will not go out of the house, because I think that reflects badly. So even if I don't go to temple, I will not do anything that would undercut the ability of other Jews to be totally observant. So my schedulers know that on Rosh Hashanah and Yom Kippur, I will not be doing anything."

He doesn't celebrate Christmas. "Actually I go to a Hanukkah party every year run by Cokie Roberts." (Roberts is a senior news analyst for NPR and used to cohost ABC News' Sunday morning show.) "Cokie, who is herself very Catholic—has a husband, Stephen Roberts, who is Jewish," Frank explains. "And she invites all her Jewish friends. Talk about intermarriage: For years, the only all-Jewish couple at Cokie's Hanukkah party would be me and Herb—my ex-lover."

I ask if he gravitates socially toward other Jews. "I do. Not consciously, but a disproportionate number of my friends are Jewish. Obviously there are connections based on common backgrounds. Now that's less so with my gay friends. But with friends my own age, more of them are Jewish."

Does the same go for his romantic relationships? "It's not been a factor," Frank replies. "I've had two relationships—one for eleven years with a Jewish man and I'm now dating a Columbian who's Catholic."

His siblings married non-Jews, but they're raising their children to be Jewish. "I'm glad that they are," says Frank, whose only personal effects in his office are photographs of his nieces and nephews and a handwritten sign from one of them: "UNCLE BARNEY'S DESK"—with the S's written backward. "My brother's divorced. He just remarried a woman whose parents are Orthodox, and my mother was told about the dress code for the wedding: no cleavage and no pants suits. She said, 'At ninety, it's very flattering to be told not to be sexy.' The invitation also said the men will dance with men, the women dance with women. I showed it to my boyfriend and said, 'See, you've got to dance with me or the rabbi will be upset.' "

When the congressman is in synagogue for a wedding or for the High Holy Days, he does feel some emotional tug: "It happens anytime I put on a tallis and yarmulke." He reads Hebrew but doesn't understand it. "Last time I was in Israel—I think I was with Gay Israelis—one of them told me that I read Hebrew with a Yiddish accent." He picks up an Israeli newspaper. "Look at this." He shows me. "It's a big article about me being gay. I can read it, but I don't know what it says." He zeroes in on one sentence. "I can read this: It says, 'Dick Cheney, *abba*'—that means 'father'—'*shel*'—that means 'of'—'lesbian.' " He smiles.

I ask if Frank has ever drawn on his religion when he was in trouble. I'm obviously thinking of the low point in his career, in 1990, when he was censured by Congress for paying a male prostitute for sex and helping him get thirty-three parking tickets dismissed. "No," Frank answers. "I think Judaism is important and that it does not survive without a strong religious component, but personally I'm just not religious. To the extent that I am consciously in charge of myself, I'm very rational. My view is that you've got to *think* your way through things."

When he mulled the notion of a political career decades ago, he believed his ethnicity would prevent him from having one. "I thought being Jewish would keep me from being elected," he says. "When I was growing up, there were very few Jews in elective office. Today, I've seen political anti-Semitism largely crumble. Being Jewish is just not a factor anymore."

Frank once said that he didn't reveal his sexuality when he was first elected to Congress (he came out publicly in 1987), but he couldn't hide his religion. "I outed myself with a bar mitzvah," he told the *Washington Post* in 1998. "It was too late to be in the closet as a Jew."

I have to ask about the time his colleague Representative Dick Armey from Texas called him "Barney Fag"—allegedly thanks to a slip of the tongue: Does Frank agree with *New York Times* writer Frank Rich's comment at the time that had the slur been "Barney Kike," there would have been more of an outcry? "Of course," Frank answers. "I think it's a para-dox in America: Anti-Semitism, I think, is pretty much verboten; only crazy people are anti-Semitic. So yes, calling someone 'kike' would be to-tally destructive. With regard to race and homophobia, it's an interesting thing: I think the country is, in fact, more racist than it is homophobic, but that we are *officially* anti-racist. I think the average American is not anti-gay but thinks he's supposed to be; and he's probably more racist than he's will-ing to admit."

Our conversation takes place just as Senator Joe Lieberman is poised to launch his candidacy for 2004, and I'm curious to know Frank's feelings about the way Lieberman dealt with his Jewishness in the last campaign. "Basically very well," Frank replies, but then goes on to criticize him. "I disagree with the suggestion that being religious makes you better in some ways than others—and that sometimes creeps in. There's a kind of tri-umphalism, but it's not specific to Joe's Judaism; you had it in Carter, you have it in Bush. But in general, I thought Joe handled it very well. I was very pleased when Al nominated him; I thought it was good for Gore, good for the Jews, good for America."

So Frank never thought Lieberman was overdoing his devoutness? "I have spoken to him generally about using religion as a vote-getter. I think that's a mistake. I don't think religiosity should be a basis for getting votes."

Is America ready for a Jewish president? "No," Frank says. "The pres-idency is unique. I think we've gotten rid of anti-Semitism everywhere but the presidency. You know, for all of the to-do over John Kennedy, he's still the only non-Protestant to be president of the United States. The presi-dency is sui generis—for blacks, for gays, for Jews, for women. And that will always be the case."

I still don't have a clear picture of where Frank's Jewish identity falls on the spectrum. "Oh, it's very important," he says. "Empirically it's very im-portant. When I'm asked what I care about in politics, the moral values that I'm looking for are alleviating poverty, fighting discrimination, and pro-tecting freedom of expression. And I think being Jewish has a lot to do with all of those."

So if ritual is absent, how would he characterize what being Jewish is about? "It's the common history of having been discriminated against, hav-ing relatives who were killed in the Holocaust. It's the experience of being unfairly treated because of who you are. That's one of the reasons that I think Jews are as supportive on gay rights as they are. Being Jewish is also about the tradition of intellectual activity—the life of the mind. Appreciation of food. By the way, I have a great story about that: I was in Berkeley, California, with my college roommate, who lives there now. And he's Jewish, and we went out to a restaurant for lunch, and the waitress came over and said, 'Do you want to know the specials?' We said, 'Yes, we do.' She said, 'Well, the special soup is puree of beets with crème fraîche.' " Frank chuckles. "You know what that soup was?"

Borscht?

"Yes! With sour cream!" He laughs. "I said to my friend, 'Charlie, that's *borscht with sour cream*!' Being Jewish is about shared experience, but it's also survival in the face of oppression, commitment to the enlightenment of the intellect," and of course it's communion over a bowl of beet soup.

Or a plate of mandelbread. Apparently, it's one of the congressman's favorites, and when the organization PFLAG—Parents, Families, and Friends of Lesbians and Gays—asked Frank's mother to contribute to their cookbook, she e-mailed them her recipe for mandelbread, a Jewish dessert that resembles biscotti. Elsie Frank did more than bake for her son: She made speeches on his behalf when he was running for office and was corralled into making a campaign ad in 1982, in which she said: *"How do I know he'll protect Social Security? Because I'm his mother."*

Richard Meier

RICHARD MEIER PHOTOGRAPHED BY LUCA VIGNELLI

"AS FAR AS I KNOW, I was the first Jewish architect in five thousand years to build for the Catholic Church."

It's a stunning fact, which was emphasized repeatedly to Pritzker Prize–winning architect Richard Meier in the fall of 2003, after he designed Rome's Jubilee Church (Dio Padre Misericordioso), commissioned in honor of the Catholic Church's two thousandth year. A tall man with a lumbering gait, Meier has led me through his white reception area, with its white models of his famed designs, to his office, where he sits in front of white cabinets behind a white expanse of desk in a white shirt with a white mane of hair.

"This church design was a rather unusual circumstance because there was a competition in which fifty Italian architects were asked to submit designs," Meier explains, his large hands folded in front of him, "and the Carriato [the Vatican] of Rome felt there wasn't one of those fifty designs that they felt was appropriate or good enough to carry on with. And so they decided to have an international competition when they invited six architects to compete for this particular project. Of the six, three were Jewish, as it turned out [Meier, Frank Gehry, and Peter Eisenmann]. I don't think that was intentional because they were all good architects. There was nothing in the Vatican's agenda that said that they required the church be done by someone of their faith. So when I won, I never thought it was particularly significant that I was Jewish. After I finished the church, then I realized."

His realization was driven, in part, by reporters who zeroed in on the historical implications of a Jew creating a place of worship for a group that once persecuted Jews. "Every article mentioned that I was a Jewish architect," Meier says. "I think partly because it coincided with the Pope's desire to open things up and recognize the Jews in a way that the Church hadn't done before." I read him a paragraph from a 1996 *New York Times* article in which architecture historian Bruno Zevi weighed in on Meier's Rome commission in *L'Architettura*, an Italian journal: "I do not think that anyone realizes the novelty of this," Zevi wrote. "You must remember that for centuries and millenniums the Jews were defined, at best, as faithless. They were accused of murder, of procuring the death of the symbol of humanity, of the Son of the Father, of the Son of God."

Meier concedes that the symbolism is "very important": "It hopefully changes people's attitudes, breaks down barriers, and promotes understanding. I think all those things are very important. They were important to me. But when you're in the middle of *working* on the project, you don't think about those things."

Now that the building is completed and populated, Meier says he can reflect on the more philosophical dimensions. "In a lot of interviews people said, 'How can a Jew design a Catholic church?' And since it's now extremely popular not only with the parish but with tourists, and since everyone seems to respond to it, I answered: 'Religion, and thinking about your religion and God, is not something that is reserved for one religion or another. It can be expressed in architecture in a way that affects all people regardless of your religion.' I think that's what happens in a church. And when you come in, the act of looking up and looking out and thinking about the world around you—not in a physical sense, but in the sense that your focus is, say, to the sky rather than to the earth—makes you think about things that are outside yourself."

I ask if, in the course of this undertaking, he thought about his own spirituality. "I thought about what it is to make a religious place; whether it's Catholic or Jewish, it didn't matter: it's a religious space," he says. "Now obviously if it were a synagogue, it wouldn't be the same because the criteria would be different, the organization would be different; you wouldn't have to have a baptistery or side chapel or confessionals or doors that don't open except on High Holidays."

In fact, Meier is unenthusiastic about synagogue architecture in general. He says that temple design has been limited by the conflicting needs of the structure. "Basically these spaces, with dual functions which were contradictory, just didn't work," he explains. "You can't make a space for worship and then also have it serve as space for bar mitzvah dinners for five hundred people."

Meier schooled himself in synagogue architecture back in the early 1960s. "One of the first things I did when I went out on my own was to help install exhibits at the Jewish Museum for Alan Solomon, who was a teacher of mine and the curator of the Jewish Museum," he says. "He made amazing exhibitions in the early sixties: the first Robert Rauschenberg show, the first Jasper Johns show, the first Ellsworth Kelly show. And the museum told him, 'On the one hand, the attendance is going crazy and we're so pleased; on the other hand, what do these exhibits have to do with the role of the Jewish Museum?'

"So Alan Solomon and I were sitting on the beach one day on Fire Island and he said, 'Everything's going great except the museum board is really pressing me to do a Jewish show.' So I said, 'Why don't we do a show on synagogue architecture?' He asked me if I'd do it and I said yes. So in 1963, I did an exhibit on the architecture of synagogues in America. There was an historical section and then a section showing what was going on at the present moment—the Frank Lloyd Wright building in Philadelphia, Percival Goodman's work, Philip Johnson's building in Port Chester. We highlighted a building that was under design, Mikvah Israel, designed by Louis Kahn in Philadelphia. The point of the exhibit was to show what was happening and also to make a commentary on it."

Is there a synagogue today that Meier thinks is . . . "Good?" He finishes my question. "There's one in Amsterdam that was built in the 1700s, I think," he replies. "And there's a tiny synagogue in Prague. It's beautiful. Tiny. It's amazing. Very moving."

If Meier was today asked to design a synagogue? "I'd be delighted," he says with a smile.

Does he think he could solve the problem he identified regarding the conflicting needs of the space? "Only by making the separation between the place of worship and the place of community," he says. I submit that even the needs for worship can come into conflict—for instance, aiming for the intimacy of a Shabbat service versus accommodating the hordes on Yom Kippur. "Well, I think that's something that really has to be addressed," Meier says. "I haven't thought about it in a long time, but I think there's ways of solving it."

Meier says he used to go to temple on Friday nights as a child. When I inquire about any brushes with anti-Semitism, he recalls one. "When I was thirteen or fourteen I wanted to go out with a girl in my class," he says, "and she said to me, 'I won't go out with you.' And I said, 'Why?' She answered, 'Because you're a Jew.' That was a big surprise to me."

Meier ended up marrying a Catholic, and his two children were raised as Jews with major Jewish holidays and Christmas thrown in; no Hebrew school. "I felt that they should know their history and be as aware as they can be without any formal education," Meier says. "When they were maybe nine and ten, I once took them to enroll them in religious school at Temple Emanu-El. After the first day they said, 'Dad we don't want to go there anymore.' I said, 'Why not?' They said, 'The kids just made us feel very uncomfortable.' They felt that somehow they weren't accepted in that situation. I figured it was probably because they'd had no religious education, so they felt out of place. So I said, 'Fine, you don't have to go.' I didn't want to force it on them. And therefore I felt whatever I can do at home to reinforce it is good."

Meier doesn't go to synagogue anymore. "If I observe the holidays now, I observe them at home," he says. "It's something which I think is for me and my immediate family; I don't feel part of a quote, unquote, 'Jewish community.' "

I ask Meier if he can describe the moment in his life when he felt the most Jewish. "Probably my wedding," he says. "Because I thought it was important—I don't know why I felt it was important—to have a rabbi there, and therefore my wife felt it was important to have a priest too—her family was fairly religious. I think it was significant because here we were, both coming together to say, 'We're going to be together, but we have a history and identity that we feel it's important to maintain.' "

I tell him that the majority of those I've interviewed are, like him, not observant, which for some begs the question of what makes someone a Jew. "If you believe you are a Jew," Meier says firmly, "then you are one."

When Meier walks me out, we stop to look at the glass-encased model of the Jubilee Church. I have to ask him whether he thinks anything can be made of the fact that so many giants in his field are Jewish, including himself, Frank Gehry, Robert A. M. Stern, Denise Scott Brown, Peter Eisenman, James Ingo Freed, Stanley Tigerman, and Eric Owen Moss. "No," he says with a shake of his head. "I mean, if you take all the good architects in the world today—and there are many—maybe five percent are Jewish. It's not like it's a profession of Jewish architects."

"Well, you have to concede that many of the stars happen to be Jewish," I tell him.

Meier smiles. "There are a few."

Ruth Reichl

DESPITE RUTH REICHL'S varied culinary exploits as restaurant critic for the *New York Times* (1993–1999) and as editor in chief of *Gourmet* magazine since then, she has never had a great Jewish meal. "It's the only food I don't much like: that sort of heavy, brown Eastern European food," she explains, leaning on her blond wood desk in the Conde Nast Building. "I don't think of it particularly as Jewish food—it's Eastern European: heavy, meaty, cooked a lot. As opposed to light, green, barely cooked."

Reichl, fifty-six, doesn't have fond memories of authentic Jewish cooking in her Greenwich Village home: Her mother, chronicled comically in Reichl's memoir, *Comfort Me with Apples*, was inept in the kitchen and couldn't have molded a matzo ball without involving mold. (Reichl has described her mother's cooking as life-threatening.) But the Reichl family wasn't inclined to whip up big holiday dinners anyway: This was a family that couldn't find their menorah each year. "We were Christmas-tree Jews," Reichl says. "Every year we hung up stockings and ate matzo brei."

Matzo brei on Christmas? "Yes. That's probably the only Jewish food we really ate."

Reichl does recall one "major experience" with Jewish restaurant food: "When my first husband, Doug, and I were living on Rivington Street, whoever was the restaurant critic at the *New York Times* reviewed Sammy's Romanian Restaurant, which my mother was thrilled to see; it was right around the corner from our apartment. So she said, 'Let's go to this place.' And we went there and ate this seriously Jewish food, and it was *awful*." Is she referring, for instance, to the chicken fat that sits bottled like ketchup on each table? "Yeah, and unborn chicken eggs and what Doug called 'steak by the yard.' "

Since Reichl is considered one of the reigning arbiters of gastronomy, I ask for her take on why Jews and food are a cliché—that notion of "food is love"? "You see it in any culture," she says. "But what my parents always said was, 'The Jews eat themselves to death and the goyim drink themselves to death.' The role that alcohol plays in many cultures, food plays in the Jewish culture. Of course, for my parents' generation, that wasn't true: A lot of my parents' friends were big drinkers."

For all the Jewish emphasis on food (I'm recalling my own Aunt Helen's entreaties to "Eat! Eat!"), I'm curious why Reichl thinks none of the top-tier chefs in New York are Jewish. She immediately rattles off accomplished Jewish chefs in England—Heston Blumenthal—and in California—Joyce Goldstein and Nancy Silverton ("She virtually *invented* pastry," Reichl says). "Oh, and there's Jonathan Waxman in New York."

So she doesn't think there's a cultural indicator that steers Jews away from the kitchen? "Well, it's true that Jonathan Waxman has an M.A. in political science or something. So I think it's fair to say cooking is not where the culture sends you. I mean, my parents were horrified that I was even *writing* about food: 'For this we sent you to college?' "

The Reichls valued religion even less than great cuisine. "My parents didn't belong to a temple," she says. "But when I was in eighth grade, my mother announced that she thought I should get some Jewish background. So she went and joined Temple Emanu-El. And she came home and announced that I was going to go to Sunday school and be confirmed. And my father said, 'How did you join the temple?' And my mother said she put down their names on the membership, 'Mr. and Mrs. Ernst Reichl.' And my father said, 'You will go and take my name off; I will not belong to a temple.' It's the only time in my life I ever saw him really put his foot down."

Her father, who was raised in an assimilated, wealthy German family and came to America in 1926, "hated religion of every kind. He thought religion had been the source of every evil in the world and he was very anti-Zionist: He believed that Israel was going to be the source of the next world war and just another reason for people to hate the Jews. So he was just adamant: 'I will not belong to a temple.' So my mother went and took his name off of the temple membership. I went to Sunday school. The next year, they sent me to a French Catholic boarding school in Canada, so I finished my confirmation by mail: I wrote my confirmation thesis on why I didn't believe in God."

It had to have been odd, being a young Jewish girl from Greenwich Village in a French Catholic boarding school. "I don't think most of those kids had ever *seen* a Jew before," Reichl says with a laugh. "But it was a much bigger issue for my schoolmates that I didn't believe in God than that I was Jewish. I remember one of my roommates saying to me, 'Oh, please believe in God.' "

Was she required to recite all the Catholic prayers? "The priest came in twice a week for catechism and I was excused. Everyone thought I was really lucky because the priest really smelled. He'd wear these long black wool cassocks and he had this incredible B.O. So everyone was really jealous of me not having to be in the classroom with him.

"I didn't speak any French when I got there and the one lightbulb moment for me was: We got up every morning and sang the Canadian national anthem first and then we recited this other thing in French. And after about six months there, I realized I was saying the Hail Mary every morning! I'd never bothered to translate it! All of a sudden one morning, I'm saying, 'Je vous salue, Marie, pleine de grâce—Oh my God.' "

Did she keep saying it after that? "No."

Reichl fininshed high school in Norwalk, Connecticut, where she was again in the minority. "It was very Italian, Polish, and it was very funny to all my friends that I was Jewish. I remember they made up this little thing: 'Boo-boo-pee-doo! Ruthie's a Jew!' "

Reichl says her mother was pleased that Ruth's first husband, Doug, wasn't Jewish. (Her second husband, Michael Singer, is). "Michael would tell you that my parents were self-loathing Jews," Reichl says. "I don't think that's true. But my mother would probably have been happier if she herself wasn't Jewish. When I told her that I was marrying Doug, she asked, 'Don't his parents mind?' "

Though she'd had a limited religious upbringing, Reichl did want to be married by a rabbi. I ask her why. "I'm Jewish," she says simply. "I didn't want to be married by a minister." Her mother had a hard time finding someone who would conduct an intermarriage, so they enlisted a Unitarian minister.

Her second wedding, to Singer, was more kosher. "Michael's mother would not have come if we had not been married by a rabbi," she says.

But her faint feelings for Judaism did not intensify being married to a Jewish man, and their son, Nicholas, was not raised with any tradition. "We asked him if he wanted to be bar mitzvahed because everyone in his class at Fieldston was being bar mitzvahed, and he said no," Reichl says. "I think Michael was disappointed, although Michael hated every second of Hebrew school. So he wasn't going to force Nick into it. Nick didn't even go to all the ostentatious bar mitzvahs he was invited to. He said they were just stupid, big, fancy parties."

I ask if it would give her pause were Nicholas to end up with a non-Jewish spouse. Reichl shakes her head: "No. I expect he will. What would give me pause—what would make me unhappy—is if he were ever not to identify himself as a Jew. But that's not going to happen."

And if he decided to raise his children as Christians? Reichl responds by relating a personal story that clearly shook her up: Her father's only sister, Lili, had "experienced part of the Holocaust," but escaped to America and decided to convert to Protestantism. Lili's son, Robert—Reichl's first cousin—married a Protestant. Robert's son, Mark, married a Catholic. Mark was speaking to Reichl about some land that they're now entitled to—land that had been confiscated during the Nazi regime that they won back through reparations after the Berlin Wall fell. "He called me and said, 'You know, one of us should go over there and look at this land.' And I said, 'I don't have time to go to Germany right now.' He said, 'Well, my in-laws happen to be going over there, but my father doesn't really want them to know about this land.' And I said, 'Why?' He said, 'Well, he doesn't really want them to know how he came to get possession of this land.' And I said, 'Wait a minute: Are you telling me that your father doesn't want your in-laws to know that he's Jewish?' And he said, 'My father's not Jewish.' "

Reichl gets wide-eyed with anger—"I mean, I was *stunned:* I said, 'I beg your pardon, but he was *one hundred percent* Jewish; he was *certainly*

Jewish enough for Hitler; as would *you* have been.' And I hung up the phone and I haven't spoken to him since. I was stunned at how furious I became when he said to me, 'My father's not Jewish.' It just came over me: 'How dare you!? I mean, this is my only living relative of my father and you're telling me he's not a Jew? How *dare* you?' "

I'm curious why she thinks it disturbed her so much. "I think it speaks to everything that is important to me: not denying this kernel of who you are. I loved my Aunt Lili very much; she was this lovely Jewish woman, whether she changed her religion or not."

Reichl describes her Jewish fealty as rooted mostly in family. "What's been most Jewish about my life is that my half-brother, Bob, moved to Israel in 1968. [We have the same mother, different fathers. He's fourteen years older than I.] So my only living immediate family are Israeli. They are all very strongly identified as Jews, but none of them has ever set foot in a temple. My brother and I really love each other and are very close, but we didn't see much of each other until my son, Nick, was born. Family is a huge thing for Israelis; and Bob knew that if anything happened to me and Michael, he was Nick's guardian. So the whole family really came back into our lives at that point. Suddenly this family connection became very strong. Bob comes to visit every few months—he's made the trip regularly from the day that Nick arrived. So this Israeli family is very present in our lives, and the Jewish identification there is very strong."

I ask if the political situation in Israel impinges on their relationship. "Yes," Reichl says with a nod. "It's major—as you might imagine."

Are the political debates theoretical or a real emotional strain? "They're a real strain," she says. "It's really hard. One year, we sponsored this Palestinian girl, brought her over here, and they really had a problem with it. They used to be very left, but as the situation gets worse there, they get more and more right wing."

Her outlook on Israel's future is grim. "My father was so strongly anti-Zionist, and I just feel like he was right. I understand wanting a refuge, but why did they have to take the one corner of the earth—? There were all these other places that would have been much more welcoming, but no, it had to be there. And now the country is going to destroy itself with the right-wing Jews. You know, for my brother to have moved there was such a blow to my father. I don't see anything good happening there."

When she visits Israel, does she feel a visceral reaction that "these are my people"? "No. About six or seven years ago, our whole family went on this four-day trip up to the Golan, white-water rafting; it was great. And at one point, we were walking through some area, and my niece's then-boyfriend was telling my son, Nick, about the history of the battles that have taken place, and I said, 'This just makes me feel like we have to take Nick to visit Civil War sites so he can see this kind of history in his own country.' And my niece's boyfriend looked at me and said, 'This *is* your country.' And I said, 'This is not my country.' That's where we part company, because I just don't feel that at all. I mean, I'm American. My identification as an American is much stronger than my identification as a Jew."

And yet she says her Jewishness is integral to who she is. "I think it's really important. Not in a religious sense, but in the sense that I'm one hundred percent Jewish on both sides and I value the culture that it has given me. It's a great tradition to come from."

And she understands why Jews tend to want to hold up their highest achievers, even after decades of assimilation and acceptance. "What we went through the last two thousand years—with other cultures trying to get Jews to stop being Jews, to give up their faith—you have to say, 'Okay: This is what we get for that. What we get for that is the right to say, *Look at who we are. Look who we have made ourselves. This is why it was worth it.* Yes, we paid in blood for refusing to kiss the cross or to eat pork and all of those things that for two thousand years the Christians made us do. But that's how we got Einstein. That's how we got Freud.' "

I tell her the conundrum for me is how Jewish identity survives if so many, like her, have steered clear of ritual and Jewish learning. What makes Jews Jews anymore?

"You know what makes Jews Jews anymore?" she answers. "The fact that the world won't let us forget. You can say till the cows come home that you're not a Jew, but the world keeps telling you that you are. And that's what makes you a Jew. What makes black people black? No matter how white your skin is, if you're a black person, the world keeps reminding you that you're black. Ultimately it's others' definition of us that makes us Jews."

Richard Dreyfuss

RICHARD DREYFUSS DOESN'T AGREE with the notion that actors like him and like Dustin Hoffman broke the Hollywood mold of the leading man. "There's always been two parallel themes in movie stardom," says Dreyfuss, sitting in gray sweatpants on a gray morning in his Upper West Side living room. "There's Clark Gable, Gary Cooper, and Robert Redford, and then there's Charles Laughton, Spencer Tracy, Edward G. Robinson, and Jimmy Cagney. If there was a mold that was busted, whether it was Dustin, Barbra Streisand, myself, or a conglomeration of all three, it was that we said to the world, 'We're Jews. And we were very proud of that part of our story.' I don't remember—before us—I don't remember anyone getting up and saying, 'And by the way, I'm Jewish.' The generation before had basically said, 'I'm going to change my name to Edward G. Robinson'; 'I'm going to change my name to Danny Kaye.' "

Dreyfuss goes so far as to say he played up his Jewishness as a way to distinguish himself at auditions. "What I always tried to do was to separate myself; to create a story more interesting than the guy standing next to me. That's how I would be remembered and get the job. So part of my story was 'Jew.' Because no one else was saying it."

Once he became famous, thanks to his roles in *Jaws* and *Close Encounters of the Third Kind*, not to mention his Oscar—the youngest actor ever (until Adrien Brody in 2003) to win the best actor category, at age twenty-nine (for *The Goodbye Girl*)—his Jewishness came up in press interviews. "It was a *thing*," Dreyfuss recalls. "It was a known deal. And I liked that." But he knew not to take the Jewish label too far. "There is always that problem: If you're an actor and you say that you're gay, you will not get heterosexual parts. You don't want to say you were raised in Beverly Hills, never went to college, and don't ride horses, because when you get the job of the Montana-born, Harvard-educated cowboy, they won't believe you. So there's always that element of, 'Don't say you're Jewish, don't say you're short, don't say you're anything. Say you're everything.' That's the actor's oath. The actor's oath is, 'Can I ride horses? Are you kidding? I was raised on a ranch!' "

Dreyfuss, fifty-eight, actually was raised in Beverly Hills from the age of eight, but he talks much more vividly about his earlier childhood in Bayside, New York. "Bayside was a hotbed of red-diaper baby, left-wing Jewish stuff," Dreyfuss says, sipping bottled water. "We left Bayside when I was eight and a half, but it was still very resonant in me. I visit Bayside like I visit a synagogue—it really has quite a heavy aroma for me." Politics *was* religion on his street. "If you had not been a member of the Abraham Lincoln Brigade [a volunteer organization that supported anti-Fascist forces in the Spanish Civil War], you better have a damn good reason," he says with a laugh. Dreyfuss's memory this morning is being cross-checked by his sister, Cathy—four years younger—who has just flown into New York after spending six months in Europe and who sits in on most of our interview sipping a café au lait.

These two siblings recall an unsubtle liberal upbringing, complete with union songs on the front stoop. "At ten o'clock at night in the summer," Dreyfuss recalls with nostalgia, "my parents would come outside with their little deck chairs, my father would bring his guitar, and someone across the street would do the same thing with another guitar, and they would start to play these union songs or old Spanish Civil War songs. A guy in the neighborhood named Joe owned his own Good Humor truck."

"Popular guy," Cathy interjects.

"He brought his truck out on those nights," Dreyfuss continues. "I can still see, in the pool of light from the street lamps, Joe—in his white uniform—giving kids ice cream. And what you'd hear is," Dreyfuss starts to sing robustly, " 'There once was a union maid' and 'Last night I heard the strangest dream . . .' This left-wing texture was, well, up our nose," he says with a smile. "And we were all Jewish."

The Dreyfusses weren't observant—Cathy hypothesizes that the Holocaust killed any notion of God in their home—but their dad insisted on some Hebrew school for his two boys. "When we moved to California, I was eight, my brother was ten, and Cathy was four," Dreyfuss says. "One day, my father sat my brother and me down and said, 'Look, I don't practice Judaism, but I feel that it is my obligation to introduce you to it. So I'm going to offer you two options; you have to do one of them, but you can choose which one. I'm not going to prejudice you in any way, I'm just going to describe them: One is bar mitzvah and the other is confirmation. Bar mitzvah is boring, it's stupid, you don't want to do that, it's dull, rote bullshit. But confirmation is where you discuss ethics and you debate and it's issues and it's history.' " Dreyfuss laughs at the obvious bias of this speech. "So I volunteered for confirmation. Little did I know that confirmation took seven years, bar mitzvah would have been only three. But I went. And I loved it."

Hebrew school taught Dreyfuss early about the Holocaust. "It was, of course, our daily bread," he says. Cathy recalls their parents warning them to always watch their backs. "They'd say, 'Never feel comfortable. The Jews in Germany got too comfortable and look what happened.' "

Dreyfuss nods. "My father had a twinkle in his eye when he talked about politics, *except* when it came to the Holocaust and anti-Semitism. Then he got deadly serious." Nevertheless, Dreyfuss says he never felt his father's fear. "I was so romantically involved with the story of the Jews in school, that to me anti-Semitism was this great compliment, this thing that obviously *little* people felt for *great* people. I was one of those secret liberal progressive Jews who believes that—Dreyfuss lowers his voice to a whisper—'*We are the Chosen People.*' We are. And even when that became not politically correct to say, I still do believe that."

Dreyfuss says his acute pride came from the Jewish chronicle of endurance. "It's a miracle that an ethnic group could stay together, using the rigor of intellect and *seckel* [cleverness], and have no military strength for the overwhelming majority of their history, and see every civilization take the bullet but us. The Romans died, the Byzantines died, the Assyrians died, the Babylonians died, the ancient Greeks died, the Medievalists died, even the Church died in a sense. But the Jews consistently retained a set of principles and ties that bound one another. And that's a unique story."

Dreyfuss regrets that he never conveyed that to his three children by his first marriage. "I had said to my first wife before we got married, 'I'd like you to convert,' " Dreyfuss recounts. "I knew that I needed to re-create the atmosphere that I grew up with." He says this was ill-conceived. "My first wife and I met under unrealistic circumstances—I was just recently sober"—he refers to well-publicized years of drug addiction—"and we weren't asking each other really important questions. I said, 'I want you to convert' and she said she would; then after we got married, she said, 'No, I won't.' So then I felt this overwhelming resentment. And then I became *really* Jewish. I mean, I began to be involved in Jewish politics, and the Israeli peace program, and stuff like that. I was so angry, I felt that my children had been kidnapped.

"It was made worse because I am naturally lazy and my Judaism can't be expressed by going to temple. It's just a generalized atmosphere that I grew up with and wanted for my kids: You jump into the pool and you're swimming around in Jewish water. So I wasn't going to demand that my children go to temple, but I wanted them to be in a Jewish household. It mattered a great deal, although the extent to which it mattered very much surprised me."

After the divorce, his ex-wife moved with their children to Sun Valley, Idaho, and Dreyfuss remained in New York. "There was no reason for them to be Jewish on a daily basis after that," Dreyfuss says dolefully. "Until then, they were Jewish just because I would come home and say, 'Jews! Come here!' " But he couldn't figure out how to maintain their identity from afar when he didn't buy into the rituals himself. "I couldn't force something long distance," he says.

His sister, Cathy, rubs salt in the wound. "I would add," she says, holding her coffee, "that from my perspective, there was something you had the opportunity to do but never made the effort to do, which would have made a big difference: making sure that the kids were brought to us for Jewish holidays. Our family has celebrated Yom Kippur, Rosh Hashanah, and Passover every year of our entire lives—either at my place, Mom's while she was alive, or Uncle Gilbert's—and *your* children have not participated."

There's an awkward pause; I'm taken aback by Cathy's directness in front of a stranger. But her brother accepts the criticism. "I think that's what I mean when I say that I'm lazy," he concedes. "I didn't understand the connection between Judaism and family until I was older. I didn't understand that going to High Holy Days services or going to Passover at my sister's was less about Judaism than it was about cousins. So yes, that was something that I certainly could have done and didn't; I didn't see the value of it at the time."

He adds that his nineteen-year-old daughter, Emily, has recently shown an interest in her heritage. "She comes to it, oddly enough, as a tourist. To me, that's such a weird thing: My children are tourists about Judaism."

Dreyfuss's second (and current) wife, Janelle Lacey, converted. "She did it on her own," he says, "but she did it, to a certain extent, to please me. She kept kosher for two years, but she's since let that go."

I can't help asking if his religion helped him in any way when he was going through "difficult times." He cuts to the chase: "You mean like the drugs? No. Was I a *shanda* [a disgrace] to my family? I suppose . . ." Dreyfuss returns to the question of whether Judaism has ever been a comfort. "I think that's what's wrong with my life. I think I've always known that there was an aspect to life that was spiritual, and that one took comfort from it or dwelt in it and it answered some anxieties. But I have never known what that was. And it was not in Judaism; Judaism was too practical."

Cathy gets up to get more coffee and Dreyfuss switches chairs. I ask him about the role that established him as a movie star in 1974: *The Apprenticeship of Duddy Kravitz*. He played an ambitious kid from the Jewish ghetto in Montreal whose moneymaking schemes get him into trouble. When the film came out, some Jewish audiences were offended by the character, which surprised Dreyfuss. "I was raised by people who I think were unflinchingly honest about their beliefs and who told the truth about being Americans, even if it hurt. We also told the truth about being Jews. So, to me, just as it was a shock to see that people didn't know about slavery until *Roots* was televised, just as it was a shock to find out that people didn't know about the Holocaust until the TV movie was made, it was a shock to find out that Jewish people didn't admit to Duddy Kravitz.

"To me, Duddy Kravitz was as normal as apple pie. He wasn't *the* Jewish character, but was he *a* Jewish character? Read Sholem Aleichem! Have *any* conversation about our history, and you know that our immigrant past can be basically summed up as: 'quiet shtetl Jews sitting there for centuries being raped and pillaged and cheated, then they pick up one day and go to New York and hustle their little asses off until their children are in college.' And that hustle, which was first criminal and then civic and then business, is an epic and known story to the world—or at least, to the Jewish world. So I read the original book, *The Apprenticeship of Duddy Kravitz* [by Mordecai Richler, 1959], and thought, 'Wow, this is the greatest part I've ever seen and I want this part so badly I could spit.' But I didn't know it was controversial until later."

He said he'd hoped the criticism would be good for box office. "I tried to fan the flames so more people would be aware of the controversy and more people would go to see the movie." Did that happen? "Not enough. The movie is a classic now because of cable, but it wasn't successful."

The film that Dreyfuss says caused him for the first time to adopt his father's Jewish paranoia was a flop called *Inserts*. Dreyfuss experienced disturbing flashbacks to World War II, which he says were not connected to the movie, but to his visit to Germany to promote it. The German accents alone made him physically sick. "Sometime around 1975 I went to Munich to do a publicity junket," he recounts. "I was being interviewed one day in a Munich hotel by this German lady and I said, 'Excuse me,' and I puked in a potted plant in the lobby."

Dreyfuss describes another experience walking into a pub in Munich with a fellow actor. "Veronica Cartwright and I are in the *Verdenhassen* [his made-up German word], and we order a *Hostebrotten* [more faux German] and a beer, and we're looking for a place to sit. It's this place with huge doors, and I admit I'm feeling paranoid. There's a German everywhere. There are seventeen Germans over there and there are sixteen Germans over here and there are German children and they're *all Germans!*" Dreyfuss shouts. "And the doors open and there in that room were a thousand men sitting with beer steins and sauerbraten"—German accent now—"und it vas suddenly the Munich beer hall of the 1923 putsch! It was it. I was *in the fucking room* and I was terrified and hate-filled and disgusted—words I can't even describe. Because it hit me at that moment: *These* people did *this unspeakable thing to my family*.

"I was in a press conference the next day and there were about thirty to fifty reporters and paparazzi types. [The accent returns] Und they were asking the qvestions, und this one voman stands up and she says, 'Mr. Drey-fuss, as a Jew, has it helped you in Hollyvood?' " He clears his throat. "I said, 'Well, it doesn't mean very much in Hollywood, but it means a *fuck of a great deal here in Germany!*' And she says, 'That was my next question: How do you feel here?' And I said, 'Hostile. I would like to *kill* everyone I see over forty-five years old.' Which made headlines all over Europe. I honestly divided it by age: If you were over forty-five, *where the fuck were you when Jews were being slaughtered?* I was serious. I would walk down the street in Munich from one hotel to another and I would think, *Where the fuck were you?*"

This emotionalism has been the engine, at least in part, behind his decades-long activism on behalf of peace in Israel, working primarily with Americans for Peace Now. "I've been involved in Jewish politics since the first intifada," he says. "If I hadn't done it, I would have felt that I was be-traying my grandmother. We were raised with a belief that you were con-nected to the world and you worked at it; *tikkun olam* ["heal the world"]. You were always going to be involved. It's just a question of how."

He says he understands people writing him off as just another leftie movie star exploiting his celebrity. "You're always ready to dismiss some-body because they're an actor," he says with a smile. "I believe there are certain rooms where I have to earn my stripes every time I walk in. I am perfectly willing to have my credentials questioned in any Jewish discus-sion, because I know what I'm talking about."

He describes Israel's moral underpinnings as especially precarious these days. "It's a question now of whether the existence of Israel will be at the cost of the Jewish ethic. Put aside democracy: Will we accept the demo-graphic nightmare which says there will be more Palestinians than Jews? There are two options: Either you share the state or you occupy a people. That's the conundrum here. I don't advocate for the end of Israel. But those are the issues that must be faced. And we've all been in denial about this for sixty to seventy years. Can Israel be a Jewish state without it being an imperial power in the region? And can Israel give up being a Jewish state without being overrun and slaughtered? There really is a slender thread coming through the hole of this needle. It's a very difficult thing. I think that the chance of mankind losing its soul, corrupting its soul, is very pos-sible if not probable. And that can certainly happen to the Jews. We can lose our soul here."

For a moment he's quiet, and I'm aware that his air conditioner is on in November. "Mankind loses and gains its soul every day," he continues. "We are part of this story. The Jews are meant to be better. Or else my life as a believer in the Jewish tale has no meaning. If the Jews are not better, if the Jews do not act and think more clearly, more courageously, more intellectually finely than others, then my love for Judaism is reduced to the love that someone has for a baseball team. Are the Jews better? Well, that's kind of elitist. But they better be. They better be."

Mike Wallace

CONSIDERING THE NUMBER OF TIMES that Mike Wallace, the correspondent emeritus of CBS News' *60 Minutes*, has been accused of being a self-hating Jew, it's surprising to hear him describe this sacred ritual: "To this day, when I go to bed at night, I say '*Shema Yisrael, Adonai Elohenu. Adonai echad*' ['Hear, O Israel, the Lord our God, the Lord is One']." It is Judaism's most fundamental affirmation of fidelity to God. "I can't go to sleep at night unless I say it," Wallace says, sitting at his kitchen table casually dressed in denim shirt and khaki pants. I ask him what he thinks that's about. "It's a mantra." He shrugs. "I *feel* Jewish; but it's an ethnic Jewishness."

Does that mean he feels Jewish when, for instance, he hears Jewish music or eats Jewish food?

"What's Jewish food?" Wallace replies.

Myron Leon Wallace, the son of Friedl and Zina Wolek, grew up in Brookline, Massachusetts. Now eighty-seven, he can still recite the names of both neighborhood temples, his rabbi, and the rabbi who later replaced his rabbi. "Brookline was an O'Connor and Goldberg town," says Wallace. "You were either Irish or Jewish. So the Kennedys lived doors away from the Wallaces and anti-Semitism, as far as I was concerned, didn't exist."

He went to Hebrew school reluctantly, was confirmed at sixteen, and always pined after Christmas. "I would cut out Santa Clauses from the newspaper—the advertisements," he says wistfully.

Wallace says he dropped any observance at the University of Michigan— "There was a Hillel foundation and I didn't want to get involved"—and joined a non-Jewish fraternity.

Once married, he celebrated the Christmases he'd always longed for, and still does to this day. "We have Christmas dinner here on Christmas Eve with all our friends—Jews and Christians and whatever. It's a wonderful place to have it."

At *60 Minutes*, while I worked there as his producer, Wallace could be depended upon to show up for work on Yom Kippur and to give plenty of grief to those of us who didn't. "People take advantage of Yom Kippur," he says, half-joking. "I haven't the slightest clue whether they actually go to synagogue. Morley's Jewish and takes it seriously, cares deeply. But for a lot of people however, who are Jewish, it's just a day off from work."

Wallace became a gossip item in the *Washington Post* in 2001, when then–"Reliable Source" columnist Lloyd Grove found him eating on Yom Kippur in the D.C. restaurant Bullfeathers. Wallace was munching a kosher-flouting ham and cheese sandwich, which he was happy to specify, "was *cheddar* and ham."

Wallace says the first time he felt prejudice was from other Jews. "The only time I was troubled by prejudice was when I was called a 'self-hating Jew' during the Syrian thing, and later by Larry Tisch." He's referring to the *60 Minutes* story he did in 1975 on Syrian Jewry; Wallace reported they were not as oppressed as was previously thought.

Tisch actually called him a "self-hating Jew"? "Sure," Wallace replies. "He didn't say it to my face, but he told other people that Hewitt's name was Horowitz, and Wallace's name was Wallach or something else. Somebody complained about our apparent pro-Palestinian, anti-Israel stance, and gave Tisch the idea that we were self-hating Jews."

I ask whether Wallace ever confronted Tisch. "You bet we did."

And Tisch's response? " 'No, no, no,' " he imitates him, " 'I didn't mean it.' "

According to Wallace's memoir, *Close Encounters: Mike Wallace's Own Story* (1984), his Syria report unleashed a torrent of calls, telegrams, and bundles of postcards to CBS, many asking, "Is Mike Wallace trying to deny he's Jewish?"

The brouhaha culminated in a confrontational meeting held at the Seagram Building in the office of Seagram's chair, Edgar Bronfman Sr.—then head of the World Jewish Congress. Wallace says, "Every damned Jewish leader in the city—and around the country—was there to get an explanation from me as to what I had done and how I came to the conclusion that Jews in Syria weren't suffering."

After much discussion, Wallace says he made his case. "I satisfied them that I was doing my job. But I was still labeled a 'self-hating Jew.' "

Eventually Wallace's take on the Syrian situation was vindicated by a subsequent *60 Minutes* piece with new interviews that substantiated the claims of the first report. But I wonder if being called an anti-Semitic Jew by other Jews bothered him at all? "At first it did, to some degree," Wallace admits. "But it comes with the territory. I am not a self-hating Jew. If I were a self-hating Jew, I would not be saying the Shema every night; I'm a Jew, and proud of it."

There were many more Middle East stories and many more firestorms. During the middle and late seventies, according to Wallace's book, he "was flayed with the charge of betraying his Jewish heritage." I ask Wallace if, through it all, he always felt he was a reporter first and a Jew second. "Always," he replies. "I've always found that doing a story about an underdog is more interesting than the other way around, and as far as I was concerned, during that period of time, the Palestinians had become the underdog. Of course I tried to make my reporting as dispassionate as I could, but I was taken aback by some of the callousness with which Israelis handled Palestinians."

I'm talking to Wallace during a period when Arab suicide missions are happening almost daily, so I ask how that affects his perspective. "Last March I went to Ramallah to see Yasser Arafat—fascinating guy. [Arafat died after we spoke—in November 2004.] Suddenly I found myself having supper with him. I put every barbed question I could to him and I realized that this man had really lost his way, that in a sense he had become a captive; he didn't have the guts to say to Hamas or Islamic Jihad, 'Knock it off.' He liked being the leader of the Palestinians, didn't want to give it up. He should never have turned aside the opportunity to make peace at Camp David. And for the first time he lost me; he totally lost me."

Wallace had built a cordial relationship with Arafat over the years. "When I first met him, back in seventy-seven, I think he didn't know what to make of this Jewish reporter. We became—quote—'friends' of a sort, and I was drawn to Arab men. When I say, 'drawn to Arab men,' I mean I found them interesting."

Wallace became close to a Palestinian named Fayez Sayegh, an erudite Arab scholar whom he met in 1957 when he interviewed him for *Night Beat*—Wallace's first talk-show program. "He opened my eyes to the plight of the Palestinians, to the life they lived," Wallace recalls. "I had the opportunity back then to talk to all kinds of people and get myself an education of sorts. I still correspond occasionally with his widow; he's been dead for a long time."

Wallace says his first trip to Israel was emotional. It was 1960, when the country was just twelve years old. "It was the bar mitzvah year," Wallace remembers. "So when the El Al plane circled before landing, down below they were dancing horas. We landed late at night and as we were driving on the road from Tel Aviv Airport to Hebron, the sun was just beginning to rise, and people were just out there in their chairs waiting for the parade that was going to take place, and I just broke down. In that moment I was very Jewish, I was very Israeli, very proud. This was a voyage of discovery for me and obviously I identified."

Despite his unsentimental reporting over the years, Wallace says he has always been "pro-Israel," and moved by its success as a tiny yet formidable nation. "I remember so well when I went to Israel toward the end of the Six Day War—I think I arrived on the fourth or fifth day." He felt personal pride in Israel's rout of the Arabs. "Because I'd never thought of Jews as fighting people. I never thought of them as independent, brave, courageous fighters somehow."

I try to pursue Wallace's feelings about the Middle East tensions today, but he hesitates. "I've got to be careful," he says. "It's hard for some people to believe that you can be dispassionate in your reporting and yet still have a feeling about any given subject. I believe in a secure and safe Israel. I also believe that if the Palestinians and the Jews would get together, that that part of the world would prosper beyond belief."

Does he support Israel financially? Wallace nods. "I established a fund at Hebrew University in Jerusalem. Ted Yates was killed there," he says, referring to a CBS reporter to whom he was close. "He was killed by an Israeli sharpshooter from the Jordanian side of Jerusalem on the first day of the Six Day War."

Yates's widow, Mary, ended up marrying Wallace in 1986, his fourth and current marriage. His first wife, Norma Kaphan, was the only one of the four who was Jewish. "I've never been attracted to Jewish women, not since the first one," Wallace confesses. Norma ended up marrying William Leonard, then a highly regarded CBS News executive, and they took the lead in raising Wallace's two children, Peter—who died at nineteen in a tragic accident when he was traveling in Greece in 1962 (he fell off a mountain)—and Chris, who is currently the host of *Fox News Sunday*. "The kids were not raised—" He starts again: "They were under the impression—at least *Chris* is under the impression—that he is not really Jewish," Wallace says, a little uncomfortably. "I mean his mother and his father are Jewish, and so is his grandmother, grandfather, and so forth. But Bill Leonard brought Chris and Peter up . . ." This is clearly sensitive terrain. "Chris married a Catholic girl and their kids are mainly Catholic. Chris doesn't regard himself—I've said, 'Chris, you're Jewish! You may not like it, or you may not want to . . .' We've had discussions about it."

Does it give Wallace pause when he considers that the Jewish Wolek/Wallace line has petered out? "Um," Wallace pauses for what feels like a long time. "I never thought about it, truly." Another pause. "I guess it's true. But my brother, Irving, is Jewish and still very involved with it. He lives in Washington and he would prefer that I was more observant than I am. My two sisters, they're both gone."

My last question is whether he has felt, at any point in his celebrity, an obligation to be "a face of Judaism"—a role model or a spokesman. "I'm not a professional Jew," Wallace says with a smile. "Everyone knows me for what I am and I'm quite content with that."

Shawn Green

COURTESY OF ARIZONA DIAMONDBACKS

MOST OF THE PEOPLE I INTERVIEWED for this book say they are rarely, if ever, asked about being Jewish. Arizona Diamondback Shawn Green, on the other hand, is pummeled with the question. That's because he's unique: a Jewish baseball star.

There have only been roughly 140 Jewish players in major league history, and just two legends: Sandy Koufax and Hank Greenberg. Green draws attention not just because of his Jewishness but because it matters to him. So much so, that in 1999, when he was deciding which ball club to join after his triumphant run for the Toronto Blue Jays, one requirement was that the home city have a significant Jewish population. "I wanted to play in a place that had a large Jewish community because I wanted to be able to have an impact," says Green. (He opted to sign with the L.A. Dodgers and is still a member of that team at the time we speak.)

An imposing six-foot-four, Green is talking to me in his uniform, standing outside the visitors' locker room in Toronto's stadium, where the Dodgers are about to play his former team, the Blue Jays. It's loud and echoey, but I can see he's used to doing interviews this way—standing up, on the fly. "L.A. was a perfect fit, since I'm from there," he says. "And it has a large Jewish community. Toronto did, too."

Raised in Los Angeles, Shawn David Green, age thirty-two when we met, has the distinction of having signed the largest contract—in total value—in baseball history at the time, 1999: He was promised eighty-four million dollars over six years. When this left-handed outfielder and first baseman was traded from the Jays to the Dodgers, he had just completed a spectacular season: 190 hits for a .309 average, 42 home runs, 123 RBIs, and 20 stolen bases in 27 tries. The year before, he stole 35 bases and hit 35 home runs.

As Green rose in stature, his religion was often the story. The *Washington Post* blared, *"An Heir Apparent Worthy of Hank Greenberg; Blue Jays Star Green Is Taking Baseball by Storm."* A headline in the *Forward* read, *"Next Boychik of Summer Reignites Koufax's Flame."*

I remind him of something he said once: "My being Jewish separates me from most players and it will separate me for my whole career." Green nods. "When I'm done playing baseball, for the people who do remember my career—not that it's going to be Barry Bonds's career—but at the end of it, people are going to remember me as, 'Oh yeah, he was a Jewish ballplayer.' Everyone has a label, and mine is pretty specific."

He doesn't shirk it. When he played for Toronto, he agreed to speak to countless Jewish organizations and fielded many Passover and bar mitzvah invitations. "One of the team doctors is Jewish and a friend of mine, so I would go with him to shul. And I guess the word kind of got out."

He is still sought after by Jewish groups in every town he visits. "I have a little bit extra on my plate when it comes to going to different cities because of all the Jewish newspapers and organizations. I try to do those interviews and meet with everyone, but I try to do them at the stadium rather than go all over God's creation."

I wonder if he ever feels it's a burden, being the "Jewish sports star," when he might just want to play ball. "I think it was a burden until I learned how to say no," he replies. "Because you can only do so much. During the season, it's really hard—it got to the point where, in every city I went to, there was a Jewish community center or some Jewish organization that wanted me to come and make an appearance or do something, and I just had to say no at some point. Otherwise my life is just baseball and making appearances and that's an exhausting way to live."

His father, Ira Green, who trained his son from the age of three, told the *Los Angeles Times* in a 2000 profile of his son headlined "Hebrew Natural" that he was weary of the religious focus. "I wish the whole thing would die down a little," he said. "Can't writers just think of Shawn as a great player and not a great Jewish player?"

However saturated Green's family may feel, Green knows he's a role model—especially for kids—and he takes that function seriously. "I missed a game for Yom Kippur in 2001," he says, referring to his well-publicized decision to sit out the season's final home game, against San Francisco. "I just thought it was the right thing to do. At the time, we were in the pennant race, so it was a big game." Obviously this echoes former Dodger Sandy Koufax's momentous decision in 1965 to sit out the first game of the World Series against the Minnesota Twins because it fell on Yom Kippur. "It always seems to come up in the big situations," Green says. "But I felt it was the right thing to do even though I'm not particularly religious. A lot of people in the Jewish communities recognize me as a Jewish athlete they can relate to, and I felt it was important to set a good example."

(In the fall of 2004 he again faced the play-or-pray conundrum on Yom Kippur: he had to decide whether to miss two crucial games in the pennant race against the San Francisco Giants: One fell on Kol Nidre night, the other the next day. After agonizing for a period, he chose to play on Kol Nidre and ended up hitting the game-winning home run. The next day, he skipped the game and went to synagogue.)

I wonder what his heritage means to him, now that he's been forced to be more Jewish than he otherwise might have been if he hadn't become famous. "That's a tough question," he says. "I've definitely learned a lot more about it since I've been playing. I think it's just a sense of pride you have about what Jewish people have accomplished, what they've been through, all the obstacles. It seems like there's never-ending struggles for Israeli people and Jewish people. It's a very strong and relentless group."

How would he explain why there's still so much excitement about a Jewish sports star today—why it's such a big deal? "I didn't know it was," he jokes, smiling. "I think the stereotype is that the biggest asset for Jewish people usually isn't athleticism," he says. "So when there are successful players in sports who are Jewish, the Jewish communities across the country say, 'See, we can do that.' It's something I can understand especially as a kid: If you're Jewish, you can relate to someone who celebrates the same holidays you do, who was raised in a similar household. That's the player that you're going to say, 'Wow; I'm sort of like him.' "

The player who inspired Green as a boy was Koufax. "I didn't see him play, he was before my time, but he was obviously the big one. And I remember hearing that Rod Carew had converted. Whether or not that's true, I don't know, but I collected his baseball cards. I remember Steve Stone was Jewish."

Green says that growing up, he wasn't as fixated on Greenberg's career (ironically, "Greenberg" was Green's original family name), but he was an expert on Koufax, who is now a familiar presence during spring training. "Every spring he comes out to Dodgertown," Green says. "He still lives down there in Florida. I talk to him about life and baseball; we really don't talk much about being Jewish athletes."

Has Koufax offered any advice about being an exemplar for Jews? "He just told me that you've got to do what you feel in your heart to do and everything else will take care of itself; you can't try to please everybody."

Green learned that lesson as a teenager when he decided to forgo college for baseball—not his mother's plan. After a straight-A high school record, ranked third in his class, he was admitted to Stanford University. Judy Green wanted him to go. "My mom was hoping that I would go to school; I actually took courses there in the winters. But my dad was kind of focused more on the professional baseball side, so there was a kind of split." (Green's father, formerly a gym teacher, coach, and medical supplies salesman, owns an indoor-batting facility, the Baseball Academy, near his home in Tustin, California.) "But then when I signed with the Blue Jays, the team said I could go to college in the off-season, and they paid for it in the contract. So it was kind of the best of both worlds." He attended Stanford for two years until he was offered the mega contract.

Judy Green was quoted in *Sports Illustrated* talking about her son's new salary. "I think our society is out of whack," she said. "When you think about what policemen, schoolteachers, firemen, and paramedics do and what they are making, it's crazy what we pay our athletes and entertainers. But I know the money won't change Shawn. I know he'll do the right thing with it."

Her son confesses it's an added pressure. "I was raised with Jewish values—just to be appreciative of what you have and know that other people are in need. Jewish people traditionally are very charitable and it's hard in some ways to be in the position I'm in because you never feel like you're doing enough, and then at the same time, you keep getting bombarded and you want to go, 'Whoa.' It's a tough mix."

The other major pull in his life these days is his daughter, Presley Taylor, born December 22, 2002. It's Green's first child with wife Lindsay Bear. "My wife's not Jewish," he volunteers. "Now that I have a daughter, we're going to expose her to both religions. I will go to synagogue on the High Holy Days, but sometimes I find it's almost harder to go because it's kind of uncomfortable for me to get a lot of attention there. It kind of all depends on how I'm feeling. Sometimes I would rather stay home and not deal with all that."

I wonder if having a child has intensified issues of identity for him. "Definitely," Green says with a nod. "I think it's great because she can learn two completely different religions and ways of life, not to mention that she gets extra holidays. I'm always of the belief that you should expose your kids to different things and let them find their way."

So he didn't feel the typical family pressure to marry a Jew? Green smiles. "It's always there a little bit," he concedes. "But you get through that fast."

When I ask about anti-Semitic jokes in the locker room, Green waves it off. "You hear things casually," he concedes, "but not any more than you would hear it if you were working in a nine-to-five job." Since he is out-numbered by non-Jews in his profession, it was a memorable moment in 1998 in Milwaukee when three Jews stood at home plate simultaneously: Green was up at bat; Jesse Levis, then of the Milwaukee Brewers, was catching; and Al Clark was the umpire. "It was right after Rosh Hashanah," Green told the *L.A. Times.* "And, after greeting each other with a laughing round of 'Hey, Yids,' we wished each other a happy new year."

Green's next interviewer is cooling his heels nearby, so I wrap it up by asking him about the symbolism of his success. Since athletics is still an area where there aren't the equivalent of hundreds of Jewish Nobel Prize winners, he must be aware that he's breaking ground. "Obviously the ground has been broken for me," Green demurs. "There's always been a Jewish player that's been the most recognized in the Jewish community. Since I've been playing, there have been some other players who have been up and down, but I understand that my role is to be that guy for this generation. And someone else will come along sometime and take the torch."

Stephen Sondheim

STEPHEN SONDHEIM PHOTOGRAPHED BY JERRY JACKSON

"I THINK JEWS ARE SMARTER than any other race." Composer Stephen Sondheim is talking to me on the telephone. He responded to my request for a meeting with a typed note that said, *"Might it be possible to do it over the phone instead of in person? I really hate to make appointments except when I have to (with doctors and dentists)."*

Did he just say Jews are smarter than any other race? "I'm prejudiced," he continues. "I identify with people who get beaten up. I'm in a profession that invites it." Meaning? "The critics."

Sondheim, whose résumé includes *Company, A Little Night Music, Sweeney Todd, Sunday in the Park with George*, and *Assassins*, grew up in the tony San Remo apartment building on Central Park West. "I grew up thinking the Jews were the world," he says. "Everybody was just Jewish. I went to summer camps where everyone was named Nussbaum."

His father was a dressmaker who "raised a lot of money for the UJA." His mother, who is described in Sondheim's biography as emotionally abusive, "was sort of ashamed of being a Jew," he says. "She claims she was brought up in a convent in Rhode Island.

"The first serious Jew I came into contact with was Lenny Bernstein." Sondheim is speaking of the celebrated composer and conductor Leonard Bernstein, whose music accompanied Sondheim's lyrics for *West Side Story* in 1957. "Lenny looked at me askance when I said 'Yum Kipper.' I grew up not knowing anything. We celebrated Christmas by buying things at Saks. You know what I mean by a West Side Jew."

Did he ever experience any anti-Semitism in his profession? "My God—in the theater? In musicals? Name me three gentile composers."

None come immediately to mind. "Cole Porter," he helps me. "He is one of the three gentile composers. But his music is actually very Jewish. He was very influenced by the Mideast—he was in the Foreign Legion as a young man. His music is very Semitic. Semitic scales. Listen to any Cole Porter song in a minor key; you'll hear it."

I wonder if he's ever considered exploring Jewish themes in his work. "Not really."

Does he have any special feeling for Israel? "My attitude toward Israel is the *New York Times*' attitude toward Israel," he replies. "Whatever they tell me is what I believe. I became aware of Israel because Lenny cared so much about it."

I can see my brief telephone time is almost up, so I try to clarify how Sondheim would characterize his Jewish identification. "It's very deep," he answers immediately. "It's the fact that so many of the people I admire in the arts are Jewish. And art is as close to a religion as I have."

Eliot Spitzer

ELIOT SPITZER, whom the *New York Times* has called "the most prominent Attorney General around," who is gearing up to declare his candidacy for New York governor when I meet him, is in his Manhattan office during a snowstorm, looking immaculate in a blue suit, white shirt, and black shiny shoes. Of course, he's at his desk in a blizzard. Article after article has been written about Spitzer's ambition and tenacity, his trophy diplomas from Horace Mann (tennis team captain), Princeton (student body chairman), and Harvard Law School (Law Review); his election at age thirtynine—in 1998—to the office of New York State attorney general, and lately, his headlines for taking on corruption in the financial and insurance industries. He's been touted for rousing a tired office into becoming an aggressive muckraker.

As for Spitzer's Jewishness, he says it can be found in his work. "On one level it pervades everything that I do," he says, sitting on a government-issue blue chair on a government-issue blue carpet. "I'm always trying to figure out what is the best way to use the capacity of this office to do something that's useful. And it's not as though one's deepest values pervade every decision like that, but to a certain extent, when I'm thinking about, 'Do I want to get involved in this issue, and if so, why, and whom do we help,' to a certain extent that does go back to my sense of what the core values of Judaism are as I understood them. I do have a sense that when I set priorities and try to articulate what it is we're doing, the reasoning stems concretely from my Jewish ancestry, as my dad conveyed it to me."

His father, Bernard Spitzer, a civil engineer who became enormously wealthy in real estate, instilled his son's hustle and acumen. (Spitzer describes his relationship with his mother—a literature professor at Marymount Manhattan College—as "the classic son-mom type," saying "She is just as intellectually acute, but was always more emotionally driven.") Family dinners in Riverdale, New York, were a place for discussion and debate: The three children took turns bringing an issue to the table. (They were also quizzed on sightseeing during family vacations.)

When I ask Spitzer how he would link Jewish values to achievement, he laughs: "I'm neurotic." He confesses that he's inherited his parents' premium on accomplishment. "I'm not necessarily comfortable with self-analytical stuff, but it's hard, I suppose, to deny that when I was growing up, there wasn't a certain set of expectations, or that I haven't passed that on to my eldest daughter at this point. My younger two are still a little young— but even my eight-year-old, who is in third grade, hasn't missed a spelling word on her weekly spelling test all year. There is a very real sense that we expect performance—always shrouded, of course, in the cliché that 'We want you to do the best you can do.' "

The academic pressure with which he was raised and is raising his own children, however, does not apply to his Judaism. Spitzer's parents, despite Bernard's training as a cantor ("He has a great voice," Spitzer says), did not take him to synagogue regularly or insist he be bar mitzvah, which his mother still regrets. "Once or twice she has voiced misgivings that I wasn't bar mitzvahed," Spitzer says, "but when I ask her why, it sort of doesn't go anywhere. So I don't know quite what to make of it." It's clear that Spitzer too feels ambivalent. "There are moments where I wish I'd had a more formalistic training. One thing that I think is symbolic of how my dad viewed it was that instead of my being bar mitzvahed, he wanted me to read Abba Eban's *History of the Jews*. That gives you a certain insight into what he considered the important aspect of the maturation process. And if my children are not bat mitzvahed, they're going to read that book, too. Because I think understanding the history and the cultural predicates of Judaism is critically important."

Spitzer's own religious parenting has been complicated by the fact that he married Silda Wall—a law school classmate—in 1987: "She's not Jewish," he says, "which is an issue that we've grappled with in terms of the kids." (They have three daughters ranging from ten to fifteen years old at the time we meet.) "I obviously feel that the children will be Jewish; they're going to Horace Mann—a school that's predominantly Jewish, they're growing up in a Jewish environment, a Jewish culture." I ask if he and his wife discussed the matter of religion before they got married. "Yeah," he says with a smile. "You know how conversations like that go. To put it in the context of a corporate transaction, it probably wasn't the deal-breaker on either side, so it sort of got pushed aside and we delayed. Even the closing documents didn't address it." So, the hurdles are being dealt with as they go along? "Yes."

He says the girls go to church only when they visit his in-laws in North Carolina. I ask if that makes him—"flinch?" he finishes my question. "I grimace. But I bear it." He seems to take comfort in the fact that at home, they're surrounded by other Jews. "My view is they're here in New York and they're growing up in a culture that is essentially a transmission to them of Jewish values. I want to take them to Israel. I don't know when I will. I've resisted going on all the political junkets; I don't want to be there with ten elected officials. I think that would cheapen it."

I wonder if he thinks his children consider themselves Jewish. "I hope—" He pauses. "They probably consider themselves *confused*, but that's like all kids. I think they are very conscious of the fact that they are Jewish, but Mommy might not be, but that's okay." All three daughters attend Hebrew school, but one has already taken her father's path. "My eldest is not being bat mitzvahed. The younger two, it remains to be seen." I asked if it was his daughter's decision. "As parents, there are choices that you lead your children to; this one I really had a more hands-off attitude because I didn't want to force it on her because I didn't think that would be terribly productive."

In addition to celebrating Hanukkah, the Spitzers do have a Christmas tree every year. He says he doesn't recall his parents ever cringing at the sight. "They know that nothing I'm doing is a rejection of how they raised me—which I think would evoke a different emotional response from a parent. If they had been much more rigorous in their purely religious training with me and I had gone somewhere else on the spectrum, that might have been difficult. But what we're doing is very much in sync with where they were."

Even without the religious foundation, Spitzer says ethnic pride fuels his professional focus on fair treatment. "We have been able to represent immigrant groups who came here—West Africans, Mexicans, Asians—who have been taken advantage of by a system where they were denied rights because they were easy targets. We are a nation of immigrants, very much like Jews in the Diaspora, who have needed to migrate, to find a home. That sense of providing opportunity is what America is all about. It's the common theme that I hope traces through much of what we do."

He confesses there have been moments where his Jewish pride has been tested. "I wouldn't be truthful if I didn't say that occasionally there have been a couple cases where the defendants were Orthodox Jews. There was a high-profile fraud case, for example, and within a certain circle of the Orthodox community, there was a lot of anger against me. People said, 'What are you, one of those Jew-hating Jews?' This defendant was someone who had given away a lot of money to the community, but he'd stolen the money he was giving. At the end of the day he pled guilty to every count of the indictment; the evidence was *that* overwhelming. So I went back to the people who had come to me and who had said things that hurt. I never let on that it hurt, but it hurt because I felt it was not only unfair but it was wrong, and it was wrong for them as Jews to think in that way. It bothered me. I looked them in the eye and I said, 'Now you understand: you were wrong. At least I hope you do, because it was the wrong way to judge me and it's bad for us as Jews when we react that way.' "

I'm talking to Spitzer before the 2004 election and before his subsequent announcement that he's running for governor of New York. He won't comment on whether he dreams of the presidency, as some—including his father—have speculated, but he does say it's "stupendous" that Senator Joseph Lieberman could be taken seriously as a candidate without his religion being the focal point. He also gets a kick out of revelations that Senator John Kerry has Jewish blood. "Next time I see him, I'll say, 'Hey! We're closer than we thought.' "

Harold Prince

WHEN PRODUCER/DIRECTOR HAROLD PRINCE, who's helped create such Broadway classics as *West Side Story, Damn Yankees, Sweeney Todd, Evita*, and *Phantom of the Opera*, was approached in 1964 by writers Sheldon Harnick and Jerry Bock to direct *Fiddler on the Roof*, he refused. "I didn't *get* any of it," Prince says, swiveling around in his leather office chair. "So I said, 'I won't do it. As far as I'm concerned, you should do everything in the world to get Jerry Robbins.' When they asked Jerry, he said, 'I'll direct it if you get Hal Prince to produce it.' "

Fiddler turned out to be the longest-running musical of its time. "But all during the entire rehearsal process, I still didn't get it," Prince repeats. "Harnick gave me a book about the shtetl, and Bock made me look at Maurice Schwartz's film version of *Tevye, the Milkman* [the story by Sholem Aleichem on which *Fiddler* was based]. I steeped myself in a lot of it, but it wasn't coming from in here." Prince knocks on his chest.

As the descendant of German Jews, Prince explains, his gut connections did not come from the poor Russian villages that *Fiddler* portrays. Yet somehow Prince and his collaborators managed to craft the definitive

Jewish portrait—a show whose musical score, including "Sunrise, Sunset," have become almost part of the religious canon.

"I think one of the things you have to realize is it was a huge success because people thought it was about family," Prince says, taking off the signature glasses that often sit perched on his forehead. "It was a hit all over the world. And when we finally reached nine thousand-whatever performances, I brought all the Tevyes to New York from all over the world—every actor who had ever played the role. And at the end of the show, they came out on stage in costume singing 'Tradition' [the show's opening song], one after another after another—a Japanese Tevye, a German Tevye, a Mexican Tevye. There they all were." Prince smiles at the memory. "The show was a success because for non-Jews it wasn't Jewish: It was about family."

However universal the appeal, however, some Jewish audiences were unhappy about it. "When *Fiddler* opened, Jerry Robbins gave his first dance teacher—an old, old man—the role of the rabbi. And he was a kind of befuddled, humorous, adorable character and Jerry loved him. The board of rabbis didn't. They sent me a telegram threatening to boycott the show if we didn't change that character. I wrote back and said, 'We have no intention of changing that character; it's created by Mr Robbins and the authors with great affection.' "

I ask what exactly the board of rabbis objected to. "They thought he was buffoonish," Prince explains. "Yes, he was an addled little rabbi. But he was adorable. You know what the character's signature gesture was? Anytime anybody in the village came to him for advice, he'd take the big book and leaf through it madly, looking for answers. And then he would do a Solomon-like thing: '*You're* right and *you're* right!'"

"The New York board of rabbis started sending me a telegram regularly every few hours for delivery. It was harassment. I barked back, 'If you continue this, I will publicize it. It's narrow-minded foolishness; stop right now.' And they did. But for a moment there, I said to myself, 'Holy God, are they going to deliver telegrams every two hours forever?' "

Prince's own Jewish affinity was ignited much more deeply decades later by a far less successful musical he directed called *Parade*. It told the true story of Leo Frank, a Jewish factory manager who was falsely accused of raping a white girl in Atlanta in 1913 and ultimately hanged for it by an angry mob. "I felt *Parade* was as close as I could get to doing *my Fiddler*," says Prince. "And when it was rejected in terms of popular entertainment, I was very hurt. Because I loved the show and still do. Its reception could have put it right where it belonged, but instead, it was completely unappreciated where it mattered."

I ask how it connected him to his Jewishness. "What did it mean to me? Everything," he says. "I related to Leo Frank. But see, that's a southern family."

Prince has southern roots because his German ancestors migrated to El Paso, Texas, stopping in New York along the way. His mother's great-grandfather, Adolph Rubin, was the second cantor of New York's Temple Emanu-El—"He wrote some hymns that they still use today," Prince says. Adolph Rubin's daughter, Ella, married and moved to El Paso, "where her husband became the president of the Bank of Juárez, Mexico!" Prince clearly gets a charge out of this. "So you see, it's kind of a weird Jewish family story!"

Harold Prince is less enthusiastic when asked about his father, Harold Smith. "I never talk about him," Prince says matter-of-factly. "My mother remarried when I was three years old, so I was raised all of my life by a guy named Milton Prince who was on Wall Street. My father was a guy I never cared much for, to be honest with you. And I never cared for his family."

I remark that "Smith" doesn't sound Jewish. "I think it may have been Goldsmith before," Prince explains.

Prince grew up in New York City—attending the Dwight School when it was called the Sachs School: "We were all Jewish there except for Truman Capote," Prince says with a laugh. "He graduated a year ahead of me."

His family never went to Temple Emanu-El for services, but to this day, they have two seats that are always set aside for them. "They're lousy locations, because they know I never come," Prince says with a laugh. "But I tell you what: I did repay them once." He's referring to the time the head rabbi asked Prince to direct a show to celebrate the temple's 150th anniversary. "There was a moment where I thought, 'You owe them this.'" Prince smiles. "'You haven't been in the doors for decades, even though someone is singing your great-grandfather's hymns every year; you owe them this.'" The rabbi said he wanted the celebration to be a revue in honor of three temple alumni. "I said, 'Which three?'" Prince recounts, "And he said,

'Jerome Kern, Irving Berlin, and Richard Rodgers.' I said, 'You bet I'll do it.' It was a very sweet evening. And that's the last time I set foot in the temple."

When one is reminded of those Broadway greats—not to mention Stephen Sondheim, with whom Prince collaborated on such musicals as *A Little Night Music* and *Sweeney Todd*—it raises the question of whether Jewishness might fuel creative talent. "Most people who are high accomplishers come from behind some psychological eight ball where they feel disenfranchised and they have to create something," Prince says. "Certainly that's true of me. It's almost true of almost everybody I know. There's that neurotic 'you either sink or you swim, and swimming's better.' So I think what you're talking about is grit and resilience, and yes, fantasy and escape. The art went to some place of escape. It is an advantage not to be born with a silver spoon in your mouth. It just is."

I pass along what Sondheim told me, in our conversation for this book, that Jews are "smarter," and how he challenged me to name a great gentile musical theater composer other than Cole Porter. "I'm so reluctant to ever go where Steve went, which is to say 'We're the best.' Somebody else better say it. Somebody who isn't Jewish. Every once in a while you find yourself in a room full of accomplished Jewish people and they feel too superior. I don't think anyone should feel superior."

And yet he does connect the success of many Jews to their ethnicity. "I could say something very arrogant—though I don't approve of it: It's a hell of an elite club. I don't take huge pleasure in saying, 'Look at us on Broadway in the musical game: We're Jewish.' But the facts are there. And all I can ever think is so much of this has to do with how a race of people—or a religious group—dealt with deprivation. They actually took an isolation that was thrust on them and turned it into an advantage. And in that isolation, they saw to it that people were educated, that their priorities included medicine, law, literature, the arts. They were passionate about taking a disadvantage and turning it to a cultural advantage—their advantage—and that's huge. Because there's another way to deal with this kind of deprivation. There are other races and religions out there and they don't always turn adversity into creativity. And we'll let it go at that."

Stephen Breyer

IT'S ONE OF THE MOST undeniably interesting components of Supreme Court Justice Stephen Breyer's Jewish identity: that his daughter, Chloe Breyer, thirty-five, is an Episcopal priest. But it's a subject he will address only cursorily. "That shouldn't be the emphasis of this," he tells me. "Chloe is a wonderful person. And she's really decent and she wrote a book on her life in the seminary; so if you want to look at it . . ." He finds a copy of her memoir, *The Close*, for me on a shelf in his stately office. "It's funky and it's interesting." He says, urging me to keep it.

I pursue the subject a little further, venturing that his daughter's religious path "is a pretty strong contrast" to his Jewish upbringing at Temple Emanu-El in San Francisco. "It is." He nods. "She's quite ecumenical. I told her—which is how I do feel about it—that what I want for her is what satisfies her and what makes her life happy. And that's what she's found."

Breyer's wife, Joanna Hare Breyer, a clinical psychologist, is Anglican (daughter of former Tory parliamentarian Lord John Blakenham), and the three Breyer children got a little of each parent's heritage. "The children went to Protestant church," says Breyer. "Not a lot, but some. And also we'd celebrate Passover and sometimes the children would go with me to

Rosh Hashanah or Yom Kippur services. So we tried to keep up somewhat in both."

I make one more attempt to get at whether his daughter's divergent, intensive religious career has been complicated for him. "She stands on her own feet," he says. "And it's her life. Moreover, she's not embarrassed about me, I hope—any more than any other child is about their parents. So what she does is great. And of course it's interesting and unusual." I assume that their dinner table conversations must be fascinating. "It's normal, family dinner conversation," he says dismissively. "I have one child who is an Episcopal priest. I have one (Nell, thirty-four, a Yale graduate) who considers herself Jewish, and I have one (Michael, thirty-one, a Stanford graduate) who considers himself not religious. So I think that really what's important is that the children themselves are satisfied with their spiritual lives. I think they are. That's what a parent wants."

He said it's what his parents wanted for him. "What my parents wanted was that I be happy," he says. "I think today the Jewish community as well as the non-Jewish community is more accepting of mixed marriages. So I think if I had been married in 1997 instead of 1967, it's possible it would have seemed a more natural thing for an intermarried couple to have fuller participation in Jewish community life. But there wasn't hostility."

We are drinking tea from a silver pot, sitting in two chairs alongside his large desk. Justice Breyer is dressed in a gray herringbone suit with a blue shirt and red tie. His round wire-rimmed glasses frame sleepy eyelids, but there is no lethargy about him; he speaks with distinct formality but also noticeable joviality. "Like most Jews—or people in any religion—being Jewish is part of my life. There we are. It's normal. I'm certain that some of my reactions— legally speaking—grow out of that heritage. Why is it that, like my father—who I think was a pretty practical person—why is it that my favorite way of looking at things is what Hillel said: 'If I am not for myself who will be for me? If I am only for myself, what am I? If not now, when?' That captures it to me. The heritage of law in this country is to make people's lives better, to make certain there's a reasonable level of social equality, to make certain people's basic freedoms are guaranteed. Everyone who is a judge in the United States traces that back to the founding of this nation, and the Jews are immediately aware that it goes far further back than that."

Breyer, sixty-six, says his Hebrew school and Jewish summer camp experiences "made an impression," though not necessarily because he re-calls any specific lesson. "You learn things in Sunday school—'justice flow-ing like the waters,' for instance. But it isn't exactly being able to attach the name of the right prophet to the right quotation. It is in discussions and the atmosphere, in learning the history of the Jews, in understanding what the holidays are about. For instance, that Passover is a holiday that com-memorates freedom. And I have to say it took place many, many years be-fore the Fourth of July. Does that make it more important? No. Does that make it original? No. It's that both as Americans and as Jews, you see in the background that same commemoration of human liberty that people in this country, and I think in the law, have a special responsibility to live every day."

Breyer, a graduate of Stanford, Harvard Law, and Oxford, does not, however, feel that his being Jewish confers any added responsibility or spotlight when it comes to his decisions on the Court. "I feel zero pres-sure. The fact that you might be ruling this way because you're Jewish, or the fact that you have to be careful to rule the other way to make certain nobody thinks you are, you know this kind of psychological you-get-so-mixed-up-you-can't-figure-out-what-is-the-real-reason-I'm-doing-this-or-that . . . I would say, luckily for me, the pressure even to get into that is, today, zero."

I ask if he was surprised that his religion was a non-issue in his confir-mation hearings—a fact reporters noted when he was nominated in May 1994. "I was a little surprised," he says. "And I would say that my parents would have been *more* surprised. I wish my parents were alive when I was appointed, but they were not, unfortunately. My mother's father came to this country at the turn of the century, and if he had thought that his grand-son would be appointed to the Supreme Court, he would have thought that was hard to believe. My *mother* would have believed it." He laughs. "But if you told my grandfather that there would be two Jews on the Supreme Court at the same time and nobody would make an issue of that, he would have found that to be impossible.

"When I was appointed, I was asked by a reporter from a Jewish news-paper, 'What do you think about two Jews being on the Supreme Court at the same time?' And I said, 'Fine.' " His intonation is markedly blasé. "Just like that; my tone of voice is important: 'Fine.' Not so unusual. Not beyond the realm of thinking. Because *that's what we're trying to achieve.* We're trying to achieve a world where, if you say you're Jewish, if you say you're black, if you say you're Hispanic, if you say you're a Muslim, 'Fine.' Just like that: 'Fine.' "

Breyer says he doesn't feel the weight of history even though his nomination marked only the second time in the Supreme Court's history that two Jews have served on the nine-justice bench simultaneously. (Louis D. Brandeis and Benjamin Cardozo presided together in the 1930s.) And he doesn't make much of the fact that, for the first time, the Court decided in 2003—at the behest of Breyer and Ginsburg—not to convene on Yom Kippur, even when the holiday falls on the first Monday in October, the date that has always commenced the fall term. "Both of us wanted that and it wasn't a problem," he says.

It is, however, a departure. When he clerked for Arthur Goldberg, the fourth Jewish justice, from 1964 to 1965, there was no special dispensation for Jewish holidays. But Goldberg celebrated them with gusto. "We used to have these great seders at his house every year," Breyer says with a smile. "He always invited all the labor leaders, and most of the seder was spent singing various songs that I think came out of the labor movement. It was great."

After Breyer's nomination, the *New York Times* did a profile in which Breyer's former colleague on the Harvard Law School faculty, Morton Horwitz, criticized him. I read Horwitz's quote to Breyer:

> The nominee has little in common with such past Jewish justices as Brandeis, Cardozo and Felix Frankfurter. Breyer's social instincts are conservative . . . If we still believe there is this social justice strand in the best version of the American judiciary, and that's what all these Jewish justices stood for, Breyer doesn't stand for that. The words "social justice" would somewhat embarrass him.

Breyer looks startled. "There, I have no idea. I would say the words 'social justice' don't embarrass me," he says. "I guess that was somebody who was opposed to my nomination; ask him."

I read Breyer a different quote about him, from the same time period—this one in a Jewish newspaper from his younger brother Charles, a U.S. district court judge in San Francisco who is still an active member of their childhood synagogue. "He's very kind," Charles said of his brother. "He has a dry, self-deprecating sense of humor. And he's a great worrier about everything, little and big. He falls right in with the [Jewish] tradition."

Breyer smiles. "He knows me better than Morton Horwitz," he says.

Aaron Sorkin

"FOR SOME REASON, in our Passover Haggadah, there were ads."

Screenwriter/playwright Aaron Sorkin has his sneakers propped on the conference table, and he's chain-smoking. "I remember that there was an ad for Maxwell House coffee—four different kinds of Maxwell House coffee—which they called 'The Fabled Four.' And every time we got to that page in the Haggadah, my brother, my cousin Dave, and I would just lose it." Sorkin laughs vigorously.

It's an odd day to be visiting Sorkin on the Warner Bros. lot because it's his last day of work as head writer and creator of *The West Wing*. After four seasons and four Emmys, he's leaving the show and his office, which is half-packed in boxes. We're talking in a nondescript room next door that has a long table and some haphazard chairs. The offices have none of the glamour that I imagined the father of a hit show would enjoy.

Sorkin is as gregarious and manic as I've heard him described—he speaks loudly, rapidly, leaving almost no dead space; even when he's between thoughts, there are a lot of "uh-uh-uhs" to fill the thinking time. Meeting him, it's utterly clear why his scripts were infamously last-minute and how he managed to engender a feeling of creative madness on the set. "My first comedy love and playwriting love was Neil Simon," he says. "I would read his plays over and over again and that rhythm got into my head. So much comedy descends from the borscht belt and those comedians who were then the first ones in live television, whether it was Milton Berle or Sid Caesar. I don't know where the enzyme to entertain a room full of people came from." He stamps out a cigarette. "Humans are going to be hopeful. We're going to entertain each other and make each other happy. So perhaps the more screwed around you get, the better you're going to get at telling jokes and singing songs."

He recounts an anecdote he wrote for a *West Wing* script to illustrate the perseverance of Jewish humor. "This story was taken from something I'd heard about Robin Williams," he explains. "A bunch of Germans came backstage to see Robin Williams after a stand-up concert of his and they said, 'You're so funny; how come we have no one like you in our country?' and he said, 'You killed them all.' "

I ask Sorkin if he ever thought about the commercial risks of creating Jewish characters, for instance *The West Wing*'s Josh Lyman (deputy chief of staff) and Toby Ziegler (director of communications). The question sets off something of a tirade in which he mocks his critics for inferring ethnicity where it doesn't exist. "These characters on *West Wing* are Democrats, and the thing that a lot of Americans find so off-putting about them is they're such smarty-pantses." Sorkin mimics his detractors: " *'They think they're so smart,' "* he whines. " 'They think they're smarter than me; they make me feel so dumb!' " His volume rises. " 'They think they're so smart with their snappy comebacks and their words that they use so fast, so smart—those *Jewish* people on the *West Wing*! It seems like everybody on the show is *Jewish!*' "

He drags on his cigarette. "It doesn't matter how many times I have Martin Sheen [as President Bartlet] talking to *priests,* quoting New Testament *scripture,* talking about how he almost went to the seminary, talking to God in the National Cathedral *in Latin*; doesn't matter how many times I do that." Sorkin shouts, " *'He's a fucking liberal smarty-pants; he's a Jew!'* " Another inhale. "So. That was a long way of answering your question. Am I aware, when I'm creating a Jewish character on the show, that most of the country is going to see them as a Jewish character and that is not going to be attractive to them? I'm aware of it, and I say, 'Fuck it; you're getting it anyway; it's not your airtime, it's mine.' "

Sorkin has never been known for reticence. When he wants to fire a shot, he unpacks the howitzer. In one *West Wing* episode, for example, he created a radio talk-show personality based clearly, in part, on Dr. Laura Schlessinger. The character was a coiffed blonde radio host who is visiting the White House and who has said on her radio program that Leviticus 18:22 unambiguously states that homosexuality is "an abomination." Sorkin lambastes her through his surrogate, President Bartlet, in the following speech, meant to illustrate the absurdity of taking biblical dictates at face value in the modern age:

> I'm interested in selling my youngest daughter into slavery as sanctioned in Exodus 21:7. She's a Georgetown sophomore, speaks fluent Italian, always cleaned the table when it was her turn. What would a good price for her be? My chief of staff, Leo McGarry, insists on working on the Sabbath. Exodus 35:2 clearly says he should be put to death. Am I morally obligated to kill him myself or is it okay to call the police? Here's one that's really important 'cause we've got a lot of sports fans in this town: touching the skin of a dead pig makes one unclean. Leviticus 11:7. If they promise to wear gloves can the Washington Redskins still play football? Can Notre Dame? Can West Point? Does the whole town really have to be together to stone my brother, John, for planting different crops side by side? Can I burn my mother in a small family gathering for wearing garments made from two different threads? Think about those questions, would you?

Sorkin's Jewishness, as he describes it, was defined chiefly by his hometown, Scarsdale, New York, which was dominated by Jews, and brainy ones at that. "When I was there, the percentage of graduates going on to college was ninety-nine-point-something; and usually the ones not going to college were going on to become the chief of police. An extremely high percentage of kids were going on to Ivy League schools." It took him a while to recognize that Scarsdale was atypical. "Before I was sixteen or seventeen, if you had asked me to guess what percentage of this country's population was Jewish, I would have told you probably about forty-five percent. And I was stunned to discover that I was wrong." He says he wasn't conscious of the Scarsdale stereotype—the ostentatious Jew. "But you knew about the size of noses and money."

Sorkin didn't go to Hebrew school, which his parents, at one point, attempted to remedy. "I can remember when my parents, neither of whom had been religious growing up (my father's parents were much too busy being Socialists) maybe twice on Sunday morning asked us to hang out at the kitchen table, and we read the Old Testament. I think they were feeling derelict in their role as teachers," he muses. "But I don't recall us ever getting past Genesis."

He decided he wanted a bar mitzvah because his friends' ceremonies reminded him of the theater, which was fast becoming his obsession. "My parents had to take me to see plays because I loved everything that I was seeing," Sorkin says, "and now I was going to bar mitzvahs and it looked a lot like theater to me: Someone was up there performing, and there was music, singing, languages, wardrobe, and an audience! So my clarion call to Judaism wasn't through Judaism as much as through theater. It was five or six weeks before my thirteenth birthday and I called a father of a classmate of mine who was a rabbi and I said, 'Rabbi, I'm turning thirteen in six weeks, and I'd like you to teach me the Torah so I can be bar mitzvahed.' He said, 'Kid, I can't teach you the Torah in six weeks; it takes years.' And I said, 'No, you don't understand. I have a pretty good ear. If you just say it into a tape recorder, I can learn it phonetically.' "

Sorkin never got his quickie bar mitzvah, but he did pursue a theatrical life that continued to be informed and shaped, in some fundamental way, by the Jews of his suburb. "I went into the world assuming that it was like Scarsdale—that there were going to be lots and lots of people who were smarter than I am. And in developing my taste for what I liked to watch or write in a play or a movie or a TV show, what I began to love was simply *the sound of intelligence*. The way a smart, passionate argument goes. Someone who could argue the other side of the argument as convincingly as they can argue their own. My brother and sister are lawyers, my father was a lawyer, I'm married to a lawyer—we're no longer married, but I *was* married to a lawyer—they all love to debate like that."

That "sound of intelligence," as he describes it, is unmistakable in

Sorkin's dialogue, though of course it's not usually coming out of the mouths of overtly Jewish characters. When I come back to the issue of whether he thinks explicitly Jewish roles don't work in Hollywood, he scoffs.

"In 1970 a network executive told James L. Brooks [the TV/film writer who created *Rhoda* and *Taxi*] there are four things you can never have on television: people from New York, Jewish people, divorced people, and people with a mustache. If you look at the television landscape now, pretty much every show takes place in New York, characters are Jewish whether they're actually Jewish or not because it's the rhythm of comedy, and it is almost a requirement that these people be single or divorced because one way or another you need to be sending these people out on dates. And Tom Selleck is doing fine with his mustache. So things change."

Another cigarette. "That said, would a studio head have passed on *Schindler's List* if Steven Spielberg wasn't attached because it was a downer and too Jewish? I'll bet you anything. And it's one of the best films ever made by one of the best filmmakers.

"It's been very recently, to be honest with you, that I've felt in a little way—I don't want to go so far as to say *in touch* with things of the past, but the slightest fingertip connection that makes you feel something. In the post-9/11 world of the entertainment industry, I've realized that, just a few short decades ago, my career would have been ended: to be a forty-year-old man, Jewish, with a political ideology considered to be liberal and with a tendency to make public, critical remarks about the president, my ass would have been hauled in front of crazy people and my bosses—the head of NBC, the head of Warner Bros.—would have been too scared to work with me."

There is a mound of stubby cigarettes in the ashtray, and it's clear Sorkin needs to get back to his last day on the job. I ask him, finally, if he sees any commonality that explains the amount of creativity that has come from Jewish people over the years. "You can say there is," he says, "but then what do you say about the Tom Stoppards, the Noël Cowards, and the William Shakespeares? I don't know what to make of it. I think creativity is a wonderfully human quality."

In other words, he doesn't think Jews are uniquely creative, and his personal imagination is not fueled by his Jewishness; if it seeps in, it's only for the good of the story. "Someone who watches the show—a fan—once wrote a letter wanting to know why, in all four of the Christmas episodes that we've done in the four seasons, does the most significant emotional thing seem to happen to a Jewish character. It's purely coincidence," he says. "I never tried to get tricky with that."

Gloria Steinem

GLORIA STEINEM PHOTOGRAPHED IN 1971 BY JILL KREMENTZ

I'VE KNOWN GLORIA STEINEM most of my life. My mother, Letty Cottin Pogrebin, and she were among the five women who created *Ms.* magazine in 1972, and their desks were next to each other in the *Ms.* offices in midtown Manhattan. My childhood memories of Gloria are of a willowy woman in bell bottoms and big glasses who always had her hair hanging like thick curtains on either side of her face. She always greeted me warmly and tap-danced at our Hanukkah parties (my mother asked guests to bring some form of entertainment and Gloria resuscitated a childhood talent). But I never felt as if I knew her. She was always just the World's Most Famous Feminist—the face of the Women's Movement—and I was proud to have some link to her.

I never knew she was half-Jewish on her father's side. (Steinem's mother was an unenthusiastic Episcopalian.) Even when she started coming to the annual feminist seders, of which my mother was one of the founders and which my sister and I attended every year starting when we were ten, I didn't really connect that she had any link to my heritage. Those seders were kind of radical because they reinvented the ritual in order to honor and include the women who were left out of the Passover story and were traditionally tethered to the kitchen during the seder. In this feminist adaptation, men were not invited, and each participant brought something for the supper and a pillow to sit on around a tablecloth on the floor. Women passed a bowl of water and a towel to wash each other's hands, and there was an orange on the seder plate to challenge some rabbi's comment years ago that "A woman belongs on the bimah [the synagogue podium] like an orange belongs on the seder plate."

I remember being aware of how special this evening felt, the eloquence of the women present. When Gloria attended, it was only validation of the importance of the event: In a room full of accomplished women, she was the celebrity—along with Bella Abzug in her signature brimmed hat—and it made an impression on me that Gloria thought Judaism was worth four hours sitting cross-legged on the floor.

"The whole idea of remaking religious ceremonies to include women I found very magnetic." Steinem has just made us tea in delicate china and settled herself in a green velvet armchair in her New York City living room with a garden out back. She has damp hair from a shower and is wearing a black shirt, black pants, and white Nike socks. "Religion in general did make me feel excluded. But it was only through the seder that I came to realize that the ceremony in and of itself was less hierarchical than Christian ceremonies; everybody read and participated. I came to appreciate the democracy of it, the cyclical nature of it, the lack of emphasis on an afterlife. The feminist seder gave me whatever Jewish education I have."

I ask if, in light of her scant Jewish upbringing, she felt comfortable at the seder. "Absolutely," she answers. "I was really moved by it and I felt that I belonged there. I didn't know the songs because I wasn't raised with them, but I felt like this was my family. A couple of times after that, I went to a regular seder and I was quite surprised: It was so much less interesting."

Even twenty-five years later, the feminist seders continue today, and Steinem is still stirred by the custom that begins each service: Every woman introduces herself by her matrilineage—i.e.: "I am Abigail, daughter of Letty, daughter of Ceil, daughter of Jenny . . . etc." "I never get over being moved by people saying the female lines of their families," says Steinem. " 'I am Gloria, daughter of Ruth, daughter of Pauline' . . . and of course, in my case, that's not the Jewish side of my family, but it doesn't matter; the truth is the same: It's for all the women who were sad over generations because they could prepare the feast but not take part in the ceremony, all the women who had no names." She also appreciates the fact that every year there's a topic chosen for its relevance to current events and the Exodus story. "There's always a theme that's earnestly discussed in terms of our life now and in terms of the tradition," she explains.

Steinem's father, whom she describes as a "gypsy" who moved his family from one trailer park to another selling antiques, was "somewhat embarrassed by the idea of any religion." He never talked about his Jewishness. Her mother, on the contrary, extolled it. "What's ironic," Steinem remarks, "is that it was the non-Jewish parent who valued it, not my father." Her mother, Ruth Steinem, presented Judaism "as a wonderful heritage and gift and great tradition of social justice and culture. And my mother also used to tell me—against all logic when it came to my father—that Jewish men made better husbands." Steinem laughs. "I mean, I don't know how she could say that, given her situation." (Steinem says her father was a ne'er-do-well, at best.) "But she still felt—my father to the contrary—that Jewish men in general were more 'family-minded.' "

Steinem's mother also made a young Gloria conscious of the Holocaust. "I remember once, when I was very little during World War II—we were still living in Michigan—that she and I together listened to a radio show about the concentration camps. I was very young, so it was quite risky, I suppose, for her to do that—but she did it in a way that didn't frighten me but impressed me with its seriousness. She said, 'You should know that this is going on in the world.'

"I remember listening to a story of a woman trying to soften a crust of bread in a concentration camp in order for her child to be able to eat it." Steinem didn't connect, however, that these were her people. "I knew from my mother that we had distant cousins who were in concentration camps—or maybe I learned that later. I just kept imagining the children; but not as connected to me."

The religious amalgam she was exposed to included her Jewish father's mother, who embraced Theosophy—translated to mean "Divine Wisdom"—which comprises a melding of religion, philosophy, and science. "Though my grandmother was culturally Jewish and belonged to Jewish women's organizations," says Steinem, "in a spiritual sense, she kind of crossed over into the more mystical part of Judaism and then into Theosophy. She died when I was five, but she influenced me through my mother, who loved her—utterly *loved* her. The only reason I ever knew that in the Bible, when Ruth says, 'Whither thou goest, I shall go, and thy people shall be my people'—that it was a woman saying it to another woman—was because my mother used to say it about her mother-in-law."

Steinem says that as a kid she went through a "fundamentalist" phase, where she was drawn to the Presbyterian church because she was afraid of the boys in her neighborhood and "it seemed that the church was the only thing that could make men peaceful." But she was quickly disillusioned: "It became apparent to me that it was a place where people seemed to be nice to each other only because Jesus told them to."

Despite her churchgoing stint, she says, religious buildings alienate her today. "There's some part of me, when I'm in any religious institution, that makes me want to lie down and take off all my clothes. Just because I think I'm not supposed to be there somehow. It doesn't really include women.

"You know this wonderful thing about how the religious institutions are built to resemble the body of a woman? Years ago, when I was at the Smithsonian, I read some author on religious architecture who casually mentioned that, of course, in patriarchal religions, the building is usually built to resemble the body of a woman. That's because the central cere-mony is one in which men take over women's power of giving birth. In a Christian church, it's especially obvious because you have an outer en-trance, an inner entrance, a vestibule, a vaginal aisle, two curved ovarian structures on either side, and then the altar in the center, which is the womb where the miracle takes place, where guys dressed in skirts say, in ef-fect, 'You were born of woman and therefore you were born in sin. But if you're good and obey the rules of the patriarchy, you can be reborn through man. We will sprinkle imitation birth fluid over your head, give you a new name, and promise you rebirth and everlasting life.' It just all pisses me off so much that I want to defile the altar at any opportunity by reasserting women's bodies, the reality of women's power to give birth."

The notion of Jewish comradeship was a foreign concept to Steinem until college. "I became aware that there was a Jewish community when I went to Smith because there was a cultural difference between me and the other young Jewish women in the dorm. They were very close to their families and would call their mothers every Sunday to discuss who they'd gone out with and what they were wearing." Steinem, whose mother had become mentally ill and dysfunctional by that time, began to associate Jewish women with supportive, involved parents. "It was fascinating, and seemed warm and enviable, but also alien.

"While I was a freshman, I was going out with a young man in Washington who was Jewish, and that, I think, was my first real understanding, because he was very much a part of the Jewish community. I actually went to a temple once with him; it was one of the High Holy Days and they had *sold tickets*, which I just found completely mind-boggling—it was like getting tickets to a movie. And also everyone was so talkative and noisy in the congregation—I was used to these very Protestant, silent ceremonies. So I was quite shocked. That was not the best introduction."

Steinem got a warmer view of Judaism in her twenties when she started dating Blair Chotzinoff, who became her fiancé, until she broke off their engagement. "He had a wonderful, accomplished family," she says. "His father had been the accompanist for Jascha Heifetz and had married Heifetz's sister. They didn't have a lot of money and they lived in a little apartment across from Carnegie Hall in New York. Leonard Bernstein was this young, awestruck guy coming by to visit, sitting at their table; it was a very seductive, creative, exciting community. I think Blair's family was mildly upset by the engagement because they considered me not Jewish, but they didn't care that much."

Nevertheless, she felt out of place in their orbit. "Blair was so handsome and sexy and interesting and creative, that I was desperately grabbing at little straws to keep my own identity in the middle of this accomplished family." Finally too uncomfortable, she played the half-Jewish card to extricate herself. "I was trying desperately not to get married because I knew that it would be a terrible error," she says guiltily. "So I think that I—I hate to say this, it shows you how desperate I was—I think I once said to them that I wanted to get married in a church. Just because I was trying so hard not to get married. And they said, 'Fine, you can do that, but we're not coming.' Which was a reasonable attitude."

Steinem's brushes with Judaism—mostly via boyfriends—didn't take hold. "The stage of my identity today is that I feel like if there's trouble for the Jews, I should be there," she says. "But if there's not trouble, I feel like I don't have to worry about it. Which is a different level of identity. Because when I see Jews doing well, I don't necessarily kvell in the same way that I do when I see women doing well. But I feel endangered when Jews are endangered; it's like I'm a foul-weather friend."

When it comes to Israel, she's a critical friend. "I have an instinct for it that I don't argue or defend: It just always seemed to me that nationalism wasn't safe. I don't know why that was—maybe because people used to say, 'If they get us all in one spot, then they'll really kill us.' Some of it was that I didn't believe in nationalism altogether. I've always had an unexplained feeling that the strength of Judaism was not to be tied to national boundaries. It was to be everywhere—to be a culture and a spirituality. Not to be a nation-state."

She tells me that her opinion on Israel led to one of her few political disagreements with my mother during their long friendship. "I once totally dismayed your mom," she says with a smile. "She will tell you about it—ask her; I think she wondered at the time if she could ever forgive me. But I really felt somehow that Israel was kind of the last punishment of Hitler. To have created a necessity so tragic, that everyone became a nationalist. At the same time I was inspired by the kibbutz and the transformation of the military to include women; I found that very inspiring."

Was there any point in her life when she wished she'd been more Jewish? "I wish I'd had the feminist seder all my life. But I don't wish I had what comes to mind in a more traditional sense when you say 'Jewish' because I think I had enough trouble trying to get over Marx and Freud."

Interestingly, at least half of her closest friends are Jewish—"which is disproportionate," she acknowledges—and she feels more simpatico with Jews. "Because there's a warmth and a vitality," she says, "and because the Jewish tradition encourages your mind to work, includes social justice, is more circular and less hierarchical." Not that she responds to every Jew who comes along. "I'm not convinced that every Jewish person in our crowd in New York has more warmth than every non-Jewish person: You know, some of them are pretty Episcopalian." She laughs.

I ask if Jewish groups have pressured her to wear the mantle more publicly. "Actually the people who have pressured me to be a Jewish symbol, you might say, are the right wing. Because they're the ones who put out all the literature saying how feminism is a Jewish plot to destroy the Christian family. And they name us all—the Jewish feminists." She says her favorite specimen of hate mail, which she kept for years, was a postcard filled to its edges with vitriolic name-calling. "It was great because it had managed to get everything on one little postcard. It said something like, 'Now that I've heard you speak, I know for sure you are a long-haired, Commie, dyke, lesbian slut who dates Negroes.' And then in the last line, it said, 'Isn't that just like a Jew?' " She laughs. "It's really fantastic—they got it *all* in there."

Larry King

"I ALWAYS LIKED SHIKSAS." CNN anchor Larry King is being driven in a Town Car from the Regency Hotel, where he slept the previous night, across town to CNN's Manhattan studio. Tall and reed thin, he's wearing Façonnable jeans, black Nike sneakers, and his trademark suspenders. "I only loved three women in my life and none of them were Jewish," says King, who has been married seven times—twice to the same woman—and is now married to Shawn Southwick-King. "When I grew up, nobody lived together; you just got married. So I got married. But in retrospect, I only loved three women in my life: I mean, in the sense where they could emotionally affect me."

Does he make anything of the fact that the three wives he genuinely loved were gentile? "Never think about it," he says with a shake of his head. "I didn't have anything against Jewish women. When I meet someone, I don't ask, 'What are you?' I'm simpatico with a lot of people. There are a lot of links between Catholics and Jews."

Did his mother care if he married a Jew? "She would have liked it if I did. But no pressure. I never saw her show an act of prejudice. For example, one of my cousins, Karen, got involved with a black guy. Her parents disowned her—her Jewish parents wouldn't talk to her. My mother? They came to her house for dinner."

King's current wife is a devout Mormon. "She believes she's going somewhere after she dies," he says. "I hope she's right." But he points out that religious leaders who purport to believe in an afterlife aren't so different from those who say they hear voices from the grave. "Sometimes we have guys on our show who communicate with the dead," King says. "They claim the dead come back and talk to you. And every time I talk to mainstream religious leaders, they say, 'Ay, those people are crazy.' I think, 'What do you mean, crazy? They're saying exactly what *you* say!' "

King was turned off to Judaism back in Hebrew school in Bensonhurst. "I didn't like the God of the Old Testament," he says. "The God that's printed there was vindictive, vain, petty, violent. Why would I want to share an afterlife with that God? And I never bought the whole story—that Moses went up the mountain and God spoke to him. I thought Moses was kind of a genius for coming up with Ten Commandments—most of which don't make any sense today. For instance: 'You can't covet.' *Everybody* covets! You don't *do* anything about it, but who doesn't covet?

"So I'm not a religious Jew—I grew up away from that. But I'm so culturally Jewish. For example, the *thought* of mixing milk and meat would cause me to throw up. I would *never* take a piece of steak with a glass of milk; I think I'd faint. I'll eat a piece of bacon. But it has to be very dry. And my mother used to bring home bacon that wasn't from a pig."

His mother wasn't Orthodox, but she kept a kosher home, lit candles every Friday night, and hosted a seder. "And we ate Chinese food on Sunday like every good Jew." King smiles. "I still do *yizkor* [tribute to the dead] every Yom Kippur even though I don't believe my mother is hearing it anywhere. I don't know if there's a God. I'm a classic agnostic, but I'm a Jewish agnostic. That is, 'Maybe there's *something*! Don't count it out!' "

He no longer fasts on Yom Kippur. "I used to. Once I made a terrible mistake. I was a big smoker before I had a heart attack, and one year I broke the fast with a cigarette. This is not smart. When you inhale it, and you haven't had anything—no food for twenty-four hours—I thought I was going to topple over. I used to go to William Safire's house [the *New York Times* columnist]; he used to do a big break-fast dinner. He'd say, 'Eat light. A little matzo ball soup first.' "

I ask about King's two young children (by his current wife), ages four and three at the time of our meeting. "They're going to be Mormons," he says, "because my wife is so devout. When we got married, I said, 'Look, since I'm agnostic, I have no right to tell you not to teach them what you believe. But give them an opening.' So if they ever ask me, I'd tell them the exact same thing I'm telling you: 'I don't buy that God, I don't know if there's an afterlife.' I'll tell them the truth. I'll take them with me when I go to synagogue on Yom Kippur and explain what it is. I hope they choose what they want. Most people believe what their parents believe. You're a Mormon because your father was a Mormon. I'm a Jew because my father was a Jew."

Would it matter if his children ultimately don't call themselves Jews? "It wouldn't be the end of the world if they don't, but I'd like them to know that they're Jewish," he replies. "Whenever we apply to schools we list them as both Jewish and Mormon. I have three grown children too—a boy, forty-seven, another boy forty, and a daughter thirty-five. The only one of the five who goes to synagogue is the boy who is forty. He's raising his kids Jewish. I have five grandchildren. Three are being raised Jewish." King pauses for a moment. "I just want my kids to be smart enough to learn for themselves and not be something by rote. I don't want to believe something just because my father believed it."

His father, a Russian immigrant who spoke fluent Yiddish, died when King was very young. "He died on the way to work of a sudden heart attack. My mother never remarried and raised the two of us: I was nine and a half, my brother was six. Before I was born, she had lost a son named Irwin who died of a burst appendix when he was six. My father was buried next to him in Beth David in Elmont, Long Island, near Belmont racetrack. A very appropriate place for my father to be buried because he used to bet the races.

"I took my dad's death badly. I took it as him leaving me. He was very close to me. I didn't go to his funeral. In retrospect I was very angry. People said all the wrong things to me: 'You're the man of the house now; you gotta take care of your mother.' I got angry at my father: Not only did he leave me, but he gave me responsibilities. But I said kaddish every morning and every night. I'd go to synagogue in snowstorms. I'd always walk in, and all the men would feel sorry for me because most of them were in their forties and fifties and here was this little nine-and-a-half-year-old boy."

King did manage to talk about his father in his bar mitzvah speech. He says the ceremony was bare bones because his mother was destitute. "We were just getting off being on relief. We didn't have a party. I had the ceremony and then afterwards we served snacks in the anteroom." He remembers studying for his haftarah—the Prophets reading that follows the Torah portion. "The rabbi had his long beard and he used to put his hands through it. When I did my haftarah all in Hebrew, he stood right next to me and it was his fingers that went down the lines as I read. I had a long haftarah. When we were just beginning to study for our bar mitzvahs, my friends and I would always look up our haftarahs—'How long's your haftarah?'—because your haftarah depends on your birthday. And I had two and half pages. Sam Finkelstein had half a page. What a break."

King once said that growing up in Brooklyn, he didn't know what a Protestant looked like. "Ninety percent of my friends were Jewish. We had a club called the Warriors. Occasionally the Italians would yell at us, 'You killed Our Lord!' So one day my friend Herbie confessed. He said, 'Okay, we killed your Lord, but the statute of limitations is up.' " King laughs.

"Since I was a kid, I never understood prejudice. I always regarded it as stupid. It means to prejudge. I don't do it when I interview. I don't expect someone to be good or bad. To judge a people by what their religion or color happens to be is self-defeating. When I came to Miami the first time, I got off the train with sixteen dollars in my pocket to try to break into radio and the first thing I saw were two water fountains: one said 'Colored,' one said 'White.' I drank out of the 'Colored.' I sat in the back of the bus where blacks were supposed to sit. I've never had a rational explanation for bigotry. Hitler took away the best of his community: The Jews of Berlin were the symphonic maestros, the medical leaders. He chased Einstein out! It makes no sense to me.

"Lenny Bruce used to say, 'There will always be prejudice, because people need people to kick around.' He was a great friend of mine. He said this in 1960: 'Someday blacks will get equal rights, and when they do, we're going to have to find someone else to pick on.' He says, 'I got it! Eskimos! We'll pick on Eskimos! Did you ever meet a bright Eskimo? Would you ever be taught by an Eskimo leader? Can you name a famous Eskimo author? No! Eskimos cause problems.' "

Larry King changed his name from Lawrence Harvey Zeiger early in his radio career in Miami. "Nowadays, they wouldn't have changed it," he says. "Today in broadcasting, any name goes. But when I started in 1957, right before I went on the air, the general manager asked me what name I was going to use. I hadn't even thought of it. He had the *Miami Herald* newspaper open to an ad: 'The King's Wholesale Liquors.' So he said, 'How about Larry King?' And I said, 'Fine.' "

When people argue about anti-Semitism or anti-Israel sentiment on his program, King says he tries to stay out of the fray. "When I'm doing my show, I'm a journalist. Do I want the Jews to survive? Of course. Do I hope there's peace in Israel? Naturally. I'm emotionally a Jew. It's like Irish New Yorkers who rooted for the IRA: I have an understanding of them."

He defends the instinctive loyalty toward one's own. "When people ask, "Why do blacks root for black athletes?"—I know the answer. I root for Jewish athletes. Why? You just want to see them do better. Any minority roots for the minority to do well. Why is that strange? If I go to the voting booth and I'm voting for the state legislature and Goldstein is running against Smith, I vote for Goldstein."

After a bout with midtown traffic, we've arrived at the CNN studios on Seventh Avenue near Penn Station. We conclude the interview in the elevator: What would he consider the most Jewish moment in his life? "Being recognized on the streets in Israel," he says. "Standing at the Wailing Wall and having a rabbi say to me, 'So what's with Perot?'

"I think also one of the most unique moments was when I addressed the graduating class of Columbia University Medical School. I stood up in the Columbia robes—I never went to college—and I said that I had this vision of my mother looking down, rubbing her eyes, looking again, and saying, 'He's a *doctor!*' "

Mark Spitz

A. B. DUFFY/HULTON ARCHIVE/GETTY IMAGES

MARK SPITZ WAS THE FIRST, and remains the *only*, Olympic athlete to win seven gold medals in one year—1972—each one breaking a world record. The fact that this champion swimmer was Jewish and triumphed in Munich, Germany—forty-five minutes from Dachau—was history making enough. But tragic events made it even more poignant: The same night he won his seventh prize, nine Israeli athletes were taken hostage by Palestinian gunmen, who killed them the following day.

"I was a Jewish swimmer at the Munich Olympic Games," Spitz recounts by phone from his Los Angeles home. "We were fifteen miles from Dachau, and here was this Jew at the games. It's important to remember that 1972 was the coming-out party for Germany; the nation was saying, 'We're here and we're not like the regimes of thirty years before. These games will be the perfect example that the German people have come full circle.' And then I go and win seven gold medals. And that night, the terrorists jump the fence and later kill eleven Israeli athletes. So there was simultaneously the triumph of my accomplishment and the tragedy of the Israelis; these two were inextricably linked."

The day after Spitz's gold sweep was September 5, 1972, and Spitz, then twenty-two, was supposed to be at a press conference talking about his feat. Instead he was rushed out of the country because law enforcement feared he might be in danger. "I left that evening because of the ensuing uncertainty of what was going on," says Spitz. "I woke up in London—I was with my swim coach—and read about the killings in the paper. It was unbelievable."

He says the symbolism of these events only intensified the public focus on his religion. "My being a Jew was put into the limelight in a very big way," says Spitz. "I had a calling of the guard to step up to the plate and recognize that I was Jewish."

Not only were journalists and Jewish groups bombarding him; Spitz says even the president was preoccupied with his affiliation. Recently released tapes of Richard Nixon's conversations, publicized in December 2003, show that Nixon deliberated over whether to make a congratulatory call to Spitz. "There was a quote from Haldeman talking to Nixon," says Spitz. "It was about how Nixon painstakingly vacillated about whether to call Mark Spitz after he won seven gold medals but elected not to do so. Do you know why? He assumed, because most Jews are Democrats, that I supported George McGovern. This was September of 1972—two months before the election—and he didn't want to align himself with Democrats by congratulating a Jewish athlete because Spitz was probably a Democrat," Spitz says with a chuckle. "The irony is that I've been a registered Republican since I've been able to vote."

Spitz, fifty-five, grew up in California and Hawaii—where his father, Arnold Spitz, put his son in the water at age two. "I was bar mitzvahed on December 7, 1963, the anniversary of Pearl Harbor," says Spitz. "I was very nervous that day, but there were only two people who knew I made a mistake during the service. I remember that because I was embarrassed. In my haftarah portion, I chanted one line twice. Only my grandfather and the rabbi knew that."

He started competitive swimming before he was ten and was named the world's best ten-and-under swimmer. At fifteen, in 1965, he went to Tel Aviv for the Maccabiah Games—an annual contest created to celebrate and encourage Jewish young people in sports—and he won four gold medals. A year later, Spitz went to compete in Germany. I ask him if it felt strange to be there as a Jew. "In 1966 I was sixteen and the war had only been over for twenty years," Spitz says. "The thought did occur to me that anyone I met in their forties could have been a Nazi at one time. It was weird to walk into a bakery and know that, twenty-odd years ago, I would have been pulled into the street and shot . . ." He pauses. "Of course your humor about that situation is a lot different when you're sixteen or seventeen because nothing happens to a seventeen-year-old."

Years later, in 1985, Spitz was asked to return to the Maccabiah Games to carry the torch. "There were three little girls, thirteen years old, who ran behind me," he recalls. "Each of those little girls' mothers was pregnant when I was in Munich. Each of their fathers was killed as one of the Israeli athletes. That was pretty emotional." Spitz is quiet for a moment. "That was the best time for being a Jew."

But Spitz says his status as a Jewish role model never fueled his athleticism. "I embraced the fact that I'm Jewish. Did that have an influence on me athletically? Zero. Does it influence younger people? Yes. Because it says that being a Jew is not something that limits you physically and athletically."

I ask him why he thinks there are so few Jewish sports stars. "There are fewer sports stars only because there are fewer Jews," he scoffs. "We have the same number of Jewish athletes proportionately as non-Jews have. Does that mean that Catholics are better than us? Hell no. It's just sheer numbers."

What about the stereotype that Jews go on to be doctors and lawyers, that they favor more intellectual pursuits? "That's not because we're smarter," says Spitz. "If you keep telling your kids to hit the books, even a dummy can get smarter."

Spitz himself was preparing to go to dental school before he abandoned that plan after the 1972 Olympics. These days, Spitz works as a stock broker and financial analyst and gives inspirational speeches. He's been married to "a Jewish girl," as he puts it—Suzy Weiner—for thirty-two years. "Early on, before I even got married, I thought about how I would raise children if I were to marry outside the religion. How would they identify with who they are and would it be good to have a split situation, where they were raised with both religions involved? I realized that that wasn't something I would be comfortable doing. So perhaps it's prejudiced, but I focused on marrying someone Jewish."

Both his sons—Matthew, twenty-four, and Justin, fourteen—went to Stephen Wise religious school starting from kindergarten and became bar mitzvah. "The funny thing is that it becomes kind of contagious," says Spitz. "When you're around a community that embraces religion, you embrace it more, too. I've been participating in this in a big way. I'm a big proponent now. I used to hate going to High Holy Days services; as soon as I got there, I was counting the minutes till I could leave. Now I look forward to going. Maybe I'm older and not as fast paced as before. Also, I'm an example for my kids. I enjoy it."

Though he never experienced any overt anti-Semitism, he's still bothered by the fact that he was not asked to participate in the opening Olympic ceremonies in either 1984 or 1996. "Look, one of the greatest honors bestowed upon someone in the Olympic games is that at the opening ceremonies they honor past notable Olympians and their accomplishments—not just the medals they won but the way they've represented their sport. These athletes would participate in the opening ceremonies, either running the torch, lighting the cauldron, or carrying in the Olympic flag. In the Olympic games in L.A. in 1984, I was thirty-four. They had two people involved in carrying the torch—both of them deserving as far as their credibility and athletic accomplishments. But Mark Spitz wasn't there.

"In the 1996 Olympic games, there were three people involved in the opening ceremonies and the lighting of the torch. And in no cases were any of them Jewish. I guess Mark Spitz didn't win enough medals to be included in that fraternity. I leave it to you to figure out why. Does it bother me? Would I have liked to? Sure. I didn't compete in the Olympic games just to win medals, become known as a Jew, and then be asked to run in the Olympic flame; I did it because I love the sport. But I noticed.

"But hey, I'm still not dead," he adds. "There's still a chance."

Alan (Ace) Greenberg

JOHN H. GUTFREUND, the former CEO of Solomon Brothers, once described Alan ("Ace") Greenberg, the former CEO of Bear Stearns, this way: "Ace is by the numbers, very black and white . . . He sees prices, he's not clouded by emotionalism."

You can say that again. My interview with him is a dramatic confirmation of that characterization. This highly respected titan of Wall Street, who made $16.2 million in 1994 and who built Bear Stearns from 1,200 employees (and $46 million in capital) into the fifth-largest investment bank—with 10,300 employees and $1.4 billion—talks in bullet points instead of paragraphs, without a wasted word or a trace of sentiment.

From his seat on the bustling trading floor (he prefers sitting amid the din to staying in his office), his strong bald head stares straight ahead—military style. He doesn't even glance at me sitting next to him when he answers my questions. Jacketless, in a monogrammed blue shirt that strains against his former football player's frame, Greenberg holds a lit cigar in his meaty grip. Its smoke fills the air and probably violates company policy.

Greenberg isn't rude; just abrupt. It's difficult to describe the staccato exchange, so perhaps an excerpt is the best illustration:

Q. Did you go to synagogue and Hebrew school growing up?
A. The whole works.
Q. Was that important to your parents?
A. If I had my choice, I wouldn't have done it. I would rather have played football.
Q. The fact that you excelled at football—was that something other Jewish boys were doing?
A. No. I was the only one. For years, in fact. Obviously it helped me a lot socially. In high school. There was anti-Semitism, no question about it, in Oklahoma City.
Q. Can you describe that a little more specifically?
A. Well, the high school fraternities didn't allow Jews in them. That wasn't easy for me. But I played football, so that kind of made up for it.
Q. Was there some sense that people gave you special treatment despite your religion because you were an athlete?
A. Yeah, I think the girls did.

Greenberg attended the University of Oklahoma on a football scholarship, and after a back injury transferred to the University of Missouri, where he received a bachelor's degree in business in 1949. When he was applying for entry-level jobs on Wall Street, he was shut out of the white-shoe firms because he was Jewish. Only Bear Stearns would take him. "In those days, it was pretty tough," Greenberg says. "But that's changed." Was the prejudice explicit? "Well, there was a certain amount of anti-Semitism even among Jews then. Some of the investment banks in New York that were prominent were Jewish—they were basically run by German Jews. But they weren't exactly looking for me either."

The war had recently ended when he began his professional life, so I ask him if the Holocaust had a strong impact on him at the time. His response is trademark efficient and unrevealing. "No, I don't think so. I obviously felt very bad about it."

Over the fifty years that Greenberg has spent advising prominent investors such as Henry Kravis and Donald Trump, he's garnered respect for his prudent, unvarnished counsel and his quirky pursuits. He is a nationally ranked bridge player and an ardent devotee of archery, pool, whittling, dog-training, and the yo-yo. Not to mention magic tricks. He's spent many Saturday mornings in Reuben's Delicatessen honing his sleight-of-hand before other "expert" amateurs. "That has nothing to do with being Jewish," he says with a chuckle. "The rabbi didn't encourage it."

Greenberg keeps glancing at his telephone, as if willing it to ring so he can get back to work. Suddenly it obliges and Greenberg seizes the receiver. "Hello?" Apparently that's standard procedure at his company: Greenberg believes no phone should ring twice before it's answered. There are other Greenberg tenets that have become Wall Street lore: his announcement that paper clips would no longer be purchased by the company—employees should reuse the ones from incoming mail; interoffice envelopes should be conserved by licking the flap alternatively left and right. Employees must pay the difference if they upgrade to first class, and there are no corporate jets or limousines. Greenberg used to distribute half-kidding memos with tips on frugality, penned by an "advisor and mentor" he invented named Haimchinkel Malintz Anaynikal. For example: "The time to stop stupidity and be tough on costs is when times are good. Any schlemiel and most schlamozels try to cut costs when times are bad." Or Anaynikal's guidance on the envelope-licking strategy: "If one has a small tongue and good coordination, an envelope could be opened and resealed ten times."

On a more sober note, Greenberg has for decades required that his top managers donate a portion of their income to charity. "Four percent," Greenberg says. "All senior managing directors. There are about six hundred of them." Has any employee ever balked at that? "One person. In the whole time we've done it." What happened to him? Greenberg grins. "Well, he's not a senior managing director anymore."

Greenberg believes there's an obligation to give back. "I think it's called a Jewish tax," he says. He has contributed generously to many college scholarships and charities such as the United Jewish Appeal-Federation. He's also established a school and a health center in Israel. "I used to joke, 'When I grow up I want to be a philanthropist because it seems to me they always have a lot of money.' So that was my goal: to be a philanthropist." Some of his causes are not exactly mainstream: for instance, his support of a dwarfism program at Johns Hopkins Hospital, or his one-million-dollar donation to New York's Hospital for Special Surgery to offer Viagra to the poor. Greenberg laughs when I inquire about that one. "At that time, Viagra wasn't covered by any of the insurance companies, and I felt it was just something that I could do for people who couldn't afford it."

The phone rings again and the boss seizes it. "Hello? Hi, Gail . . . So what can I do?" Greenberg is famous for cutting to the chase: *What's the bottom line?* He discourages small talk, and doesn't seem to engage in it himself. He's even alert to distractions: When I try to rummage unobtrusively in my bag for my last page of questions (he's running through them like water), Greenberg notices and barks, "What do you need?"

Q. Once you had your own family, I wonder to what extent you maintained the childhood traditions with which you were raised—?

A. Maintained them.

Q. How important was it to you that your two children feel Jewish?

A. Very.

Q. How did you pass that on?

A. Oh, just in conversations with them, trying to explain the culture and how important I felt it was.

Q. Was it important to you to marry a Jewish woman?

A. My first wife was, my second wife is not.

Q. And your children—?

A. My daughter married a Jew; my son did not and they got a divorce. I don't think religion played any part in it whatsoever.

Q. Did you care if they married outside their religion?

A. No. I wanted them to just be happy. Sometimes Jews marry Jews and they're unhappy, right?

A former bachelor-about-town, escorting the likes of Barbara Walters or Lyn Revson, Greenberg has been married since 1987 to Kathryn A. Olson, nineteen years his junior, who was until recently a supervising attorney at the Benjamin N. Cardozo School of Law at Yeshiva University in New York, specializing in the legal rights of the elderly poor. Press accounts say Olson has softened Greenberg.

A trader named Mitch stops by Greenberg's work station. "Can I get you to do a quick meet-and-greet?" he asks.

Greenberg replies: "Sure; what time?" Mitch: "Say, two-thirtyish?" Greenberg seems delighted: "The guy from John Hancock? That's fine. Shake-and-bake, right? Okay, Mitch; that's fine."

I see that my sliver of Greenberg's attention span is thinning, but I want to finish by asking one mushy question: Where does being Jewish fit into his sense of self? I'm surprised by his instantaneous response: "Well, it's first and foremost. Everybody knows I'm a Jew—there isn't anybody I do business with who doesn't know it. If my name was O'Reilly, I might be embarrassed by somebody saying something against Jews, but it doesn't happen with a name like Greenberg. They may think it, but they don't say it." He laughs and stamps out his cigar. I thank him for the interview. "That's it?" He looks genuinely surprised. "If you have any questions, call me."

Charles Grodin

"I WAS ACTUALLY THROWN OUT of Hebrew school," says Charles Grodin, the actor/writer/director/talk-show host who asks me to meet him in an empty Broadway theater before a rehearsal. "It's because I asked questions if I didn't understand what was going on. It wasn't the only place I was thrown out of around that age, and always for the same reason. I think I always asked questions politely, but my persistence alienated people. Still does." Grodin, who grew up in Chicago in an Orthodox family (his grandfather was a rabbi and Talmudic scholar), speaks in run-on sentences. ("I'm the kind of interview," Grodin confesses, "where you just say, 'Hello,' and I'll answer you for an hour.")

"I changed Hebrew schools and there was a fellow named Rabbi Morris Kaplan who was the father of my closest friend and he became the head of the League of Rabbis in Los Angeles and he was a spellbinding storyteller and he would tell all the stories from the Old Testament and he wrote my bar mitzvah speech and, because a lot of my family was from Chicago, it was a triple bar mitzvah in Chicago and because he wrote a very good speech and I delivered it adequately and it was the date of the birth of Israel, it got applause, which is inappropriate in a synagogue, but I think that's where I first got the idea to go into show business; I said 'Oh, that's a heck of a feeling right there.' And that was it."

Grodin believes he got more than a taste for theater out of Hebrew school. "I think my whole value system came from Hebrew school," he muses. "That you're supposed to be honest, to look out for other people, not to sit around and bad-mouth people or find things wrong with people, and that's what I've really carried forward. It was all part of what I absorbed in Hebrew school and what I observed in my house."

He left home—and Jewish observance—when he was eighteen, and gives his own kids more culture than ritual. "I'm now doing it with my son who's fifteen. Today I made him a Nova Scotia salmon bagel—cream cheese, onion, tomato—and he said afterwards, 'Boy, you really know what you're doing.' Now I'm going to have to see how tough he is: I'm going to do herring and sour cream with him and see if he can handle it."

His current wife—his second—joined a temple in their Connecticut neighborhood. "I don't go to the synagogue," he says, "but I was talking to my wife yesterday, and told her that my two main goals right now are to figure out what I can do to make some kind of a contribution to the well-being of other people, and to also try to somehow connect with nature. I know that sounds pretentious—but I've never been good at stopping and looking at anything. Those are the two things that provoke me and I—I don't know, does that have to do with Judaism? I don't really know, it's just a way of being. You know, I read in one of the weekly magazines yesterday that Nelson Mandela was equating Israel with Iraq, since they both have nuclear weapons, or they might. I think the more anti-Semitic talk or the more anti-Jewish feeling I hear, the more Jewish I get."

Grodin himself has never felt any anti-Semitism. "No one thinks I'm Jewish; I don't look it. And I haven't heard much prejudice around me, although I do get the sense sometimes with some people that there's just an underlying assumption that the Jewish person is going to do you in. I feel the opposite: that it's much more likely you're going to get help from Jewish people, that Jewish people are going to be more sensitive. So I don't really get it."

Grodin did get a taste of Jewish sensitivity when there was a Jewish outcry over the film *The Heartbreak Kid* (1972), in which he played a Jewish man so obsessed with a shiksa girl—played by Cybill Shepherd—that he abandons his wife on their honeymoon. "I was the only person who seemed to see that the film would be taken as anti-Semitic," Grodin says. "I definitely saw it that way. Initially I was just so excited to be playing a lead in a movie. But I was the only one that said, 'You know, they're going to hate this guy.' Everybody else thought I was just being self-protective. The first review I saw of that movie had a headline that said 'You'll hate him, love the movie.' But it bothered me, and I was living in an Upper West Side building at the time with a lot of Jewish people who commented that the movie was anti-Semitic because of my behavior of leaving a Jewish wife on a honeymoon for a gentile girl. When I was doing the role, I never thought of 'Jewish' and 'gentile,' I thought of a girl who was driving me crazy and who looked like, you know, happiness is just around the corner. But there was ultimately resentment from Jewish audiences."

Mirroring the film, Grodin's first wife was not Jewish, which he said disappointed his parents, Ted and Lena. "It was disturbing to my mother and to my first wife's mother as well," he says. How did he navigate that? "I just went ahead and got married anyway," he replies. "You know, a rabbi once told me that the children of mixed marriages are the biggest anti-Semites, which turned out not to be true at all."

Grodin says he didn't care a wit who his grown children married. "I think it's so daunting to find somebody you could be married to. If that person turns out to be an Indian or a black person or something other than Jewish, so be it. My daughter is married to a non-Jewish fellow, and I pushed for the marriage. I just thought he was remarkable, and he is."

Are Grodin's close friends Jewish? "Well, let me see . . . I've actually got a top-ten male friend list that I talk about for numerous reasons and let me just examine it; I never thought of it that way." He runs them through in his head. "Number one is not Jewish, two is, three is, four not, five not, six not; I'd say it's about a split fifty-fifty." So he doesn't find his Jewish pals inherently more compatible? "I'm friends with Phil Donahue, I'm friends with Regis Philbin, I'm extremely compatible with them."

Grodin donates time to causes both Jewish and otherwise, but his Jewish loyalties, he says, get seniority. "I definitely lean in that direction. If there were two functions, I'd go to the Jewish one." And though he's not an intense Jew, he'll occasionally draw the line at ecumenism. "I'm emceeing an event that the Kiwanis is giving in Connecticut for Christmas and now they're telling me, 'We're going to begin by all of us singing

Christmas carols,' and I didn't say anything at the time, but I probably won't sing them."

He says his consciousness of the Holocaust never leaves him, in part because his family lost relatives. "Just coming from Brest-Litovsk, which, depending on the year, was either in Russia or Poland around that time, there's no question: I have a powerful connection to that event. Oddly enough, any time I went to Barney Greengrass [the bagel and lox fixture on Amsterdam Avenue] when I used to live in Manhattan, or sometimes when I go into this beautiful Jewish deli where I live now, I don't know why, but at that moment I think of people in the camps and say to myself, 'Oh my God; *look at all this.*' "

Kitty Carlisle Hart

KITTY CARLISLE HART PHOTOGRAPHED IN 1977 BY JILL KREMENTZ

KITTY CARLISLE HART, doyenne of New York's theater society but perhaps best known for her fifteen years as a panelist on the TV show *To Tell the Truth*, is dressed formally for Easter lunch when I meet her on a Sunday morning. The ninety-five-year-old answers her apartment door in a bright lime green suit, low black heels, a double strand of pearls, pink lipstick, and fingernails to match. With her proper appearance, patrician accent, and fancy name, Hart is not exactly the Jewish archetype.

"They changed my name when I went on the stage," warbles Hart—formerly Katherine Conn—sitting primly on her velvet couch, a small black purse at her side as if she's waiting for a bus. "I found the name in the phone book. I originally wanted 'Via Delia,' but I was persuaded against it."

For all of her personal accomplishments as a singer and actress, Hart derived much of her early stature from her marriage to Broadway legend Moss Hart, director of *My Fair Lady* and *Camelot*, and coauthor—with George S. Kaufman—of *The Man Who Came to Dinner* and *You Can't Take It with You*. She was acting with the Marx Brothers in their 1935 classic film, *A Night at the Opera*, when she met her future husband for the first time. He was looking for a leading lady for his musical *Jubilee*, written by

Cole Porter. "I didn't get the part"—she smiles—"but I got the man." Not easily, she adds. "It took me nine years!" She almost giggles. I kept thinking, " 'He'd be so perfect! He's Jewish, I'm Jewish, I've seen all of his plays, I think they're wonderful, he's never been married, neither have I. Why doesn't he think of marrying me?' "

They were wed in 1946 by a justice of the peace in a small ceremony. "Moss said if we had a big wedding, we'd have to invite a thousand people," she recalls. She says he knew as little about being Jewish as she did. "He cared about it politically," she says. "He cared about it in terms of a consciousness of injustice."

They celebrated no Jewish holidays, except of course when they were invited to Passover at the home of a prominent fellow thespian. "I once went to George Gershwin's for—what was it called where they read and put the matzos out?" she asks. "A seder," I offer. "Yes," she says with a nod. "Gershwin and Oscar Levant [the composer and actor] decided to do the whole seder in music. It was so wonderful! They sang and did the whole thing in jazz." Who else was there? "I remember Robert Sherwood," she muses, mentioning the playwright, "but I don't remember anybody else."

Hart was definitely aware of her religion being heavily represented in her profession. "Everybody in the theater was Jewish except Cole Porter," she declares.

Looking back, does she make anything of that or feel it was pure coincidence? "I think there are times when a whole flowering of some kind of an art form occurs. It happened in Greece when they built the Parthenon; they never did anything great after that. It happened with the flowering of opera in Italy. Jews had the American musical theater. And people don't know how to do it anymore."

Hart was raised by a socially ambitious mother, Hortense Holzman Conn, who was cold and unaffectionate. In Hart's 1989 autobiography, *Kitty*, she writes: *"the moments of physical closeness were so rare that when I was fifty years old, I was still trying to crawl into her lap."* (Hart's father, Joseph, a gynecologist, died suddenly in the 1938 influenza epidemic.)

Hortense was determined to obscure their Jewishness. She sent her daughter to Miss McGehee's finishing school. "It's the chicest school in New Orleans," she says. "Very grand; they call me an '*alumna*.' " She was conscious, as a child, of being different. "I felt peculiar at Miss McGehee's," she says. Her classmates knew she was the only Jew. "They didn't want to eat lunch with me. They said it was because my mother sent my lunch with French bread."

Hart says her mother wanted desperately to gain entrée into gentile society, and when they moved to Europe, Hortense managed to figure out how. "It was through music and bridge," she explains. "Bridge in those days was 'Open Sesame' to society."

And did Hortense successfully penetrate the upper crust? "Oh yes," Hart assures me, her hands folded in her lap. "I came out in Rome *and* in Paris."

But the party was short-lived. "We 'passed' as gentiles for years because it was easier to get up in society," Hart says. "But then we lost what little money we had in 1929 and we came back to America. I had to get a job to support my mother. That was the best thing that ever happened to me; I was nineteen or twenty years old. I got a job in the Floradora Sextet—I was going to sing—" Hart sings in a fragile voice that trills with age: *"Oh, tell me pretty ladies, are there any more of them like you?"*

During the Second World War, she entertained the troops around the country—"I always sang 'The Star-Spangled Banner' "—and she only gradually became aware of the hatred against Jewish people. "I went to a dinner party," she begins. "In those days, everybody dressed up for dinner parties. And they were talking about the Jews in a way that was just awful. It was unbearable. And I got up in the middle of dinner and I said, 'I am Jewish, and I won't sit here and listen to this kind of talk for another five minutes.' And I left. The bravest thing I ever did."

Her stories are told in patchwork—with loose threads of Jewish identity dangling here and there. Another snippet: "I once got into a taxi in New York with my mother"—she's laughing at the memory already—"and after she dropped me off, the driver turned around and said to my mother, 'That's Kitty Carlisle, right?' And my mother said, 'Yes.' And he said, 'Is she Jewish?' and my mother said, 'She may be, but I'm not.' " She laughs again.

One of the few times she went to synagogue was when her mother died. "My children were very small, and I wanted to give them a sense of finality. I didn't want to have this poor lady just disappear out of their lives. So I decided to take them to Temple Emanu-El on a Friday for the service for the dead. And I said to my son, Chris, 'This is the home of your forefathers.' And he looked up at the rabbis and said, 'I only see three of them.' "

Despite the fact that she raised her children with Christmas and without Hebrew school, she seems to have silently preferred that they marry Jews. "Catherine is married to an Episcopalian, and my son, Christopher, is married to a Catholic," she says. I ask if she ever cared that they marry Jews—or told them she cared? "No," she answers quickly. So she didn't care? Hart pauses. "I'm not prepared to say," she says.

Hart's Jewish identity is obviously hard to pinpoint, but the strongest signpost of her connection comes in her sense of peril—a suspicion that Jews could be targeted again. "I always felt that the time would come when we would have our packs on our backs and be pushed out. I said to Moss one day, 'Darling, where will we go when we get pushed out of this country? I have my pack on my back; are you ready?' He said, 'Well, let me think about it. I tell you what: We'll go to the Gobi Desert. They have the best music, they have the best philosophers. Then again, who will fix the toilets?' That made me laugh so hard, I forgot about my fears."

Norman Lear

ARCHIE BUNKER WAS A RACIST, sexist anti-Semite, but his creator, Norman Lear, reminds us he was all talk. "There was nothing violent about his attitudes about anything," Lear says. "He was more fearful than anything else. I mean, he wouldn't light a cross on a lawn or be any part of that. But his invective would cover the landscape."

Lear says there are too many instances in *All in the Family*'s nine seasons on the air to recount the times Archie knocked the Jews, but in one episode, he needed a Jew: When Bunker feigned injury from a minor traffic accident in order to recover insurance, he wanted to hire a Jewish attorney to help him win. "He went to Rappaport, Rappaport, and Rappaport or something like that [it was actually Rabinowitz] because he wanted the smartest lawyer, so he wanted a Jew," Lear recounts. "And of course, when the law firm sent somebody out to the house, the attorney was, from first blush, anything but Jewish. This lawyer explained to Archie that since his firm knew the neighborhood, they figured Archie couldn't be Jewish: 'So of course they sent me: I'm the house goy' " (a reference to the designated gentile who would turn the lights on and off for an Orthodox family during Sabbath).

Lear sits at a wooden table in his spacious Beverly Hills office, looking relaxed in a blue chambray shirt, vest, and rimless glasses. There is no overt evidence that this is the man who made $485 million when he sold his company in 1985 or that he fits a description from Chicago's Museum of Broadcasting Communications: "*No single individual has had more influence through the medium of television in its 50-year history than Norman Lear.*" Despite a producing career that's spanned four decades and included iconic series such as *Sanford and Son, Maude, The Jeffersons, Good Times,* and *Mary Hartman, Mary Hartman,* plus some debacles along the way, he appears to be a very youthful, hearty eighty-two-year-old, perhaps by necessity: In addition to his three children and five grandchildren from his first two marriages, at the time we meet he now has eight-year-old twins and a fifteen-year-old son by his third wife, Lyn Davis.

"I was thrilled to see Benjamin bar mitzvahed," he says of his teenager. "His mother's not Jewish, and I would not have insisted. It was *his* decision and that thrilled me. But I have no interest in the formal processes of the religion. When I infrequently go to a gospel service, I'm more comfortable there than I am in synagogue. I think Jewish services are stiff and dull and awkward."

Lear grew up poor in Hartford, Connecticut; on Passover, his grandparents "came with their dishes" from New Haven. The Lears moved to a small apartment in Brooklyn just in time for his bar mitzvah celebration. "I remember a bathtub full of soft drinks and beer and ice," Lear says with a smile. "And a bunch of fountain pens. And two-dollar bills."

Lear says his brand of Judaism is social consciousness. "I will say this about my own Jewishness." He leans forward. "I was inordinately aware of anti-Semitism in the world. I listened to Father [Charles] Coughlin on the air as a kid—I don't remember how old I was. And I listened to a fellow by the name of Carl MacIntyre out of New Jersey who was a Protestant Jew-hater. And I had a nose for anti-Semitism unlike any other. *People for the American Way* came directly out of that nose."

He's referring to the organization he started in 1981, which became an influential watchdog safeguarding constitutional freedoms. He founded this group after spending hours watching ministers Jimmy Swaggart, Jerry Falwell, and Pat Robertson on television—preparation for a screenplay he was writing which, he says, was going to "savage" their profession. Lear recalls his revulsion watching these evangelists: "I thought, 'Not in my

America,' " he says. " 'This is really dangerous.' And so I decided to create a TV spot—a sixty-second commercial which ended with a fellow saying, *'They can't tell you you're a good Christian or a bad Christian depending on your political point of view: That is not the American way.'* So somebody suggested, 'Call the organization "People for the American Way." ' " Lear chuckles. "I'm on sort of a rant here, but it all began out of this Jewish nose."

That Jewish nose isn't sensing rampant anti-Semitism these days, but it's still wary. "While I feel absolutely at home and fully integrated in this country, history teaches that one's guard should be up," Lear says. He is also watchful of the behavior of Israelis. "I remember the first time I started to read the word 'humiliation' in newspapers: 'Arabs being humiliated at roadblocks.' I know just enough about uniforms and humanity to know that, no matter who they are, some percentage of people in uniform will behave very badly. So there had to be some truth in those accusations of Israeli abuses from the beginning of the settlements. And to the extent that Jews caused humiliation, I was very upset."

Lear makes it clear he thinks religious allegiances are obsolete; he has a vision of creating harmony via our television screens. "I think when the hardware, the technology becomes available, one of the most helpful things that could occur—by 'helpful' I mean to bring together races, religions, and so forth—would be an international Sunday morning service. It would be closer to gospel, but it would be universal gospel—music from every discipline everywhere in the world—which was all about that which unites the human of the species, not the stuff that divides us like, 'I worship this way, you worship that way.' "

How would he square his proposed melding of religions with the joy he felt when his son chose to become a bar mitzvah? "It's not easy," he concedes. "What I want to maintain are the memories of my grandmother Hannah Rachel and all the gorgeous little fresh-to-this country Jews. But you see it's only *my* memory; my kids don't have those memories. And you can't pass those on. They die with me. My memories of Friday nights with the spanking white tablecloth and the candles and so forth . . ." He trails off.

"We live at a time when, I don't know how many dozens of times in the course of a year, I'll have a conversation with my wife about how difficult it is to pull the family together in our *own* home. We have three kids: The twins are eight, Benjamin is fifteen. They are so bloody *busy*. It used to be just the *father*'s late." In other words, family togetherness—which he connects to Jewish scenes of his childhood—makes him want to keep certain rituals afloat. "I could cry remembering how my grandfather took an hour and a half for the Passover ceremony that used to bore the shit out of us," he says with a laugh, "but now I reflect on it, how sweet it was."

So he carries that tradition on, albeit without religious content. "At my seder this year, we did a reading of Justice Learned Hand's speech about liberty, and then we talked about how it applies to everything that's going on in the world," he says. "It was the best seder service I can remember. My kids *got* it." He pauses. "I realize that I haven't answered your question." He has, in his way. It's what I've heard from so many: They reject Judaism—and often religion in general—but they can't let go of feeling Jewish. "I'm sure others have expressed to you the enormous pride in the contributions the Jewish people have made anywhere one cares to look," Lear says, "except perhaps ice hockey. But medicine, science, music, *comedy*—my God."

He says his proudest Jewish moment was watching his son hold the Torah, but other Jewish snapshots resonate, too. "Eating my grandmother's matzo balls. Just remembering her stooped over the oven and her soup . . . The smell." His eyes water. "I cry easily. Jews are wet. I like that. There are wet people and dry people. Jews are wetter."

David Copperfield

DAVID COPPERFIELD, the nation's most successful magician—who has won nineteen Emmy awards, ranked number 43 on Forbes' Celebrity 100 list of 2003 (earning fifty-five million dollars), been knighted by the French government, waxed at Madame Tussaud's, and licked on postage stamps in four countries—has just asked his assistant to order him Kentucky Fried Chicken.

When I first arrived at Copperfield's high-rise apartment on a sweltering June day in New York City, his assistant opened the door and closed it almost as fast, telling me that the air-conditioning was out and the interview would take place across the hallway in the "Sky Terrace"—a private common room for tenants with wraparound views of the city. To my frustration, I'd stolen only a fleeting peek of Copperfield's foyer before the door closed; I glimpsed antique arcade games aglow in the darkness. (Copperfield collects and restores these toys.)

As I settle myself on a beige sofa in the earth-toned Sky Terrace, Copperfield pads in in bare feet, dressed in a spotless white Polo crew-neck sweatshirt and immaculate jeans. His polish, even in a casual setting, is consistent with his personality, at least the one he reveals to me: smooth, glib, chary.

I ask him to tell me about his Jewish upbringing.

"Ask me specific questions," he instructs.

"Did your family celebrate all the Jewish holidays?" I ask.

"I think so," he says. "I went to Hebrew school four hours a week up through my bar mitzvah. I hated it, of course."

Did he tell his parents he wanted to stop? "No. I didn't think it was an option. It was part of the program. But I'm happy for the experience now and if I'm lucky enough to have children someday, I'll do the same thing for them—to give them a sense of purpose and place. Part of who I am is based on the fact that we're taught that we have to fight a little harder, we're constantly challenged; as a people we're told 'no' all the time. And you have to just believe in yourself, no matter what's thrown at you."

David Copperfield—born David Seth Kotkin—remembers that his bar mitzvah made him sick with anxiety the night before. "I was sweating with a 102-degree temperature," he recalls. "Midnight turned into 3 A.M., then 4 A.M. I had ice cubes on my head because I was so nervous about remembering my haftarah. At the time you had to learn it from a record, there were no cassette tapes; so the cantor would actually cut an LP for you. I took that LP to my non-Jewish summer camp and learned my haftarah by LP. There were no headsets. I was playing it in my room the way they broadcast reveille."

Copperfield, forty-nine, dropped all Jewish observance after his bar mitzvah. "Even though my mother was born in Israel—she moved here when she was five years old—there was no motivation to continue it. There was nobody pushing me along to do it. The focus changed." He says he's not the type who sticks with things. "I lasted in college for three weeks; I went to Fordham University, which is a nice Jewish school; I'm joking—it's a kind of Jesuit school. I dropped out after three weeks, and twenty years later they gave me an honorary doctorate. So my Jewish mother got to see me become a doctor—even though it was the honorary kind."

I tell him I read an interview he gave the *Cleveland Jewish News* in which he related doing magic to being Jewish. "What did I say in the article?" he asks me. I read him his quote: "*We are taught throughout childhood not to take 'no' for an answer; it is possible to turn 'no' into 'yes' and that is what magic is all about."*

Copperfield looks at me. "It's my quote, so you can use it again," he says with a smile. He grabs my list of prepared questions out of my hands. "I'll say it again right here." He starts to reread his own quote aloud. I ask him if he could elaborate instead. "I think every human being to a certain degree is persecuted," he says. "We're taught in the Jewish culture the same story over and over again, whether it's in *Fiddler on the Roof,* the Holocaust, or the Maccabees: that we have to rise above persecution and do our best. Magic is about making people dream and taking impossible things and making them happen; taking things that aren't supposed to be and turning them into something beautiful. Houdini was a Jew; I'm a Jew."

I ask if he's ever thought about the nexus of being famous and Jewish. "For me, I'm a little fearful sometimes if I'm in various countries that there will be a crazy person that will be a Jew-hater and want to make a point. And I'm not trying to make any political stands. I'm just trying to help people dream and grow. So that crosses my mind. My parents are always a little bit nervous because I have shows everywhere in the world and I'm pretty popular in a lot of countries that are anti-Jew." Which countries? "I don't really want to talk about that," he says.

"So I don't deny being Jewish," he continues. "But I don't really push it. Not because I don't believe in who I am, I just think there are people out there who will make up their own scenario in their heads, especially now."

He also thinks that highlighting one's religion distracts from one's work. "If Danny Thomas was known as a Lebanese guy, I think we'd be focusing on that," Copperfield says. "Casey Casem: Arab guy. But it should be about his Top 40 Countdown. Winona Ryder: I think it's pretty cool that she's Jewish: hot-looking girl, really talented. I don't think it's a matter of hiding it; but not emphasizing it just allows people to focus on their work. I'm trying to think—the people who are non-Jews that are famous, do we talk about their religions? Do we know what Halle Berry is?"

I ask if he would be uncomfortable being known as a Jewish star? "My answer would depend on the political climate, just for the safety of my family. I can do more good as a person that is apolitical and I can make more people happy and have people escape more than as a person that is becoming symbolic."

He says he's very comfortable performing in Germany, where he has broken records for sold-out crowds. "I was engaged to a German girl for six years," he adds, referring to supermodel Claudia Schiffer, with whom he broke up in 1999 after a much-publicized romance. "In Germany, they make such a big deal of the Holocaust and teaching the Never-Again mentality—they drill it into people's heads. So they overcompensate."

I speculate that planning a life with a German woman could have raised issues for someone Jewish. "It didn't," he says quickly. "It matters in one sense: I hope that when I settle down with somebody whom I can trust and trusts me, that our children can be brought up Jewish and go through the same torture I had when I was a kid. Because I think it did do me good at the end of the day. I've had a few long-term relationships—some famous, some non-famous, and most people have been agreeable to that idea."

His assistant lets him know that his fried chicken has arrived. I ask, finally, why he changed his name to Copperfield when he was starting his career. "I don't know," he says absently. "I didn't think Kotkin was a catchy enough name."

So it wasn't that Kotkin sounded too Jewish?

"Do you think it sounds Jewish?" he asks. "I don't."

Morley Safer

MORLEY SAFER, the seventy-four-year-old, wizened newsman, is reclining on a well-worn leather couch in his handsome carriage house, smoking the cigarettes he's never quit, and sipping coffee he can't do without—even on Yom Kippur. "I'm not a total hundred percent faster as I once was," he says with a smile. "I do have coffee. I need it. Giving up coffee would be cruel and unusual." Aside from caffeine, fasting is not a hardship. "I never eat breakfast anyway and not much of a lunch," he explained. "But I remember the agony of it as a kid. I mean, *agony*."

He and his wife, Jane, are not observant, but they do go to synagogue each year. "Then we go for a long walk. I think the sheer disengagement, even if one didn't go to synagogue, does make you think. Which is hardly a punishment once a year, and in fact, may be a bonus. It's not exactly wearing a hair shirt or flogging your back or climbing one thousand steps on your knees."

Safer grew up in Toronto, where he experienced some anti-Semitic incidents he prefers not to talk about: "I don't want to go into all that," he says, stubbing his cigarette out in a large ashtray.

His family observed a modified Shabbat—attending Saturday services, then a matinee. The only holiday he still celebrates without fail is Passover. "We've been doing it for the last thirty-odd years, since Sarah was born," he says, referring to his only child, who is thirty-four when we talk. "It's an interesting, really jolly mix of people." Not all the guests are Jewish. "I think it's about evenly split," Safer says. "And the most insistent ones—the ones who start calling weeks before, saying, 'We haven't been invited yet'—tend to be the non-Jews." He chuckles.

For the traditional meal, the Safers order their gefilte fish from Rosedale Fish and Oyster Market on the Upper East Side—"it's the oldest fish market," Safer tells me, as if that should be obvious to any true New Yorker—but he's still in search of the perfect lump of pike. "I've yet to find gefilte fish that is as close to the one my mother made," he says wistfully.

Sarah was sent to Hebrew school, he says, so that she'd be equipped to spurn Judaism with intelligence. "You've got to know what you're going to reject," Safer says. "You should not be allowed to reject something without learning it first." Today she is non-observant. "It was her choice," he says. "Would I like her to come to synagogue on Yom Kippur with us? She has once or twice. But I can't impose—she's a thirty-whatever-old woman. As a young woman she kind of rejected it, probably more strenuously than she does now. She has a son—our first and only grandchild." Sarah's husband is a Russian Jew, but they chose not to circumcise their son. "I would have wanted it because it's such an ancient tradition," he says. But he didn't pressure her. "There's nothing more destructive than that."

The Safers never celebrated Christmas, and I ask if he has any reaction to Jews that do. "I find it a little alien, but I'm not a tyrant on these things. I find excessive Christmas stuff kind of gives me the willies anyway. And I hate Christmas in New York because of what happens to the city. I mean, you can't get a cab, the weather is lousy—you freeze your ass off, and there is no joy in it. I love the idea of it—the idea of charity and all of that.

"I'll tell you a story," he continues. "At the office, you always get presents for the people you work with around the holidays. I'd been doing it for the thirty-three years I've been at *60 Minutes*; I always give a couple of very good bottles of wine, or one very good bottle of wine and one very good bottle of spirits or malt. And it was just fascinating: One year, it was at the height of the homelessness crisis, and I said to my staff, 'Look, I have a thought: What I would love to do is go and buy food and gloves and scarves. And we'll distribute the stuff and then all go and have a nice supper together.' They looked at me like I was crazy: 'What? That's the worst idea you ever had.' I was devastated," he says with a laugh. I tell Safer they probably couldn't stand the idea of giving up their malt liquors. He nods. "Here I am, engaging this holiday with the kind of heart that you're supposed to have. And people were appalled."

The doorbell rings. "That's our dog coming back from her walk," he says, looking suddenly like a thrilled little boy. "Come here, Dora! We have a houseguest! Dora!" Dora runs to Safer and they canoodle each other. "Hello, my little lady; here's my sweetie pie," They clearly have a mutual admiration. I try to pat her casually, despite my complete awkwardness with animals, and think of the right thing to say. "She's so clean," I manage.

"She likes you," Safer says with a smile. "She loves loving. I warn you." After some genuine ardor from her owner, Dora pads away, ostensibly to seek a second breakfast.

As Safer fetches a bottle of Pellegrino water from the open kitchen, I ask him whether he thinks being Jewish has affected his reporting in any way. "I think, after all these years, and having spent a lot of time covering Middle East wars and covering Israel between the wars, you really are able to detach when you do this work.

"But I remember the first time I went to Auschwitz—it was probably in the fifties. I was working for the CBC [Canadian Broadcasting Corporation], doing a half-hour documentary on Poland. This was after the food riots—late fifties, early sixties—and the full horror had really been revealed. That was just one of the most powerful moments in my life. The camp hadn't been museum-ized yet; it was in many respects not much different from how it was left.

"And it was also very powerful the first time I went to Germany, which was even earlier. I remember getting off the plane in Frankfurt and hearing that sound of the guttural language." He pauses. "And you think, 'There but for a few years . . .'—this was 1954 as opposed to 1944—it's not that much time."

So, would Safer say that his Jewishness is a significant part of him? "Oh yes," he responds. "It's who I am. I think it's an important part mainly for what many people may regard as secular reasons, though I don't think they're entirely secular. That is, I think it leads to a more contemplative kind of life. I think it gives you a very, very clear idea of ethics, which I'm not suggesting I may practice. But I certainly have a clear idea. Which is why I never understood why they go through this charade now of *teaching* ethics. You can't teach ethics. You have to be a zombie not to know the difference between right and wrong. I think that a Jewish background does give you a very, very strong sense of doing the right thing."

William Shatner

STAR TREK'S CAPTAIN KIRK used to recite the four questions and lay tefillin during morning prayers. That's difficult to imagine. William Shatner's image has never been exactly Jewishy. He's sandy haired and barrel chested—his bearing, at the height of his fame, was that of a classic leading man. "There was a whole thing where people would say, 'Funny, you don't *look* Jewish,'" Shatner recalls. "The racial stereotype bothers me to this day. I'm very sensitive to it; I find it offensive."

Today, at seventy-three, he looks like he actually could play the archetype if he wanted to; he's got the paunch and the weathered face. But he's still a far cry from Tevye.

My interview with him turns out to be brief—our scheduled L.A. meeting unexpectedly conflicts with a rehearsal for a benefit performance he's appearing in that evening. The Shakespeare Festival/LA, whose mission is to connect the community to the classics, is producing a reading of *Two Gentlemen of Verona*. Shatner's assistant, Robin, tells me to meet her at the David Geffen Theatre and promises to grab Shatner during a rehearsal break.

When I walk into the theater to watch a run-through, my eyes have to adjust to the star wattage on the stage. Dressed casually, in shorts, jeans, and flip-flops, are Tom Hanks, his wife, Rita Wilson, Robin Williams, Billy Crystal, Martin Sheen, Christina Applegate, Drew Carey, and Shatner himself, perched unobtrusively on a wooden stool among the megastars. His button-down black shirt doesn't deemphasize his girth and he appears to be sweating under the lights, but he looks happy to be in such A-list company. Williams, Crystal, and Hanks are the jesters—constantly injecting silliness that makes everyone break into giggles; Shatner laughs along but doesn't initiate any of the shenanigans.

When there's a pause in the rehearsal, I finally get some time with him in the theater lobby, both of us leaning on a high refreshment table. "I was brought up in a Conservative Jewish home in Montreal," he tells me, "and compared to the United States, Conservative there is pretty much like Orthodox here. My mother had a kosher home and I went to Hebrew school until I was bar mitzvahed and I did tefillin for a few years. And in the context of those times, there were some really tough fights between the Jews and some of the population, generally in places that wanted the Jews out— a club that didn't allow Jews, or areas that didn't sell homes to Jews. What I was mostly aware of was that kids were jumping on me at school and I had to fight. Sometimes two kids at once.

"I recall the worst moment was when I was playing football for the high school and it was Yom Kippur and I had to stay home instead of practice. And the coach replaced me because I missed practice and I never got my position back. And I remember to this day being really hurt because we were a really good championship football team. I was a back and I loved football."

He says he didn't try to convince his parents to let him skip Yom Kippur services; he knew by that age it was sacrosanct. "It wasn't a choice," he says matter-of-factly. "It was Yom Kippur." Schoolyard ridicule was also a given. "When I would go to Hebrew school after regular school, I'd walk on the opposite side of the street to the shul and then look both ways and run across the street and run into the synagogue before anybody could see me," he recalls. "There was some kind of unspoken feeling of oppression. Being Jewish was difficult as a kid. I got the strangest questions about what we Jews did in the chapels. My non-Jewish friends were filled with bizarre knowledge about things we did with dead cats and blood. I mean, just the strangest things that, looking back, I wonder what the parents must have thought about Jews; because they're clearly where the misinformation was coming from."

He says he feels no vindication having become a star. "I wish I could say that I felt some sense of satisfaction that the kid who had to fight for his life on the streets of Montreal sure showed those bullies after achieving some measure of celebrity, but I've long since forgotten the humiliation. It's probably—in fact likely—lodged in the recesses of my brain and affects my behavior to some degree. Being humiliated for any reason will leave a scar, but my adult life has taken over and I no longer think of what it was to be a boy on the streets of Montreal. On the other hand, I'm acutely sensitive to people being mutilated—emotionally or physically—because they are Jewish, and this has stayed with me all my life."

He never denied his religion, but he didn't advertise it, either. "There were many times when I kept silent about being Jewish as I got older, when Jewish jokes were told," he confesses. But he says he wasn't closeted when he became famous. "I've made no secret of it," he insists, "and a lot of people know I'm Jewish now." Really? I tell him I haven't found that to be true. Shatner rethinks it. "Perhaps they would be surprised," he says with a shrug. "So is Mr. Spock." He smiles, speaking of his former *Star Trek* colleague, Leonard Nimoy. "He's Jewish as well."

Unlike Nimoy, who based his Vulcan greeting on a Jewish blessing, Shatner never incorporated any Jewish signs on the Starship *Enterprise*. "I never knew what Leonard Nimoy was doing with his forked fingers," he says now. "I tried in vain to fork my fingers but always got a singular raised digit that was always misinterpreted."

Shatner has, however, been developing a film comedy with a Jewish theme: "It's a glorious idea," he explains, "in which a young group of people who come to the aid of some folks sitting shivah decide to start doing that as an occupation to make money. That is, they find a person who is mourning their loved one and help them in a variety of ways while they are sitting shivah. They call themselves guess what? The Shivah Club." The project is currently in limbo, or as Shatner puts it, "in a state of vibrating stillness": "It's out there on the many highways that lead to producers who have money," he says. The idea came to Shatner when he was mourning his third wife, Nerine, who was found to have drowned in their Los Angeles pool back in August of 1999, with alcohol and Valium in her system.

But aside from this project, Shatner makes it clear that his faith isn't at the forefront of his identity. "I'm Jewish because my mother was Jewish and because my background was Jewish and I understand Jewishness. I like the comfort food of Jewish dishes and the lilt of the language—people speaking English in a kind of Jewish lilt is a kind of familiar, homelike sound." But it's not at the center of who he is. "I would say it's like twenty-five percent of my life. It's a four on a scale of ten in terms of influence right now."

He says he dropped the rituals because they didn't make sense to him. "I didn't understand the effort to be Jewish. I am Jewish, and the formalities—although I recognize the necessity of keeping them up, because it's what being Jewish is—by the same token, there's more to being Jewish. So I'm Jewish without the protocols."

The actors are called to resume rehearsal and Shatner returns to the stage.

Linda Fairstein

LINDA FAIRSTEIN PHOTOGRAPHED IN 1994 BY JILL KREMENTZ

"JEW BITCH."

That's what Linda Fairstein was called when she was prosecuting some of her most high-profile cases as head of the Manhattan Sex Crimes Unit for twenty years. "Interestingly, I heard it first during the Robert Chambers trial." She refers to the 1986 case in which eighteen-year-old Robert Chambers killed eighteen-year-old Jennifer Levin in Central Park in what came to be known as "The Preppy Murder." "Robert Chambers was Catholic and very warmly supported by the Catholic clergy, who first bailed him out," says Fairstein, now a best-selling author of the Alex Cooper crime novels. "Jennifer Levin was 'The Jew' and she was called that in very derogatory terms. A lot of Robert's friends called me 'The Jew Bitch' in and out of the courtroom when I passed them every day. It was about the ugliest thing I'd ever heard."

She heard it again during the Central Park jogger trial in 1989—where five black teenagers were accused of accosting a young jogger in a brutal attack, also in Central Park. "Whenever I came or went from the courthouse, that's what they called me. And this was done by the black and Hispanic advocates for the defendants." I ask if it upset her. "I was certainly fazed. But I always had a phalanx of detectives around me. What it brings strikingly home is how frightening it is when it happens and people don't have the kind of protection I had. And it was disturbing how it resonated with people who want an easy catchphrase."

It was a far cry from her law school days at the University of Virginia, when the few Jews and blacks there became close friends, in part because of their common ground. "There were only a handful of Jews in my law school class, a handful of women, and a handful of African Americans," says Fairstein, sitting on her hunter green couch wearing a blue blazer with gold buttons and what looks like a man's gold watch. "Within the first two weeks of school, the Jews and the blacks sort of found each other and bonded."

When she was being called names by blacks during the jogger trial, did part of her want to trumpet her enduring law school friendships as evidence to the contrary? "It would never have occurred to me," she answers. "I remember growing up with that 'some of my best friends are Jews' kind of thing. I mean, what's the point? In those trials, it was more important for me to simply say, 'Look at the facts.' "

Fairstein's no-nonsense instincts were instilled, she says, by her Jewish father: "The importance of one's name and integrity came from him," she says. "There were just things that Jews didn't do. If a bad event happened and a Jew was responsible for it, there was a tremendous sense of shame in our home."

She brought some of that shame on her father when she first prosecuted a Jew. "In 1977, I prosecuted a dentist from Westchester who practiced in Manhattan, named Marvin Teicher, who had been accused, and was convicted at trial, of sexually abusing women who he had drugged for dental procedures in his office. It was the first case I'd had that got high-profile media attention, and it pained my father that this was a Jew. On top of the shame of doing what this dentist was doing, this was bad for the Jews."

Fairstein, fifty-five, is the product of an interfaith marriage. Her mother was Episcopalian by birth and converted when she married Fairstein's father. Their romance is the stuff of movie scripts: "They met while working in the same hospital—she was a nurse, my father was a young doctor. She was pretty, he was handsome. They fell madly in love. Her conversion was really to please his parents, who were devastated at the idea that their son was going to marry a Christian. They got married in June of 1943 in Norfolk, then went by bus to Virginia Beach for a honeymoon. Soon after, my father was shipped out to the South Pacific. It was a war story like a lot of people have from my generation, where the father was away for a long time. My brother was born while my father was in the South Pacific, and so my father never saw his son until he was eighteen or twenty months old. My father wrote to my mother almost every day. She's got this chest of letters from the war that I would love to do something with. I used to love to read them."

Fairstein's mother took her conversion seriously, becoming a dedicated temple member, though she still put up a Christmas tree every year. Young Linda didn't question a Christmas tree in a Jewish home. "When you're a kid, you just do things and you don't think much about it until you're nine or ten and somebody criticizes or makes fun of it," Fairstein says.

She quit Sunday school when she felt personally insulted by the teacher. "He was explaining that Judaism passes through the mother: you're not Jewish unless your mother is Jewish. He said that although ours was a Reform temple, his personal belief was that converting didn't make my mother a Jew. So therefore I was illegitimate. I came home outraged and defiant. I just said, 'I'm never going back there.' "

Fairstein says her perspective on her mother's conversion changed dramatically when she was ten or eleven years old. "Like most girls that age, I read Anne Frank for the first time and it changed everything. It made me do everything from starting my own 'Dear Kitty' diary to having the nightmares about 'Could this happen again? Could this happen here?' That was the first time that I realized it was remarkable that my mother had the courage to become Jewish. To think back to a time where people were killing Jews, I felt so proud that she embraced a man's faith because she loved him."

Fairstein has great nostalgia around Jewish ritual and her dad. "On Friday we would drive to temple and my mother would drive home ahead of us. I would take his hand and walk home. I like to do things today that remind me of him." Like fasting. She says he used to fast, in part, as a symbolic gesture. "He had this old-fashioned sense that as a visible Jew in the community—the town doctor—he should be seen in temple. So I still go and I still fast. There are things like that that I do that are just a little tip of the hat for my father."

Fairstein herself was married relatively late—at age thirty-nine—to Justin Feldman, an attorney who helped run Robert F. Kennedy's 1964 senate campaign. "I married Justin, who is Jewish and whose first wife was Christian. She didn't convert." I ask if Fairstein had been looking for a Jewish man. "Sort of. Intellectually I was drawn much more to Jewish men. I know it's stereotypical generalizing, but I love the intelligence and often the spirit of caring, the sense of family."

And she finds herself feeling a reflexive protectiveness over preserving the Jewish people. "I do very definitely have a concern about it," she says. "You know, from silly things like looking at the Sunday *New York Times* wedding announcements and seeing who we're losing. I hate to read that a Jew got married and 'the ceremony was performed by a Buddhist minister . . .' You know, when it's not a rabbi performing the ceremony, it's a sign to me: 'We've lost one.' "

She herself has lately been more drawn to ritual, suggesting to her husband that they join the Hebrew Center on Martha's Vineyard, where they have a second home. "It's become more and more important in my life as I have gotten older," Feinstein says. "It's something I've become more fiercely proud of. I haven't talked to many people about it, but I actually reflect on it a lot."

In fact, she intends to have her fiction's protagonist, Alex Cooper, begin to grapple more with her religion. "One of the only personal things about that character which is true to life is that she's Jewish and her mother was Christian. I use that background, though I haven't explored it terrifically and I want to. But from the moment I created Alex Cooper, I very definitely wanted her to be Jewish." I ask why. "Because I'm proud of it too," she says with a smile. "And it made her smart."

Paul Mazursky

"HALVAH IS PROBABLY the closest thing I have to being religious," says director/actor Paul Mazursky, sitting in an office so spartan it looks temporary. "I've been on a diet for twenty years, but if you give me a piece of halvah, it's over; I'm going to eat it."

Mazursky, seventy-five, writer and director of *An Unmarried Woman*, *Down and Out in Beverly Hills*, and *Tempest*, among other films, is acting these days in Larry David's *Curb Your Enthusiasm* on HBO. "I don't have a good psychological explanation for why I'm Jewish," he says from under his baseball cap. "I was born eating kreplach and matzo brei and lox. The Jews don't make good main dishes, by the way. They're only good at making what you call 'fore spice'—the stuff before the meal. And some of the desserts. Ruggelach is a treasure."

The Brooklyn-raised Mazursky calls his parents "Holiday Jews" and says his grandmother went to synagogue, but his grandfather stayed home. "I found him eating one day on Yom Kippur while Grandma was in shul, fasting. I was five or six years old. He was eating pickled herring. I said, 'Grandpa, why is Grandma fasting while you're eating?' He said, 'Because I'm hungry.' And that told me everything that I had to know about religion."

Mazursky says his wife isn't Jewish, but she wears a Jewish star "because she likes Jews, she likes Israel." As for himself, he's "anti-religious": "For me, religion is one of the things that's ruined mankind and continues to do so every day. Something that used to have meaning and importance has emerged as 'I'm different than you,' 'I'm better than you,' and it's endless. We're now in a world situation that I find in many ways the worst I've ever remembered it."

A messenger enters the office to deliver a package and apologizes for the intrusion. "That's okay," Mazursky tells the messenger, who is black. "We're talking about Jews. Do you know any Jews?" A nod. "What are you?" Mazursky asks. "Catholic," the messenger replies. "That's nice," Mazursky says.

Mazursky's two grown daughters, Jill and Meg, did not marry Jews, but Jill is sending her five-year-old daughter, Molly, to a Jewish school in Los Angeles. "Here's a good story," Mazursky says. "Molly comes home from school one day and I said, 'Did you learn anything special today?' She said, 'I learned a' "—he's trying to remember a Hebrew word—"it wasn't a 'mitzvah,' but some word for 'song.' I said, 'How does it go?' She says"—he suddenly bellows approximated Hebrew—"*Chai ditz shoi la shoi balla bu!*" He smiles. "I started to cry. I literally started to cry. All the Jewish stuff came out of me. I felt, 'Oh, this is a Jewish kid!' That was fabulous beyond belief. And Steve, the husband, turned purple."

I ask him which of his movies he would consider Jewish. "Well, of course *Enemies, A Love Story:* It's about a tortured Jewish guy with three wives, who escaped the Holocaust by hiding in an attic. There are about three meals in that movie that are particularly Jewish. See it again and pay attention to the food."

What about *Bob & Carol & Ted & Alice?* "Nah. That's why it was a hit. If there are Jewish characters, you have very little chance of being a hit. However, *The Producers* is a big hit, so I'm making a huge generalization. But generally speaking in Hollywood, they've always been nervous about big-time Jewish stuff. The ones who are most uncomfortable are Jewish executives. Not the goyim. My movies were usually backed by goyim."

Would he be bothered if someone described him as a Jewish director? "I don't think I would be bothered, but it wouldn't be a fair description. I'm an American director, I'm an American actor, and I happen to be culturally Jewish and very proud of it and I don't hide it. I've never hidden it in my work."

Mazursky does feel wistful that the "old-fashioned stuff" he cherishes from his childhood has been lost from Jewish life. "It's not the same now," he says. "You wouldn't be surprised to see a rabbi in New Balance sneakers, a good jogging outfit, and a hip yarmulke singing Yiddish rap. But we still have the great clichés: Jews still want for their children a great education.

"You know the great joke about the first female president? A Jewish girl becomes president and she says to her mother, 'You've got to come to the inauguration, Mom.' The mother says, 'All right, I'll go, I'll go. What am I going to wear? It's so cold. Why did you have to become president? What kind of job is that? You'll have nothing but tsuris.' But she goes to the inauguration, and as her daughter is being sworn in by the chief justice, the mother turns to the senator next to her and says, 'You see that girl up there? Her brother's a doctor.' "

Ellen Goodman

ELLEN GOODMAN PHOTOGRAPHED IN 1987 BY JILL KREMENTZ

BOSTON GLOBE COLUMNIST ELLEN GOODMAN, who won the Pulitzer Prize in 1980 for distinguished commentary and whose column is syndicated to over 450 American newspapers, says her thick blond hair used to tag her as gentile, especially in the dating scene at Radcliffe. "It was more of an issue that nobody knew that I was Jewish; I had a neutral name—Holtz—and that blond hair. Coincidentally, I was paired with a roommate who was Jewish. She introduced me to artichokes."

How Jewish does she feel now? "It's sort of like when someone says, 'Are you a feminist?' and they think you should duck under the table. But my answer to 'Are you a feminist?' is 'Sure; I'm part of a hundreds-of-years-old tradition of women who believe in equality.' If someone says, 'Are you Jewish?' that's also a question rarely asked by someone who is thinking positively. Particularly when we were kids. I remember, when I was in sixth or seventh grade, being pushed on the way home from the swimming pool—'The Tank,' as we called it—by some Irish girls. I don't remember whether I told my parents or not."

Does she recall being frightened? "The thing that I've never been quite sure of is why I didn't run away. I guess it was an issue of twelve-year-old dignity."

Goodman is eating a chicken pita sandwich at a round wooden table in her quiet second-floor office close to Harvard Square. She says she was raised by a German-Jewish father, an attorney, who became more involved in Jewish life as an adult. "He developed what I would describe as a 'they're-going-to-kill-you-for-it-anyway-so-you-better-know-something-about-it' attitude," says Goodman. "The weirdest part of his Jewish activity was that in 1948 or 1949, he became National Commander of the Jewish War Veterans. (He was in the army but never went overseas.) He thought there should be a Jewish military group for the image of the Jews."

Her father worked on John F. Kennedy's campaign for the U.S. Senate in 1952. "My Uncle Mike referred to my father as 'Vice President in Charge of the Jews.' He and Kennedy became quite close at that time; my parents went to [Jack and Jackie's] wedding. My mother describes herself as 'the only person who changed for the Kennedy wedding at a gas station in Rhode Island.' Everyone else who went to the wedding was rather fancy."

Goodman is very close to her daughter, Katie, who she says "bagged Hebrew school early on," partly because Goodman didn't push it. "I think at some point I wanted that weekend time with her. I wasn't very committed and she wasn't all that interested. But we've always celebrated family Hanukkah, Passover, Rosh Hashanah, and Yom Kippur."

Katie married a man Goodman describes as a "Catholic-Baptist-Buddhist combo." She's not sure how her grandson will be raised and won't say whether he had a bris. "I don't discuss my grandson's penis in print."

Did she wish that Katie had married a Jew? "It's complicated. None of the children of the next generation in our family married Jews. In fact, I think the only one who will eventually have a Jewish life partner is my cousin, who's gay. His partner is converting to Judaism. In some ways I think he cares the most. But it was not important to me. However, it would have been important to me that she not marry someone who took *another* religion very seriously. For her to have married a very religious person—or even an Orthodox Jew—would have probably freaked me out."

Goodman finishes her sandwich and, before I go, tries to sum up her view of Jewish identity. "When Madeleine Albright's linkage to Judaism came out, I remember thinking that her parents could have been self-hating, self-denying Jews; a lot of people had that reaction. But her parents could also have been people who didn't want to be defined by something they didn't believe in and so chose to convert or redefine themselves. Or they could have been totally secular people. So if you define them and her as Jewish, are you doing what the Nazis did, which is to make Judaism a race? If you don't, are you then denying a connection with an ancient tradition and group? If you insist on being connected to the past, what does it mean? I'm not being very articulate about this.

"Unless you are a true believer, should you maintain a connection based on—quote—'blood'? What do you think religion is? What do you think ethnicity is? It's endless. So a lot of people give it a good leaving alone. A lot of people deal with it as a serious part of their spiritual life and a lot of people leave it alone. I'm somewhere in that mush. Someone asked me once, 'Do you pray?' And I said, 'No, I don't pray.' On the other hand, I've been on an occasional plane when I've given a little Shema. When the plane goes down, I may be saying a Shema."

Jeff Zucker

WHEN JEFF ZUCKER, president of NBC Universal Television Group, who oversees NBC's news, cable, and entertainment, was struggling with colon cancer in 1996 at the age of thirty-one, he found himself reaching for faith. "I think we all use religion and God at convenient times, let's be honest," he says in his large office in Rockefeller Center. "I think when I was sick, I definitely talked to God. I did do that. I probably talked to God in a way that I probably never did before or haven't enough since."

Did it make him more religious? "I think a lot of people find comfort and solace in God or religion in times of trouble. And you don't have to be over-religious to want to ask somebody else for help. Whether you can see them or not. I think you always want to believe that there is a greater being."

While Zucker was in treatment, he and his wife, Caryn, went to Temple Emanu-El to speak with the junior rabbi who married them. "I thought she was helpful," he says. "She just gave us comfort."

Recently he's been more drawn to Jewish ritual, spurred by fatherhood, not cancer: "It's been less about when I was sick and more about having children," he says. "I do want my kids to have a sense of belonging to something they can hang on to and believe in—having a community. I think being Jewish is really that community."

He says that view is shared by his wife, Caryn Nathanson, a former associate producer for *Saturday Night Live*. I ask if he thinks it's easier to be married to another Jew. "Totally. I think that if you grow up Jewish in Miami or New York or anywhere else, that there's a common thread of understanding and values that are implicit."

Before he was married, was it important to him to find a Jewish wife? "I think I always knew that I would," he replies, though he says he was more ecumenical in his dating years. "I think all Jewish guys like dating the shiksas," he says with a smile. "But I don't want to insult you."

Zucker grew up in Miami, where he was bar mitzvah and confirmed at Temple Israel—"the most Reform synagogue in South Florida." His family's weekly tradition was Hebrew school and football. "After Sunday school, my folks would pick me up and we'd go to the Dolphin game," he recalls.

He said he didn't miss a Christmas tree, in part because Miami isn't exactly a winter wonderland that time of year, and he used to fast on Yom Kippur though he doesn't anymore. I ask him why not. "I don't know," he answers. "Now that I have children, I would like to get back into doing it."

He's currently a member of Temple Emanu-El in New York, and says his kids received an early dose of Jewish education in preschool at the 92nd Street Y. "Every Friday they would have prayers," he explains. "So they know a little bit about Friday night Shabbat dinner. They know they're Jewish."

How would he answer his children when they ask him what it means to be a Jew? The rapid-talking television executive pauses for the first time. "I think it means that we believe there's a God who looks out over all of us." Another pause. "A large part of Judaism is the type of home you have and the feelings that are expressed there and the expectations that are around you. And it ties us to a tradition and a way of living that our grandparents and their grandparents lived."

I wonder if, when he was sick, he made any bargains with God; especially after the cancer returned three years following the first bout. Zucker shakes his head. "No bargains. But you're always reaching out in times of need. And just because you can't see Him, doesn't mean He's not there."

Neil Simon

NEIL SIMON PHOTOGRAPHED IN 1970 BY JILL KREMENTZ

MARVIN NEIL SIMON ONCE WROTE that he dropped his first name when he realized that "Marvin Simon" would never "be announced on the public address system at Yankee Stadium as playing center field for the injured Joe DiMaggio." In a phone interview from Los Angeles, he says he did not grow up in "what you would call a really Jewish home." His parents kept separate dishes for the High Holy Days and tore off pieces of toilet paper before the Sabbath arrived, so they wouldn't have to "work" on the day of rest. That was about the extent of it. "They ate the right food," he adds.

Simon soured on religious education when he was chastised for asking what he thought was a reasonable question in Hebrew school. "The rabbi was telling us about Adam and Eve and their children, Cain and Abel," Simon recalls. "He said Cain slew Abel and then went out into the world and wherever he went, people shunned him. And I said, 'What *people*? You just told us they were the only human beings on earth.' The rabbi said, 'Shut up.' " Simon pauses. "Things like that are what discourage you from having a religious background."

He also disliked that the subject Hebrew school seemed to care most about was tuition. "The rabbi would say to me, 'You got the money? Did you give us the money yet?' It's very possible and probable that the place I went to in Washington Heights was not a very good place of learning."

Simon also found observance too demanding. "I think one of the things that put me off a little bit was the amount of time you had to spend to be a good Jew," he says. "The amount of times you had to go to synagogue." His older brother, Danny, went more often. "He had more fear of it," Simon recalls. "My brother would sleep next to me and I remember hearing him at night praying, 'Please, Jewish God, give me this; please, God, give me that.' I thought it was interesting because I said, 'Look; he's making selections.' "

In Simon's memoir, *Rewrites*, he recounts the family's annual visit to shul on the High Holy Days and how his father insisted he recite the prayers in Hebrew. "I would say, 'I don't know what the Hebrew means.' He answered, 'Do what I say. God doesn't understand English.' "

Simon, seventy-seven when we speak, says the anti-Semitism he saw in his Bronx neighborhood—"there were always street fights"—paled by contrast to his later stint in the army. "In the army, I knew that I was Jewish because they would tell me so," he says. "That was when I really got it. It struck me as being so hypocritical and kind of stupid that the guys who were the cooks—who were to me the dumbest group of all the guys that I met—were putting us all down for being Jewish."

In *Biloxi Blues*, the third of Simon's autobiographical trilogy about a Brooklyn Jewish family, the main character, Eugene Jerome (played on Broadway by Matthew Broderick), goes to boot camp and learns that the same American soldiers who are champing at the bit to kill Nazis also happen to hate Jews. When the character Joseph Wykowski ridicules Eugene's fellow private, Arnold Epstein, Eugene does nothing. "I never liked Wykowski much and I didn't like him any better after tonight," Eugene confides to the audience. "But the one I hated most was myself because I didn't stand up for Epstein, a fellow Jew."

This Pulitzer Prize–winning playwright—with more than thirty plays and twenty films to his credit, including *Barefoot in the Park, The Odd Couple, The Sunshine Boys, The Goodbye Girl*, and *Brighton Beach Memoirs*—chose to re-create one of his first comedy-writing jobs in his script for *Laughter on the 23rd Floor*. It was based on the writing team of Sid Caesar's *Your Show of Shows*, which included Simon, Carl Reiner, Larry Gelbart (who later created *M*A*S*H*), Mel Brooks, and Caesar himself. "Almost all of them were Jewish," he says. "It was just familiar and it made things easier. There would be things that were very funny that were said in the room that would come from a place familiar to us all. If a guy came from Ohio, it would be hard for him to catch up."

He sounds annoyed when I ask him if he thinks American humor has been shaped in large part by Jewish humor because so many comedians are Jewish. "I have such a hard time talking about this and my answers are always the same," Simon replies. "Even having difficulty talking about it says something about what my background was like."

But Simon has often been described as a Jewish playwright. "I always felt that people were trying to pinpoint clues and say, 'Is this a Jewish play?' and I never thought of that. Even though I thought my characters were sometimes probably Jewish. *Barefoot* wasn't Jewish. *Come Blow Your Horn* was." I ask if he's bothered when critics or commentators analyze the Jewishness of his work. "It only bothers me in that not all the plays are about that," Simon answers.

He also resists speaking about his personal life. It's well known that he was deeply distraught when his first wife, Joan Baim, died of cancer in 1973 after almost twenty years of marriage, leaving their two daughters, Nancy and Ellen. In his memoir, he writes about his helplessness watching his wife slip away. *"I looked for the God I hoped existed but was too cynical to believe in. It did not, however, stop me from asking Him to point me in the right direction, as I mumbled silent prayers on the carpet of my office in the late-night hours when Joan was asleep."*

When I ask him whether his daughters feel Jewish, he says, "The youngest one—who's now forty—started to look into it for herself in college and went to synagogue for a long time to see what she could get out of it. She wouldn't talk to me about it much; she just felt that maybe she'd missed something."

I can tell that Simon is ready to get off the phone. When I ask my last question—how much it matters to him to be Jewish—I assume he'll brush me off; but his answer surprises me. "It matters to me like my hands matter to me," Simon replies. "It's there."

Al Franken

AL FRANKEN PHOTOGRAPHED BY OWEN FRANKEN

SITTING WITH AL FRANKEN at his dining room table with a bowl of cashews laid out by his buoyant wife, Franni, I ask him whether he was *Saturday Night Live*'s go-to guy on whether a Jewish skit was in bad taste. "Remember *Lorne*'s Jewish," says Franken, speaking of SNL creator and executive producer Lorne Michaels, "so sometimes I'd have to get stuff past *him*.

"My comedy partner, Tom Davis, and I would do this thing called 'The Franken and Davis Show,' where we'd walk out in costume to introduce the sketch we were about to do and then never actually do the sketch. And we did one once where Tom and I came out in Gestapo uniforms and my parents come out in overcoats with Stars of David on them—old European, tattered overcoats"—he's laughing already—"and my dad said to me, 'Alan, we've decided not to do this sketch.' And I go, 'What are you talking about?' And he says, 'I don't know; I just feel I can't do it. It's not in good taste. I'm sorry that I've waited till now, but I can't do it.' And then I got angry at my parents for refusing to do the sketch, and that was the end of the sketch.

"I remember Bernie Brillstein, Lorne's manager, was there watching during dress rehearsal, and I guess Bernie objected to it and that resonated with Lorne and Lorne said, 'Al, we can't do this. You just can't do it.' So we scrapped the sketch. Afterwards he said, 'Don't ever make me cut your parents again.' " Franken laughs. "So Lorne was a little bit more sensitive on the Jewish issue than I am."

There was also the time when Franken went on "Weekend Update" with anchor Dennis Miller to report on the most negative political ads of 1994. "In the skit, I introduced an ad that [Lieutenant Colonel] Ollie North ran against [former Virginia senator] Chuck Robb on Christian television and it said"—Franken assumes his ominous-attack-ad voice— " 'Chuck Robb is against school prayer. And no wonder: *He's a Jew.*' " Franken guffaws. "And Dennis goes, 'Chuck Robb isn't Jewish!' and I said, 'Dennis, *you* know that; *I* know that; *but it's a close race.*' " Another chortle. "And Lorne was like, 'Oh, Al, I don't know about that.' So we cut that joke and my heart always aches that we cut it because I love that line."

I ask Franken why he thinks so many top comedians happen to be Jewish. "There are funny gentiles too," he says, adjusting his trademark glasses, "but there is a certain thing in Jewish culture that honors humor. Lenny Bruce said there's this tradition of the charming Jew—meaning the funny Jew. It started with the pyramids: There was one Jew who didn't want to carry the stones and so he would just be charming instead." He laughs. "Am I proud that there are funny Jews? Yeah."

But Franken says it's impossible to define humor—Jewish or otherwise. "It's never funny when you talk about it," he says. "Obviously there's a lot of self-deprecation in it."

That certainly applies to Franken's book *Why Not Me? The Inside Story of the Making and Unmaking of the Franken Presidency* (2000), which chronicled his fictional effort to become the first Jewish president and his rapid implosion. In the book, candidate Franken hails from Christhaven, Minnesota, and proclaims, "I am not going to be president of the Jews. I am going to be president for all Americans, Jews and anti-Semites alike."

"Part of the whole idea of the book," Franken says with a chuckle, "was that my character was misguided in every possible way." He picked an imaginary all-Jewish cabinet, for example, including Attorney General Joel Kleinbaum, Treasury Secretary Peter Steingarten, and Health and Human Services chief Harold Lipsky. "And I chose Joe Lieberman to be my vice president," Franken continues, "which would be an incredibly stupid thing for a Jewish presidential candidate to do—to pick another Jew—but that's part of the comedy." Franken writes that he selected Lieberman to "balance the ticket, since he's Orthodox and I'm Reform."

I ask Franken what he thought of the real Joseph Lieberman's vice presidential candidacy in 2000: whether he agreed with those who felt the senator came off as holier-than-thou when explaining his faith. Franken is diplomatic: "He could have laid off it a *little*."

But does Franken think the country is ready for a Jewish president? "I always tell this joke that I believe Colin Powell could have been president if he had run in '96, and that led me to conclude that the first Jew to be elected president will have to be a four-star general. So it gave me the idea that we should find a high-ranking Jew in the military and start grooming him for a run in the White House. I did a little research and, unfortunately, it turns out that currently the highest-ranking Jew in the military is the comptroller of the U.S. Coast Guard." Another guffaw. "That's my 'Is-it-possible-to-have-a-Jewish-president?' joke. But seriously: I do think if it's the right Jew at the right time . . ."

Unlike many Jews I spoke to after the 2004 election, Franken does not view America as a hyper-Christian nation that's less hospitable to Jews. "I think this strain of evangelical Christianity isn't anti-Semitic," he says. "It's just very, very judgmental and intolerant and narrow-minded and in some cases, angry and cruel. But I don't think it's toward Jews as much as it is toward the rest of the world; toward Muslims, for example. It's a very scary mind-set to me, not as a Jew so much but as a person."

Franken's daughter, Thomasin, has dropped in for a visit and is greeted warmly by her parents. "Hi honey!" Franken calls out. "Oh, my baby's here!" cries Franni. A graduate of Harvard—her dad's alma mater—Thomasin is currently a teacher in the Bronx. "Would you call yourself Jewish?" Franken ambushes her while she still has her coat on. "I would," Thomasin replies, staying to chat amiably for a moment before joining her mother in the kitchen.

"I don't think I ever told my kids, '*You're Jewish!*'" Franken explains. "They just think they're Jewish." Franni, he explains, is a "lapsed Catholic." "When the kids would ask me growing up, 'Am I Jewish?' I'd say, 'Well, you're half-Jewish, so you're kind of Jewish and you live in New York on the Upper West Side, so you're Jewish!' When my daughter was five or six, my brother asked her, 'What's the advantage of being half-Jewish and half

Christian?'—thinking she'd say, 'You get to celebrate both Hanukkah and Christmas.' And instead, she said, 'If someone asks you if you're Jewish, you can say no.' My brother was both amused and a little shocked by that."

He says Franni was observant until they got married. "She comes from a very Irish Catholic family," he says. "We met freshman year in college. She would stay over in my room and then go to Mass on Sunday morning, which I thought was odd. But she, more than I, made the conscious decision: 'The kids aren't going to be Catholic.' And I said, 'Okay.' " He laughs.

Franken grew up in Minnesota's St. Louis Park—dubbed "St. Jewish Park," Franken says, because of its heavy concentration of Jews. He was confirmed in a Reform synagogue. "I remember being in a carpool to go to temple and not particularly liking confirmation class. I would have preferred to have slept." He laughs. "My father was slightly more observant than my mother in the sense that he liked to be an usher at temple. I liked some of the music: 'Ein Kelohenu.' And I also liked Rabbi Shapiro. Everyone who was confirmed got to have a meeting with Rabbi Shapiro, and when it was my turn, I asked him, 'Why exactly should I believe in God?' and he said, 'It's easier.' And I said, 'Boy, that doesn't convince me at all.' " He laughs.

His parents held a seder every year and celebrated a low-key Hanukkah. "We'd get a quarter every night," he recalls. "Or socks."

In tenth grade, Franken went to a private academy, the Blake School, in Hopkins, Minnesota, which required a coat and tie and attendance at morning chapel. "In later years, when I used to visit Minnesota and talk about Blake, I'd say that it was founded around the turn of the century as a school for Protestant boys, which it was, and that they started letting Jews in during the fifties to keep the SAT scores up. I'd say that and I'd get a laugh. About three years ago, they had their centennial, and as part of it, a history teacher researched a history of the school. She calls me up and says, 'You know that joke you tell when you come to town about the Jews and the SAT scores? It's truer than you can possibly imagine.' "

Franken recalls two scrapes with anti-Semitism at Blake. "During morning chapel, you'd sit in these pews and sing two Protestant hymns. 'Onward Christian Soldier'—Jesus stuff. I didn't mind it at all except that I didn't sing the hymns when I first got there because I'm Jewish. So one day, I'm about to leave math class, and Mr. Lundholm—Harold

Lundholm—says to me, 'Mr. Franken, could you stay after class?' and I said, 'Sure.' And everyone leaves, and he says to me, 'I notice you don't sing the hymns in chapel.' I couldn't believe he said this. I said, 'Well, yeah.' He said, 'I'd sing the hymns if I were you.' And I said, 'Okay, well, the thing is, I'm Jewish and the hymns are Christian and I wouldn't want to undermine the sanctity of the songs by singing something that I don't believe in.' And he said, 'You want to go to a good college, right?' and I said, 'Yeah.' And he said, 'And your math grade is going to be very important?' And I said, 'Yeah.' And he said, 'I'd sing the hymns.' So from then on, I sang the hymns."

The second episode occurred in "The Senior Room," which Franken describes as a recreation/study room for seniors only. "One morning we walked in and scrawled all over the walls were things like 'Hitler was right,' and some swastikas. *That*, I thought, was very serious, and I went to the headmaster and he didn't take it seriously enough. He basically said, 'Well, boys will be boys.' So I made a big stink out of it. At the time some friends and I were writing an underground newspaper—*The Blakely Barb*—so we did a really scathing piece."

I ask Franken if, now that's he's out front politically and often a target of derision from those who disagree with him, he ever feels that a personal attack is also a shot at his ethnicity. "Only when it literally is," he says. "You get mail or e-mail that literally says 'Die, Jew.' That's pretty unambiguous."

Franni comes in to offer me another Diet Coke and points out the gift Franken received as a child from his temple. "This was my confirmation Bible!" he says. "Open up and see all the rabbis' signatures," Franni urges. Franken starts flipping through the rest of it. "Oy! I didn't know they had this section: '*Deaths*.' " He shows me the page and laughs.

Coincidentally, only two weeks before my visit, Franken had returned to his childhood temple in Minnesota to give a speech. "Rabbi Shapiro came," he says proudly. "He's like eighty-eight now. I was very surprised and glad to see him; I really felt an emotional tie to my rabbi. I spoke for maybe an hour, then had a question-and-answer session, and then the synagogue's new rabbi said, 'Rabbi Shapiro will ask the last question.' He was seated in the audience of the sanctuary and they gave him the hand mike and he just said to me, 'I'm proud to be your rabbi.' And I just cried. I went down and hugged him."

So if someone were to ask Franken how important is being Jewish to him, how he'd rank it among the components of his identity—husband, father, American, and so forth? "Well, it's important to me," he replies. "Is it more important that I'm a Jew or an American? American. Is it more important that I'm a Jew or a husband? I'd say husband. Jew or father? I'd say father. Jew or New Yorker? Jew. Jew or Minnesotan? Minnesotan."

Diane von Furstenberg

IN ALL HER YEARS in the spotlight as a successful fashion designer, arbiter of style, and chic fixture of New York night life, Diane von Furstenberg never publicly discussed the fact that her mother was a Holocaust survivor. And she wasn't prepared to change that when she walked to the podium at an Anti-Defamation League event in 1981 to receive their Woman of Achievement Award.

"I had just gotten back from Bali," she says, dressed in a leather jacket in her plush office that feels more like a boudoir with its pink walls and electic art.

The morning of the ADL benefit, von Furstenberg called her assistant. "I said, 'Oh my God, do I have to do this?' And she said, 'Yes, these women are your customers.' I had no idea what the Anti-Defamation League was, only that they had decided to honor me. And it's only when I started to thank them at the podium that it all just came to me; I found myself saying, 'Eighteen months before I was born, my mother was in

Auschwitz.' To hear myself say that was a revelation to me. That's when I realized that I had somewhat of an obligation to talk about it."

She also decided to write about it. In her memoir, *Diane: A Signature Life*, she described her mother, Lily Nahmias, who in 1945 at the age of twenty-one was freed from the Neustadt-Glewe concentration camp. "My mother rarely talked about the camps during my childhood in Brussels," she wrote. "I remember the numbers that were tattooed on her arm from two of the three camps she had been in, but after a while she had the tattoos removed because it annoyed her to have people constantly remark on them."

"I would hear her talk about her experience when I was growing up," says von Furstenberg now, shifting in her black suede pants on her leather sofa. "It was always there. But to me, she would only talk about the good things: the camaraderie; only the good things."

I ask von Furstenberg if she had a sense of being Jewish growing up. "Not at all," she says as she shakes her head firmly. "Because I was born too close to the war." Her point is that survivors like her mother often disengaged from Judaism after their horrific experience. "It was never something I addressed at all."

Still, she writes in her book, "The Holocaust has shaped my character from inception." I read her that quote. "Well yes," she says. "It's very much who I was. My mother was a total miracle. She weighed forty-nine pounds at the end of the war, she was not supposed to be alive; but she did make it, she survived, she married my father. She wasn't supposed to have a child, but I was born healthy eighteen months later . . . a total miracle. Everybody comes with a certain DNA; that was my DNA. So my responsibility or duty or thankfulness means that I have to take that energy and live it. And be thankful for it. So yes, I do think that it makes me very much who I am."

Her mother told her one story as a child which became a defining parable for the way to live life. On the train to the camp, her mother befriended an older woman who offered much-needed maternal comfort. When the Nazi guards eventually separated prisoners into two lines, Lily Nahmias clung to her new older friend. But an officer forced the women apart despite Lily's protestations; her friend went into a separate line. As it happened, the group Lily was desperate to join was sent to the gas chamber, while she was spared. "From this sad event," von Furstenberg writes, "my mother drew the life lesson that you never really know what's good for you. What may seem to be the absolute worst thing to happen to you can in fact be the best."

"It's a story that I always heard," she explains now, "and it's a very strong story. It didn't traumatize me. But it is a story that I use a lot when people complain. I say, 'You know what? You never know.' "

Von Furstenberg, born Diane Simone Michelle Halfin in Brussels on December 31, 1946, absorbed her mother's resilience and clearly has drawn on it repeatedly—during the divorce from her first husband, Prince Egon von Furstenberg, when her business plummeted in the 1980s, when she was diagnosed with tongue cancer in 1994. "Whatever happens, my mother always told me, you just deal with it and turn it around. There's not even an alternative. There's always something good. The one thing that I think is most valuable that she taught me is that fear is *not* an option. She would just never allow me to be afraid, and as a result, I was never afraid. It's the best gift she could have given me."

After the ADL honor, von Furstenberg became very involved in fundraising for the Holocaust Museum in Washington, D.C., and invited her mother and two children, Alexandre and Tatiana, then twenty-three and twenty-two respectively, to join her at the opening in April 1993. I assume the visit must have been emotional. "Well, we made it very light and we turned it into a field trip. I went with my kids. I didn't want it to be heavy."

She writes more expansively about accompanying her mother into the new museum: "I held her small hand tightly as we walked quickly through the original gate of Auschwitz with its sign: ARBEIT MACHT FREI ('Work makes one free'). I did not want her to break down. The four of us were silent as we walked through the museum, keeping our feelings under control. My mother's example had taught us not to give in to sorrow . . .' "

She says now that, in its way, this particular evening felt like a victory: "There we were, the four of us, and for my mother it obviously meant so much; she had survived, she was there with her daughter and grandchildren. It's only afterwards when we came back that I know it affected her, and for a few days, it affected me too."

The intercom in her office suddenly blares, "*Diane?*"

She calls out, "Yes?"

"Libby from *Inside Story* wants to confirm the interview with you tomorrow at six?"

Von Furstenberg goes to check her calendar on her desk, which sits in front of her Warhol portraits, and checks her calendar. "That's right," she affirms.

It's the holiday season and the flurry of orders and sample sale preparations can be felt even in this third-floor oasis above the design studio.

I ask von Furstenberg if she raised her children with any religion. "No," she replies. "My children were actually christened because of my husband. But I don't like religion. I think it's destructive. I believe in God. I have my own personal relationship with God." She goes to synagogue once a year. "Yom Kippur is something I do *alone*, with nobody else, because I believe that my relationship with God is mine and mine only. And I do fast. I do that."

Her marriage in July 1969 to Prince Eduard Egon von und zu Furstenberg—who hailed from the Agnelli family, which owned Fiat— was somewhat controversial. "They didn't like that I was Jewish," she says of Egon's relatives, "but my husband didn't care." Egon's father attended their wedding ceremony but refused to go to the reception. Did that trouble her? She shrugs. "I felt bad for him. I didn't feel bad for me."

She is a proponent of intermarriage across all backgrounds. "I think the more people mix, the better we are," she says. "It's better for the blood, people look better. I like that."

Her phone is ringing, the intercom is buzzing, and I realize I have to let her get back to work. As she walks me out, I ask how she'd respond if someone asked her what religion she is.

Von Furstenberg pauses a moment. "I'd say I was born of Jewish parents," she says, "and I'm Jewish. But I don't like religion. There are a lot of things about the Jewish faith that I like; what I like the most is that you're responsible for yourself. You take your life in your hands and you're responsible for your actions. There are a lot of things that I like about it . . . I do carry and honor the strength of my mother. I'm thankful that she was saved. And I want to be buried as a Jew; very simply."

Epilogue

A FUNNY THING HAPPENED on my way to finishing this book:

I became more Jewish.

I'm not saying I now keep kosher or daven every morning. What I mean is that I've become more stirred by Judaism—more impatient to understand it, more surprised by how preoccupying it is, less baffled by those who prioritize it. Judaism became a richer piece of my life.

Over the course of the last two years, as I listened to one prominent person after another describe how onerous Hebrew school was, how readily they left religion behind after their bar or bat mitzvah day, how boring they find synagogue, how unaffected they are by prayer, the more I felt drawn to understand the religion myself. The more I heard Jewishness described as a gut connection, a shared history, a value-system, a vibrant culture, but not in terms of ritual or liturgy, the more I felt pulled toward exactly those things: the scaffolding of this obstinate tradition.

During these many varied conversations, I never felt disapproving when someone told me they were indifferent to the religious aspects of being Jewish; on the contrary, I related to the sentiment. But it also made me want to investigate what so many people, including myself, had rejected or never opted to explore.

I trace this bend in the road, in large part, to Leon Wieseltier. I walked out of his Washington office at the *New Republic* feeling dazed and provoked. I took his rebuke of "slacker" Jews as a personal challenge: How could I make choices regarding my faith, let alone pass on a legacy to my children, when I knew so little about it? I'll never forget his response when I pointed out that for many of the people I'd interviewed, observance takes a lot of time out of already busy lives. "Oh please," he'd scoffed. "We're talking about people who can make a million dollars in a morning, learn a backhand in a month, learn a foreign language in a summer, and build a summer house in a winter . . . We're talking about intelligent, energetic individuals who master many things when they wish to."

I know I can never hope to make a million dollars in a morning, but I also know I manage to make time for things that count. I schedule my life around my son's baseball game, my daughter's art class, a particular yoga instructor. When Wieseltier said, "It's all about what's important to you. It's about motivation and will," I felt the proverbial lightbulb go off over my head: "You should make time for this," I told myself.

So I started studying Torah. Every Thursday morning, a young rabbi named Jen Krause—a brainy, spirited, and blessedly unpretentious teacher—met with me and a friend over coffee and for ninety minutes we dissected the Torah portion of the week. The process was demanding and emboldening, not just because I grasped the Jewish chronicle in its entirety for the first time, but because I realized that simply reading the story of the Jewish people was the key to the club. Keeping up with each week's chapter—being guided by a scholar and discussing it with a friend—was my entrée into a world that had long felt closed and overwhelming. Suddenly, I had a place at the table, and no question was too simple or sacrilegious. I realized I was entitled to this narrative, too—it was mine as much as anyone else's—and by wrestling with the text, I watched it come alive. What I'd assumed would be heavy lifting (an assumption that had kept me from taking any first step) wasn't arduous at all.

I discovered for myself why the Bible narrative endures: how each chapter is packed with upheaval and spectacle, how every verse can launch a conversation, why there's so much room for disagreement. I'm sure veterans of Torah study will roll their eyes at my elementary Eureka!, but the juiciness of the text was, frankly, news to me. The missteps of the patriarchs and matriarchs were also resonant; it was instructive to look at ancient self-interest and selflessness with a contemporary eye.

When the Passover holiday arrived, I actually felt equipped to tell my kids the Exodus story. I went to the West Side Judaica store and bought a "Bag O' Plagues," which included a plastic locust (God sent pestilence as one penalty for Pharaoh's intransigence) and a frog that hops (God also sent a barrage of frogs). I prepared a playlet for the family seder, with my nephew playing Moses, my son Pharaoh, and my daughter and niece Israelite slaves lugging fake bricks in the desert. As we rehearsed, minutes before the seder began, my brother-in-law's seven-year-old niece announced she wanted to join in. Inspired by her red tights, I assigned her the role of the Red Sea. When she parted her knees for Moses' passage to freedom, relatives rolled with laughter, and I realized we should probably find a more G-rated simulation next time.

When the High Holy Days arrived the following autumn, I found myself volunteering to run the children's services for our congregation in Connecticut. As I spent weeks designing the kind of ceremony I'd been trying for years to find for my own kids at other synagogues, I became a bit obsessed. I pored over Internet High Holy Days lessons, ordered twenty plastic shofars online for the kids to blow, found painted wooden apples for the children to pretend to "slice," and purchased every Rosh Hashanah and Yom Kippur storybook listed on Amazon.com. When I couldn't find a children's song that explained the holiday in fundamental terms, I wrote one: "The Sorry Song," so named because the theme of the holidays is atonement. ("Oops, I had a tantrum. Oops, I threw my food. Oops, I didn't listen to my parents and was rude." You get the idea.) The kids ended up learning the lyrics with my rudimentary guitar accompaniment, and after children's services we were invited to sing my new composition for the entire congregation.

At the Kol Nidre service, I was given the honor of opening the Torah ark. It didn't matter that the ark in our provisional temple is pint-sized; I was trembling when I wrapped a tallis around my shoulders for the first time in my life and approached the bimah.

I RSVP'd *yes* for the first time to a Sukkoth gathering one week after Yom Kippur. I'd never helped build a sukkah before, let alone eaten under one, and two years earlier the idea of devoting a Saturday morning to that enterprise would have been unthinkable. But there I was, feeling choked up as I watched my children take the *lulav* (branches) and *etrog* (citron) that were passed around and shaking them toward the four corners of the world.

I started reading my son a chapter from the *Children's Illustrated Jewish Bible* (foreword by Rabbi Joseph Potasnik) each night. Its compact, dramatic storytelling and stormy illustrations are perfect for a second-grader. Ben is riveted by the stories, and I'm not surprised: Few other children's chapter books are as action-packed. What novel offers an evil serpent, a deadly flood, brother killing brother, father sacrificing son, son tricking father, stone spouting water? I'm glad to see that Ben is turned on by the Bible, but I'm also a little relieved: *This isn't medicine*, I think to myself—*he likes it*. This is a road we can take together. Where it leads doesn't matter to me—only that he and my daughter become engaged in the Jewish story sooner—and more naturally—than I did.

The final rung on this strange ladder was my decision to become bat mitzvahed when I turned forty last May. With Jen's help, I boned up on my hazy college Hebrew, learned the singsong melodies used to recite Torah, and prepared a brief talk about the Emor portion of Leviticus. I'm sure some of my friends thought I'd gone off the deep end, but for some reason this didn't strike me as extreme. It felt as if I'd been unwittingly headed toward this rite of passage, albeit at a glacial speed, for a long time.

When I first met the diplomat Richard Holbrooke, he asked me why I'd chosen this book topic, and I stumbled over an explanation, admitting that I myself was struggling with the same questions of identity that I was probing with famous Jews. "So this is therapy for you," he said. "We're therapy." I balked at his comment at the time. But maybe, in a roundabout way, he'd hit on something: I may not have consciously conceived this project to confront my own confusions, but it certainly has had that effect.

I started this book because I was genuinely curious about how being Jewish—that unique amalgam of ritual, Israel, Holocaust, matzo, Torah, and Seinfeld—sits with people who live public lives, who are among America's success stories. But every person I spoke to made me look at myself: my childhood, my children, my marriage, my faith or lack of it, my education or ignorance, my connection or indifference. Every one of these conversations was a prick at my conscience. I personalized each person's story. And no matter the gulf in stature between us, each person felt fundamentally linked to me.

I realize this epilogue is personal: Even after talking to more than sixty Jews, I don't think it's my place—nor am I equipped—to make broad, authoritative summations. I could proclaim that most Jewish public figures aren't publicly Jewish; that most have abandoned customs, intermarried, or don't seem very worried about Jewish continuity; that all of them feel unshakable Jewish pride. But I don't know any of these things with any scientific or sociological certainty. What I do know is that being Jewish is powerful and, in a sense, unavoidable—whether one embraces it or leaves it on the shelf, whether one lives a visible life or an anonymous one. And that, in the process of writing this book, it's become more vital to me than I ever expected.

Acknowledgments

TO ALL THOSE PEOPLE WHOSE HELP AND ENCOURAGEMENT WERE INCALCULABLE: Dan Algrant, Jamie Alter, Lisa Belzberg, John Bennett, Candice Bergen, Jeremy Coleman, Marcia DeSanctis, Nick Dolin, Rachel Dretzin, Noah Emmerich, Marshall Goldberg, Jane Harnick, David Holbrooke, the Jordan family, Esther Kartiganer, Billy Kingsland, Deborah Kogan, Edward Klaris, Lorin Klaris, Itamar Kubovy, Rabbi Irwin Kula, Al and Lori Leiter, Miranda Levenstein, Tom Levine, Marvin Levy, Michael Lynton, Joshua Malina, Steve Nemeth, Kenneth Nova, Lucie Perry, Holly Peterson, Richard and Lisa Plepler, David Pogrebin, Christy Prunier, Michael Ravitch, Gretchen Craft Rubin, Ira Sachs, Dani Shapiro, the Shapiro family, Annie Silberman, Joshua Steiner, Alexandra Styron, Chris Taylor, Julie Warner, Pamela Weinberg, Phyllis Wender, Hanya Yanagihara.

Special thanks to:
JILL KREMENTZ—for her generosity and kindness
RABBI JEN KRAUSE—for her teaching and uncomplicated friendship
LETTY COTTIN POGREBIN—for her tireless advice and constant example
BERT POGREBIN—for his unflagging enthusiasm
ROBIN POGREBIN—for her editorial counsel and for finding the title
DIANNE CHOIE—for her diligence and good humor
DEB FUTTER—for her astute guidance, gusto, and early faith
DAVID KUHN—for his daily wisdom and extraordinary capacity to make things happen

Photo Credits